The Segu Tukulor Empire

Ibadan History Series

Published by Northwestern University Press

Christian Missions in Nigeria 1841–1891
by J. F. A. Ajayi

The Zulu Aftermath
by J. D. Omer-Cooper

Published by Humanities Press

The Missionary Impact on Modern Nigeria 1842–1914
by E. A. Ayandele

Britain and The Congo Question 1885–1913
by S. J. S. Cookey

The Sokoto Caliphate
by Murray Last

Benin and The Europeans 1485–1897
by A. F. C. Ryder

Niger Delta Rivalry
by Obaro Ikime

The International Boundaries of Nigeria
by J. C. Anene

Revolution and Power Politics in Yorubaland 1840–1893
by S. A. Akintoye

Power and Diplomacy in Northern Nigeria 1804–1906
by R. A. Adeleye

In preparation

The Warrant Chiefs
by A. E. Afigbo

The Evolution of The Nigerian State
by T. N. Tamuno

The New Oyo Empire
by J. A. Atanda

For further details of the books in this series
please consult the publisher.

Ibadan History Series
General Editor J. F. A. Ajayi, PhD

The Segu Tukulor Empire

B. O. Ọlọruntimẹhin, PhD
Department of History, University of Ibadan

Humanities Press

First published in
the United States of America 1972
by HUMANITIES PRESS INC.
303 Park Avenue South
New York, N.Y. 10010

SBN 391-00206-6

Printed in Great Britain

To 'Funmi and little 'Jumọkẹ.

Contents

Contents

Contents

Maps

Plates

The publishers are grateful to Messrs. Aubanel of Avignon,
France, for permission to reproduce the photograph on plate 3.

Abbreviations

ANSOM	Archives Nationales, Section d'Outre-Mer, Paris
ASAOF	Archives du Sénégal – Fonds de l'AOF, Dakar
BCAF	*Bulletin du Comité de l'Afrique Française*
BN	Bibliothèque Nationale, Paris
CAD	Centre of Arabic Documentation, University of Ibadan *Bulletin: Bull. CAD*
CEA	*Cahiers d'Etudes Africaines*
CEHSAOF	Comité d'Etudes Historiques et Scientifiques de l'Afrique Occidentale Francaise *Annuaires et Mémoires du . . . : Ann. et Mém. CEHSAOF* *Bulletin: Bull. CEHSAOF*
IFAN	Institut Fondamental d'Afrique Noire, formerly Institut Français d'Afrique Noire, Dakar *Bulletin: Bull. IFAN*
ISH	Institut des Sciences Humaines, Koulouba, Bamako
JAH	*Journal of African History*
JHSN	*Journal of the Historical Society of Nigeria*
MAE	Ministère des Affaires Etrangères, Paris
SOAS	School of Oriental and African Studies, London *Bulletin: Bull. SOAS*

Preface

This book is an attempt to fill a gap which exists in our knowledge of the nineteenth-century history of the Western Sudan. Although the Tukulor have for long played a key role as leaders of religion and purveyors of ideas, and an understanding of this role is a *sine qua non* to an understanding and appreciation of movements and events in the Western Sudan, particularly in the nineteenth century, the Tukulor have hitherto received little attention in historical and other forms of scholarship. This study is a modest contribution in the historical field to the pioneering studies of the Tukulor recently started by two Tukulor sociologists.[1]

Perhaps the title needs some explanation. *The Segu Tukulor Empire* is adopted in contradistinction to the earlier Segu empire which was Bambara, and also to emphasise that the study transcends the Tukulor in their Futa Toro homeland and sees them in their role as empire builders and rulers. Consequently, the book deals with the process of political unification, administration and politics in the Western Sudan under the leadership of the Tukulor. The Tukulor created their empire through a protracted, violent revolution that lasted from 1852 to 1864, and they were to rule the empire wholly or in part first, under the founder and leader of the Tijaniyya in the Western Sudan, al-ḥājj 'Umar b. Sa'īd Tall, and later, his son, Aḥmadu b. 'Umar Sa'īd Tall, until the French conquest in 1893.

The analysis of the Tukulor revolution and empire necessarily involves a discussion of the roles of the Tukulor aristocracy as well as those of opposition groups both within the Tukulor political class and non-Tukulor nationalities like the French, the Bambara of Segu and Ka'arta as well as the Cissé Fulani of

1 Abdoulaye Bara Diop, *Société Toucouleur et Migration*, IFAN (1965); Yaya Wane, *Les Toucouleur du Fouta Tooro* (*Sénégal*), IFAN (1965)

Masina. The image of the Tukulor empire that one gets is one of a strife-stricken entity gallantly striving to survive and establish some order at the same time as it had to cope with so many violent confrontations. Fighting was endemic first because the empire was created through the medium of a protracted revolution in which fighting was inevitable for a number of reasons. Secondly, the Tukulor experience demonstrates that it is easier to conquer than to govern. Ruling the emergent empire was made difficult partly because the Tukulor regime lacked legitimacy in its relations with the conquered nationalities and partly because its ruling group suffered from succession problems and endemic conflicts of ideologies which it had been possible for the earlier revolution to contain, canalise and direct against other groups. Conflicts arose over practical problems of power and position and over concepts as to what constituted the 'right' political and social system. The resolution of anti- and intra-Tukulor conflicts necessitated civil war from time to time. Moreover, unlike the earlier, more fortunate Sokoto empire, the Tukulor empire came to grips with advancing French imperialism and continually clashed with it from the beginning till it collapsed. Faced with so many problems which found expression in a near-permanent state of violence, and given the fact that it existed in the period of, and struggled continually against, the high tide of European imperialism, it should not be surprising that the Tukulor experiment in large-scale political and social integration did not last longer than it did. The Tukulor needed more time than they had to consolidate the achievement of their revolution by building a coherent and strong state.

This work is founded upon a Ph.D. thesis which I submitted to the University of Ibadan in 1966. Once more, I wish to express my gratitude to the Federal Government of Nigeria who awarded me the scholarship that made the study possible. I also wish to repeat my gratitude to those who in one way or the other contributed to my training at that stage. In particular, I am grateful to Dr Robert Gavin, now of Ahmadu Bello University, Zaria, for his constant encouragement and helpful comments while I was writing the thesis. In preparing this work I received useful advice and constructive criticism from several people. In particular, my thanks go to Professor E. A. Ayandele, University of Ibadan, Professor John D. Hargreaves, University of Aberdeen, both of whom read the whole manuscript and gave me the benefit of their

experience. I am also grateful to Professor J. F. Ade Ajayi and
Dr R. A. Adelẹyẹ, University of Ibadan, for finding time to read
the first two chapters and make helpful comments on them.
Mr Wilson Aiyepeku helped in preparing some of the maps.

In addition to the acknowledgements already made in the
footnotes and bibliography, I am grateful to the following persons
and institutions: Professor Vincent Monteil who as Director of
the I.F.A.N., Dakar, during my stay in Senegal provided me
with free lodging and made research facilities available to me at
his institute; the staff of the archives of Senegal, especially M. J.
Maurel and Mlle Le Toux; the staff of the Archives Nationales
(Section d'Outre-Mer), rue Oudinot, Paris; the staff of the
Archives du Ministère des Affaires Etrangères, Quai d'Orsay,
Paris and the Bibliothèque Nationale, Paris; the Institut des
Sciences Humaines, Bamako, Mali and the staff of the Africana
Library, University of Ibadan, for their cooperation and help at
various times. Lastly, I am grateful to M. Seydou Tall, then of
the Ministry of Education, Bamako, for putting me in touch
with members of his family at Segu, and the latter for their
cooperation and help during my investigation at Segu.

B. O. O.

Ibadan, 1970

1 The Western Sudan at the Emergence of the Tukulor Empire

The events associated with the Tukulor empire provide the central theme of the nineteenth-century history of the Western Sudan as far east as the Niger bend. Apart from the fact that the Tukulor empire absorbed many of the states and chiefdoms that had existed in the area before its rise, it exerted great influence upon developments in neighbouring states. This was due in part to the vastness of its size and to its strength relative to the others. Until the emergence of Samori Ture's state later in the century, the Tukulor empire was the largest and most powerful state in the Western Sudan. At its greatest, it spread along the river Senegal and included the Niger river basin northeastwards to Timbuktu. It covered the present area of the Republic of Mali (excepting the largely desert areas north of Timbuktu), the Moorish emirates which now form the southern part of the Islamic Republic of Mauritania, the Dinguiray province in the northern part of the Republic of Guinea and parts of modern Senegal.

The history of the Western Sudan in the second half of the nineteenth century is largely the history of the interaction between the Tukulor empire, including the groups which it incorporated within it on the one hand, and the states which were its neighbours on the other. Of these, the states of the Senegal valley occupied a special position. Their connections with the empire were unique, resulting, as they did, from their ethnic, cultural, common historical experience and religious identity with the rulers of the empire. In a cultural and historical sense, the people of the Senegal valley states, especially those of Futa Toro, and the rulers of the Tukulor empire belonged to the same community. And although most of the Senegal valley did not actually fall under its rule, the creation, growth and collapse of the Tukulor empire were lived through as a common experience by the people of the two areas. The Tukulor of Futa Toro, as of other Senegambian states, and those closely associated with the government of the Tukulor empire belonged to the same society. One should bear this in mind for a proper understanding of the history of the Tukulor empire, as of the Western Sudan generally. For example, one must realise that the struggle and wars associated with the rise of the empire were, for Futa Toro and the other Senegal valley states, essentially internal struggles and civil wars between sections of the same community and, indeed, in some cases, between members of the same family who were split over issues. This fact explains the sustained interrelationship of the politics of the two areas throughout the latter half of the nineteenth century. For the founders of the Tukulor empire and their lieutenants, Futa Toro was home, and they had developed, like those who remained at home, through a common process of cultural and political socialisation. Some of their ideas and practices were influenced by this fact.

The relations of the Tukulor empire with the other states and groups were not as close as those with the states in the Senegal valley. Generally speaking, however, as with the latter states, the relations between the Tukulor empire and these other states and groups were partly a product of their individual histories. A brief sketch of the historical background of the states of the Western Sudan is therefore necessary for an understanding of our subject.

Before the emergence of the Tukulor empire in mid-nineteenth century, the area had been occupied by several states and chiefdoms. Among these were large states like the Ka'arta Massassi and Segu Bambara kingdoms, and the Fulani Caliphate in Masina, all situated east of the Senegal river. In the Senegambia there were, among others, the states of Jolof, Futa Toro, Futa Jallon, Bambuk, Bondu and Khasso. Before the establishment of the Tukulor empire which absorbed many of them, the states were independent of one another, and they had different sociopolitical systems. Their individual identities were sometimes reinforced by ethnic and religious differences. In spite of their individualism and independence, however, the Western Sudanic States had, long before the nineteenth century, established economic and political relations with one another as well as with the outside world. Their participation in the trade with the Maghrib and Europe through the trans-Saharan caravan routes comes readily to mind. Within the Western Sudan itself, relations

between states were facilitated by the cultural and political influence of the Mande group of people, especially the widespread
use of the Mande group of languages practically over the whole
area.[1] There was also the cultural and historical unity represented
in the Fulani, a people who were (and are still) to be found in
almost every state in West Africa from the Futa Jallon and
Senegal eastwards across to Northern Nigeria.[2]

The states which we are considering were not only involved in
the events which resulted in the establishment of the Tukulor
empire, but also socio-political situations prevalent within them
from mid-nineteenth century onwards had their impact on
developments within the empire. Some of the dominant factors
in the history of the area at this time were the rapid social and
political changes, leading to instability within and between states,
the existence of a lively tradition of proselytising and religious
revivalism, and the existence of European, notably French,
settlements and trading posts along the Atlantic coast and in the
Senegambia. The following brief survey of the history of some of
the states mentioned above is intended to illustrate the roles of
these factors in determining the pattern of events both at the
founding of the Tukulor empire and during its existence.

JOLOF

Jolof[3] is reputed to be the oldest state in the Senegambia. At its
apogee, it had a federal structure embracing Walo, Kayor, Baol,
Sin-Saloum, Dimar and a part of Bambuk. The original inhabitants of the area are thought to have been Sérères, who were
joined later by the Wolof. Later still, before the tenth century,
Tukulor and Moorish populations migrated into the area. As a
result of the migration and settlement of various peoples in the
state, the population of Jolof became heterogeneous. Heterogeneity remains a marked feature of the population up to the

1 See Labouret 'Les Manding et leur langue', *Bull. CEHSAOF*, 1934;
  Goody, 'The Mande and the Akan Hinterland', in Vansina, Mauny
  et al., eds., *The Historian in Tropical Africa* (1964), p. 193; also Goody,
  'The influence of the Mande in West Africa', *ibid.*, pp. 91–3
2 Harris, 'The Kingdom of Fouta Diallon' (Ph.D. thesis, 1965), pp. 17,
  23ff
3 'Jolof' refers to the country while 'Wolof' refers to the people and the
  language.

present time. It has been estimated that contemporary Jolof population comprises Fulani of the Dyeeri stock (constituting about three-quarters of the total population), the Wolof (about twenty per cent) and the Moors (about five per cent).[1]

Walo is said to be the first original Jolof state from where the other Wolof chiefs migrated. Like the other parts of Jolof, it was situated in a fertile area of the Senegal valley. The fertility of its territory derived from the annual rich deposit of silt (described as *Waalo* in Fulani in contrast to the dry land of the up-country called *dyeeri*).[2] Walo was originally a Sérères Kingdom which, about the tenth century, was governed by the Dya-Ogo dynasty. Subsequently, however, various other ethnic groups moved in and occupied Walo. Among these were Fulani and Wolof. This mass population movement into Walo has been explained as resulting from the activities of the Almoravids[3] and the effects of the capture of the empire of Ghana towards the end of the eleventh century.[4] The swamping and displacement of the Sérères by other ethnic groups is attested to by Professor Murdock who says: 'Around the eleventh century . . . the Berbers, pressed from the north by the Arabs, pushed the Wolof southward to near the mouth of the Senegal river, and the latter in turn partially displaced the Serer.'[5] But Murdock, apart from giving the fact that the Sérères are now to be found mainly in the region of Sin-Saloum, does not give reasons for the reported population pressure. However, part of the explanation lies in the general search for settlement in the agriculturally suitable areas of the Senegal valley, a common socio-economic factor that accounted for movements of peoples in most of the Senegambia and the concomitant heterogeneity of the populations of the states in the region.

1 Boutillier, Cantrelle *et al.*, *La Moyenne vallée du Sénégal* (1962), p. 15; Monteil, 'Le Dyolof et Al-Bouri Ndiaye', *Bull. IFAN*, B, xxviii, 3–4, 1966
2 Monteil, ed., 'Chronique du Walo Sénégalais (1186?–1855) par Amadou Wade (1885–1961)', *Bull. IFAN*, B, 3–4, 1964, pp. 440–1
3 The Almoravids were a militant group of religious revivalists who preached a doctrine of purity and the annihilation of the unfaithful. The name—Almoravid—was derived from *al-murābītun*, meaning 'people of the hermitage'. Under their leader Abdullahi ibn Yasin, the Almoravids proclaimed a 'holy war', conquering several places in the Western Sudan between 1042 and 1147.
4 Monteil, ed., 'Chronique du Walo . . .', p. 445
5 Murdock, *Africa: its peoples and their culture history* (1959), pp. 265–6

States and major nationalities in mid-nineteenth-century Western
Sudan

From its nucleus in Walo, the Jolof empire eventually emerged. It was probably founded around 1434 by a Mandingo, Dyolof Mbing, after whom the state took its name. During the life of the empire, the overall sovereign was the *Buurba-Jolof*. The component states were each governed by a *lamaan* who was responsible to the *Buurba*. The villages were headed by either a *dyambuur* or an *arDo* in the case of Fulani settlements. An early nineteenth-century observer claimed that the *Buurba-Jolof* was a feudal despot whose subjects were mainly pagans.[1] But it has been established that the real power in the state was wielded by the Council of Kingmakers (*Dyaraf Dyambuur*) presided over by the chief elector or 'Grand Dyaraf' known as the *Dyaraf dyureg*. It was the latter who received all complaints from the people and would later bring them to the notice of the *Buurba* only if necessary. Moreover, the Council of Kingmakers, seven in number, was usually consulted on all important matters by the *Buurba*. The component states were also largely autonomous in the running of their local affairs.[2] This shows that power was more diffused than has been suggested and there was little, if any, room for despotism.

Up till the sixteenth century the empire was governed as a united entity. Its economy was based on agriculture, for which it was particularly suitable because of its location. It spread over a fertile part of the Senegal valley, extending to the sylvo-pastoral sector of the arid Ferlo which was especially suitable for the cultivation of gum. As already pointed out, the fertility of the country attracted migrant populations in search of settlements where they could both grow their crops and tend their cattle. By the nineteenth century the Moors had become the main carriers of the gum trade, notably with the Europeans. Moreover, the existence of gum plantations in Jolof had become the main attraction for the traders, especially with the French who constituted the most important interest group in the trade.

But Jolof did not last long as a united entity. The imperial fabric was broken in the middle of the sixteenth century with the secession of Kayor. The *lamaan* of Kayor asserted his independence after fighting victoriously against the *Buurba*. There-

1 Mollien, *Voyage dans l'Intérieur de l'Afrique aux sources du Sénégal et de la Gambie fait en 1818* (1822), i, p. 148
2 Monteil, 'Le Dyolof . . .', pp. 602–4; Brigaud, *Histoire Traditionnelle du Sénégal* (1962), pp. 47–52

after, he vainly attempted a conquest of the other component units, but failed. In the process, however, the *Buurba* had been weakened and it was easy for the other *lamaans* to declare themselves independent in their various areas. They subsequently took the new title of *damel* (king) and continued to struggle for supremacy, one against the other. For this reason, Jolof, at the emergence of the Tukulor empire in the nineteenth century, no longer meant more than the area effectively controlled by the *Buurba*, and this varied from time to time. In spite of the break-up of the empire, however, the *damel* of the successor states still conceded some respect to the *Buurba-Jolof* whose moral and spiritual pre-eminence they recognised. But as a state it lacked the socio-political cohesion that it needed to be able to resist external invasion.

FUTA TORO

Futa Toro (or Senegalese Futa) was situated along the valley of the Senegal river, sharing its borders with the Jolof states in the west and the Brackna and other Moorish groups to the north. Futa Toro was a federation of the following principalities, each of which was dominated by a particular clan: Dimar, Toro, Lao, Irlabé-Ebiabé, Bosséia, N'Guénar and Damga. Its favourable location in one of the most fertile areas of the Senegal valley was an important factor, as in other states, in its social and political history.

The struggle for the possession of the land in the area was often connected with the struggle for the control of political power. In any case the two could hardly be separated in an agrarian society like Futa Toro. From the Middle Ages to the nineteenth century, the political history of Futa Toro has been largely an account of the establishment of successive states. In the search for fertile lands, various peoples, notably the Fulani, Tukulor, Wolof, Moors, Bambara and Sarakole, had come to live in Futa Toro. Each group had, at one time or another, taken part in the struggle for political power until the eighteenth century when the Tukulor became dominant both in terms of power and number.

The earliest state in this area, known to Arab geographers as Tekrur, was probably established in the eleventh century. Tekrur was absorbed into the Mali empire by about the fourteenth century and was ruled as a vassal state under a Mandingo-SouSou dynasty until the sixteenth century, when political power in the area passed on to the Denyanke Fulani under the leadership of Saltigi Koli Tengella, also known as Kikali.[1] The assumption of control by Koli Tengella paved the way for closer links between Futa Toro and Futa Jallon, between which areas the Fulani, Tukulor and other ethnic groups migrated back and forth henceforth.[2] With increased mobility of people came greater contact and spread of ideas, which tended to draw the two areas closer.

With the establishment of the Saltigi dynasty, the Denyanke Fulani dominated the various populations of Futa Toro. They based their rule on Fulani princes placed at the head of extensive fiefs. The dynasty established a strong administration, with headquarters at Goumel on the right bank of the Senegal. Among the best-known rulers of the dynasty were Boubakar Siré I, Samba Boe, Samba Done, Boubakar Siré II, Gelongai and Soulé Boubou.[3]

But the period of Saltigi domination was marked by political and religious conflicts which were tied to agrarian questions. The Denyanke Fulani were non-Muslim, and because of this the Tukulor, who were ardent Muslims, resented their domination. Partly for religious reasons, therefore, the Tukulor worked for the overthrow of the Denyanke political power. Opposition groups to the Denyanke also had economic grievances. There was, for instance, the question of land distribution which was so vital to the economy of the area. In the seventeenth century, the Saltigi rulers tried to solve the land problem, but they failed. For instance, under Suley Ndyay, one of the last Saltigi, efforts were made to redistribute land. These efforts failed, and conflicts continued to divide the population until the Tukulor revolution,

1 Boutillier, Cantrelle *et al.*, *La Moyenne vallée du Sénégal*, p. 17; for evidence that Denyanke rule began in 1515; Brigaud, *Histoire Traditionnelle*, pp. 9, 11–12; A. B. Diop, *Société Toucouleur et Migration* (1965), pp. 14–15; Harris, 'The Kingdom of Fouta Diallon', pp. 9–11; Niane, 'A propos de Koli Tenguella', *Recherches Africaines*, no. 4 (Oct.–Dec. 1960), pp. 33–6
2 Harris, 'The Kingdom of Fouta Diallon', p. 11
3 Wane, *Les Toucouleurs du Fouta Tooro* (*Sénégal*), 1969, p. 11, for a discussion of the duration of the rule of the Saltigi dynasty and the length of the reigns of the individual members.

which began *c.* 1769 under the leadership of Suleyman Bal, resulted in the fall of the Saltigi.[1]

The leader of the Tukulor revolution, Suleyman Bal, was a native of Bode (in Toro). He arrived from pilgrimage during the reign of the last Saltigi ruler, Soulé Boubou. Suleyman Bal preached conversion to Islam, but this was rejected by Soulé Boubou. Eventually Suleyman Bal found himself at the head of the various interest groups which were opposed to the Denyanke regime for economic, political and religious reasons. Unfortunately for the Denyanke, Bal's revolution came at a time when the soldiery of the state, the Colyabé, felt alienated and were in revolt. Many of the nobles also deserted the regime for their own reasons and later proposed Suleyman Bal as head of the state. Although Bal refused the offer, he remained at the head of the revolution until the Saltigi dynasty fell, *c.* 1775. He proposed another religious leader, Abd al-Qādir b. Hammadi, as head of the state and the latter was elected almamy after Bal's death.

Abd al-Qādir completed the subjugation of Futa Toro and established a new regime based upon the Muslim idea of government. But he did not rule for long. The nobles soon plotted against him and had him assassinated *c.* 1804.[2] Abd al-Qādir had, in the meantime, succeeded in establishing a theocratic rule headed by almamies. Thus from Bal's revolution dated the establishment of the imamate system[3] in Futa Toro.

After Abd al-Qādir the almamies were elected by a council of clan heads who were powerful feudal lords in possession of large territories. The almamies were, as a rule, all from Toro and had

1 De Crozals, 'Trois états foulbés du Soudan occidental et Central, Le Fouta, le Macina, l'Adamaoua', *Annals de l'Université de Grenoble*, viii, 1, 1896, p. 296; Diop, *Société Toucouleur . . .*', p. 14; Brigaud, *Histoire Traditionnelle*, pp. 20–2

2 Kane, 'Histoire et origine des familles du Fouta Toro', *Ann. et Mém. CEHSAOF*, 1916, pp. 333–40; Smith, 'The Islamic revolutions of the 19th century', *JHSN*, ii, 2, 1961

3 Almamy is probably a corrupt form of the Arab word *al-imam*: he who leads the believers in prayers. From the eighteenth century onwards the word acquired the additional meaning of the political and religious head of the Muslim Community and is therefore synonymous with *amir al-muminīn*. In this sense it is the title of the head of the government of the Futa Toro confederation from the establishment of the imamate system onwards. A second sense in which it is used is as a title for the head of each of the component units of the confederation. Cf. Wane, *Les Toucouleurs du Fouta Tooro*, p. 211

to be renowned for their piety.[1] But to understand the subsequent history of Futa Toro, some understanding of Tukulor society is necessary.

The organisation of Tukulor society revolved around two main forces: the clan and the caste systems. Within the society the largest form of association and relationship was the clan, subdivided into lineage groups, a sort of extended family. Each clan embraced all who traced their descent to a common ancestry. Within each clan members owed one another social obligations and responsibilities. Members occupied the same area of land within the country and defended their common interests jointly against other clans. In particular they owned landed property in common and protected or sought to expand it against other clans. Such groups as the Bosséia, Lao and Toro occupying well-defined areas of the Senegal valley are examples of clans. The head of each clan was often also a big feudal lord with considerable political powers. Over the centuries, the clans acquired a measure of autonomy and Futa Toro soon became a loose federation of such groups.

In spite of their internal cohesion, the clans were sometimes dislocated. Dislocation was sometimes caused by conflicts between groups or by demographic pressures, as well as the search for new lands for cultivation and pasturage. In such cases dislocation occasionally resulted in expansion by segmentation of the existing lineages. The new settlements resulting from such an expansion were more often than not constituted by a reunion of several segments of the lineage groups. As in the primary group, the segmented groups usually recognised new lineage heads through whom social and spiritual contacts were maintained with other members of the clan. Alliances between clans were common and were usually based on economic cooperation, marriages or political connections.

The other important factor for the social and political organisation of the Tukulor society was the caste system. The castes were characterised by heredity, endogamy and/or professional specialisation. They constituted closed groups and maintained relations with one another on a hierarchical basis. Social relations, especially questions of domination and subordination, were defined

1 Coindard, 'Notes sur les indigènes du Tamgüe dans le Fouta Jallon (Guinée Française)', *Ann. et Mém. CEHSAOF*, 1917, p. 350; Diop, *Société Toucouleur*, p. 14; Mollien, *Voyage*, i, p. 352

essentially by the castes to which people belonged. There were three broad castes, of which the *rimBé*, consisting of the free men, was the most important.[1]

Among the *rimBé*, the *toroBé* (singular, *torodo*)[2] formed the superior group. They represented the religious aristocracy who led Futa Toro in its religious wars and conquests which have had so much impact on its history. The *toroBé* occupied a dominant position since the establishment of the theocratic regime founded by Suleyman Bal, himself a *torodo*. It was from among them that the almamies and their electors were chosen. The most important families and the owners of the largest estates in the country were mostly *toroBé*. The most powerful among them occupied positions not dissimilar to those of European feudal lords.

It was within this organisational framework that the political life of Futa Toro continued during the imamate period. The establishment of the imamate system represented a change of government. But the economy of the country remained as it had always been, based on the possession of land in the Senegal valley. The new leaders of Futa Toro were Muslims and there-fore, as far as religion was concerned, their interests were comple-mentary. The economic and political interests of the different clans continued to be competitive. A desire to protect individual interests while maintaining the state as an entity was perhaps the main consideration which governed the politics of Futa Toro during the imamate period. As the account will show, emphasis seems to have been placed on preserving the rights and privileges of the constituent clans. The result was a weakening of the central authority, and consequently the creation of a situation in which the various groups engaged in continual feuds in an attempt to satisfy their particular interests.

After the almamy Abd al-Qādir the elected almamies were simply title-bearers. The main power was exercised by the heads of the clans who, as a council, acted as electors and could make or unmake almamies. Each of the electors had hereditary rights over a particular section of the country, and their positions did not depend on the person elected as almamy. On the other hand the almamy was very often no more than a tool in the hands of

1 Diop, *Société Toucouleur*, pp. 19–23. The three castes are discussed in detail, pp. 23ff
2 Literally, *toroBé* means 'those who pray together'. This is an obvious reference to their role as religious elites.

the clan chiefs. To ensure that power remained in their own hands, the electors usually adopted several devices. For instance, in electing an almamy they always looked for someone who could easily be controlled among the marabouts. It is clear from this that what the council usually wanted was a nominal head who would leave them with the real power. All acts of government were done in the name of the almamy; but it was found by observers early in the nineteenth century that the almamy would not dare do anything without consulting the council or, at least, Aldondou and El-Imama Sire, both of whom at that time had a sort of pre-eminence over the other members of the council.

For this reason the almamy, supposedly the supreme authority in the country, was indeed in a weak position *vis-à-vis* the clan heads. In 1818 alone three almamies were installed and deposed in quick succession. Famine and similar public affliction very often served as excuses for deposing an almamy. Because of his weakness in relation to the chiefs, the almamy was usually more of a mouthpiece voicing the orders and wishes of the council than an effective leader or ruler. He lacked any independence of action. But although theoretically real power lay with the council, it was wielded only when there was broad agreement among the chiefs. Sovereign authority was not likely to be exercised on an issue that was unpopular with the chiefs, since their interests were competitive. The almamy and the chiefs being what they were, the sovereign power of the state was in flux much of the time. Real and effective exercise of authority from the centre took place only rarely.[1]

Since each of the seven chiefs comprising the council was the *de facto* supreme authority in his own domain, it is obvious that real and effective power was located only in each chief when acting individually as head of his own district. The almamy and the council were no doubt symbols of the unity of the various groups and should therefore have been able to give the affairs of the country a central direction. But this could happen only when no one's interests were injured: that is, only when the chiefs were unanimous. In any situation, unanimity as a basis of government can hardly be a workable proposition. This means that effective, consistent central administration was, in the Futa Toro situation, near-impossible.

1 Kane, 'Histoire et Origine . . .', pp. 342–3 for a list of thirty almamies; Diop, *Société Toucouleur*, pp. 20, 23; Mollien, *Voyage*, pp. 352–4

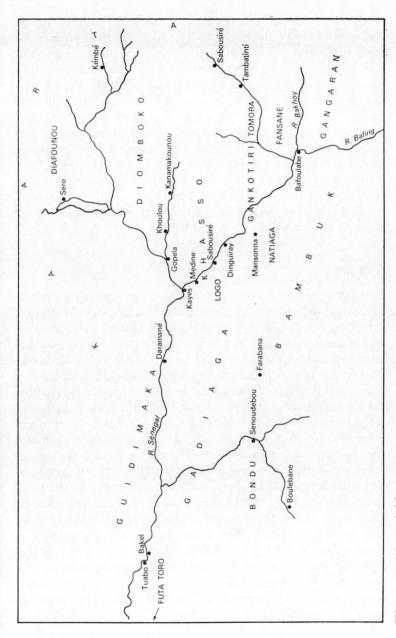

Khasso and its neighbours

13

The weakness of the centre explains the relatively strong positions of the sectional chiefs. The resultant rivalry for economic and political power among the clans explains much of the war and the attendant political disunity and instability that bedevilled Futa Toro right up to the coming of the French and the emergence of the Tukulor empire. The social and political instability which plagued the country explains why it was easy for external factors to play important, and often divisive and decisive, roles in the affairs of Futa Toro. The competition between 'Umar and the French for influence and control in Futa Toro was typical. This will be shown in the discussion of 'Umar's revolution in the Senegambia.[1] The impact of this social and political system on the administration and politics of the emergent Tukulor empire will be discussed below.

FUTA JALLON

Futa Jallon, situated south of Futa Toro, was similarly governed by several ethnic groups, especially non-Muslim Mandingo dynasties, before the eighteenth century. During this period of non-Muslim rule there also existed pockets of Muslim Fulani (mainly herdsmen) who belonged to the Qādiriyya brotherhood. The system of government operating in Futa Jallon during the period seems to have been similar to that which was evolved by the contemporary Saltigi dynasty in Futa Toro. In Futa Jallon the supreme authority was originally a council of thirteen members. Members of the council were usually men of advanced age, and credited with wisdom. They were elected through a collegiate system involving two stages. First, the villages in a particular area would be represented in the assembly for the area. Each area assembly would then send representatives (two or three, according to the number of military chiefs in the area) to the Supreme Council. The Supreme Council had exclusive direction of political and religious affairs. It also acted as the highest court in the country. The seat of government in this period was at Foucoumba. The council took decisions unanimously, especially on questions of war and peace.[2] This, as usual, made the functioning of government delicate and difficult.

1 See Chapters 3 and 4
2 Hecquard, 'Coup d'oeil sur l'organisation politique, l'histoire et des moeurs des Peulhs du Fouta Dialon', *Revue Coloniale*, Nov. 1852

Apparently the Futa Jallon system worked like that of Futa Toro, under which clan heads, acting as electors of the central authority, gave prior consideration to their own particular group interests. As members of the council developed their own group interests, they showed considerable concern for preserving intact their individual authority and privileges. Acting as the supreme tribunal of the land, the council often abused its powers, using its authority to effect the elimination of renowned persons who were potential rivals for power and prestige. As the council became oppressive and overbearing, discontent against it became so widespread that it was possible for an able and clever chief, Ibrāhīm b. Nuhu, to exploit the situation to his own advantage. As friction over land and cattle rights with the Baga, Diallonke and other groups increased, and skirmishes became more frequent it became evident that the time was ripe for a revolution. Those with political and economic grievances gave their support to nine Karamokos who, as representatives of nine different Fulani settlements, met at Pita to organise a jihād against all non-believers, especially the Baga, Diallonke, Tanda and Landouma.

The jihād against the non-Muslim regime and groups took place under the leadership of Alfa Ibrāhīm b. Nuhu in 1725.[1] It was probably inspired by men from Futa Toro. This view seems corroborated by the evidence that Ibrāhīm Nuhu was aided by men of the Irlabe lineage group from Futa Toro, especially the leader Modi Maka Maoudou. This should be understandable in view of the links between the two areas, which had been increasing since the sixteenth century, and the known Tukulor tradition of going to places outside Futa Toro to prosecute religious wars.[2] There is also evidence that at this period, many Qādiriyya Muslims had migrated from Masina as militant proselytisers making converts in Upper Guinea and Futa Jallon area.[3]

With the success of Nuhu's revolution, an imamate system of

1 Guébhard, *L'Histoire du Fouta Djallon et des Almamys* (1909), pp. 8, 9, 11; Gouilly, *L'Islam dans l'Afrique Occidentale* (1952), p. 67; Harris, 'The Kingdom of Fouta Diallon', pp. 23ff; Smith, 'The Islamic revolutions of the 19th century', p. 173; Rodney, 'Jihād and social revolution in Futa Jallon in the eighteenth century', *JHSN*, iv, 2, 1968

2 Coindard, 'Notes sur les Indigènes du Tamgüe . . .', p. 350; Diop, *Société Toucouleur*, pp. 49–50

3 Hopewell, 'Muslim Penetration into French Guinea, Sierra Leone and Liberia before 1850' (Ph.D. thesis 1958), pp. 3–4

government, similar to that of Futa Toro, was established. Ibrāhīm Nuhu also became the political and religious head, with the title of almamy. He worked through existing institutions at first. He allowed the traditional council to continue to function, but made sure that it would serve his own purpose by packing it with his supporters. The seat of government was, however, transferred from Foucoumba to Timbo. But, as in Futa Toro, the establishment of a new polity did not guarantee peace in Futa Jallon. The revolution appears only to have provided a new context within which the struggle for dominance by the various socio-political forces could be carried on.

Ibrāhīm Nuhu was succeeded by his son, Alfa Karamoko, who carried on his work. Karamoko himself left behind him two sons, both notoriously ambitious to rule. With the struggle for power between them came division into the state. The older of the two, Yoro Pade (also called Sori) succeeded first in getting into power. But when he was away to wage war on infidels (that is, non-Muslim Mandingo elements who had not as yet accepted the new regime), his younger brother, Ali Alfa, seized power. The struggle which then ensued led to the division of Futa Jallon into two hostile camps which came to be named after the rivals – Soriya and Alfaya respectively.[1] Subsequently, Futa Jallon was afflicted with political struggles fought out in wars which endangered the stability and unity of the state. These wars raged on till the middle of the nineteenth century.

In the tussle for power, the leaders of the principal chiefly families, called 'elders', acted as advisers to the almamies and played decisive roles. As in Futa Toro, they were capable of getting almamies elected or deposed. In 1827, for instance, in cooperation with opposition groups led by one Aḥmadu of the Soriya party, the elders caused the reigning almamy, Yaya, to be deposed, and by 1831, as a result of the confusion which followed, Aḥmadu got himself proclaimed almamy. But as he did not belong to any of the ruling families, he was regarded as a usurper. The Irlabé group in Timbo refused to recognise him. He was rejected by the noble families of even the Soriya party. In an effort to get Aḥmadu deposed, an Alfaya-Soriya coalition was forged for once. Aḥmadu was killed in the war which he afterwards fought against the coalition. He had reigned for only a little over three months.

1 Hecquard, 'Coup d'oeil . . .'

Following the death of Aḥmadu, Bubakar, from the Alfaya side, succeeded to the imamate and ruled till he died in about 1840. But although he reigned for nearly nine years there was no peace in the country. The period was marked by continual armed rebellion organised by the Soriya groups. Civil wars persisted not so much because of the rivalry for power but because wars had become for many people a profitable venture through which fortunes were made.[1]

Futa Jallon was still in the political trouble caused by the Alfaya-Soriya wars when 'Umar, who was to lead the Tukulor revolution, returned from his pilgrimage. Of the connection between the Futa Jallon situation and the career of 'Umar, André Arcin's explanation is worth noting. According to it, 'Umar's success in rapidly recruiting a large following was due to endemic conflicts reflected in the political instability of the state, hatred between ethnic and political groups and the existence of war-mongers whose fortunes lay in continuing the wars – a situation from which the population at large was eager to escape.[2] The adherence to the cause of 'Umar by many disciples should not be surprising. Political instability had meant a disruption of the economic and social life of the country. And 'Umar came not only preaching religious reform but also offering means of peaceful and gainful employment through his commercial activities.

After the death of Bubakar in 1840, 'Umar even took part in settling the Alfaya-Soriya rivalry. Along with some others he proposed that the post of almamy should alternate between the two parties every two years. But because of the enormous difficulties involved in operating the settlement feuds continued within and between the two parties. These made the political situation in Futa Jallon as confused and precarious as ever before. In 1850–51, for example, there were civil wars to determine which of two cousins, 'Umar and Ibrāhīm, both of the Soriya faction, would be the almamy. The struggle lasted several months until it was settled in favour of the former.[3] By this time the Tukulor revolution led by 'Umar was about to start from neighbouring Dinguiray. The Tukulor revolution was to create more complications for Futa Jallon.

1 Arcin, *Histoire de la Guinée Française* (1911), pp. 101–2
2 *Ibid.*
3 ANSOM, Sénégal iii, 8, Rapport de M. Hecquard sur son voyage dans l'Intérieur, 1852

KHASSO

Khasso was originally a Malinke (Mande) state stretching along the two banks of the river Senegal, between the Senegambia and the Massassi Bambara state of Ka'arta. By the eighteenth century, however, Khasso came under the domination of some Fulani from Futa Jallon. Thereafter the Fulani conquerors formed the ruling elite, while the population remained mainly Malinke. The first Fulani ruler of Khasso was Demba Sega who established his headquarters at Médine.

What is known of Khasso history followed the familiar pattern common to the Senegambian states. Demba Sega's descendants engaged in a cut-throat struggle for power up to the middle of the nineteenth century. As a result of the civil wars, Khasso became politically weak and unstable and suffered fragmentation into small units, each of which later conducted its affairs in almost complete independence of the others. By the middle of the nineteenth century two of these units had assumed prominence over the others. These were the groups under Dyoukou Sambala with headquarters at Médine, and Logo with headquarters at Sabousiré. Some of the others were Khoulou, Natiaga and Fansané.[1]

The division among the rulers of the various Khasso principalities was such that they hardly ever came together for common action, even when this was necessary against external threat. Consequently they often fell prey to invaders and soon became virtual tributaries to neighbouring states, especially to the Bambara Massassi Kingdom of Ka'arta. In return for the protection afforded them, Ka'arta continued to collect tribute from the Khasso states until it was itself weakened by civil wars between the Bambara Massassi rulers and their subjects and could therefore no longer continue to exact payment of fixed tribute. But since the Khasso groups were still at loggerheads with one another, Ka'arta continued to provide help for some against the others. Whenever help was provided the protected province would pay tribute, while the opposing province would be made

1 ANSOM, Sénégal i, 41b/402, L. Faidherbe à son Excellence, Monsieur le Ministre de la Marine et des Colonies, Camp de Médine, 1 Oct. 1855; see also Monteil, *Les Khassonké* (1915) for information on the history and social structure of Khasso.

to pay indemnity. By the middle of the nineteenth century when the French were already established on the Senegal, spreading their activities to the country, and the Tukulor were launching their revolution, Khasso was still in the throes of civil wars. In 1848, for example, the political strife between the ruler of Médine, Sambala, and his brother, Tounka, led to the Khassonké being further divided into warring camps. L. Faidherbe gave further details of this state of affairs about seven years later, in 1855, when he reported that up till the arrival of 'Umar in the country, Sambala, ruler of Médine, was still at war with the provinces of Khoulou, Magui, Dinguiray, Makakingue (under Tounka) and the part of Logo that was under the control of Niamodi, based at Sabousiré. In this war, Sambala of Médine had the support of some other provinces like Natiaga, Fansané, and Tomora.[1] By the time 'Umar had started his revolution, Khasso presented the picture of a war-torn fragile state, which would easily break up before an external invasion.

KA'ARTA AND SEGU

The Bambara kingdoms of Ka'arta and Segu had the same origins. Before the emergence of the Bambara as the dominant group in the Western Sudan, the area had been under the influence of the Mali empire of the Soninke. The last Soninke king of Segu before the Bambara came into prominence was Siramakha Keita, who lived at Markadougou. Before his death, however, the Bambara had become so powerful and influential that by about 1670 they had no difficulty in gaining control of political power in the country. The Bambara who later ruled in the area were descendants of Khaladian Koulibali. According to the myth of origin Koulibali had seven sons, who scattered all over the Sudan, sharing control of the country between them. Of the descendants of Koulibali, two were very distinguished: Massa, ancestor of the Bambara Massassi; and Souma, the father of Bitto.[2]

After Koulibali's death, a struggle for power and civil war

1 ANSOM, Sénégal i, 41b/402, 'L. Faidherbe à son Excellence . . .', pp. 4–6
2 Tauxier, *Histoire des Bambara* (1942); Labouret, 'Les Manding . . .', pp. 37–9

broke out among the Bambara. Bitto, also called Tiguitto, founded Segu-Koro.[1] He got the state of Segu under his control and proceeded to chase out the descendants of Massa, particularly Sey Bamana. Sey Bamana himself went to found the kingdom of Ka'arta, and was its first ruler. Ka'arta subsequently became known as the kingdom of the Bambara Massassi (that is, the kingdom of the descendants of Massa).[2]

Segu and Ka'arta had similar social and political institutions. In both states, the *fama* (king) traditionally came from among the descendants of Koulibali, and succession belonged to the brother of the reigning king, and not to the son. By the eighteenth century both kingdoms had become powerful. The most notable of the Segu Bambara kings of the eighteenth century was N'Golo, who ruled for about thirty-seven years (*c.* 1753–90). Not only did he establish firm Bambara control over the Segu state, but he also succeeded in keeping Masina in vassalage. He made Timbuktu pay tributes and waged wars on the Mossi.

Mansong succeeded N'Golo. But his reign was marred by wars arising from the competition for power between him and his brother, Nienancoro. In the process Nienancoro solicited and received aid from the Massassi ruler of Ka'arta, Daisé Koulibali. But because he had greater resources to keep a large army continually active, Mansong won. Because of the role of Ka'arta in the struggle in Segu, relations between the two Bambara states became strained. Mungo Park visited this area in 1796 and found that the armies of Mansong were fighting the Ka'arta kingdom. The wars arose from the desire of Mansong to avenge the military and moral aid which Daisé, the Massassi ruler, gave to Nienancoro at Nyamina. In these wars, the Ludamar Moors were involved first for, and later against, the invading Segu forces.[3]

Ka'arta was powerful, militarily, especially in the eighteenth and early nineteenth centuries. Daisé Koro (end of the eighteenth century) and Mamadi Kandia (1845 onwards) were important among Massassi rulers who built up the power of Ka'arta. But like other kingdoms in the neighbourhood, the country became

1 Segu-Sikoro, capital of Bambara Segu empire, was one of four different settlements called Segu.
2 ASAOF, 1G195/9, Lt Sagols, Notice générale sur le Soudan – Administration, mai 1897; Mage, *Voyage dans le Soudan Occidental 1863–1866* (1868), p. 398
3 Mage, *Voyage*, pp. 401–3; Gwynn, *Mungo Park and the Quest of the Niger* (1934), pp. 99–105

weak because it was torn by internal wars. Opposition to the Massassi regime came notably from among the Diawara and the Kagoro peoples. The insurrections were still being fought up till the coming of 'Umar's revolution and as will be seen later, even in spite of the ravaging campaigns of the latter.

In the nineteenth century, before the establishment of Tukulor rule, Ka'arta and Segu were separated by Beledugu, a wide stretch of land occupied by the Beleris Bambara and the Mandingoes, both branches of the Mande stock. Beledugu was a conglomeration of small groups of villages each of which had its own separate government, and the only occasions for cooperation among them were to fight external aggressions. In their subsequent resistance to Tukulor rule, they were an effective, near-complete barrier separating Segu from the Ka'arta section of the empire. In this area, the political system was decentralised, there being no such overall sovereign as the *fama* in Segu and Ka'arta.[1]

MASINA

Adjacent to the Bambara Segu Empire, to the east, was the state of Masina. The first known rulers of Masina were the Songhay under Sonni Ali, who conquered Jenne and established his rule over a large part of the area around. The Songhay empire under the Askia dynasty was conquered by the Moroccans in 1591.[2] The other parts of Masina were under the rule of a non-Muslim Fulani dynasty, the Rari. The Rari dynasty were reduced to vassalage by the Bambara of Segu who conquered Masina in the period of anarchy which followed the decadence of the Moroccan political influence in the Timbuktu-Jenne area. From the Bambara conquest in the seventeenth century to 1818 the Rari dynasty ruled Masina as a vassal state of Bambara Segu kingdom.[3] Ardo Diko was the last of the rulers before the revolution launched by the Cissé in 1818 ended the dynasty and Segu vassalage in Masina.

1 Qlọruntimẹhin, 'Resistance movements in the Tukulor empire', *CEA*, 29, 1968; ASAOF, 1G124, 'Pays du Ka'arta: Historique'; Gouilly, *Islam dans l'Afrique*, p. 64; Labouret, 'Les Manding . . .', p. 43
2 For more details see Rouche, *Contribution à l'histoire des Songhay*, *Mém. IFAN*, 29, 1953
3 ASAOF, 1G158/2, 'Notes sur l'histoire et la situation actuelle du Macina', Le Résident, Ségou, 1 Mar. 1892, pp. 1–2

The 1818 revolution in Masina was inspired by ideas which were similar to those which animated the jihad of 'Uthmān b. Fodiye among Hausa kingdoms and their neighbours. The leader of the revolution was Aḥmad b. Muḥammad Lobbo Cissé Al-Masini, a devout and austere Muslim who was also apparently the head of a community of Muslim scholars ('*ulamā*'). He drew inspiration from Sokoto and had support not only among scholars but also from some Muslim notables in positions of political power. Obviously because he regarded Sokoto as a model, Aḥmad Lobbo had sent emissaries to 'Uthmān b. Fodiye as early as 1815 or 1816. The aim of the mission was to seek advice from the latter on the validity of his projected jihād against the Fulani Rari dynasty in Masina.[1] The jihād was accomplished, however, before the emissaries returned from Sokoto so that it could be said that Sokoto's influence in the revolution did not go beyond providing inspiration.

The jihād which resulted in the establishment of the Cissé dynasty started between March and May 1818. In the wars the reigning *fama* of Segu, Dah, aided his vassal, Ardo Diko. But in spite of the military assistance from Segu, the Cissé armies defeated the forces of Ardo Diko in successive battles, until the latter were finally routed at the battles of Nokouma and Geri. With the fall of Ardo Diko, Aḥmad Lobbo Cissé assumed control of the country under the title of Shaikh Aḥmadu.[2]

Once established in Masina, Shaikh Aḥmadu quickly extended his rule over Jenne and Timbuktu. Under the Shaikh, the Cissé converted Masina into a base for the propagation of Islam into neighbouring areas. But their encounters with other states are not to be explained only in terms of their desire to spread Islam, of which the Shaikh was the protagonist in the region. The establishment of Cissé rule in Masina was a violation of the political interests of Bambara Segu in the state. Many of the crises which later faced the Cissé both within and outside Masina are to be explained in terms of reactions against them from peoples on whose interests they trampled. For example, apart from the Bambara Segu state, there were communities within Masina, including sometimes even influential Muslims in commercial Jenne, who

1 William A. Brown, 'Towards a Chronology for the Caliphate of Hamdullahi (Masina)', *CEA*, 31, viii, 3, 1968
2 For more details on the Cissé period in Masina, see Hampate-Ba et Daget, *L'Empire Peul de Macina 1818–1853* (1955)

valued their Segu connections and were prepared to defend them against the new regime. The reactions of the Segu rulers to events in Masina and the enthusiasm of the Cissé to spread Islam, and with it their own political power, largely influenced the course of events in the internal as well as external affairs of Masina up till the eve of 'Umar's Tukulor revolution.[1]

Internally the administrative system adopted was very much dictated by the need to curb widespread and continual uprising. For defence reasons, Shaikh Aḥmadu changed his capital from Nokouma, which was subject to inundation, to Hamdallaḥi ('Praise be to God'), which occupied a better strategic position. Shaikh Aḥmadu was faced with armed resistance from various ethnic groups within Masina, the most redoubtable being the Tuaregs and other peoples from Timbuktu. In an effort to consolidate his position, Shaikh Aḥmadu directed a series of wars against Timbuktu until about 1831, when he achieved the first victory. But even after 1831 the Timbuktu forces, especially those of the Tuareg, did not entirely submit to Cissé rule. While the struggle for supremacy between the Cissé and the Tuareg was raging in Timbuktu, the Kounta tribe led by the Bakkā'ī family maintained an equilibrium between the two forces until a pact was concluded in 1846. Sidi Aḥmad al-Bakkā'ī, the head of the family and of the Bakkaiyya branch of the Qādiriyya brotherhood, helped to arrange the compromise solution by which Timbuktu was recognised as part of the Masina caliphate, but was left with a good deal of internal autonomy. Part of the agreement was that Timbuktu was not to be subject to military occupation, and would have the right to retain part of the taxes collected in and around it.[2]

As soon as the internal situation in Masina permitted him Shaikh Aḥmadu embarked upon campaigns to expand his area of authority. While the wars against the Oulibé, Ighuillade and Tademeket Tuareg of the Timbuktu region were still on, the Shaikh also led military expeditions to the Mossi country and to the Bambara Segu state. The declared purpose of these expeditions was the spread of Islam. But most of the operations failed and therefore did not lead to the expected result. For example the wars against the Mossi did not achieve the subjection of the

1 ASAOF, 1G301/1, Sénégambie-Niger – Cercle de Bandiagara par Ch. de la Bretesche, 15 Oct. 1903
2 Dr Tautain, 'Tombouctou', *Nouvelle Revue* 1 fevrier 1885, pp. 631–7

people as had actually been hoped. Instead, Masina forces, led by such army leaders as Abderrahman, Aḥmadu Sheik, Aḥmadu Lobo and Gourorro Malado, suffered several reverses.[1]

As has been explained earlier the conflict with Segu did not result from religious considerations only. While the Cissé harped on the aspect of religious duty involved, it was obvious that from the point of view of Segu the struggle hinged upon the need to restore its socio-political and economic interests in Masina. Here the struggle was more protracted and difficult, producing no decisive results in the reign of Shaikh Aḥmadu. The campaigns were continued by his successors, Aḥmadu Sheik (1846–53) and Aḥmadu b. Aḥmadu (1853–62). The latter was engaged in the wars against Segu right up to the time that 'Umar launched his campaigns. For instance, in 1858 he personally led the Masina forces to the conquest of Sanamadougou, a village directly opposite Segu. The campaigns of the Masina rulers were also carried to Ka'arta where, in the reign of Aḥmadu Sheik, expeditions were sent to Bakhounou and Kingui provinces. Masina forces were also sent to aid the Jawandos in their rebellion against Bambara Massassi rulers of Ka'arta.[2] Masina's military involvement in Ka'arta could be seen as an attempt to subvert the Bambara rulers – an extension of the war against Segu. This background of conflict between Masina and Segu is important as it will help our understanding of Masina's attitude in their later clash with al-ḥājj 'Umar. It contrasts with the mistaken suggestion that Aḥmad b. Aḥmad, ruler of Masina, was an 'accommodator' of non-Islamic practices and that he 'had achieved an understanding' with the powerful pagan Bambara of Segu, each agreeing to abstain from interference in the other's internal affairs'. That this suggestion could not be valid is borne out by the same writer who on the following page cites evidence to show that Aḥmad b. Aḥmad, among others, regarded himself as a Mahdi.[3]

1 *Ibid.*; Hampaté-Ba et Daget, *L'Empire Peul, passim.*
2 ASAOF, 1G122/1, Underberg, 'Notes sur l'histoire du Macina', Ségou-Sikoro, 10 Oct. 1890, pp. 15, 17, 23
3 See Willis, 'Jihād fī Sabīl Allāh: its doctrinal basis', *JAH*, viii, 3, 1967, pp. 401, fn 24 and 402

INTERSTATE RELATIONS

Reference has already been made to the fact that there was considerable social and political mobility among peoples from various
states, especially between Futa Toro and Futa Jallon as well as
Masina. In addition to the type of relations which resulted from
such mobility, considerable trade relations existed between the
various states of the Western Sudan before the beginning of
Tukulor rule. There were also trade connections between the
Western Sudan and the states of the forest belt on the one hand,
and the Sahara and North Africa on the other. Long-established
commercial centres of the Western Sudan included Timbuktu,
Jenne, Nyamina, Sansanding, Bamako, Boure and Kankan.
As might be expected, the wars that were often fought in this
period had damaging consequences for the economic activities
of these centres. For instance the wars between Bambara Segu
and Masina had disastrous effects on Jenne and Timbuktu,
especially on their status as commercial centres. The wars
continually interrupted communications between these places
and Nyamina, Sansanding, Bamako and Boure, whence came
the bulk of the gold traded in the Western Sudan.[1]

In spite of disturbances, however, relations were never completely broken. Economic ties were fairly strong. Futa Jallon
and Futa Toro engaged in frequent, lucrative commercial relations. Kankan traded in slaves and gold dust with Futa Jallon.
The Sarakole were renowned as great carriers of trade all over
the Western Sudan. Gold from Boure, Kankan and Wasulu,
was an important factor in the commercial life of the Western
Sudan. The Mandingo traders also served as carriers of trade
between the Western Sudanese states and Sierra Leone, Gambia
and the French establishments in Senegal. E. Mage, on mission
to Segu, came across petty traders and artisans from Sierra Leone
in the various markets of the Western Sudan in 1864.[2]

Kolanut was another very valuable article of trade carried
mainly by the Diulas. For centuries trade in this commodity

---

1 Caillie, *Travels Through Central Africa to Timbuctoo; and Across the
   Great Desert to Morocco, performed in the Years 1824–1828*, i, (1830),
   pp. 445–6
2 Mollien, *Voyage*, ii, pp. 193, 199; Mage, *Voyage*, p. 188

had served as an important link between the Western Sudan and the coastal regions of West Africa. From Ashanti kolanuts were conveyed north-westwards to Sansanding, Segu and Timbuktu, and north-eastwards across the Niger to Kano and Bornu. Some of the kolanuts were also re-exported to the Sahara and North Africa.[1] The Moors and the Arabs were very important for their role in the gum trade, and in the trade in sugar, dates, cowries, incense, oriental perfumes and copper bracelets. Means of transport were not lacking: bullocks and boats were plentiful.[2]

EUROPEAN INTERESTS

The earliest European contact with the Western Sudan was made by the Portuguese between 1443 and 1460. By the first date Portuguese explorers had arrived at Cape Blanc and two years after in 1445 they established a trading post in the southern limits of the Sahara on the island of Arguin in what is now Mauritania. Arguin soon became Portugal's main trading base in West Africa and the Portuguese erected a fort on the island to protect their traders, sailors and fishermen who had been attracted to the area by the abundance of fish just off the Cape. The construction of the fort which was begun either in 1448 or 1455 was not completed until 1482.[3] But the Portuguese remained attached to the island because they hoped that from there they could intercept the flow of gold being traded by the Moors along inland routes with Berber and Arab people to the north. They were soon disillusioned, as their hopes about the commercial potentialities of Arguin proved exaggerated. However, Portuguese merchants traded such European goods like cloth, linen, wheat pots, combs and glasses for pepper, gum Arabic, salt, gold and slaves, but by the 1470s their main commercial interest had shifted to the areas south of the Senegal river. Even then Arguin was not just abandoned and it was to be occupied not only by the

---

1 See Boahen, *Britain, the Sahara and the Western Sudan: 1788–1861* (1964) for a full treatment of this theme.
2 ASAOF, 1G184, 'Renseignements historiques sur le Sansanding et le Macina', Capitaine Bellat, Sansanding, mars–avril, 1893, pp. 20–2
3 Cultru, *Histoire du Sénégal du XVe Siècle à 1870* (1910), p. 179; Gray, *The Gambia* (1940), p. 9

Portuguese but also the Dutch and later the French for nearly three hundred years.[1]

In the meantime, Portugal established a new base at Elmina in present-day Ghana in 1482. Elmina was to prove a more important base for commercial activities than Arguin or any other post they built on the mouth of the Senegal river and in the Senegambia. In 1488 the Portuguese made an unsuccessful attempt to build a fort among the Wolof of the mouth of the Senegal in an effort to establish contact with the famed Timbuktu and drain some of the gold trade of the interior to their trading stations on the coast. After 1488 they made more efforts to establish bases in the interior in a continued endeavour to tap the interior trade routes, but the opposition of the indigenous population to Portuguese intrusion generally frustrated the effort. In particular, although some Portuguese traders were reputed to have become established in the gold-producing Bambuk, they had to abandon the country shortly after because of the hostile reactions of the people.[2]

Although the Portuguese had an early start over the other European groups in the penetration of the Western Sudan, they did not achieve any significant result, partly because they had to abandon some of their posts and partly because they were absorbed through a process of acculturation into the indigenous population. An example of the latter case were the Portuguese elements who settled in the Cape Verde in present-day Senegal. During the sixteenth century the Portuguese were significant as settlers mainly at Portudal and Joal in the Casamance area: they also had outposts in places like Rufisque and Beziguiche. They appear to have had more fortune in settling and trading in the Gambia. In the latter place, they settled and traded at Tankular, Bintang, San Domingo Sika and other places.[3]

While the Portuguese were trying with varied successes to establish bases, other European nation groups also emerged to compete for the trade of West Africa especially from the sixteenth century onwards. The first to follow the Portuguese example seem to have been the Castilian traders who were said

1 Wood, 'An archaeological appraisal of early European settlements in the Senegambia', *JAH*, viii, 1, 1967, p. 43
2 *Ibid.*, p. 45; Blake, *Europeans in West Africa 1450–1560* (1942), pp. 1, 22, 24
3 Wood, 'An archaeological appraisal . . .', pp. 45–6; For details of Portuguese activities in this region see Rodney, *A History of the Upper Guinea Coast to 1800* (1970), chs. III and IV

to have visited the Guinea coast in 1453–54 and 1492, after which date their attention was diverted to the New World and its riches. The Dutch, the British and the French joined early in the sixteenth century, though like the Castilians they did not as yet establish posts. But the presence of several European groups soon resulted in competition for the trade of the area. Early in the seventeenth century the Dutch began to threaten Portugal's position all along the West Atlantic coast. The British and the French later joined in the competition.

As far as the Senegambia and the Western Sudan were concerned the competition between the British and the French was the most significant. It remained almost a permanent feature of the history of the area from the seventeenth century to the nineteenth. Merchants of both countries were interested in the gum trade, of which the Moors were the principal carriers, as well as in the other items of trade from other areas of the Western Sudan. The Mandingo traders served as carriers of trade between the Western Sudanese states and the British settlements in the Gambia and Sierra Leone as well as with the French establishments in Senegal. The Diula were prominent in the kolanut, gold and salt trade between the coastal states and the interior. The competing interest in the trade of the area accounted largely for the protracted rivalry which the British and the French engaged in to oust each other from the coastal settlements which served as gateways to the interior.

The French established first at Saint Louis (Senegal) in 1637, and the following year they began building a fortified station at the mouth of the river Senegal.[1] New settlements were subsequently established at Goree Island, Rufisque and Joal – places where the Portuguese had settled at one time or the other. In the eighteenth century, with Saint Louis (1638) and Goree (1678) fortresses serving as bases on the coast, the French penetrated further into the interior by means of a series of forts and posts. Some of these forts, like Fort St Pierre (*c.* 1714–20) were situated far inland, especially on the Faleme River in Galam, near the gold-producing area of Bambuk.[2] Between 1697 and the beginning of the nineteenth century the French had built forts and minor posts in such places as Bakel and Matam. The British, for their part, colonised the Gambia from about 1661 onwards.

1 Cultru, *Histoire du Senegal*, p. 42
2 Wood, 'An archaeological appraisal . . .', p. 50

As a result of rivalry between the two, Britain took Saint Louis and Goree Island from the French on three occasions before 1817 when she finally returned them to the French.[1] Henceforth the French remained the dominant European group in the Senegambia and for the rest of the nineteenth century they were to devote their attention to expanding not only their economic interests but also their political influence in the Senegambia and the Western Sudan generally. The attempt to do this to the exclusion of all other comers partly explains the continuation of the rivalry between them and the British for the rest of the century.

In the commercial sphere, the French had attempted to exploit their presence on the coast since the seventeenth century. In 1696 the Compagnie Royale du Sénégal, Cap Nord, et Côte d'Afrique was incorporated, to handle French commercial activities and make French presence in the area meaningful.[2] Working from this base, and in spite of vicissitudes, the French developed their commercial interests until by the beginning of the nineteenth century they conceived of the Senegambia as a hinterland necessary for the legitimate development of their colony of Senegal. At first working with the Moors but later against them, the French were firmly established in the gum trade. It was to foster this and other economic interests that the French Government sent various missions to the Senegambia and parts of the Western Sudan. For instance in 1818, G. Mollien visited the Senegambian region to find routes linking Senegal with the Gambia and Bambuk, and to ascertain the extent and richness of the gold mines in the latter place.[3] In 1828 M. Duranton was on a similar mission to Bambuk and Khasso.[4] M. Hecquard was also sent to investigate the usefulness of the waterways as means of communication and to establish commercial relations with the Segu Bambara empire.[5]

1 See Ọlọruntimẹhin, 'The Western Sudan and the coming of the French, 1800–1893', in J. F. Ade. Ajayi and Michael Crowder eds., *A History of West Africa*, vol. ii (forthcoming) for details.

2 Ly, *La Compagnie du Sénégal* (1958), pp. 87–214 for details of French activities in the Senegambia in this period; Ritchie, 'Deux textes sur le Sénégal (1673–1677)', *Bull. IFAN*, B, xxx, 1, 1968, pp. 289–353

3 Mollien, *Voyage*, vols. i and ii contain details of this mission.

4 Hardy, 'Un épisode de l'exploration du Soudan – L'Affaire Duranton 1828–1838', *Ann. et Mém. CEHSAOF*, 1917, pp. 413–36

5 Hecquard, 'Coup d'oeil . . .'

As French economic interests grew efforts were made to protect them. At first this was done through treaty agreements with
indigenous rulers;[1] but in addition fortified trading posts were
built along the river Senegal. Between 1820 and 1854, the French
established fortified posts (forts) at Bakel (1820), Dagana (1821),
Merinaghen (1822), Lampbar (1843), Sénoudébou (1845), and
Podor (1854). At the beginning, the posts were conceived of as
trading centres which also afforded protection to French persons
and property in and around them. Between 1854 and 1855 the
French Government ordered the building of eight more fortified
posts from Richard Toll to Médine, a development which testified
to the expansion of French economic interests in the Western
Sudan. The gum trade had become very important, and the
French were eager to establish a monopoly over it. They were
now becoming impatient with the Moors, the intermediaries
in the gum trade, and were fighting wars against them with a
view to limiting their share of the trade. The French now began
to talk of the need to maintain 'French authority' both on the
right bank of the Senegal, where trade was largely carried on
with the Moors, and on the left bank, where they traded with
the local inhabitants and with the people from the interior.
Following the inauguration of this new policy under Governor
Protet, other posts were built at Médine (1855), Matam (1857),
Aere (1866), Ndiagne (1866), Klur-Mandoumbe-Khary, Khoulou
and Talem in 1867. Henceforth these posts ceased to be mere
trading stations; they were now conceived as serving to maintain
French authority and political influence along the river Senegal.[2]
   This aggressive imperial policy naturally provoked hostility
towards the French from the indigenous populations. In many
areas, French posts were subjected to attacks. The French also
had to wage wars against the Moors whom they were trying to
push out of the gum business. For instance, in 1854 the French,

1 For examples of such treaties, see 'Traité de paix et d'amitié conclu à
   N'gulo le 8 mai 1819 avec le roi et les chefs du Wallo'; 'Traité de
   paix et d'amitié conclu à St Louis le 7 juin 1821, entre la France et le
   Roi des Trarzas'; 'Traité conclu, le 20 avril 1842, entre le Roi des
   Bracknas et M. Caillé, délégué du Gouverneur du Sénégal' etc. in
   A. J. H. de Clercq, *Receuil des traités de France 1861–1919*, pp.
   202–3, 270–5, 619
2 ASAOF, 13G23/13, 'Notes sur les postes militaires du Sénégal et de
   sa dépendance', 19 July 1867; 13G33/4, 'Considérations générales sur
   l'état des postes du fleuve au moi d'août 1875'

in addition to fighting the Moors, had to face some of the Tukulor in war. At Dialmath alone in that year, they had to fight against about 2,000 Tukulor forces.[1] The hostile reaction of the indigenous populations was understandable. From being the protectors of the French, they were now being told to accept French authority. With the spread of hostility against them, the French soon found that they were ill-equipped to execute the policy launched by Protet. The policy failed almost inevitably and the need for a change seems to have been accepted by the French Government, who replaced Protet with Louis Faidherbe later in 1854. By the time Faidherbe assumed office as Governor, French commercial and political relations with the states of the Western Sudan had fallen into chaos. The state of war had virtually paralysed French commercial activities.

But the state of war between the French and the neighbouring states did not change with Faidherbe's[2] appointment. As was clear from the instructions given to him on appointment, the French Government had not renounced its imperial objective of establishing spheres of influence over the areas where they traded. He was told that his appointment was not meant to mark the beginning or continuation of a bellicose era, but rather that his main mission was to see to the peaceful expansion of commerce through the exploration of new avenues. This was a realisable task which was, however, made impossible by the political task which he was asked to perform. He was to impress upon the people among whom the French traded that the French were always ready to use force to back up their claim to political authority in their countries, especially in the areas bordering on the Senegal from Saint Louis to the Cataracts of Félou.[3] In effect, the French were claiming political authority over the territories adjoining the river Senegal.

Faidherbe's attempt to realise these objectives necessarily involved a continuation of the state of war left over by Protet's administration. Faidherbe, who had commanded the battalion

1 Hardy, *Histoire de la colonisation française* (1928), pp. 169–71, 202–3
2 General Louis Léon César Faidherbe, b.1818, served in the French army in Algeria before coming to Senegal. In Senegal, first a Marine Engineer, later Governor, from 1854–61, and 1863–65. Subsequently, after career in the French army, was Deputy and Senator in French Parliament: d.1889
3 ANSOM, Senegal i, 4/C, 'Le Ministre à M. le chef de bataillon du Génie, Faidherbe à Sénégal', Paris, 9 Nov. 1854

of troops stationed at St Louis under Protet, continued the war against the Moors and some of the other riverain peoples. The indigenous populations continued to base their relations with the French on the earlier treaty agreements and they fought to preserve their independence of the foreigners. They insisted on the French paying tribute over the land on which their posts were built.

After a while Faidherbe sought to deal separately with the states, apparently in the hope that he would thereby be able to isolate and defeat the Moors. In this bid he entered into negotiations with the almamy of Futa Toro over the payment of tribute, while continuing the war against the other states. He was, however, shocked to discover that there was cooperation between the states in their efforts to preserve their independence and rights against the French. To the request that Futa Toro should deal with the French separately, Faidherbe was told that Futa chiefs were having consultations with the chiefs of the Trarza and Brackna Moors, the almamy of Futa Jallon and others. Confronted with a united front in this way, Faidherbe concluded despondently that '. . . cela semblerait annoncer un commencement de concert, de ligue contre nous'.[1] The power of the French was based on naval boats operating during the high waters of the Senegal. They could therefore not afford campaigns against hostile neighbours who were united against them during the dry season. This situation had hindered the progress of the French, and by the end of 1854 they were in a stalemate in their relations with the Senegambian states.

Nevertheless Faidherbe saw in the Western Sudan an indispensable vast hinterland that should serve the commercial needs of France in Senegal. But given the emerging Tukulor empire in the Western Sudan, and the fact that the new French policy was not popular in the Senegal area, penetration inland by force of arms was out of the question, especially since the outcome of the wars already started against the Moors and others was still uncertain. Since the French were still bent on achieving their objective, another approach was called for. This was provided by the internal political situation in Senegalese Futa and by the various resistance movements against the evolving Tukulor empire. From 1854 onwards the French became part and parcel

1 ANSOM, Sénégal 41b/551, 'L. Faidherbe à M. le Ministre de la Marine et des Colonies', St Louis, 26 Dec. 1854

Al-Shaikh Ahmadu, Head of the empire 1864-1893

Muhammad Aguibu, emir of Dinguiray until 1891

of the politics of the states in the Senegal area. They tried to exploit the confused situation in the area to their advantage. Further inland, by using their posts in the river as bases, they also soon became involved in the politics of the emerging Tukulor empire.[1]

SUMMARY

In the foregoing analysis of mid-nineteenth-century history of the Western Sudan, certain issues stand out clearly. There was the question of land connected with the location of the Senegambian states in the fertile, arable areas of the Senegal valley, particularly in the areas of the valley which were very suitable for the cultivation of gum, an important article of trade in the area. The significance of the location of these states for the history of the Western Sudan lies in the fact that the fertility of the area easily attracted migrant populations in search of a settlement where they could grow their crops and tend their cattle. Conflicts often arose as population groups settled in areas coveted by other land-hungry peoples. The influx of peoples in search of fertile land often led to the population of the states becoming heterogeneous, as in Jolof. Notable among the settlers in Jolof were the Moors who, by the beginning of the nineteenth century, had become the most important carriers of the gum trade, especially with the Europeans. The struggle for land similarly affected Futa Toro which up to the nineteenth century was a federation of several principalities, each of which was dominated by a particular clan competing with one another for dominance.

The struggle for the possession of land was often connected with the struggle for the control of political power. For instance, from the Middle Ages to the nineteenth century, the political history of Futa Toro was largely an account of the rise and fall of regimes. In the search for fertile land, various peoples, notably the Fulani, Tukulor, Wolof, Moors, Bambara and Sarakole had come to live in Futa Toro and each group had, at one time or the other, taken part in the struggle for political power, until from the eighteenth century, the Tukulor became dominant in terms

1 See Chapter 4 for an account of the struggle between the French and the Tukulor in the Senegambia.

of power and number. The need to possess political power as a prelude to exercising control over the economy of the area must have been obvious to the contestants. The dissolution of the Jolof empire resulted from similar developments as in Futa Toro.

In other states instability resulted from naked struggle for political power between rival groups in the ruling dynasties. Typical of this was the instability caused by the Alfaya-Soriya struggle in Futa Jallon and the dynastic struggle in Khasso. In both states the people were divided into feuding groups up till the time that al-ḥājj 'Umar emerged to establish the Tukulor empire. Ka'arta and Segu Bambara kingdoms were relatively stable in spite of the insurrections from subject peoples, like the Diawara and Kagoro, which plagued the former, and the wars of the latter with Masina.

Another important factor in the history of the Western Sudan was the tradition of proselytising and religious revivalism. In Futa Toro the tradition of Islamic proselytisation could be dated back to the eleventh century with the establishment of Tekrur. The imamate systems in both Futa Toro and Futa Jallon resulted from the eighteenth-century revolutions led by Suleyman Bal and Ibrahim Nuhu respectively. Tukulor rule in Futa Toro dated from the Bal revolution of 1775. The tradition was still very much alive by the beginning of the nineteenth century. The religious leaders of Futa Toro and the main agents for the propagation of Islam in the Western Sudan were the *toroBé*. They were reputed for their role in toppling the non-Muslim Denyanke rule in Futa Toro and for aiding the revolutions in Futa Jallon and other adjacent territories. 'Umar's family belonged to the *toroBé* group and was part of the religious leadership. In Masina also the Cissé successfully led a revolution against the non-Muslim dynasty in 1818 and thereafter established an Islamic theocracy. The wars between Masina and Segu resulted in part from the desire of the Cissé to spread Islam and their own rule to neighbouring states.

Thus, it is clear that the Western Sudanic societies were by mid-nineteenth century in a remarkably dynamic state, susceptible to rapid changes. By mid-nineteenth century, all the factors enumerated above had led to one major development – instability of the Western Sudanic societies. Upon this came the complications brought about through the activities of competing Europeans, of which the French were dominant. The latter, in an effort to increase their share of the commerce of the Western Sudan, were seeking to acquire political power in the area of their operations. The result was that they tried to undermine the independence and authority of the states with which they had relations and the states concerned naturally became hostile. To protect their sovereignty, they had to fight a series of wars against the French. These wars, coupled with the difficult internal situations in the various states, absorbed the energies and attention of the participants at a time when the Tukulor revolution was already being launched.

2 'Umar b. Sa'īd Tall and the Beginnings of the Tukulor Revolution

The founder of the Segu Tukulor empire was 'Umar b. Sa'īd Tall, popularly known as al-ḥājj 'Umar. The fourth son of his father, 'Umar was born in the village of Aloar (or Halwar) in Futa Toro around 1794.[1] His father, Sa'īd Tall, was a learned marabout[2] who brought up his children in strict Islamic traditions. The family belonged to the *toroBé* social group. As such they formed part of the superior caste which, in the Tukulor society, provided the political, religious and social aristocracy. Traditionally, the *toroBé* supplied the *literātī* and agents for the spread of Islam not only among the Tukulor but also outside the society. They were responsible for the revolution that overthrew the Denyanke dynasty and for establishing a theocracy in Futa Toro in the eighteenth century. With the establishment of the imamate system of government, the *toroBé* became the dominant political and social class since it was from their group that almamies and their electors emerged. But apart from the fact that 'Umar was born a member of the group that provided the Tukulor society with its political and religious leadership and that, like other children of his father, he followed religious instructions, little else is known of his youth. The little that is

1 A. Le Chatelier, *L'Islam en Afrique Occidentale* (1899), p. 167. 'Umar's hagiographer, Muhammad Aliou Tyam, puts the date at 1794. But Mage, *Voyage*, p. 231 erroneously gives 1797 although his own evidence that 'Umar was sixty-nine years old at the time of his death in 1864 suggests that he was probably born earlier.
2 Sa'īd Tall was not only learned, he was also regarded as pious. 'Umar's mother was said to be Adama Ayse Caam. 'Umar was said to be the last of the ten children of his mother. The others were Fatimata, Ibrahima, Umakala, Jeynaba, Sire, Mokhtar, Tafsiru Atumaan, Alfa Ahmadu and Ceerno Haadi. See Wane, 'De Halwaar à Degembere ou l'itinéraire islamique de Shaykh Umar Tal', *Bull. IFAN*, B, xxxi, 2, 1969, pp. 445–51, also Ouane, *Pérégrinations Soudanaises* (n.d.), p. 179

known is recorded by one of his Tukulor *talibés*[1] and admirers in a two thousand verse poem in Poular. In this hagiography, 'Umar is idealised as a born saint who never did anything wrong. According to this version both his saintly birth and divinely ordained career had long been prophesied.[2]

Like the vast majority of Muslims in the Western Sudan at the time, 'Umar's family belonged to the Qādiriyya brotherhood and he probably grew up a Qadiri. He obviously received the usual education in Islamic theology and jurisprudence. He acquired a high reputation for his learning. He grew up at a time when the Tijāniyya brotherhood was just spreading to the Senegambia. This latter brotherhood was founded towards the end of the eighteenth century and its founder, Aḥmād al-Tijānī, died only in 1815. Founded in the present area of Algeria, Tijāniyya spread to the Western Sudan through Fez and Mauritania.[3] The main agents for its spread into the Senegambia were the Moors and Berbers from nearby Moorish emirates, but also probably missionaries from the Sharifian empire of Morocco. There is a tradition which claims that 'Umar was initiated into the Tijānī brotherhood by Sidi 'Abd al-Karim al-Naqil of Timbo.[4] This implies that he had been converted from the older Qādiriyya *ṭarīqa* into Tijāniyya as a youth.

He seems to have become a prominent figure by 1825, and he had obviously made his mark as a religious leader – a marabout. In that year he was already preparing to undertake the pilgrimage. In this connection, he visited Saint Louis, Senegal, to solicit the aid of the Muslim community there. It was usual for intending pilgrims to ask for alms to augment their own resources for undertaking the pilgrimage which, because of the distance and poor communication system, was normally a costly,

1 The *talibés* were the Tukulor aristocracy, leaders of their clans.
2 Tyam, *La Vie d'El-Hadj Omar, Qacida en Poular* (1935). These attributes appear to have been shared by other jihād leaders in the Western Sudan. See on 'Uthmān b. Fodiye, F. H. Elmasri, 'The Life of Shehu Usuman dan Fodio before the jihād', *JHSN*, ii, 4, 1963; Adelẹyẹ *et al.*, 'Sifofin Shehu: an autobiography and character study of 'Uthman b. Fudi in verse', *Bull. CAD* ii, 1, 1966
3 Paden, 'The Influence of Religious Elites on Political Culture and Community Integration in Kano, Nigeria' (Ph.D. thesis 1968) for a discussion of the spread and branches of the Tijāniyya in West Africa.
4 Salenc, 'La vie d'Al Hadj Omar, traduction d'un manuscrit de la Zaouia tidjaniya de Fez', *Bull. CEHSAOF*, 1918, p. 410; tr. Gaden, Qacida, p. 8

protracted and hazardous venture. Saint Louis was at this time a
strong Islamic centre and the main commercial centre in the
evolving French colony of Senegal. It was a converging point
for Muslim traders from the Moorish emirates and the Senegambia. It was natural, therefore, that 'Umar, a *torodo* marabout,
should go there to preach and appeal for alms. It is not known
how much following he had at this time either in Futa Toro or
Saint Louis. He received generous donations, however, from the
Muslim population of the city and with these and other resources at his disposal, he was able to start off on the pilgrimage
in 1826.[1] He was apparently the pilgrim whom Clapperton met at
Sokoto and referred to rather prematurely, as an al-hājj on
7 November 1826. This would seem to be the case because
Clapperton claimed that the *al-ḥājj*, like two others, had only
recently arrived in Sokoto from Futa Toro and Timbuktu.[2]

On his way to Mecca 'Umar stayed for about seven months in
Sokoto and two months in Gwandu, both centres of the caliphate
which 'Uthmān b. Fodiye had created earlier in the century. The
Sokoto caliphate had been founded and led mainly by a community of Toronkawa Muslim scholars who, as their name
suggests, traced their descent to Futa Toro.[3] 'Umar's hosts in
the Sokoto caliphate were Muḥammad Bello, Fodiye's son and
successor, and Abdullahi, Bello's uncle and co-ruler of the
caliphate. That he stayed so long in the caliphate may be explained in terms of the close ethnic affinity and identity of
interest as a scholar which he shared with the community in
Sokoto. He could also have stayed so long in order to reinforce
himself materially and spiritually before continuing his journey.

While on the pilgrimage 'Umar travelled widely and studied
in several places, particularly in Mecca and Medina. In the
process he deepened his knowledge of Islam and gained wide
experience of other lands. He was introduced into the circles of
the leaders of the Tijāniyya, receiving instruction from Muḥammād al-Ghāli Abū Talīb in Medina. It is also claimed that the
founder of the Tijāniyya, Shaikh Sidi Aḥmād al-Tijānī, appeared
in a vision to Muḥammād al-Ghāli, commanding him to initiate
'Umar and invest him with the powers and authority of a

1 Carrère and Holle, *De la Sénégambie française* (1855), p. 192
2 Hugh Clapperton, *Journal of a Second Expedition into the Interior of
   Africa* (1829), pp. 202, 235
3 Last, *The Sokoto Caliphate* (1967), p. lxxii

muqaddam[1] as well as the *khālifa*[2] (deputy) of al-Tijānī in the Western Sudan. This order was carried out and 'Umar became *khālifa*. Thereafter, continues the story, he was secretly given an *istikhāra*,[3] a formula of prayers which would always indicate to him the right line of action and lead him out of all difficulties. After the initiation and investiture ceremonies, as well as the endowment with special powers, 'Umar was ordered not to stay any longer in Medina, but to 'go and sweep the countries to the West'. This order was subsequently interpreted as an injunction to wage a jihād against the states of the Western Sudan.[4] The essence of this story of his experience in Medina is to emphasise the divine nature of his power – he was endowed with the *baraka* and *istikhāra* – and to show that he was divinely appointed to purify Islam in the Western Sudan under the aegis of the Tijāniyya *ṭarīqa*.[5]

The pilgrimage was obviously significant as the period when he was equipped for his later role as the leader of the Tijāniyya in the Western Sudan. The story of his experience in Medina could be seen as a direct claim to superiority to, and leadership

1 Gerteiny, *Mauritania* (1967), pp. 74–5. Below the Shaikh comes the *muqqadam* or *khālifa*.

2 Martin, 'A Mahdist document from Futa Jallon', *Bull. IFAN*, B, xxv, 1–2, 1963, p. 51. The author regards this document which gives information on 'Umar's appointment as a *khālifa* as of doubtful authenticity. Whatever may be the nature of the document, however, the story of 'Umar's appointment was widespread and there could be no doubt that he was so accepted in the Western Sudan at the time.

3 *Istikhāra* was a special formula (there are various kinds) of prayers the origins of which had been traced back to the Prophet. Each formula was used as a way of securing divine guidance and approval for the possessor's enterprises and was also relied upon to help the owner out of difficulties. For a discussion of the idea of *istikhāra* see I. Goldziher, 'Istikhara' in *The Encyclopaedia of Islam* (Leiden, 1913 and 1960), ii, pp. 561–2

4 Tyam, *Qacida*, pp. 10–13

5 The *baraka* was a blessing said to be inculcated by Allah in the persons of his Prophet and saints. It was believed that the *baraka*, like *istikhāra*, consisted of extraordinary powers which Allah was said to have bestowed upon Shaikh Aḥmad Al-Tijānī, the founder of the Tijāniyya, through the medium of the Prophet. 'Umar's charisma was based on these two sources of extraordinary powers. He was reputed to have successfully used his powers of *istikhāra* in the Hijaz, Bornu, Sokoto and later in various parts of the Western Sudan. See Willis, 'Jihād fi Sabil Allah: its doctrinal basis in Islam and some aspects of its evolution in 19th-century West Africa', *JAH*, viii, 3, 1967, 406

over, all those who had otherwise been initiated to the Tijāniyya earlier on in the area. Apart from his socialisation and claims as a Tijānī, the period of his pilgrimage was also important for the opportunity which he had to be exposed to other formative influences which were later reflected in his outlook and activities as a jihād leader. Prominent among these influences were the ideas and activities of the Wahhābiyya in Central Arabia. The Wahhābiyya was a militant and violent movement which fought in the eighteenth and nineteenth centuries for the 'revival' of the true faith. The Wahhābīs were dedicated to bringing about 'a return to the pure and primitive faith of Islam purged of heresies and accretions'.[1] It would seem that 'Umar's knowledge and experience of this movement was partly responsible for the violent neo-Kharījite[2] method which he later adopted in the Western Sudan. This tendency has also been noted with regard to the outlook of the Sokoto jihādists whose achievements certainly influenced 'Umar.

On his return journey from the Middle East 'Umar reached Sokoto in 1832. He was to remain there for the next seven years as a guest of the Khālifa, Muḥammad Bello. The latter gave him one of his daughters, Mariam (sometimes also Aissatu), in marriage, as well as adequate grants to help him settle. Abibu, who, after the founding of the Tulukor empire, later ruled the Dinguiray emirate, was born of this woman. 'Umar also married a Hausa woman, an ex-slave referred to in some documents as Fatma or Nene Dade Satourou, in Sokoto. This woman was the mother of his eldest son and successor to the headship of the Tukulor empire, Aḥmadu.[3] Earlier on he had stayed for a while in Bornu and had also married into the ruling family. His Bornu wife, Mariatu, was the mother of Aguibu[4] who was later to play a prominent role in the Tukulor empire.

1 Muḥammad Al-Hajj, 'The Fulani Concept of Jihād – Shehu Uthmān dan Fodio', *Odu*, i, 1, 1964, p. 47; Holt, *Egypt and the Fertile Crescent* (1966), pp. 148–55
2 See Abun-Nasr, 'Some aspects of the 'Umari Branch of the Tijāniyya', *JAH*, iii, 2, 1962, pp. 329–31; also Waldman, 'The Fulani jihād: a reassessment', *JAH*, vi, 3, 1965, pp. 333–55 for doubts expressed on the validity of the theory of Kharijism in relation to Sokoto.
3 Houdas, trs. al-ḥājj Saʿīd, in *Tedzkiret en Nisiam fi Akhbar Molouck Es-soudan* (1901), p. 308; Mage, *Voyage*, p. 234; Mademba, 'La dernière étape d'un conquérant', *Bull. CEHSAOF*, 1921, pp. 479–80
4 De Loppinot, 'Souvenirs d'Aguibou', *Bull. CEHSAOF*, 1919, p. 25

'Umar's long stay in, and connections with, Sokoto were clearly significant in his formation and evolution as a religious leader. In addition to his earlier experiences he was surely influenced by the ideas and activities of the Sokoto community under the leadership of Muḥammad Bello. He must have been inspired by the ideas which led to the founding of the caliphate. He was obviously very close to his host and patron, Muḥammad Bello. He took part in some of the wars which Bello fought against resistance elements in the state. He became important as the author of powerful charms (*grisgris*) which were considered instrumental to some of the victories which the Sokoto army scored in the continual wars to preserve the caliphate. His experience in Sokoto was significant for the opportunity which he had to be practically involved in the politics and wars of a state which grew out of an Islamic revivalist movement and, in this connection, for his exposure to the tradition of violence as a means of pursuing the objectives of the jihād. Although his patron, Bello, died on 25 October 1837, 'Umar continued to live in Sokoto until the second year of the reign of Bello's successor as *khālifa*, Muḥammad Atiq (Atiku). He left Sokoto finally in December 1838.[1]

At his departure 'Umar was a rich man with a large following. He had also obviously become one of the leading men in the Toronkawa community. He had a large number of slaves, many of whom accompanied him on his return to Futa. Some of his slaves later on attained positions of importance and helped to make his revolution, which resulted in the creation of the Tukulor empire, a success. For instance, during the campaigns and in the early years of Tukulor rule Mustafa, an ex-slave, commanded Tukulor forces at Nioro in Ka'arta.[2]

On his homeward journey, 'Umar went through the Muslim caliphate of Masina, staying as a guest of the ruler, Shaikh Aḥmadu, for about nine months. The latter, a devout Muslim of the Qādiriyya *ṭariqa*, like his Sokoto neighbours, also received 'Umar generously at his court until the latter left some time in late 1839.[3]

In continuation of his journey home 'Umar reached the

---

1 Houdas, trs. al-ḥājj Sa'īd, in *Tedzkiret*, pp. 303, 328; A. Le Chatelier, *l'Islam en Afrique*, p. 168
2 Mage, *Voyage*, p. 234
3 Tyam, *Qacida*, p. 20, v. 107

neighbouring Bambara kingdom of Segu. The *fama* of Segu, Tiefolo, at first detained him,[1] apparently because he considered him dangerous. There is, however, a seemingly apocryphal story according to which 'Umar's detention in Segu had been engineered by Shaikh Aḥmadu, the Cissé ruler of Masina. This story appears to be an attempt to explain the subsequent hostility and war between 'Umar and the caliphate of Masina in terms of causes dating from the time of 'Umar's return from the pilgrimage.[2] The story cannot be true, since there is clear evidence that the Cissé rulers treated 'Umar well, and that was partly why he stayed as their guest for as long as nine months. Furthermore, the alleged duplicity or collaboration between Segu and Masina would be incompatible with the hostile relations, indeed state of war, which had existed between the two since the establishment of the caliphate in Masina. Rather than accept this explanation of 'Umar's detention by the non-Muslim *fama* of Segu, it is necessary to look for another which is more consistent with the facts which 'Umar himself was likely to have known of the relations between Segu and Masina. The *fama*'s action could be seen as a demonstration of his hostility to Masina and those associated with the Cissé regime. 'Umar was an important Muslim leader who, for months, was known to have been a guest of the Cissé ruler, the Muslim neighbour who since 1818 had been at war with Segu. 'Umar was, because of this connection, *persona non grata* in Bambara Segu. Hence his detention.

After his release by the *fama* he continued his journey and arrived in Futa Toro late in 1840. He did not stay long in Futa Toro however. Rather he moved with his disciples to Futa Jallon where the almamy, Bubakar, allowed him to settle and establish a *zāwiya*[3] at Dyegounko, near Timbo, headquarters of Futa Jallon.[4]

1 Delafosse, *Haut-Sénégal-Niger* (1912), ii, p. 293
2 Oral evidence at Segu, 1965
3 A *zāwiya* is a self-contained religious community which operates like a nursery of men for the expansion of the faith to be undertaken, if necessary, by force of arms. Ordinary people visited the *zāwiya* to receive instructions from the founder and to get the blessing of his *baraka*. See Trimingham, *A History of Islam in West Africa* (1962), p. 157
4 Tyam, *Qacida*, pp. 22–3, vv. 123, 125, 128. It may be recalled that Almamy Yahia had been deposed in 1827. Thereafter Bubakar became almamy. He died in 1840, a little while after 'Umar's arrival in Futa

From this time to about 1848, 'Umar remained at his *zāwiya* at Dyegounko. His reputation as a saint, a *sūfī* and *khālifa* of al-Tijānī spread quickly throughout the Western Sudan. His wide travels, experience and sophistication certainly added to his prestige. His followers soon increased, partly with the coming of those who believed in his supernatural powers and therefore came seeking holiness and salvation. To this group of believers 'Umar, as *khālifa* and head of the Tijāniyya in the Western Sudan, had supernatural powers and was prodigious in knowledge. He held all powers, especially the *baraka* – believed by Muslims as the divine benediction, the source of happiness, holiness, wealth and salvation. This attitude was typical of the unflinching faith of devotees towards the Shaikhs in the various *zāwiyas* in the Western Sudan.[1] He was quickly surrounded by *talibs* (students) who came wanting to learn the mysteries of the religion. 'Umar's movement spread quickly also partly because he was building upon the efforts of Tijānī marabouts who had already been spreading the *tarīqa* before his return to Futa. Indeed he sent some of his own sons to some of these marabouts for training.[2]

At Dyegounko 'Umar continued to recruit and teach his disciples Tijāniyya ideas.[3] Simultaneously, using his disciples and slaves, he ran a large trade, selling goods to, and buying guns and gunpowder from, the British in Sierra Leone and the British and French trading posts and agents in Rio Nunez and Rio Pongas. He had trade connections with the French merchants in Saint Louis and the French trading posts along the river Senegal. He traded in gold dust from Bouré and other areas. His caravans, like others, were often armed for security. Moreover he had faithful slaves who cultivated his farms and filled his barns with grain. He soon became very rich and popular. With the increasing number of his disciples and with the arms and ammunition at his disposal, he also became powerful and influential. As has been pointed out, he eventually became involved in

---

Jallon. It is not known why Yahia was hostile to 'Umar; but the friendly disposition of Bubakar, Yahia's rival might explain it.

1 Gerteiny, *Mauritania*, p. 74; Trimingham, *A History of Islam*, p. 157
2 Loppinot, 'Souvenirs d'Aguibou', p. 26; Delafosse, *Haut-Sénégal-Niger*, ii, p. 308
3 See Chapter 1, on Futa Jallon; Wane, 'De Halwaar à Degembere . . .'

settling contemporary political problems such as the Alfaya-Soriya dynastic power tussle.[1]

'Umar was a highly learned and sophisticated scholar, who appeared to have gained easy acceptance as the leader of the Tijāniyya in the Western Sudan. He devoted a good deal of his time to writing on various subjects, especially on doctrines and the need to revive Islam in its supposedly pure form. Among his major works were *Suyuf al-Sayyid* . . ., *Al-Rimah* . . ., *Hadiatu Muslibin* . . ., *Al-Makasidu Saniya* . . ., *Bayanu Mawakahar* and *Al-Fatiyu.* . . .[2]

His writings and teaching clearly reflected his discontent with the existing religious systems in the Western Sudan. These are divisible into two broad groups, Islam and the traditional religions. 'Umar was dissatisfied with the practice of Islam where this was the religion of the people, as in Futa Jallon and Futa Toro where a long tradition of Islam existed. In both places, as in most areas of the Western Sudan, the Qādiriyya was the dominant brotherhood to which Muslims belonged, though there were other brotherhoods as well as a sprinkling of Tijanīs, products of the earlier phase of conversion of which 'Umar was part. Most of the political, religious and social elites of the Senegambia were Qādiri. In Futa Jallon and Futa Toro in particular the Qādiri leaders were heirs to the eighteenth-century revolution which resulted in Islam becoming the state religion and in the establishment of the Islamic theocracy of the almamies. The Cissé of Masina were a product of the early nineteenth-century revolution. In other words, the Qādiri Muslims in these areas were a part of the tradition which sought to establish an Islamic society and government on the model of the ideal as preached by the Prophet and the archetype as practised by the first four Caliphs. As adherents of this ideology, the Muslims had succeeded in overthrowing the non-Muslim dynasties in Futa Jallon, Futa Toro and Masina, and assumed leadership of the society. Having won the war, they were confronted with the important task of translating the objectives of the revolution into reality. In trying to do this it must have become obvious that though governments could be broken through the employment of violent military tactics, this in itself would not guarantee the success of the victors in imposing their ideology on the society. As with other ideologies, the success of the search for the estab-

1 See Chapter 1 on Futa Jallon   2 Oral evidence at Segu, 1965

lishment of the archetype of Islam was a factor of other variables, notably the relative potency of other ideologies and interest groups in the society. As a foreign cultural and religious phenomenon being spread to other environments Islam has to contend with the indigenous cultural, political, religious and social systems. Violence, which had invariably accompanied the jihād in the Western Sudan, might inflict traumatic pains on the indigenous systems; but it had never succeeded in wiping them out. This has always meant that Islam was spread not on virgin lands, but in confrontation with continuing indigenous political, religious and social ideas and practices. In the Senegambia and Masina, as in many other societies, Islam has developed through a process of interaction or intertwining with the various primary religions and other aspects of the cultures of the peoples adopting it. For this reason there had, unavoidably, taken place some grafting of elements of pre-Islamic ideas and practices with Islamic tenets and practices.[1] Islam was accepted in stages and the search for the re-enactment of the archetype necessarily became a slow, gradual process which entailed efforts in educating the people and unceasing missionary activities. While the process was continuing purists would always find practices which either represented adaptations or departures from the ideal as recorded in the Qur'ān, the *Sunna* and *ḥadīths*. It was therefore not surprising that when, after his pilgrimage and long stay abroad, 'Umar returned to the Western Sudan he was dissatisfied with the practice of Islam. His dissatisfaction was due in part to lapses observable among Muslims in the various areas, and partly also to a desire to convert existing Qādiri into Tijāniyya which for him represented a purer form of Islam.

On the need to reform Islam by removing the lapses in its practice it would appear that 'Umar and the Qādiri leaders did not disagree. So much is clear from the friendly reception which was given him on his arrival, first as guest of the Cissé and finally in Senegambia, especially in Futa Jallon, where the almamy allowed him to build a *zāwiya* at Dyegounko. For as long as his activities were peaceful and he was concerned mainly with recruiting converts to the Tijāniyya there was no trouble. He was probably seen as another Tijāniyya missionary who, like those

---

1 See for an illustration, Gerteiny, *Mauritania*, p. 74, where it is stated: 'In Mauritania Islam is intertwined with African magic and occultism . . .'

before him, was competing peacefully with the more dominant rival Qādiriyya. Reform was of common interest to all in so far as it meant a search for improvement in the quality of Islam as practised in society so that it could come closer to the ideal. In a sense, this was the preoccupation of the scholars and theologians of all brotherhoods. But the differences between 'Umar and the others became evident before long and created a gulf between them.

The first major difficulty appears to be the difference of outlook. While the others accepted the difficulty, if not the impossibility, of establishing the ideal and were therefore more tolerant of the shortcomings in the people's practice of religion, preferring to bring about desired changes peacefully through continuing education in the tenets and practice of the religion, 'Umar, the newcomer, highly educated and very sophisticated, was more impatient if not actually iconoclastic. As a *Ṣūfī* and legist he was in a doctrinaire manner committed to transforming the existing state to the ideal. Consequently, he demanded a total involvement in Islam such as has never existed anywhere else[1] outside perhaps the native home of the religion and in the early days under the first four caliphs known as *al-khulafa al-Rashidun* (the rightly guided caliphs). It was partly the attempt to translate this ideal into reality against various cultural and social factors which necessarily caused strain between 'Umar and his community on the one hand and the rest of the society on the other.

'Umar's attitude and career should also be seen in relation to the fact of Tijāniyya's exclusiveness and militancy against the others and, as a concomitant, the criticism and even dislike which the others displayed towards it. The Tijānis believed themselves morally and spiritually superior to all other groups of Muslims. Indeed, as a Tijānī 'Umar, like Muḥammad ibn. 'Abd al-Wahhābi, the founder of the Wahhabi movement, regarded all Muslims except his own followers to be in schism.[2] With this attitude, 'Umar was determined, lapses or not, to change the Muslims in the Western Sudan, most Qādiriyya, to Tijāniyya

1 For a discussion of this idea, see the introduction to my article, 'Anti-French Coalition of States and Groups in the Western Sudan 1889–1893', *Odu* (new series), no. 3, April 1970

2 Holt, *Egypt and the Fertile Crescent*, pp. 148–55, 179–80, 233, 247, 286 and 292; for Wahhābi ideas and activities, Al-Hajj, 'The Fulani Concept of Jihād –', p. 47

and he would not consider anything other than this as right.

As for non-Muslim areas, like the Bambara Segu and Ka'arta, 'Umar's detestation was even greater. Such areas were simply *dar al-harb* and like most Muslim leaders he wanted at all costs to make them accept Islam. Against such states, a jihād was a canonical duty.[1]

Apart from the purely spiritual dissatisfaction which his teaching reflected 'Umar also found much that was repugnant to him in the political and other institutions of the Western Sudan. As a *sūfī*, who imitated al-Ghazālī, he considered kingship and similar political institutions as standing for secular despotism and its concomitant oppression as revealed in uncanonical or heavy taxation, arbitrary application of the law and moral decadence – vices which to him made the societies concerned a complete antithesis of the caliphate which was rightly guided and just.[2] 'Umar conceived his mission as that of recreating the ideal community which was rightly guided and just. To do so he eventually embarked upon a jihād on the model of the Prophet.

By 1846 he had ceased to operate just from his base at Dyegounko. In that year he began a tour of Futa Jallon, Futa Toro, Bondu and the Jolof states. During the tour he devoted much time to preaching and making converts to the Tijāniyya. But he also acquainted himself with people and events in the areas, and tried to prepare the ground for the physical outbreak of his jihād. Thus he established contacts with the French at their posts along the Senegal river and tried to reach an understanding with their officers about his projected mission. In 1846 he met Lt-Col. Caille, the director of political affairs under the governor of Senegal, M. de Gramont, and had negotiations with him at Donnai. Similarly, in 1847 he met M. Hecquart, commandant of the French post at Bakel. The discussions between him and the French political officers centred on the need to make Futa Toro and other Senegambian states safe for commercial activities. 'Umar is reported to have promised to 'pacify' the Senegal valley and re-establish harmony among its diverse peoples. As a way of achieving this he announced his intention to fight against the 'unbelievers' as soon as possible. Probably to win the sympathy of the French for his war plans, he affirmed his friendship to them

1 Smith, 'Islamic revolutions of the 19th century'
2 Willis, 'Jihād fī Sabīl Allāh –', p. 41, n. 2

and promised to stop the wars then raging in the Senegal valley, that the various peoples were fighting to protect their sovereignty and trade rights, if the French would build him a fort to support his authority.[1] The basis of his relation with the French at this time was their common concern for trade.

It was in the interest of the French that the wars should end; but they had no means of effecting this.[2] 'Umar, on the other hand, seemed to have the military means[3] of enforcing peace in the turbulent areas. Hence his friendship was valued by the French who wanted trade with minimum involvement in military installations and garrisoned posts. It should be no surprise, then, that his plans were quite acceptable to the French in 1846–47. This episode contrasts with developments later when the jihād was raging. Then, under L. Faidherbe, the French considered 'Umar's activities as detrimental to their commercial interests and relations between the two sides became hostile.[4]

In the meantime, although 'Umar had successfuly manoeuvred the French to support his plans, the rulers of Futa were not deceived about the danger which he represented to their regime. After his tour he decided to return to Dyegounko. But the almamy of Futa Jallon, frightened by the forces at his disposal, attempted unsuccessfully to prevent him from re-entering his territory.

'Umar stayed at Dyegounko for another eighteen months, during which time he continued the religious instruction of his followers. But relations between him and the almamy at Timbo worsened. In the eyes of the ruling elite he was subversive of authority and his position and role at Dyegounko had become identical with those of the lineage group chiefs who, with their centrifugal tendencies, were contributing so much to the difficulty of organising Futa Jallon as a centrally controlled state. With the wealth and forces at his disposal and the revolutionary ideas he was preaching he was clearly seen as a threat to the position of the

1 Carrère et Holle, *De la Sénégambia française*, p. 195; Tyam, *Qacida*, pp. 24–6; Mage, *Voyage*, pp. 235–6
2 Hardy, *Histoire de la colonisation française* (1928) for an explanation of French official policy as it affected the trading posts in the Senegal valley at this time; also Hardy, *La Mise en valeur du Sénégal de 1817 à 1854* (1921)
3 'Umar's military organisation is discussed below.
4 See chapter 4 on the Franco-Tukulor struggle for control of the Senegambia.

Muhammad Aguibu as Chief under French rule

Koundian: an example of the war towns on which the Tukulor defence system was based

almamy. Since his activities had resulted in a state of tension and hostility between him and the almamy, 'Umar continued the process of declaring the jihād by emigrating – performing the *hijra*. He led his followers to establish a new centre at Dinguiray on the frontier between Futa Jallon and Diallonkadougou. This was in 1848.[1]

Dinguiray henceforth became the centre from where he organised the revolution which resulted in the creation of the Segu Tukulor empire.

His denunciation of the religious system in the Senegambia necessarily implied a condemnation of the dominant elements in the existing social and political systems.[2] In his own country of Futa Toro, for example, the religious leaders were the same as the political rulers of the communities. But as Muslims they were mostly Qādiriyya. Their acceptance of the Tijāniyya brotherhood would involve the acceptance of 'Umar's claim to be the *Khālifa* of Tijānī in the Western Sudan. This, of course, meant a renunciation on their part of their positions as political and religious leaders of their communities in order to give place to 'Umar. The position was the same for the almamies of other Senegambian states as well as for the Cissé rulers of the theocratic state of Masina. As it turned out the existing ruling elites refused to make such a heavy sacrifice only to change their identity as Muslims from being Qādirī to become Tijānī. The prospects must have appeared more frightful to the ruling groups in the non-Muslim states. 'Umar's condemnation of all showed him up as a revolutionary and he was recognised as such by those with interests in the preservation of the existing systems.

1 Tyam, *Qacida*, p. 26
2 That 'Umar detested the incumbent Muslim rulers is exemplified by this statement said to have been made by him: 'I do not frequent the courts of kings, and I do not like those who do. The Prophet has said "The best rulers are those who visit the learned men, and the worst of the learned are those who visit the rulers".' Salenc, 'La Vie', p. 422 cited by Willis, in review of Abun-Nasr, *The Tijaniyya*, Bull. *CAD*, ii, 1, 1966, p. 46. 'Umar's attitude is more clearly spelt out in the statement 'only he is Amīr al-muminīn who scorns the path of inactivity and compromise, and by word and deed vindicates the claims of a dynamic sharia against its enemies . . .', Sir Hamilton Gibb in *Studies on the Civilization of Islam* (ed. Shaw and Polk, 1962), pp. 147–8. Against this background, it is obvious that 'Umar regarded the position of the incumbent Muslim rulers as compromised and invalid, hence the rulers were legitimate targets of his revolution.

Indeed, the situation seemed ripe for a revolution. As already indicated, many of the states were at this time racked by tension and strife traceable to socio-political and religious factors. 'Umar profited from the existence of socio-political disorder, the causes of which could be attributed, rightly or wrongly, to the existing rulers. One could argue that without these socio-political conditions, his propagation of Tijaniyya brotherhood could not have resulted in a revolution. It will be recalled that the fact that he was a Tijānī did not lead to hostility between him and his hosts, Muḥammad Bello and 'Atiq, and the society in Sokoto, all Qādiriyya, during his long stay there from 1832 to 1838. There also he certainly tried to convert people to the Tijāniyya sect as the claim that he converted Muḥammad Bello and other leaders of the Sokoto empire indicates. He appears to have been ambitious to rule in Sokoto after the death of Muḥammad Bello. This ambition was probably responsible for the strained relationship between him and 'Atiq who succeeded Bello. The evidence from 'Umar's descendants is that he was considered a likely candidate to rival 'Atiq for succession to the caliphate. The rift with 'Atiq was not settled until after he had left Sokoto in December 1838.[1] Obviously, he could not have led a revolution in Sokoto in spite of the difference between his *ṭarīqa* and that of his hosts mainly because the social and political situations there made this impossible. The Sokoto community was predominantly Qādiriyya and controlled and wielded the military power. Against it 'Umar's following was not only small, it was also relatively insignificant.

Some writers have tried to explain 'Umar's prestige and success in terms of the supposed differences between Qādiriyya and Tijāniyya *ṭarīqa*. Of the Qādiriyya leaders who ruled before the emergence of 'Umar, it is said that they perpetuated in Islam the privileges of the tribal aristocracy and thereby created and maintained barriers between themselves and the ordinary believer. It is then said that 'Umar's strength came in part from the fact that the Tijāniyya which he preached broke these barriers and created a new value system based on individual talents. This idea is logically concluded by the claim that the Tijāniyya had a revolutionary character and was relatively more democratic than the Qādiriyya.[2]

1 Oral evidence at Segu, May 12, 1965
2 See, for example, Suret-Canale, *L'Afrique noire. Occidentale et Centrale*

The idea of egalitarianism has meaning for the Tijāniyya only in the sense in which all Muslims accept the equality of all believers before Allah. In this belief the Tijānīs do not differ from other groups of Muslims. But in terms of organisation brotherhoods, including the Tijāniyya, are essentially hierarchical in structure. The relationship between the *muqqadam*, or the *khālifa*, *ṣūfī* shaikhs and the various other categories is essentially one between the superior who knows and directs and the learner who accepts instructions from the master. In the situation, there could be no question of equality between the leaders and the ordinary believer.

Apart from this fact the interpretation cannot be accepted also because it rests on certain wrong assumptions. The first is that the Tijāniyya was a new phenomenon introduced by 'Umar; but as I have pointed out, evidence exists that the brotherhood had spread to the Senegambia even before 'Umar went on his pilgrimage and that he himself was first initiated into it in Futa Toro. It is strange therefore that Tijāniyya did not induce such egalitarian developments before 'Umar's revolution. There is also the assumption that all or most of those who took part in the revolution understood the doctrinal points of differences between the Qādiriyya and Tijāniyya, as well as the supposed social and political ideas that separated them. The fact should be appreciated that those who were equipped to know were to be found mostly among the ruling elites who opposed 'Umar. Of course, knowledge was the property of the directing elites. The claim that the Tijāniyya was more democratic presupposes that 'Umar's movement indeed led to the establishment of a revolutionary social and political organisation from the point of view of the ordinary people. As will be shown later on, this was not so.

There is no doubt that a good proportion of his following was mobilised to action by their faith and search for religious fulfilment. But if one were looking for the sources of strength and the appeal of 'Umar's revolution, especially for an explanation for the

---

(1961), pp. 191–2; also Hargreaves, 'The Tokolor empire of Ségou and its relations with the French', *Boston University Papers on Africa*, ii, 1966, p. 29 where the author speaks of a 'streak of social egalitarianism in 'Umar's preaching that won him much support among artisans and small traders in the settlements'.

involvement of the masses, it would be better to regard the religious factor as a precipitant or the occasion for action. A clear explanation for the appeal which his movement had for the common people lies in the historical antecedents, particularly the confused socio-political situations in the various states, which exacerbated the conditions of the common people who suffered most the effects of demographic crises, land shortage and other economic and social problems. There is hardly any evidence that the common people understood the differences between the Qādiriyya and the Tijāniyya. It is therefore difficult to prove that their mobilisation to action derived from such an understanding. In a different way, however, religion could be said to be important: that is, for people who had suffered a long period of privation, while the civil wars and political struggles lasted, 'Umar's movement must have assumed the character of a sudden advent of a millennium. But one must not exaggerate the position of the common man in the movement, even though he could be important in the fighting force. In status, he was usually dependent and lacked resources of his own. For this reason, he was normally within the power domain of his employer or patron, for whose cause, more often than not, he fought. It could therefore be said that the significant elements in 'Umar's movement, as in similar revolutions, was the patron or employer – usually a member of the political class and social aristocracy. It was he, not the commoner, who usually had and used the vital tactical power.[1] In 'Umar's revolution, the significant elements came mainly from among the *toroBé* who dominated Tukulor society. As in other such movements, the commoners and peasants were generally conservative and little inclined to embracing revolutions.

A group of commoners who were obviously significant in the movement comprised the free men who had been displaced as a result of the protracted strife that afflicted the societies. They were usually ready to pitch their camp with any party that was succeeding and from whom they could make economic gains. In a sense, they were not a stable group, but rather people who were ready to change their loyalty as and when circumstances made it necessary. At the start of the revolution, they were like

---

[1] See Wolf, 'On peasant rebellions', *International Social Science Journal*, xxi, 2, 1969, pp. 286–93 for a similar analysis of the involvement of the common people in twentieth-century revolutions.

unallocated political and military resources which 'Umar capitalised and mobilised for action.[1]

'Umar was a revolutionary mainly in the sense that he sought to overthrow holders of power among the political class. There is no evidence that he was eager to up-turn society by abrogating its regulatory forces like the clan organisation and the hierarchy of castes. He was a *torodo* and therefore a member of that class of aristocrats who were supposed to have created barriers between them and the ordinary believers. As will be made clear later his immediate lieutenants during the revolution and the principal administrators of the emergent empire came mostly from among the *toroBé*. The social significance of 'Umar's movement lies essentially in the fact that it offered a new context within which men of the same politically and socially important class could carry out their usual competition for power. This explains why, although he was repulsed by those actually exercising power, his immediate assistants came from the same social class who were aspiring to positions of power and for whom his movement offered opportunity for new status. Many of those who joined him at Dyegounko and on the *hijra* to Dinguiray were notables and leaders in their own right.

The hostility of the ruling elites to the increasing strength, including military capability, of 'Umar and his *jamā'a* led to the *hijra* from Dyegounko to Dinguiray. 'Umar realised that to lead a revolution against the ruling groups, he needed more time and greater facilities than were available to him at Dyegounko where he was virtually under the control of the almamy of Futa Jallon.

On a religious plane, the *hijra* was a vital stage in the process of declaring the jihād.[2] 'Umar likened the situation which con-

1 See Eckstein, 'On the Etiology of Internal Wars', *History and Theory,* iv, 2, 1965, for an analysis of various elements that could be found in a revolution.

2 The *hijra* marks a definite stage in the process of declaring a jihād. The first *hijra* was that performed by the Prophet from Mecca to Medina on 15 July 622. See Levy, *The Social Structure of Islam* (1957), pp. 2, 5. A jihād is a form of religious propaganda to spread Islam. It could be carried out either by persuasion or by the sword. Primarily, since the jihād aims at expanding the *dār al-Islam*, it is directed against non-Muslims and not as it appears to be the case with 'Umar's movement, at least at the beginning, against Muslims who are separated from one mainly by the fact of their belonging to a different brotherhood in Islam. See Khadduri, *War and Peace in the Law of Islam* (1955), pp. 51–83; Levy, *The Social Structure of Islam*, pp. 191, 222, 254, 294,

fronted his community at Dyegounko to that which confronted the prophet at the beginnings of Islam. There were parallels between the designations he gave his followers (*Muhājirin* and *Anṣār*) and those which the Prophet applied earlier on. In all his activities at Dinguiray and throughout the military phase of the jihād, he consciously strove to duplicate the model set earlier on by the Prophet.

'Umar's revolution aimed at the destruction of the existing system and interests. To do this involved the creation of new ones. People who saw their interests in the new order naturally rallied round the movement. In each state, therefore, the revolution generated conflicts between the existing and newly created interest groups. The internal conflict and confusion which the movement created in the various states made the revolution assume the character of a civil war. The strength of the movement lay partly in the fact that it provided a common forum for people with diverse interests and ambitions to fulfil.

'Umar's community in Dinguiray was made up of people with varied backgrounds, including nobles, scholars, adventurers and peasants in the service of their patrons. The common factor which distinguished the *jamā'a* from other groups was their acceptance of 'Umar's leadership and, with it, Islam of the Tijāniyya *ṭarīqa*. As a group they constituted real unity only to the extent that members shared common beliefs and aspirations. For several reasons, the degree of involvement of the members in the pursuits of the norms and aspirations of the movement varied.[1]

Although from the start recruits came from many parts of the Senegambia, the dominant elements in the movement were the people from Futa Toro, especially the *toroBé* group to which 'Umar himself belonged. Prominent among the earliest recruits

---

and 455. The only justification which 'Umar, like the earlier jihādists in the Western Sudan, had for attacking Muslims was that he correlated the jihād with the wars of 'apostasy' (*ridda*) which took place after the death of the Prophet. But 'apostasy' in the *Sharī'a* law is interpreted as the act of complete reversion to heathenism or a total renunciation of the faith and practice. See Al-Hajj, 'The Fulani concept of jihād . . .', p. 51 for further discussion.

1 See Ọlọruntimẹhin, 'The Interactions of Islamic and Pre-Islamic Concepts in Tukulor Constitutional Evolution' (unpublished seminar paper, 1969), for a detailed discussion of the limitations on the ideas of the oneness of the Islamic community as well as the inadequacy of the idea of Islamic revolution.

were scholars like Alfa 'Umar Tierno Baila, from Lao, and Alfa 'Umar Tierno Bole from Bosséia. There were also Alfa Abass from Bosséia and Tierno Aḥmadu 'Ali Djelia from N'Guénar.[1] Not only were these people learned, they were also leaders in their own right. Many must have been attracted to 'Umar because of his charisma. But there were others who saw the revolution as a new opportunity for adventure through which they hoped to gain new land for cultivation and pasturage and attain political power.

Migration and adventure in search of land and new settlements had already become a feature of life in both Futa Toro and Futa Jallon. Many people came to join 'Umar under their clan or lineage group leaders. For example, the almamy of Bosséia came at the head of the people drawn from his clan. Cases like these were examples of the expansion of clans through the segmentation of existing lineage groups to which reference has been made earlier. In a sense 'Umar's movement provided another expression for the Tukulor tradition of migrating for the purposes of propagating the religion and making conquests.[2] Right from the beginning the Tukulor constituted the core and leadership of the *jamā'a*. The *'ulamā'* were mainly *toroBé* shaikhs. It was in this way that the revolution acquired clear Tukulor characteristics from the beginning, and this became a permanent feature because of the constant addition of new recruits coming from Futa Toro to reinforce the revolution.

'Umar's search for the establishment of an ideal Islam was not new to many of his supporters. In Futa Toro and Futa Jallon similar movements had resulted in the establishment of theocracies in the eighteenth century. Some of 'Umar's immediate lieutenants were products of this earlier tradition. But in addition to their Islamic background, they owed their culture and positions to their socialisation within the context of certain indigenous ideas and institutions which antedated Islam in Tukulor society. Indeed, some of them exemplified the unison between Islam and such pre-Islamic ideas and institutions. In a broad sense the spread of Islam in the wake of the eighteenth-century revolution was due largely to the fact that the theocracy which resulted from it was largely in harmony with Tukulor pre-Islamic concepts of the ideal society and government. Judging

1 Oral evidence at Segu, May 1965
2 Diop, *Société Toucouleur*, pp. 49–50

the attitudes and activities of the members in the revolution and in the emergent empire, one can identify two groups in the *jamā'a*. The first comprised the members who seemed dedicated to the 'revival' of the ideal Islam, and the second those who, though they were committed to the spread of the Tijāniyya, also thought of re-creating Futa Toro ideals of government and society. For the latter group Tijāniyya and Futa Toro systems were not incompatible, and they were at best only half heartedly committed to 'Umar's ideal of establishing the 'perfect' system. From the organisation and other events of the revolution it appears that the latter group were predominant in the community.[1]

At Dinguiray, 'Umar intensified his teaching and continued to prepare his followers for the launching of the revolution.

His first task seems to have been the turning of his centre into a strong military base. This he did by building a strong fortress and accumulating large quantities of arms and ammunition bought mainly from French traders in and around the posts on the Senegal and from British traders from Sierra Leone and the Gambia. He also had among his men African smiths who helped in manufacturing large quantities of guns and ammunition as well as repairing them for the use of his army.[2] Moreover, he recruited many followers whom he prepared psychologically through religious instruction for the part they were to play in the projected military campaigns. The recruits to the Tijāniyya were made to believe that they were the elect of Allah and that by fighting in wars against unbelievers they were assured of salvation and divine grace.[3] Many of the early recruits to the jihād army were men from Futa Toro who came as clan contingents under their separate leaders.

From the military point of view, the importance of recruits led by nobles from Futa Toro lay in the fact that these men brought their own arms and ammunition and constituted small

1 See Olọruntimẹhin 'The Interactions of Islamic and Pre-Islamic Concepts . . .', for details.
2 Carrère et Holle, *De la Sénégambie française*. An example of such men was Samba N'diaye who spent many years at St Louis where he learnt several trades. July, *The Origins of Modern African Thought* (1968) discusses the background of some of the men like the mulatto Paul Holle.
3 Abun-Nasr, 'Some aspects of the 'Umari Branch of the Tijāniyya', pp. 329–31

'armies' under the leadership of their lineage heads. As long as these 'armies' served 'Umar loyally they would be assets. On the other hand, having come in groups from Futa Toro as distinct bodies, they retained their traditional intergroup rivalry and their interests, apart from the common purpose of spreading religion, remained competitive. Therefore, in the organisation of his forces, 'Umar's problem lay mainly in integrating the Futa Toro groups with the recruits he had got elsewhere, and at the same time keeping all loyal by satisfying or reconciling their various interests.

His first military organisation was rather simple, since it was based largely upon the contingencies of the moment. As has been pointed out, his first set of followers had come mainly from Futa Toro, as well as from Futa Jallon, and they had different interests to pursue. Some of the groups had been at war with one another back in Futa Toro. 'Umar seems to have realised that in the situation the greatest fighting effect would be produced mainly by grouping together only those who were used to working together.

According to Alioun Tyam, 'Umar organised his army into five groups. The first comprised the N'Guénar, incorporating recruits from N'Guénar, Bosséia, and Worgo group of villages in Futa Toro. The second group had the Irlabé recruits as its core, and included men from Lao and Ebiabé. The recruits from Toro and Bondu formed the third group. The fourth, called Dyoun-fouto, acted as guards and consisted mainly of Fulani from Futa Toro and Hausa recruits. The fifth, called Mourgoula, was the group recruited and led by Alfa Usman,[1] one of the leaders from Futa Toro.

During the campaigns more troops were recruited and the problem of organisation became more difficult. At first the difficulty was met by placing the new recruits in the existing groups. Thus the recruits from Ka'arta – the Diawara, the Massassi and the Kagoro, for example – were joined on to the N'Guénar. The recruits of Khasso origin, as well as those from Diafounou and the Fulani from Bakhounou, were incoporated into the Irlabé group. Those from Guidimaka, like those from Bondu, were absorbed into the Toro contingents. The Fulani from Futa Jallon were the greatest single contingent and could therefore not be put all in one group. The majority of them, however,

1 Tyam, *Qacida*, p. 148

joined the Irlabé, while the others joined the Mourgoula, led by Alfa Usman. In this way each group gradually became heterogeneous in terms of the origins of its troops. This was to become more marked with the extension of the area of campaign.

For purposes of tactical operations each group was divided into three arms, namely, the front-guard; the inner corps, charged with attacking fortresses and keeping the flag; and the outer corps, which served as a sort of reserve charged with defending the flanks of the group, especially during attacks on fortifications. While on the march, as when in camp, each corps ensured its own security by choosing particular members to fulfil specific functions.[1]

'Umar's soldiers were maintained mainly out of the booty of war. After a campaign the canonical one-fifth of the booty (*Khums*) was usually taken to 'Umar and the remaining four-fifths belonged to the commander of the particular campaign and his men.[2] This rule must have been difficult to apply because there would be occasions when the quantity of booty taken would not be known. Nonetheless, the general needs of the revolutionary forces were provided out of the booty accumulated from campaign to campaign. Such booty often included personal effects, food and, more significantly, slaves, horses and weapons, which were very useful for the continuation of the war.[3]

With the extension of the military commitments, the need for more soldiers became acute, and reinforcements were always drawn from the Futa Toro and Futa Jallon areas through agents commissioned by 'Umar. These reinforcements often came in units under their own leaders and were sometimes assigned to tackle particular difficulties in specific areas. As 'Umar came under pressure, the desire for centralised control of the forces became secondary to the need for fighting an urgent battle. By the time the wars had spread to Ka'arta, his forces had become very large and the operating units quite numerous. According to Abdoulaye Ali, one of 'Umar's lieutenants and war leaders,

1 *Ibid.*, pp. 148–9
2 For example after his return from the campaigns in Koniakary, the commander, Tierno Moussa, sent to 'Umar the *al-Khumsu* – one fifth of the booty. In distributing the booty, 'Umar and his army leaders seem to be adhering to the Islamic rules, see Khadduri, *War and Peace in the Law of Islam*, pp. 118–33
3 M. Sissoko, 'Chroniques d'El Hadj Oumar (2e Cahier)', *L'Education Africaine* (*Bulletin de l'Enseignement de l'AOF*), janvier–juin, 1937, p. 12

there were about twenty such units, with one Alfa 'Umar as a sort of general and probably next in rank to Shaikh 'Umar himself. Other units of the army were commanded by Coli Modi, Tierno Haimoutou, Alfa Daibou, Al-ḥājj Aḥmadu, Sambounna, Tierno Djibi, Tierno Aḥmadu Oumakali, Tierno Khalidou, Abdoulaye Haoussidji,[1] Abdul Salam, Abdoulaye Ali, Al-ḥājj Sire, Djoubairou Boubou, Tierno Abdul, Alfa Usman, Modi Muḥammad, Fakhaou, Suleyman Baba Raki and 'Umar Lamine.[2] These commanders were the leading disciples of 'Umar, and were mostly *toroBé*. Some of them were also responsible for bringing their own troops from Futa Toro. For instance Tierno Haimoutou, Alfa Daibou, and Alfa Usman brought their own troops.[3]

The attitude of the Muslim rulers in the Senegambia has been explained in relation to the events which led to the *hijra*. The fact that 'Umar was intensifying his preparations for war at Dinguiray signified his determination to precipitate a crisis at all cost. For those who had previously accepted Islam, 'Umar's revolution could have been seen as an internal crisis resulting from a conflict of ideologies within the same broad cultural milieu. For the non-Muslims, however, the problem was one of total revolution which called for a complete rejection of their religion and way of life. Acceptance of Islam, especially in its puritanical Tijāniyya form which 'Umar was advocating, could only lead to a complete negation of their own culture and philosophy of life. Moreover, the dialogue between Qādiriyya and Tijāniyya Muslims was impossible and was in any case meaningless so far as non-Muslims were concerned. Worse still, once 'Umar launched the revolution at Dinguiray, the campaigns just extended like a wild fire, ravaging people who had never had a chance to consider the issues involved. There is no evidence that 'Umar made any sustained effort to convert people peacefully outside the Senegambia before they were subjected to a military offensive which they were not adequately prepared to resist. Perhaps for 'Umar no other justification for total war was required after the original injunction which he had at Médine to wage a jihād in the Western Sudan. One may also add that his large-scale campaigning was probably influenced by his experience in Sokoto,

1 That is, Abdullahi, native of Hausaland or from the Hausa country.
2 Sissoko, 'Chroniques (2e Cahier)', pp. 6–13
3 *Ibid.*, p. 13

earlier on, where the latter, military phase of the jihād had taken place on a similar pattern with the wars spreading like wild fire once hostilities had broken out.[1] But as far as the besieged people were concerned, 'Umar's revolution was an external aggression which, if it succeeded, could make life meaningless. For the non-Muslim groups in the Western Sudan, therefore, the desire to preserve what was meaningful to them, in terms of religion and culture generally, was what motivated the opposition to 'Umar's Tukulor revolution. It also made them launch and sustain resistance movements even after the establishment of the Tukulor empire.[2]

1 As in Sokoto, once the war had broken out, it spread to other areas outside the Senegambia where some effort had been made to convert people through preaching. In most of the areas where campaigns were waged, no attempts are known to have been made at persuasion before people were confronted with war of conquest. As in Sokoto, 'Umar conquered a vast territory and created a large empire in the process of the jihād.

2 Olọruntimẹhin, 'Resistance movements in the Tukulor empire'

3 The First Phase of the Revolution in the Senegambia and Ka'arta, 1851–57

FROM DINGUIRAY TO DIALLONKADOUGOU

This chapter aims at discussing the expansion of 'Umar's Tukulor revolution from its base at Dinguiray to other parts of the Senegambia and the Bambara Massassi kingdom of Ka'arta. 'Umar's forces conquered many of the states in the Senegambia and Ka'arta and laid the foundation of his state during this phase of the revolution. But some of the victories recorded during this period soon proved illusory. For example, hopes of constituting the Senegal valley states, especially his home country Futa Toro, into the nucleus of his empire[1] were disappointed in spite of initial military victories. As is evident from the events of this period in the Senegambia, 'Umar's movement was no more than a catalyst, producing a chain of reactions and interactions, the end product of which bore little relation to the nature or objective of the movement which unleashed the developments in the first instance. An important aspect of the period was the emergence of formerly anti-French Muslim elements in the same camp as the French who were spearheading the crusade against 'Umar and his revolutionary forces. This particular development was against the trend of the immediate history of the area, especially the troubled Franco-African relations, which encouraged 'Umar in 1846–47 to ask and hope for French assistance against many of the states.[2] The development also disappointed the expectations of many of the participants in the movement.

1 There seems no doubt that 'Umar intended to found his empire on the Senegambia. This is born out by his activities from 1846 onwards, particularly between 1854 and 1859. Some of these events are treated in this chapter and others in chapter 4. The evidence overwhelmingly negates the suggestion that he was not interested in waging a jihād in the Senegambia and that he was concerned principally with fighting the French in the area. For this suggestion see Fisher's review of Jamil Abun-Nasr, *The Tijāniyya* ... in *Bull. SOAS*, xxx, 1, 1967. For a more accurate view see, Willis, 'Jihād fī Sabīl Allāh ...', *JAH*, viii, 3, 1967
2 See Chapter 2, pp. 47–8

This phase of the revolution also shows some of the more permanent features of the movement and the empire which emerged from it. Among these features was the predominance of Tukulor elements in the organisations and ideas which directed the revolution. Some of these elements were in conflict with those who were overtly concerned with producing an archetype of Islamic society and government. As will be seen later, 'Umar's success lay partly in his ability to harness conflicting ideologies and groups and make them serve his purpose. Of course, in the process, compromises were made which could not have satisfied purists on either side. This phase shows the dominance of those Tukulor elements who represented *pre-* or *non-*Islamic traditions and ideas of society and government. They appeared to be in the ascendancy by the close of this phase of the movement, as could be seen from the organisation and operation of the army, as well as the form of administration which 'Umar set up. At the same time, there were indications that 'Umar meant to apply Islamic ideas in the government of his emergent state and that the concessions to essentially Tukulor pre-Islamic concepts of government reminiscent of Futa Toro were probably meant to tide over the uneasy time which his revolution was undergoing. Of necessity, Tukulor predominance continued to manifest itself in the reliance on Futa Toro not only for reinforcements and supplies for the army, but also for the administration of the conquered territories.

A notable feature of the revolution which became evident during this phase was that in all the campaigns 'Umar's strategy was a combination of political manoeuvre and military offensive. His political weapon consisted in cleverly exploiting the existing internal divisions in the various states, with a view to finding allies among those who were opposed to the ruling groups within each state. In this way the revolution often assumed the character of civil war, since by allying with some groups against others issues which had been internal to those states automatically became grafted to the objectives of the revolution. Events in Ka-'arta, Khasso and the other Senegambian states will illustrate this point clearly. In these cases the masses who were involved in the particular stages of the movement could only have seen it in terms of their own affair, even though for 'Umar and his immediate lieutenants the events could have been seen in terms of their desire to revive Islam in its supposedly pure form.

Wholesale destruction of populations and pillaging of the property of the vanquished featured in this phase. As the chroniclers of the movement repeatedly made clear, 'Umar and his men saw nothing wrong in these activities. If anything they were regarded as positive evidence of divine sanction for their effort to spread the *dār al-Islam*, in the process of which it was sometimes expedient to destroy the infidels. The ability to do this and the employment of supernatural means, which also featured, were accepted as proofs of the divine nature of their mission. Moreover the invocation of supernatural forces in warfare was a normal practice in many African societies.[1] Indeed, this could be seen as an aspect of Islam which is in consonance with African traditions.

As has been mentioned earlier,[2] since his *hijra* to Dinguiray, 'Umar had devoted a good deal of his time and attention to building up the nucleus of his revolutionary army. Under standably, this was not an exercise which could have made his hosts and neighbours think that he and his men could possibly have meant well towards them. Indeed, the military build-up soon reached such proportions as to cause alarm among the people of the neighbouring states about their own safety. In particular Diallonkadougou (or Tamla), the host country, experienced a state of alarm which bred tension in the relations between them and 'Umar's *zāwiya* at Dinguiray. When viewed against this background of tension and uncertainty about the future which 'Umar's preparations caused one can understand the hostilities which followed.

The tension which resulted from the situation created by 'Umar had by 1851 begun to be expressed in armed clashes. In that year there were skirmishes between 'Umar's forces and those of Guimba, the ruler of Tamla. Similarly, the almamy of Timbo (Futa Jallon) became increasingly apprehensive of 'Umar's plans and strengthened his defences in readiness for any eventuality. In spite of all the apprehension and war preparations, however, serious fighting did not break out until 1852 when 'Umar

---

1 Sissoko, 'Traits fondamentaux des sociétés du Soudan Occidental du XVIIe au début du XIXe siècle' *Bull. IFAN*, B, xxxi, 1, 1969; also Griaule, 'Philosophie et religion des Noirs', *Présence Africaine*, 1950, pp. 307–21
2 See Chapter 2, p. 56 f.

claimed that he had been instructed in a vision to begin his campaigns against the 'unbelievers'.[1]

Before then the skirmishes which took place between 'Umar and the forces of Tamla appear to have been no more than the product of a pre-emptive measure which the ruler of the latter state took to protect his people against Tukulor hostility. It appears there were three notable clashes before the outbreak of a major war. The three encounters were led on the Tamla side by Namouda, the commander of Guimba's forces. The encounters appear to have been aimed at getting 'Umar and his men to evacuate their base at Dinguiray, hence Namouda attacked the military base at Dinguiray on the first three occasions. 'Umar's community seems to have been able to absorb the effects of these skirmishes as they responded to their leader's appeal to remain calm in the face of what was regarded as provocation. But they suffered a grievous loss in the third encounter in which one of 'Umar's military commanders, Abdullahi from Khoulou, was killed. Even then 'Umar and his men did not evacuate Dinguiray as Guimba had expected. In their determination to achieve this objective Tamla forces changed their tactics, resorting to economic warfare, and raiding the cattle of the Tukulor and the Fulani.[2] This led to the escalation of the skirmishes and the beginning of a full-scale war against Tamla. The pastoral Fulani are very much devoted to their cattle, which sustain their economy and serve as their main source of livelihood.[3] A cattle raid was therefore interpreted as an expression of Guimba's determination to force the *jamā'a* out of Dinguiray, where their presence had become a danger to the existence of their neighbours. 'Umar's response was to meet Guimba's pressure with force. He mobilised his forces into action, informing them that he had had a vision authorising him to wage a jihād against the unbelievers. It was in this way that the pre-emptive action taken by Guimba developed into total war, not just between 'Umar's revolutionary forces and Tamla, but also between the former and other states in the Senegambia and Ka'arta.

The divine revelation which 'Umar claimed to have received through a vision had the purpose of confirming the conviction of

1 Tyam, *Qacida*, p. 32; Le Chatelier, *Islam en Afrique*, pp. 176–7
2 Sissoko, 'Chroniques d'El Hadj Oumar et de Cheikh Tidiani (1er cahier)', *L'Education Africaine*, no. 95 juillet–decembre, 1936, p. 244
3 Stenning, *Savana Nomads* (1959)

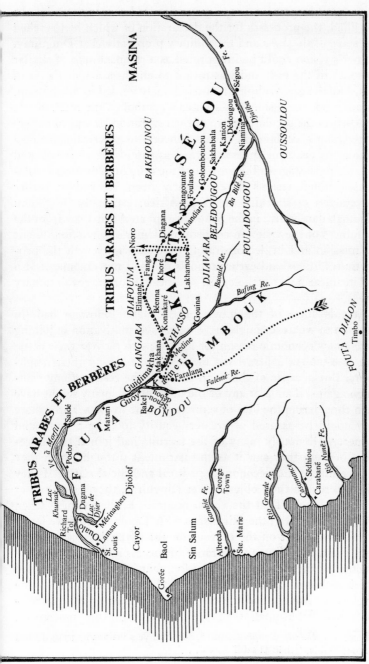

Croquis du théâtre de la guerre d'Alhadji, 1856

'Umar and his *jamā'a* that they were indeed chosen to undertake the jihād, the processes for the declaration of which had reached the stage of the *hijra* and the military preparations at Dinguiray. 'Umar's vision could be interpreted as a re-enactment of similar episodes in the past and was meant to emphasise Umar's claim that, like the early caliphs, he was divinely guided in his mission. In addition, the vision was seen as a symbol of the religious, as opposed to the secular, nature of the revolution. It was to underline 'Umar's declaration of his concern to re-create the ideal Islamic government and society as was supposed to have existed at some pure stage in the growth of the religion. Mystical revelations through visions have similarly been invoked in earlier movements of the kind in West Africa, especially by Shehu 'Usuman dan Fodiye in the Sokoto Caliphate.[1] But apart from the usefulness of the vision in confirming 'Umar's convictions about his mission and in demonstrating his conformity with the prophetic traditions and earlier models of jihād movements, it also had its immediate psychological significance for the revolutionary forces.

At this stage of the movement 'Umar's followers had, in addition to whatever might have been their motivation in joining him, a new economic reason for fighting – to recover their cattle and re-establish a firm basis of existence *vis-à-vis* their neighbours. But because of the uncertainty of the result of any campaign against Tamla or any of the other states, many might have been considering the idea of returning home to Futa Toro where they could be assured of greater security to their persons and property. Obviously many of the recruits had joined the movement because they saw it as an instrument through which they could enhance their economic, political and social status. If they failed to realise their objectives at Dinguiray, they would prefer to return home. That the vision occurred at the moment when reverses suffered in the skirmishes with Tamla could have had a debilitating effect on the movement was psychologically significant. First, by giving an assurance of success and confirming the sanctity of the mission, the development of any adverse trend which earlier failures could have caused was arrested. The divine revelation certainly had the effect of strengthening the commitment and determination of the followers for the movement.

1 Last, *The Sokoto Caliphate*, p. 10, for Fodiye's visions in 1789/90 and 1794; Willis, 'Jihād fī sabīl Allah . . .'

Henceforth the idea of fighting Allah's wars would salve the consciences of the forces, and the economic and political gains which victories would bring could be counted on to keep their interest alive.

The Tukulor continued their campaigns against Tamla with a surprise attack at night. The people were fast asleep when 'Umar's forces descended on them. A ferocious massacre took place and seventy-seven were taken captive. These were later brought to 'Umar who ordered that they be executed immediately. The Tukulor naturally ascribed their success to the will of Allah who had ordained that the enemy should be asleep during the attack. 'Umar's followers were also happy because they had escaped with only slight injuries, had recovered their cattle, and had even secured considerable booty.[1]

It was after this operation that 'Umar, for the first time, used his forces as a regular army. It was first led by Modi Muḥammad Diam, described as being one of his most intimate lieutenants.[2] 'Umar at this time declared his intention to subjugate the whole state of Tamla. Accordingly, for a start, he launched a ferocious campaign against the villages of Labata and Sountou.

The nature of 'Umar's campaigns is clear from the account of the operation against Sountou by Abdoulaye Ali, an eye-witness and participant who says: 'Sountou fut cassé et pillé, tous les habitants de ce village tués à l'exception de quatre conservés comme prisonniers; des cases furent brûlées, d'autres démolies.'[3] On the whole 'Umar would seem to have placed emphasis on large-scale, sometimes total, massacre, and on the acquisition of booty. Statements similar to the one quoted feature regularly in the accounts of 'Umar's revolution, as given by *talibés* like Abdoulaye Ali and Aliou Tyam, the writer of the *Qacida*,[4] which is a court history compiled under 'Umar's son and successor, Aḥmadu.

Side by side with 'Umar's determination to subjugate Tamla went his desire to acquire the military and economic assets of the state, assets which he hoped to use in prosecuting his campaigns against other states. For instance, the long siege against Tamba, capital

1 Sissoko, 'Chroniques . . .' (1er Cahier), pp. 244–5
2 *Ibid.*, p. 245
3 *Ibid.*
4 Tyam's *Qacida* is full of stories of large-scale massacre of people and the burning of towns and villages.

of Tamla, was undertaken with a view to gaining control of its fortifications and their military installations. Tamba was a well fortified village around which eight concentric walls had been built for defence. It was situated on an escarpment with natural defence features. It obviously had a strategic value for 'Umar's future operations, since it lay at the point of intersection of routes linking Futa Jallon with the Bambuk and Bondu. Control of Tamba and its natural fortress offered an impregnable base from which attacks could be launched against parts of Futa Jallon, Bambuk and Bondu.[1]

The conquest of Tamba proved a difficult task. Part of the problem was with the inherent weakness of 'Umar's organisation. For instance, after four months of siege the danger in using ethnic origins as a basis for the organisation of the army was painfully demonstrated. After the first expedition had returned without any concrete achievements, 'Umar decided to send two companies to attack the village. One of these companies was made up of Futa Toro recruits, while the other comprised Fulani. Both companies were put under the operational control of Modi Muḥammad Diam, but sectional jealousy inevitably came into play. The Futa Toro group, in an obvious effort to demonstrate their superior position and to arrogate to themselves the credit and praise for conquering Tamba, pressed Modi Muḥammad Diam for permission to attack Tamba alone.[2] By this act the *toroBé* were not seeking glory only; equally involved was the material gain to be acquired by the group to the exclusion of others. In the event the Futa Toro elements, though inadequately equipped or prepared, went ahead to attack Tamba, but failed. It was joined later by the other company, but even then the combined forces did not succeed in breaking Tamba; they could only take some booty back with them to Dinguiray. The experience of the Tukulor forces on this occasion demonstrated how risky it could be for them to indulge their sectional interests, and emphasised the need for concerted action in subsequent campaigns.

The various expeditions against Tamba failed to subjugate it until 'Umar himself took control of the operations. In the last and decisive siege seven of the eight walls which surrounded Tamba were broken; but in spite of three days' effort, the Tukulor

1 Carrère et Holle, *De la Sénégambie française*, p. 196
2 Sissoko, 'Chroniques . . .' (1er Cahier), pp. 245–6

forces failed to break the eighth and innermost wall which proved to be the strongest. The soldiers had to withdraw to Dinguiray to recoup. While they were away Guimba, apparently finding further defence impossible, sent a mission to 'Umar to offer his submission. He requested, however, that because of his submission and for the security of his people, the invading forces should be withdrawn to Dinguiray. 'Umar, whose forces had failed to break the eighth wall, agreed to withdraw his men. But he left two of his *talibés* – Suleyman Sarankoule and Tierno Boubakar – at Tamba to represent his authority and observe the activities of Guimba.[1]

Despite the precautions taken by 'Umar, Guimba managed to escape with all his family, servants and property into the neighbouring state of Menieng, where he sought refuge with the ruler, Bandiougou, at the latter's capital, Goufonde. But Bandiougou treacherously put Guimba to death and appropriated all his property with his wives and children. Guimba's escape was regarded by 'Umar as a betrayal of the confidence reposed in him. But on receiving news of the act of Bandiougou he sent his two *talibés* at Tamba to him, asking for a return of all the belongings of Guimba which he had appropriated. 'Umar's envoys were assassinated by Bandiougou. This was the signal for the extension of the jihād to the small state of Menieng in 1853.[2]

The campaign against Goufonde, the Menieng capital, was led by 'Umar himself. Goufonde surrendered after seven days of siege. The fortress was broken down and many of its inhabitants, including the ruler were put to death. Prisoners and booty were also taken away from Goufonde by the victorious jihād army. The conquest of Goufonde could be regarded as the end of the first stage of the military campaigns involved in this phase of 'Umar's revolution. After the Goufonde operation 'Umar retired to Dinguiray where, with his followers and army, he remained for eight months without any fighting.[3] Apparently this period was devoted to reorganising the army and consolidating the successes thus far achieved.

During the campaigns in Tamla and Menieng factors that were to influence the fortunes of the revolution were beginning to be

1 *Ibid.*, p. 246
2 ASAOF, 1G63/2, 'Notice sur El Hadj Omar', Saint-Louis, 25 May 1878; also Sissoko, 'Chroniques . . .' (1er Cahier), pp. 246–7
3 Sissoko, 'Chroniques . . .' (1er Cahier), p. 249

prominent. It was becoming clear, for instance, that 'Umar
would continue to need reinforcements from Futa Toro if he was
to succeed in the campaigns. The killing of Guimba by Bandiougou was also an indication that the existing bad relations
among the petty states would weaken their resistance and so
contribute to the success of the invading Tukulor forces. Also
evident from the experience of the first stage of operations was
the continued hostility of the almamy of Futa Jallon, based at
Timbo. This was shown by the action of almamy 'Umar (Oumarou) in detaining the reinforcements being led to 'Umar at
Dinguiray. 'Umar's brother, Alfa Aḥmadu, was leading a contingent of *toroBé* recruits from Futa Toro across Futa Jallon to
assist in the capture of Tamba. But Almamy 'Umar arrested
Alfa Aḥmadu and his men, detaining them at Timbo. The
recruits were allowed to desert one by one until Alfa Aḥmadu,
the leader, was left alone. He was not badly treated in Futa
Jallon, but he could not reach 'Umar at Dinguiray. The majority
of the recruits who escaped detention returned to Futa Toro
instead of continuing towards 'Umar at Dinguiray. Thus almamy
'Umar's action frustrated the attempt to supply reinforcements
to the revolutionary forces at Dinguiray. It was not until after
the submission of Guimba that other *toroBé* recruits were led to
'Umar by Alfa Ali Djelia. Also after the conquest of Goufonde
additional reinforcements were brought to 'Umar from Futa
Toro by Alfa Oumarou b. Tierno Baidavii (better known as
Tierno Baila).[1]

Early in 1854, 'Umar moved from Dinguiray to Tamba, which
he renamed Dabatu[2] (Taïbatu) in imitation of the Prophet
Muḥammād. This marked the beginning of the next stage of
operations in which Bambuk, Bondu and Khasso were to be
attacked. Hitherto he had been campaigning against the Mandingo people. In Bambuk, Bondu and Khasso he would be
fighting against the forces of states under Fulani, Sarakole and
Muslim rule. He would also be coming into contact with the
Moors who, as Muslims, would be fighting his forces for political
and economic reasons. The Moors, as has been noted, were very

1 *Ibid.*, p. 248
2 *Ibid.*, p. 249; Taïbatu was one of the names by which the Muslims
designated the town of Medina in Arabia. By renaming Tamba
'Taïbatu' 'Umar was apparently invoking the memory of the Prophet
and re-enacting the latter's activities.

important in the Senegambia for the trade in gum and other commercial activities, as well as for their role as agents for the spread of Islam. For the strategic reasons already discussed in relation to the siege of Tamba, 'Umar used Dabatu as his base for this stage of his campaigns just as he had used Dinguiray for the earlier stage. From Dabatu he sent some of his disciples to look for reinforcements in Futa Toro. At the same time he sent others to barter elephant tusks for arms and ammunition at the French post at Bakel.[1]

CAMPAIGNS AGAINST BAMBUK

In June 1854, 'Umar moved from his camp at Dabatu to invest Soulou,[2] a group of villages south of Koundian in Bambuk. The siege of Soulou was launched from three directions at the same time. Soulou was overrun and, after remaining there for eight days, 'Umar directed his operations against Koundian on the river Faleme, about fifteen leagues south of Bafoulabe.[3] After a day's march from Soulou, Koura, the ruler of Koundian, met 'Umar on the way and made his submission without resistance. 'Umar had Koura's head shaved as a mark of his submission, and they both entered Koundian together. With the surrender of Koundian, a garrisoned fortress, a major obstacle had been overcome and the campaign against the rest of the country continued relatively easily. Koura, the chief, even served as a guide to Tukulor forces in their campaigns in the other parts of Bambuk, especially up to Dialafara in the neighbourhood of Koundian.[4]

From Dialafara some of the invading forces moved into other parts of Bambuk, attacking the populations on their way; other forces were dispatched to ravage Dieladougou province. 'Umar also led attacks on Gadiaga passing over Diokhiba and Sormang, while another section of his army was sent to attack Makhana,

1 Tyam, *Qacida*, p. 43
2 Soulou is probably the same place referred to as Souloudie in Sissoko's translation of Abdoulaye Ali's account, see Sissoko, 'Chroniques . . .' (1er Cahier), p. 249
3 Tyam, *Qacida*, p. 44; Sissoko, 'Chroniques . . .' (1er Cahier), p. 249
4 Tyam, *Qacida*, p. 45; Sissoko, 'Chroniques . . .' (1er Cahier), pp. 49–50

a Sarakole village midway between Bakel and Médine on the left bank of the Senegal.

The invasion of Bambuk took place in the middle of the rainy season and 'Umar's troops collected plenty of food crops along with other types of booty.[1] The fact that Umar took the people of Koundian and other parts of Bambuk by surprise explains in part the easy victory he won over them. After the inhabitants of Koundian had been easily defeated, those of the neighbouring village of Dialafara took fright and fled from their homes. The Tukulor forces under the command of Modi Muḥammad Diam went in pursuit of the fugitives, caught up with some in the mountains, and defeated them in the encounter that followed, killing many and capturing others. Operations led by the same man and by Abdul Houdake and Elimane against other villages were carried out much in the same way.

The timing of the invasion also put the invaded at a serious disadvantage. The operations took place during the rainy season when communication between the various places was difficult and tardy. Even the invaders, in spite of their preparations, also experienced serious communication problems. For instance, they were held up for three days at Dialafara where the waters of the Faleme had risen high and the ford they had counted upon for crossing the river had disappeared; and when, on the third day, 'Umar successfully led his troops across the river, they regarded the achievement as a miracle.[2] For Muslims miracles were a way of expressing the Shaikh's *baraka*: but as already explained, they were also a familiar pre-Islamic weapon invoked in parts of Africa. But for a people who had not been prepared for war and were suddenly faced with an army 1,100 strong, the handicap was greater. No mobilisation of forces was possible in the short time, and even where the forces were available, they had to operate under very difficult conditions. It was also during the harvest season when the people were engaged in their farm work. It is no wonder then that the Tukulor invaders won an easy victory over their opponents.

1 ASAOF, 1G63/2, 'Notice sur El Hadj Omar', Saint-Louis, 25 May 1878; Tyam, *Qacida*, p. 245; Sissoko, 'Chroniques . . .' (1er Cahier), pp. 249–50
2 For the account of the miracle which 'Umar performed at Dialafara, see Sissoko, 'Chroniques . . .' (1er Cahier), pp. 250–1

CAMPAIGNS AGAINST KHASSO AND BONDU

After Bambuk had been subdued 'Umar carried his campaigns
into Khasso, a country which, as has been noted, had been riven
by civil wars since 1848. These campaigns were directed from
Sirimanna which was first attacked for three days before it was
subjugated, with 600 men killed and 1,545 taken prisoner. 'Umar
camped at Sirimanna until the end of the harvest season after
which he continued the operations by sending contingents
against the neighbouring villages. Modi Muḥammad Diam led
expeditions against Sougouyafara and adjacent villages such as
Kassakou; Elimane Donnaye, Muḥammad Linile, and Abdoulaye
Ali also led expeditions to various other places. Abdoulaye Ali, for
instance, took part in the attack on Counsili, where the Tukulor
forces carried away the cattle of the Khasso inhabitants.[1]

While operating in Khasso 'Umar was greatly helped by the
reinforcements which he continually received from Futa Toro.
He received, for instance, a contingent of about three hundred
men, armed with guns and led by Usman Boubou, from the
village of Singo in Futa Toro. After the defeat of Dyouku
Sambala, ruler of Khasso, at Médine, 'Umar again sent for
reinforcements from Futa Toro through Ahmadu Ali Dyelia, a
torodo, Alfa 'Umar and Kalidou Elimane Bokar, also a *torodo*
from Aeré. This was in September 1854.[2]

In terms of number, discipline and armament, 'Umar's
Tukulor forces were superior to the resisting Khasso forces.
This, in part, explains his success against Dyouku Sambala,
leader of the Khasso defence. Probably more important as an
explanation of the success of the Tukulor invaders was the fact
that Khasso was still fighting its internal civil wars, which had
begun in 1848. It will be recalled that the warring parties, both
before and after 1848, had always felt free to invite aid from
outside, especially from Ka'arta, against the opponent. The
Tukulor invasion was not seen as a common threat which called
for joint action and the pooling of resources in defence of the
state. Rather, one of the factions led by Kartoum Sambala
saw 'Umar as a useful ally against the party of the nominally

1 Tyam, *Qacida*, p. 45
2 *Ibid.*, pp. 45–6; Sissoko, 'Chroniques . . .' (1er Cahier), pp. 251–2

paramount ruler, Dyouku Sambala of Médine. This meant a polarisation of Khasso into anti- and pro-'Umar factions. The result was the Tukulor domination of a large part of the state.

The Sambala family was Muslim. The issue which divided the members of the Khasso ruling dynasty was political not religious. 'Umar found allies in Khasso not because of his religious appeal but because of his political utility value as conceived by Kartoum Sambala. The role of Kartoum Sambala in making possible the establishment of Tukulor rule in Khasso was evident to contemporaries; Faidherbe referred to him as: 'Celui-là même qui attira Alhadji dans le Khasso, lui livra la plus grande partie du pays.'[1]

The reinforcements which 'Umar had been collecting after the surrender of Dyouku Sambala were meant for the operations against Farabana, a settlement with a garrisoned fortress, where 'Umar was expecting a very strong resistance. By the time the Tukulor forces reached Farabana, they were about 12,000 strong. Before reaching Farabana, however, 'Umar's reputation as a religious leader and outstanding warrior had already spread all over the Senegal basin, and a body of admirers already awaited him there. Farabana was at this time a powerful principality. Its power was based on the maintenance of a large body of soldiers who had established their reputation for successfully repulsing the armies of Bambuk, Bondu, and Khasso. 'Umar aimed at gaining control of Farabana because it was militarily strategic, and so would be an asset to him in his subsequent operations. If not controlled by himself, Farabana was likely to be a barrier to his progress in the Senegal valley and a source of embarrassment to him even in the areas already conquered.

His approach to the Farabana problem was largely diplomatic. The people who admired him were already a powerful group in Farabana before the revolution spread there. This fact, coupled with the considerable forces at his disposal, helped him to realise his objective. While he was still at Sirimanna, 'Umar had invited the leaders of the Farabana community to discussion during which he appealed to their fighting zeal, telling them the need and usefulness of fighting a holy war; and in the end he success-

1 ANSOM, Sénégal I, 43(a), no. 463, L. Faidherbe à Monsieur le Ministre de la Marine et des Colonies, Saint-Louis, 29 Aug. 1857

fully persuaded them to stay with him. They thus accepted his leadership.[1]

With the agreement of the Farabana leaders, 'Umar sent a marabout to rule the Farabana fortress while the military men stayed with him, assisting in planning the 'holy war'. While 'Umar was playing on the warlike inclinations and ambition of the Farabana military leaders, the marabout sent to their fortress had enough time to create the right conditions to establish 'Umar's influence and to create a definitely pro-'Umar party in the place. At this point 'Umar felt strong enough to order the destruction of the fortifications at Farabana. This was at a time when he could risk direct military confrontation with Farabana, since the latter was now divided. The order to destroy the fortress further divided the Farabana leaders, with the 'Umar party ready to obey, and the others, less powerful, resisting. In the end 'Umar had his way and the fortress was destroyed. Those who could not agree with him left Farabana for the neighbouring villages in Khasso, Galam and Guidimaka. In this way 'Umar acquired control of Farabana without having to fight. He later built his own fortress in the town, amassing there considerable quantities of armament and converting it into a military base, like Dinguiray and Tamba (Dabatu).[2] It seems fairly obvious at this stage that 'Umar's strategy was to guarantee his conquests through a system of defence centred around a chain of fortresses.

But while 'Umar was away in Farabana, Dyouku Sambala of Médine, tried to reorganise his forces with a view to overthrowing the Tukulor rule in Khasso. 'Umar had left one of his *talibés*, Modi Muḥammad Diam, at the village of Makhana, from where he was to observe the activities of Dyouku Sambala. As part of his plan, however, Sambala organised a revolt against Diam at Makhana and simultaneously arranged for a recruitment of forces from among the Moors along the banks of the river Senegal and in Ka'arta.[3] Earlier on in 1854 Sambala had not cooperated with the French in the negotiations which the latter initiated for the establishment of a fort at Médine. At that time the negotiations had broken down over the exacting conditions imposed by Sambala and which the governor of Senegal could not accept as they

1 Carrère et Holle, *De la Sénégambie française*, p. 199
2 *Ibid.*, pp. 199–200
3 Sissoko, 'Chroniques . . .' (1er Cahier), p. 253

were described as 'trop exigeants'.[1] Now with the threat to his position from 'Umar, Sambala indicated his willingness to reopen negotiations, because he realised that association with the French would stand him in good stead in the struggle ahead. On the other hand, by establishing himself at Farabana, 'Umar had come very close to the French stations at Sénoudébou and Bakel, and his huge military build-up was disquieting to all his neighbours around. But although he handled the situation diplomatically, sending to reassure the French of his friendship and of the fact that he was only concerned with fighting 'unbelievers', meaning he was not against the French who were a people of the 'Book', henceforth, the Moors and the French became important factors in the revolution.

In spite of his assurance to the French, which enabled 'Umar to concentrate on quelling Sambala's efforts in Khasso for some time, the French were frightened by his activities at Farabana, especially from November 1854. In that month, Protet, the French Governor of Senegal, ordered the reinforcements of the garrison at Bakel and the improvement of its defences. These steps were regarded as protective measures taken to insure French interests against a possible attack from 'Umar, who was no longer trusted.[2]

'Umar used Farabana as a base from which he directed his operations with a view to establishing his rule over the Senegambian states, including Futa Toro and Futa Jallon. His prestige had increased enormously as was reflected in the respect with which he was treated from many quarters. He soon began to arbitrate in disputes of various types and from different states like Guoye, Kamera, Bondu, Khasso, and Guidimaka. Some of these states had internal disputes and others external disputes. Disputing chiefs even came to him from Futa Toro, more so because he already had some Futa chiefs as his lieutenants and army commanders. He was probably encouraged by all these as his pronouncements showed. For example, he gave clear indications that he intended to establish his own rule over Futa Toro itself, thereby virtually declaring war on the ruling élites and incumbent

1 ASAOF, 13G23/4, 'Rapport sur la situation générale de la colonie fait à M. le Gouverneur du Sénégal et dépendances par M. Verand, Commissaire de la Marine, Gouverneur, p.i, Janvier, 1854
2 Tyam, *Qacida*, p. 49

leaders of the religion in the area. Similarly he announced his plans to extend his jihād beyond the Senegal to other parts of the Western Sudan. Hence he appealed for support in the war he intended to fight against Ka'arta. Again his hope was that the bulk of his men would come from Futa Toro. Therefore he appealed promising that he would satisfy whoever joined him later on when his rule was established in Futa Toro.[1] His appeal yielded dividends and soon afterwards, using reinforcements from Futa Toro, he directed operations against Bondu, at that time a Muslim state, and fought battles at Makhana and Gadiaga. From Bondu, by attacking the village of Sollou, 'Umar spread his campaigns to Guidimaka and was thus campaigning in the area around Kayes and Médine.[2]

By the end of 1854 'Umar's campaigns were already causing widespread commotion in the Senegal valley. There were disturbances, as a result of which occurred large-scale migrations of people in various directions. The movements of people affected not only Futa Toro from where 'Umar's recruits came, but also Galam and Bondu which were reported to be:

> dans ce moment très agités, soit par des dissensions entre les chefs, soit par Alaghi, qui prend l'ascendant de chef religieux, soit encore par ces bandes armées du Fouta, qui ont quitté leur pays, parce que déchirés eux-mêmes par des désunions et des haines, qui dès la possession de Podor, ces hommes ne se croyaient plus en sûreté dans leurs propres villages.[3]

1 Carrère et Holle, *De la Sénégambie française*, pp. 201–3
2 ASAOF, 15G108/3(1) 'Médine 1855', Saint-Louis, 15 Oct. 1855; Tyam, *Qacida*, pp. 49–52
3 ASAOF 13G23/3 'Rapport sur la colonie adressé par Prôtet au Gouverneur', Dec. 1854, p. 25. It is worth noting here that contrary to the picture of a nationalist protecting the African interest which has been painted of 'Umar, his campaigns in this area at this time had the effect of hampering the heroic effort of the various states to defend their sovereignty against the French. As has been noted in chapter 1, about two thousand Tukulor forces fought the French at Podor in 1854. Shortly afterwards, they had to cope with 'Umar's revolution which undermined the existing régimes in the area and created social and political instability. Thus the people were besieged by two expanding imperialisms, one indigenous, the other foreign. The reactions of the people to the new situation are discussed in chapter 4. For the Franco-Tukulor confrontation at Podor see Chapter 1, p. 31. For a typical, though wrong, presentation of 'Umar as a nationalist, see Samb, 'Sur El Hadj Omar (à propos d'un article d'Yves Saint-Martin)', *Bull. IFAN*, B, xxx, 3, 1968, pp. 803–5

As is clear from this account, people were moving about because of their sense of threatened security caused by a number of factors, particularly the effects of 'Umar's revolutionary activities. Meanwhile 'Umar spread his activities in several directions after consolidating his position in Farabana. He attacked some unsubdued parts of Khasso and dragged in Ka'arta by operating in areas that were under its protection. All the time 'Umar continued to operate from Farabana. From there he sent a part of the accumulated booty, particularly the confiscated property of the defeated chief of Makhana who had unsuccessfully attempted to revolt, to Dabatu for storage. From Makhana Modi Muhammad Diam was sent to attack Guidimaka while 'Umar himself led attacks on the district from another front. Reinforcements were sent to Diam at his temporary camp at Tafsirga, and Guidimaka itself did not resist for long before submitting. 'Umar then absorbed the defeated troops into the Tukulor forces hitherto commanded by Diam, and thereafter personally assumed overall control of operations against the other villages in the district.

After Farabana 'Umar camped successively at Dramanya and Moussaba before he reached the village of Bougourou. This village was directly opposite Soutoucoule[1] where Ka'arta forces, sent to protect Guidimaka and Makhana against the invading Tukulor, were camping. After halting for a day at Bougourou the Tukulor took the offensive against the forces of Ka'arta. Thus Ka'arta's attempt to protect its dependency, Guidimaka, was made the occasion for declaring war against it by 'Umar. The battle of Soutoucoule was bloody but ended with Ka'arta forces routed and Soutoucoule rased to the ground. The Ka'arta forces fled and were pursued by the Tukulor up to Khoulou. In the battle that followed the Ka'arta forces were said to have lost 1,730 men and 20 horses captured.[2]

Khoulou was a small Khasso state which had been a protégé and tributary of Ka'arta. For its protection the Bambara had maintained a cavalry force there. With its conquest, therefore, 'Umar could be said to have subjugated the greater part of the amalgam of states that made up Khasso, especially the parts that remained on the side of Dyouku Sambala of Médine in the dynastic feud that had divided the country. From Khoulou

1 Soutoucoule was situated on the east bank of the Senegal opposite Kayes. Cf. Sissoko, 'Chroniques . . .' (1er Cahier), p. 254n.
2 Sissoko, *ibid.*, p. 254

'Umar sent one of his lieutenants, Alfa 'Umar, to Médine with orders to bring all the belongings of the inhabitants. This was done. But 'Umar allowed the inhabitants of Médine who had been brought along to return to their homes. The treasures amassed were sent to Dabatu (now being used as a treasure store) under escort commanded by Abdoulaye Haoussidji and Tierno Djibi.[1] Among the Khasso states which were loyal to Dyouku Sambala and which were subjugated were, in addition to Médine, Logo and Natiaga. The states which were on the side of Kartoum Sambala in the civil wars that had been raging before the Tukulor revolution were, however, on the side of 'Umar, not by conquest, but by an alliance which they had been using against Dyouku Sambala[2] in what was in effect a continuation of the civil war in the state.

CAMPAIGNS IN KA'ARTA: 1855-57

From Khoulou the campaigns were carried to the province of Koniakary, an integral part of the Ka'arta kingdom. Thus began the direct assault against Ka'arta itself. This stage began in May 1855 when 'Umar entered Koniakary and ended in early 1857 when he left Ka'arta for the Senegambia.

When the Tukulor forces entered Koniakary in May 1855 'Umar's first task was the building of a strong fortress as a base of operations against both the Bambara and a section of the Moors of Ludamak, led by one Ouled Embark. 'Umar once more sent for reinforcements from Futa, where he had good response to his troop recruitment drive. On this occasion the Lam Toro even left Toro to join 'Umar in Ka'arta.[3]

After overrunning the village of Koniakary itself, 'Umar moved on to the village of Ainassigana which was besieged for two nights before the villagers were subjugated. The battles against Yaguéna, and especially Yelimane and Madina, two large villages each with an estimated population of 9,000, were protracted and bloody. But these places were eventually conquered and a

1 ANSOM, Sénégal I, 41b/334, Louis Faidherbe à Monsieur le Ministre de la Marine et des Colonies, Saint-Louis, 27 July 1855; also Sissoko, 'Chroniques . . .' (1er Cahier), p. 254
2 ASAOF, 15G108/1, 'Poste de Médine 1853–1879', p. 1
3 ANSOM, Sénégal I, 41b/223, Louis Faidherbe à Monsieur le Ministre de la Marine et des colonies, Saint-Louis, 24 May 1855

large number of people were massacred or taken prisoner. The effect of these battles would seem to have been disastrous even for the victorious Tukulor forces because thereafter 'Umar withdrew his forces to Fanga, where they had to camp for about forty days in order to reorganise and have time to recover from the losses suffered.[1]

The Tukulor were this time campaigning in the height of the hot and dry season and in an area of poorly wooded savanna. One of their greatest problems, therefore, was how to find water both for the troops and for their animals. This basic need would appear to have dictated the direction of the Tukulor's march. Efforts were made to camp near water spots, such as Kassa where they camped after leaving Fanga. From Kassa the march was continued by way of Kabara to the pool of Dioka, and thence to another pool, Coumake. Before reaching Coumake, however, the troops had suffered greatly and were nearly dying of thirst. Small wonder, then, that the discovery of water in this place was regarded as a miracle performed by 'Umar through his divine powers,[2] an act which, as on the first occasion, raised the morale of the troops and inspired them with absolute confidence in his leadership.

From Coumake waters the Tukulor army reached Karabarou (or Karakoro). But before this time an epidemic had decimated the forces of Ka'arta. This development, like the miracles, was seen as a manifestation of 'Umar's extraordinary powers. The *fama* of Ka'arta, Mamadi Kandia, lacked adequate forces to sustain his resistance to 'Umar because of the ruinous effect of the epidemic. Therefore, on the advice of his military chiefs, and faced with the dangers of an almost certain defeat, Kandia made his submission to 'Umar at Karabarou. From thence the Tukulor army proceeded to take control of Nioro, the capital, using the N'Guénar contingents as the advance guard, with the Irlabé and ToroBé camping at different sides of the city walls.[3] The use of the Futa Toro elements in such major assignments emphasises their significance as the dominant group in the revolution. After Nioro had been captured 'Umar ordered the destruction of the

1 Sissoko, 'Chroniques . . .' (1er Cahier), pp. 254–5
2 *Ibid.*, p. 255
3 ANSOM, Sénégal I, 41b/324, Louis Faidherbe à son Excellence Monsieur le Ministre de la Marine et des colonies, Saint-Louis, 27 July 1855; Sissoko, 'Chroniques . . .' (1er Cahier), p. 255

shrines dedicated to the practice of the indigenous religion. He himself took part in breaking down the shrines he found in the palace of the *fama*. He also ordered a change from the traditional to the Muslim mode of living, involving abstinence from drinking alcohol and not marrying more than four wives.

In making their submission the Massassi Bambara chiefs had expected to be left in peace thereafter. They were now not only forced to make a sudden and drastic change in their way of life, but were also deprived of their property. Confronted with the loss of their political and spiritual independence and of their means of livelihood, the Ka'arta rulers again decided to fight the invaders who represented an alien culture and unprovoked aggression in their midst.[1]

Similarly the Diawara (a Mande group) and some Moorish groups had aided 'Umar in his wars against the Massassi rulers of Ka'arta either in the hope of regaining their independence of the Massassi or of enjoying some economic benefits. With the occupation of Nioro by the Tukulor, these various groups realised that support for 'Umar meant selling themselves to a more powerful and apparently more oppressive master. Such support was soon regarded as a tactical error, and rather than remain its allies, they decided to fight for the overthrow of the new Tukulor regime. Consequently the occupation of Nioro, rather than marking the final submission of Ka'arta kingdom, was just a landmark in campaigns that were henceforth to become more bloody, with the resistance more determined. In the ensuing battles, however, the various anti-Tukulor groups rarely fought together. The Massassi rulers organised their forces and fought independently of the Diawara and the Moors; and, although the Tukulor were now recognised as a common enemy, the hostile relations between the various groups did not for that reason cease. For instance, the factions that had existed among the Moors of the Ludamak emirate continued, with the faction led by Ouled Embark opposed to, and that of Ghoize cooperating with, 'Umar.[2]

The Diawara were the rulers of Ka'arta before the Bambara Massassi came to conquer them, hence the Diawara had allied with the Tukulor against the Massassi. They saw in 'Umar's revolution an opportune event through which they could be rid of their Massassi rulers. As soon as the Massassi had been

1 Ọlọruntimẹhin, 'Resistance movements in the Tukulor Empire'
2 ANSOM, Sénégal I, 41b/324 of 27 July 1855

conquered at Karakoro in Kingui, however, the majority of the Diawara considered their purpose achieved and therefore lost interest in continuing the wars. They now wanted to retake possession of their country. To 'Umar's appeals that booty should be collected and shared according to Islamic laws, only a minority responded, the others choosing to keep what they had gathered since the appeal to Islamic laws meant little to them.[1]

The Diawara soon took up arms against the Tukulor when it became clear that 'Umar intended to establish his rule over them. Hostilities began with a successful attack by the Diawara in which they recaptured cattle and other property seized by the Tukulor soldiers. Subsequently they were defeated in the Kingui district in June 1856,[2] but continued a sporadic struggle against the Tukulor in other parts of Ka'arta.

While the war was being fought against the Diawara 'Umar made sure that Nioro was solidly prepared to serve as a base of operations for future encounters in Ka'arta. During the operations of 1856 it became clear that he did not regard breaking the Diawara resistance as the most urgent task; rather he was pre-occupied with building fortifications and amassing arms and ammunition.[3] These preparations were made against the clashes that were certain to occur not only with the resisting Massassi Bambara but also with the Moors. Both of these opponents were more menacing than the scattered Diawara.

ROLE OF THE MOORS

There were several reasons for the involvement of the Moors in 'Umar's revolution. As has been noted, the French had been fighting trade wars against the Moors in the Senegal valley. The

1 This episode illustrates the difficulty, if not the impossibility, of sharing booty collected during a jihād or any revolutionary war. A revolution necessarily involves diverse elements many of which may only be marginally committed to the ideals or norms of the initiators of the movement. To expect all to respond in the same way to norms or laws, such as the one relating to the administration of war spoils, is to be unrealistic. As in this case, the leader of the movement may not have firm control over the activities of a good number of those in the band-wagon of the movement.
2 Tyam, *Qacida*, pp. 83–7
3 ASAOF 15G108/4(40), Paul Holle, Le Commandant du Poste à Médine à M. le Gouverneur du Sénégal et dépendances, Médine, 17 Feb. 1856; also 15G108/4(46) of 29 Feb. 1856

participation of some Futa Toro chiefs in the wars[1] had in turn led to the formation of an anti-French, Tukulor-supported party among the Moors. In the wars against this group the French had had to fight the Tukulor of Futa Toro, some of whom had, by the end of 1854, migrated to 'Umar for protection and support. As part of this struggle the pro-French party among the Moors became automatically involved in the wars against 'Umar's Tukulor revolution. Later on, there was a political aspect to the dispute that divided the Moors.

One of the conditions which the French had to satisfy before they could carry on their trade in the Senegambian region was the payment of royalties to the various rulers, including those of the Moorish emirates. The Moors, as the principal carriers of the gum trade, also made such exactions on the French merchants as they thought necessary from time to time. But the political division among the Moors prevented an efficient collection of these royalties and tributes. Disputes often arose over who had the right to collect them. For instance, in 1854, among the Brackna, there was a dispute between Sidi Eli and Muhammad Sidi over the right of collection. Such a dispute was very often only another expression of the dispute over the right to political authority. Even after the civil wars that sometimes took place to settle this, whoever won was not necessarily successful in exercising the right to collect the tribute, since the French might still be unwilling to pay. The French on their part found it in their own interest to ally with one group against the other, thereby ensuring the non-payment of dues. Thus, although the pro-'Umar Sidi Eli won the civil war among the Brackna in 1854, he still had difficulties in making the French pay.[2] The French regarded the paying of tribute as humiliating and would rather fight than pay. This had been made clear in the ministerial instruction given to Faidherbe on his appointment, and Pinet-Laprade was later to complain against the payment of what he described as 'des tributs humiliants que nous étions obligés de payer à tous les états riverains du fleuve et de la côte'.[3] To achieve

1 See Chapter 1, pp. 30–2 for evidence from Faidherbe of an anti-French alliance in which the Tukulor and the Moors participated.
2 ANSOM, Sénégal I, 41b/551, 'L. Faidherbe à M. le Ministre de la Marine et des colonies', Saint-Louis, 26 Dec. 1854
3 ANSOM, Sénégal I, 51C; 'Exposé général de la situation de la colonie', Pinet-Laprade, Saint-Louis, 1 Sept. 1855

their objective, which was to trade freely, the French would ally with one group to fight the other. As in the political struggle, the pro-French Moors were in the circumstances anti-Tukulor. Whenever the Moors got involved for this motive, that is, the realisation of victory in their internal political and economic struggle, their fighting for or against the Tukulor was often limited to their Moorish principalities or to the adjacent Tukulor states.

But the establishment by 'Umar of political control over Ka'arta affected the Moors in another way. Because of the aridity of their original homeland the Moors had always been in need of well-watered and fertile land for the cultivation of crops and the raising of animals. In search of this they had been pushing down the Senegal river area, defeating and displacing the indigenous inhabitants, especially the Wolof. In the process they had come into conflict with the French. The defeat inflicted on the Moors by Faidherbe in 1854 severely limited their expansion along the west bank of the Senegal. Consequently, they had turned their attention to the eastern side of the river, where they succeeded in establishing their hegemony over the indigenous populations, some of whom were turned into tribute-paying vassals. But the establishment of Tukulor rule in Ka'arta meant for the Moors the extinction not only of their political influence but also of the material benefits derived from their recent conquests. The areas in which the Moors had some political influence, but which were now being absorbed into 'Umar's empire, included Guidimaka, Diafounou, and Diomboko. The Moors, naturally, decided to fight the Tukulor to preserve their interests.[1]

In their wars against the Tukulor the Moors sometimes fought in collaboration with other anti-Tukulor forces, like the Diawara; but they also fought alone. From May to June 1856, for instance, the Moors in conjunction with the Diawara fought against Tukulor forces led by Alfa 'Umar. The battle of Bassaga was also remarkable in this period for the cooperation between the Moors and the Diawara.[2] At Sakili, and later at Toguel and Hofoure,

1 ASAOF, 15G108/4(69), Paul Holle à M. le Gouverneur du Sénégal et dépendances, Médine, 2 July 1856; also 1D137, 'Rapports de colonel Archinard, 1er Partie, 1892–93', p. 4

2 ASAOF, 15G108/4(65), 'Paul Holle, . . . à M. le Gouverneur du Sénégal et dépendances', Médine, 18 June 1856; also Sissoko, 'Chroniques . . .' (2e Cahier), in *L'Education Africaine*, janvier–juin 1937, p. 7

however, the Moors fought alone. In these encounters their losses were reported to have been heavy. For example, apart from losing some of their fighters, forty-four camels and eighteen horses[1] were captured from them by the Tukulor.

'UMAR'S REVOLUTION AND THE FRENCH OFFENSIVE IN THE SENEGAMBIA (END 1854–DECEMBER 1856)

As already indicated the French under Governor Protet had by the end of 1854 put themselves on the defensive in relation to the Tukulor. Louis Faidherbe, who succeeded Protet with the declared objective of expanding and strengthening French economic and political interests in Senegal, also began to consider 'Umar's revolution as boding ill for the realisation of his mission. This idea was gradually confirmed by the events of 1855. At that date 'Umar would appear to have come to the conclusion that the French represented a barrier to the spread of his influence, especially in the Senegal valley. This would explain the fact that by the middle of 1855 his forces had carried out attacks on French trading posts in various places, including Guoye, Kamara, Guidimaka and Bondu. 'Umar's Tukulor supporters had also attacked French posts in Khasso, in and around Bakel, Sénoudébou, and the village of N'Diayebe.[2] All these activities demonstrate the invalidity of Yves Saint-Martin's suggestion, that 'Umar's intention at this time was peaceful.[3]

The French, naturally, wanted to avenge these acts of hostility but they could not at the time engage in any immediate direct conflict with 'Umar. The situation was seen as one calling for a struggle on a large scale against the Tukulor in the Senegambia and more time was therefore needed to prepare. The French director of external affairs recommended to the governor that, for a start, the most pressing task at Bakel was the achievement of an alliance or friendship with anti-Tukulor forces such as the Sarakole traders, and the populations of Guidimaka and Bondu, and of the territories surrounding the posts along the river Senegal. In addition, he pointed out the need to make communi-

1 Sissoko, 'Chroniques . . .' (2e Cahier), pp. 8–9
2 ASAOF, 13G33/1, 'Le Directeur des affaires extérieures à Monsieur le Gouverneur du Sénégal, Saint-Louis, 28 July 1855
3 Saint-Martin, 'La Volonté de paix . . .'

cations between Bakel and Médine secure, and thereby reduce the difficulties encountered at the French trading posts. In pursuance of this policy the director of external affairs promised to do 'tout mon possible, pendant mon séjour à Bakel pour détacher du parti d'Alaghi les Sarracolets, les Guidi-Maka et une bonne partie du Bondu'.[1] The director hoped to do this without involving the French in hostile actions against the people in general. Such an involvement was in any case unnecessary because it had become clear that some of the people had only been forced to commit hostilities against the French, and some had in fact offered restitution for the pillage of French traders and trading posts. But apart from the reason given by the director, there was also the fact that the French were not at this time equipped for any general hostile involvement with their neighbours.

While looking for allies, the French were also eager to present a deterrent to their opponents. The strategy was to be a mixture of wooing and intimidation depending on the particular people being dealt with. With respect to Guidimaka, their offer to pay restitution for pillage committed was to be accepted, even if the payment was not enough, and friendly relations were to be maintained with them meantime. The same attitude should apply to the people of Guoye and Kamera, both having large Tukulor and Sarakole populations, if they brought proposals similar to those of Guidimaka, or had chiefs with whom the French could deal without fighting. The measure applied to the Dowich Moors was dictated partly by the conviction that their chief, Bakar, had conducted himself amicably towards the French during the time they were under attack. Bakar was therefore to be paid the rents due to him and, in addition, was to be given a few kilogrammes of gunpowder which he could, with some profit to the French, use against 'Umar's revolutionary forces.

With Bondu a tougher line was proposed. There the French already had an ally in one of the princes, Amady Sa'ada. Sa'ada had broken off relations with 'Umar and had come to Bakel to furnish the French with information on the movements of his Tukulor forces. Indeed Sa'ada was the leader of a distinctly anti-'Umar group with wide support spreading to the Bambara kingdom of Ka'arta. As the French director noted, the group 'est formé de tous les villages, existant entre Bakel et Sénoudébou

[1] ASAOF 13G33/1 of 28 July 1855, *op. cit.*, p. 3

et il est lié par sa famille avec les Bambaras près desquels il nous servira de bon intermédiaire'.[1] Hence in Bondu the French were interested in encouraging and maintaining the pro-French group in power. To this end the French forcefully deposed the reigning almamy, 'Umar Sane, and installed Amady Sa'ada in his place.

Such an action strengthened the position of Sa'ada and his group *vis-à-vis* the pro-'Umar group. To further weaken the pro-Tukulor forces at a time when 'Umar was absorbed in the wars in Ka'arta, 'punitive' expeditions were carried out against villages under pro-'Umar chiefs. This was at a time when most of these chiefs were taking part in 'Umar's campaigns in Ka'arta. The villages concerned succumbed easily to the French cause, represented by Amady Sa'ada. In relation to the states around Bakel and Dagana, it was decided that the chiefs and others who had led contingents to al-ḥājj 'Umar would be prevented from returning to their homes. Others not so prominently involved on the Tukulor side would be permitted to return, on the strict understanding that they would thereafter recognise only French authority, and that at the first sign of betrayal their villages would be destroyed and they themselves executed; on the other hand, if they conducted themselves well, they would be protected like Frenchmen.[2]

The French policy just sketched was translated into practice from the middle of 1855, a time when 'Umar was himself in need of reinforcements in Ka'arta, and therefore could not have given adequate protection to his followers in the Senegambian area. The people themselves, faced with the French operations, were at first uncertain what to do. They were afraid of the punitive measures the French were ready and equipped to take against them if they remained pro-'Umar and hostile. But they also feared the possible consequences which total alignment with the French could involve if and when 'Umar returned from Ka'arta. In the prevailing circumstances, however, it was logical that the French should have their way, since they were not adequately opposed.[3]

Again, in pursuance of the same policy, the French opened fresh negotiations with Sambala over the establishment of a fort at Médine in Khasso. It may be recalled that 'Umar had, by the

1 *Ibid.*, p. 4
2 *Ibid.*, pp. 5–6
3 ASAOF, 13G33/1 of 15 Jan. 1855, p. 10

end of 1854, defeated Sambala and other chiefs supporting him and that subsequently in his bid to regain his independence Sambala had reopened negotiations with the French. These negotiations resulted in the conclusion of an agreement on 9 September 1855, by which Sambala granted about five hectares of land to the French for the building of a fort in return for the payment of 300 guinea pieces. This amount was payable in three instalments, the first not later than 31 December 1855. It was further agreed that thereafter, an annual rent of one hundred guinea pieces would be paid.[1]

In spirit this agreement symbolised a defensive alliance, uniting the French with Sambala against 'Umar. To make the alliance really useful the French endeavoured to unite all areas of Khasso in the anti-'Umar group. Khasso had been divided into two broad groups by the feud in the Sambala ruling family. The hostility between the groups explains in part the alliance of one side with 'Umar and the Tukulor and of the other with the French. Realising the weakness inherent in this division, the French tried to get the family, and therefore the state, united in close relationship with themselves. Accordingly, the commandant of Médine was instructed that: 'Quant aux haines de famille qui divisent le Khasso, éteignez les autant qu' il vous sera possible de manière à avoir des alliés, bien unis en cas de besoin, et qui ne puissent tourner le dos à la première querelle.'[2] Unfortunately the feuding parties could not be united and it became clear that a trial of strength was still to come. By the conclusion of the agreement with Sambala and the building and maintenance of a fort at Médine the French became definitely committed to the anti-'Umar group in Khasso. Consequently, the attempt by 'Umar later on to subjugate Sambala and his pro-French group inevitably involved the French and the Tukulor in a direct confrontation.[3]

Meanwhile, in accordance with their policy of suppressing pro-'Umar groups, the French sent an army of 250 under the command of one Alioun Sal to attack the village of Detié in

1 ASAOF, 15G108/3(2), Acte de vente passé entre M. Faidherbe, Gouverneur du Sénégal et Sambala, Chef du Khasso, Médine, 29 Sept. 1855
2 ASAOF, 3B77/124(2), E. Bouët, Directeur des affaires extérieures à M. le Commandant de Médine, Saint-Louis, 9 Apr. 1856
3 See Chapter 4

Bondu. This, it was claimed, was to inflict punishment on Bondu for an alleged assassination of stranded French sailors. The attack took place on 25 December 1855 and the killing of the population was on such a scale that it was reported that 'la population a peri tout entière'.[1]

Thus by the end of 1855 the French were convinced that their policy was yielding encouraging results. It was reported that Khasso remained loyal to the French and that in other places the war against pro-'Umar territories was continuing with vigour and with advantage to the French. Bondu was reported to be making peace moves, indicating its willingness to accept a pro-French almamy, Boubakar, son of Almamy Sa'ada, and to abandon 'Umar. In Bambuk the Malinke population was reported to be determined more than ever before in their resistance to 'Umar.[2]

For the year 1856 Faidherbe believed that since the struggle was going well for the French they should continue to exploit the situation as in 1855. Faidherbe's main concern was with the development of French commercial interests, especially through the Moors, and the exploitation of the mineral resources of the Upper Senegal. On this point he did not see 'Umar's wars in Ka'arta or the involvement of the Senegambia in 'Umar's revolution as detrimental to French interests. Rather he even saw 'Umar's campaigns as advantageous since they kept him off the scene in the Senegambia. Against this background Faidherbe, early in 1856, remarked that there was no hope of peace returning to the Senegambia for a long time but that there was nothing yet to worry about. The gum trade, he continued, was doing better than ever before, and even if the wars of 'Umar were to last for eternity, the French would still be able to exploit the Bambuk mines. In the meantime the French should strike mercilessly at 'Umar's forces anywhere they dared to confront them.[3]

Faidherbe's strategy sufficed so long as 'Umar was deeply involved in the Ka'arta campaigns. But with the news that he was

1 ASAOF, 13G33/3(1), 'Le Directeur des affaires extérieures: Bulletin du Haut du Fleuve', Saint-Louis, Jan. 1856
2 ANSOM, Sénégal I, 41b/15, Louis Faidherbe à M. le Ministre de la Marine et des Colonies, Saint-Louis, 14 Jan. 1856; also same to same in Senegal I, 41b/37 of 28 Jan. 1856
3 ANSOM, Sénégal I, 41b/185, 'L. Faidherbe à M. le Ministre', Saint-Louis, 24 Apr. 1856

succeeding against his Bambara opponents, the inadequacy of this 'wait and see' policy began to dawn upon the French. They suddenly realised the need to settle with their enemies in the Senegambia in order to be in a stronger position to meet any move that 'Umar might make. Reconciliation with some of the enemies was seen as a means of reducing the difficulties of the French in the Senegambia. But to facilitate the settlement of their problems severe 'punitive' expeditions were also planned against some of their more difficult enemies.[1]

While thus making efforts to control the Senegambia the French were also trying to keep 'Umar in Ka'arta in a bid to postpone direct confrontation with him for some time. In pursuance of this objective emissaries were sent to him, offering to recognise his sovereignty over Ka'arta on condition that he limited his activities to that country. It was calculated, however, that, should 'Umar reject the offer, war with him would become a necessity in the near future. To prepare for such an eventuality Faidherbe ordered that the French posts along the river Senegal be reinforced with men, arms and ammunition.[2]

'Umar did not reply to the offer made to him and it was assumed that he was for war. It was also assumed, however, that he was not likely to declare any war until the dry season when the French expected to be able to use their fortified posts effectively.

Although they were making preparations for war, the French were in fact eager to limit their military commitments. They wanted to avoid creating the impression that they were against Islam as such. Therefore they explained to the Muslim population in Saint Louis and in the Senegambian area that although they had to fight 'Umar, they had nothing against Islam. This assurance was necessary in order to reduce the support which 'Umar was likely to get from the Muslim population in his wars against the French. Another reason was that the French did not in any case have the resources for conducting military campaigns on a large scale. Faidherbe himself explained the basis of his policy when he said: 'Nous sommes juste assez forts pour

1 ASAOF, 13G23/3, L. Faidherbe à M. le Commandant, Saint-Louis, 12 June 1856
2 ANSOM, Sénégal I, 41b/185 of 24 Apr. 1856, *op. cit.*, also Abun-Nasr, *The Tijāniyya*, p. 116

résister à nos ennemis extérieurs et la moitié de notre force consiste dans le concours de ces musulmans contre lesquels on conseille inconsidérément d'agir.'[1]

As has been said, 'Umar was not able to play any direct role in the events taking place in the Senegambia since 1855 because of the campaigns in Ka'arta. In 1856, his position became even more difficult and the situation in Ka'arta more absorbing because apart from fighting against the forces of the Massassi Bambara, the Diawara and the Moors, he also had to fight battles against the troops of the Segu Bambara rulers and those of Masina. As early as August 1855 the Bambara ruler of Segu had sent troops to Ka'arta to help the Massassi in their resistance to the Tukulor,[2] and battles were fought in Diagounté district on the border of Ka'arta and Segu.[3] Masina forces fought against the Tukulor in Ka'arta up till 1857. 'Umar's situation at this time was critical enough to make him order reinforcements from Futa Toro again. In response to his needs about two hundred cavalry men from Futa Toro reached Ka'arta to join his forces in January 1857.[4]

'Umar succeeded in defeating the forces of Masina, Segu and the Moors in Bakhounou early in 1857.[5] This victory gave him some respite from his engagements in Ka'arta. Thereafter, he decided to turn to the French menace in the Senegambia, especially in Khasso where the French had established the fort at Médine late in 1855. Before leaving Ka'arta, however, he established some administration under the control of his *talibés* and relatives, with Alfa 'Umar as the supreme chief of the military and civil administration.

Ka'arta was divided into districts or emirates, each under a

1 ASAOF, 13G23/5, L. Faidherbe à M. le Commandant, Saint-Louis, 12 June 1856, pp. 4–5
2 ASAOF, 13G33/1, Le Directeur des affaires extérieures à M. le Gouverneur du Sénégal, Saint-Louis, 15 Aug. 1855
3 ASAOF, 15G108/3(16), Le Commt du Poste à Monsieur le Gouverneur du Sénégal, Médine, 30 Nov. 1855; also 13G33/3(3), 'Nouvelles du Haut Fleuve: Le Directeur des affaires extérieures', Saint-Louis, 9 Jan. 1856
4 ASAOF 15G108/5(92), Paul Holle, le Commandant du Poste à Monsieur le Gouverneur du Sénégal et dépendances, Médine, 11 Jan. 1857
5 Sissoko, 'Chroniques . . .' (2e Cahier), p. 8

talibé who was often also a military leader. The following territorial divisions and appointments were made:

District	Administrator
Koniakary	Tierno Djibi
Diafounou	Djoubairou Boubou
Kaniareme	Tierno Ahmadu
Yoguire	Modi Muhammad Fakhaou
Diala	Suleyman Baba Raki
Ka'arta Bine	Tierno Khalidou
Guémoukoura	'Umar Lamine
Diagounté	Abdullahi Haoussidji
Bakhounou	Abdullahi Ali (Abdoulaye Ali)[1]

Other places where 'Umar maintained officers included Guémou and Guidimaka.[2]

With Ka'arta thus controlled 'Umar was able to leave the country for a while in order to address himself to the French challenge in the Senegambian states.

1 Information used here comes from the account originally compiled by this man who was an active participant in the revolution.
2 ANSOM, Sénégal I, 41a, L. Faidherbe à son Altesse Impériale le Prince Napoléon, Saint-Louis, 30 Aug. 1858; also Sissoko, 'Chroniques . . .' (2e Cahier), p. 8

4 Resistance to, and Failure of, 'Umar's Revolution in the Senegambia, 1857–1860

'Umar's return from Ka'arta was a demonstration of his determination to reassert his authority and consolidate his control over areas which he had conquered in the Senegambia between 1852 and 1855. But as has been shown in the last chapter, while he was engaged in the Ka'arta campaigns, various groups, spearheaded by the French, had emerged to neutralise or even wipe out the achievement of the revolution in their various areas. The activities of these anti-'Umar groups spread over the various states in the Senegambia and to achieve his objective 'Umar would have to struggle against opponents in several areas. The competition between him and his opponents split the populations of these areas into warring factions, each acting according to its attitudes to, and involvement in, the revolution. Because the struggle deeply affected the populations it became protracted and assumed the character of a civil war. The struggle began in Khasso with the siege of Médine in which 'Umar and his men encountered the Khassonke under Dyouku Sambala and the French.

With Ka'arta conquered and organised under the control of his *talibés*, 'Umar left for Khasso in February 1857. Since early 1855, when he left Khasso for the campaigns in Ka'arta, the pro-Tukulor forces in Khasso had diminished in strength while in contrast the anti-Tukulor forces, led by Dyouku Sambala of Médine and strongly supported by the French, had been growing. The anti-Tukulor elements became more confident after the establishment of the French fort at Médine in September 1855. At this time pro-'Umar Tukulor power in Khasso was based in the districts of Logo and Natiaga. From these bases pro-'Umar elements continued the struggle even when 'Umar was still engaged in Ka'arta. They sent armed contingents to attack

93

territories under anti-Tukulor rulers, especially Diatrimady and Fassané, in 1856, but they were easily repulsed.[1] As has been noted, civil wars had rent Khasso into two broad camps since 1848. With the revolution of 'Umar and the intervention of the French came external forces with which the warring factions allied as a means of achieving their respective objectives. Against this background the confusion which the civil war, grafted to 'Umar's revolution, had caused was to be further confounded by the Franco-Tukulor struggle for power. It was to oust the French from their position of power in Khasso, and generally in the Senegambian states, that 'Umar decided to attack Médine in 1857. This step was particularly necessary from 'Umar's point of view because the French had proved that, operating from their base in this area of the Senegal valley, they could be a danger to his position in Ka'arta. For instance the French had in 1856 aided Dagaba against the Tukulor in the wars in the Koniakary area of Ka'arta.[2]

Also Dyouku Sambala, ruler of Médine, backed by the French, had been leading a group of Khasso chiefs against the Tukulor since 1856. In pursuance of his anti-Tukulor policy, Sambala made efforts to detach from 'Umar his followers in Khasso, especially notables like Demba Sambala, a brother of the Médine ruler. He did not, however, achieve much success in this direction as there still remained a large body of partisans of the Tukulor in Khasso under the leadership of Kartoum Sambala who was deeply involved in the dynastic struggle against his brother in Médine. More seriously, however, Dyouku Sambala engaged in building up an army which he planned to use in attacking Diomboko district of Ka'arta. In this connection, he contracted alliances with certain chiefs in Bambuk and with some anti-Tukulor Bambara elements from Ka'arta.[3] By January 1857, the situation in Khasso was becoming almost impossible for 'Umar's supporters. At that time some of them had to evacuate their villages. Indeed in January 1857 the inhabitants of three villages in the neighbourhood of Médine emigrated to the right bank of the Senegal so as to have the protection of the

1 ASAOF, 15G108/1, 'Poste de Médine, 1853–1879'
2 Sissoko, 'Chroniques . . .' (2e cahier), p. 12
3 ASAOF, 15G108/5(92), Paul Holle, le Commandant du Poste à Monsieur le Gouverneur du Sénégal et dépendances, Médine, 11 Jan. 1857

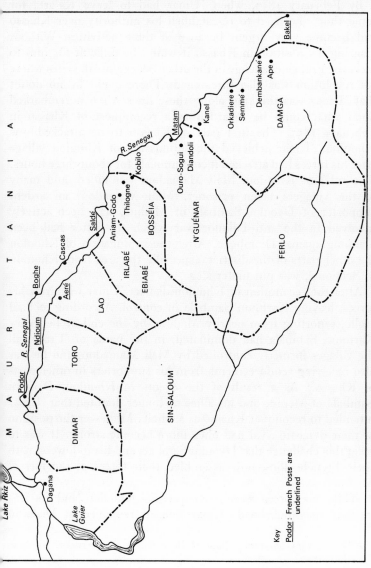

Futa Toro, showing the component groups and the French posts on the Senegal

Tukulor conquerors in Ka'arta.[1] The villagers were those who were loyal to Kartoum Sambala.[2]

By February 1857, when 'Umar had to leave Ka'arta for some time, the need to re-establish his authority over Khasso had become very urgent because of these activities. Without insuring his position in Khasso it would be difficult for him to meet the French challenge in the other Senegambian states where his revolution was also threatened. There could be no doubt that 'Umar was thinking along these lines when he embarked upon what could be regarded as a reconquest of Khasso in February 1857. The first part of Khasso to be attacked was Khoulou. 'Umar achieved the submission of Khoulou village after his forces had attacked it continuously for about three hours. The ruler of Khoulou, Mali Mamadou, was killed, and many of the villagers taken prisoner. Mali Mamadou, an ardent supporter of Dyouku Sambala of Médine, had been actively involved in the anti-Tukulor war which the latter had been planning against Diomboko. After the subjugation of Khoulou the other parts of the district, especially the area from Khoulou to Setajoulé, was put under siege.[3]

After the reconquest of Khoulou district 'Umar withdrew his forces, leaving Kartoum Sambala in control. According to Paul Holle, reporting from nearby Médine, by the end of February Kartoum Sambala had dominated, in the name of 'Umar, all the villages formerly controlled by Mali Mamadou, and he was also receiving reinforcements from his supporters in other parts of Khasso.[4] As a result of the events in Khoulou, Dyouku Sambala of Médine and his allies no longer doubted that 'Umar intended to reconquer Khasso as a whole. Moreover the position of their dynastic rival had once more become strong. It was to meet this challenge that Dyouku Sambala and his followers, with their French allies, now assembled their forces at the fort of Médine.[5]

While his forces were reconquering Khoulou and its immediate neighbourhood 'Umar himself remained at Diala in

1 ASAOF, 15G108/5(100), Paul Holle à M. le Gouverneur, Médine, 23 Jan. 1857
2 ASAOF, 15G108/5(118), same to same, 30 Jan. 1857
3 ASAOF, 15G108/5(118), same to same, 22 Feb. 1857
4 ASAOF, 15G108/5(120), same to same, 5 Mar. 1857
5 ASAOF, 15G108/5(118), same to same, 22 Feb. 1857

Ka'arta. In view of his imminent campaigns in Khasso, Diala occupied a strategic position. It provided a vantage point from which he could keep the movements of his enemies – the Bambara, Dyouku Sambala and his supporters – under surveillance. Also the success of the anti-Tukulor war on Diomboko, being planned by Dyouku Sambala of Médine, depended mainly on adequate collaboration between himself and his allies among the Bambara and in Bambuk. 'Umar's presence in Diala, however, made it almost impossible for Dyouku Sambala to collaborate with the Bambara and the Bambuk chiefs. Consequently Sambala could not receive the promised contingents from Bambuk and Ka'arta; neither could he help Mali Mamadou when the latter was being attacked at Khoulou by 'Umar. It was reported that the Bambara and the Bambuk chiefs could not come to Médine with their contingents because 'Umar, at Diala, was a threat too near them, and so they had to be on their guard. Because of this situation Dyouku Sambala was virtually compelled to stay at Médine with his little army, described by Paul Holle as 'son peu du monde',[1] which he intended to use to defend his position against 'Umar rather than take the offensive. The whole situation in Médine therefore looked critical for Dyouku Sambala and his supporters in Khasso. Their only consolation lay in the strength of their allies, the French.

The French had entered into a treaty with Dyouku Sambala in September 1855, several months after the latter's territory had been overrun by 'Umar (see p. 88). It was on this treaty that they based their presence in Médine, as well as their hostility to 'Umar. Their main interest was in gaining control of the commercial activities and potentialities for which Médine was the centre. With the threat of extinction looming over Dyouku Sambala and all that he represented, the French, whose fortunes were bound up with his, became anxious about their position. It was realised that the economic and political interests of the French would be in danger if 'Umar succeeded in removing Dyouku Sambala and installed in his place his anti-French brother, Kartoum Sambala. This eventuality seemed so real to Paul Holle, commander of the fort at Médine, that on 5 March 1857 he sent urgently to Saint Louis, asking the governor for directives regarding the military action he should take.[2]

1 ASAOF, 15G108/5(120), same to same, 5 Mar. 1857
2 ASAOF, 15G108/5(127), same to same, 5 Mar. 1857

While awaiting instructions, Paul Holle and M. des Escartes, Captain of the *Guet N'dar* (a dispatch-boat moored off Médine), resorted to acts of hostility against 'Umar's supporters. M. des Escartes, for example, had three Khassonkés brought to him from the village of Tamboukane, and, after ascertaining that they were 'Umar's supporters, had them shot dead as enemies.[1] Holle had a Fulani herdsman resident at Médine shot on the pretext that he was one of two herdsmen who had attempted to desert to the Tukulor side with the cows entrusted to their care.[2] Eventually Holle received orders to mobilise the garrison at Médine in readiness for the Tukulor menace. This was after he had again sent an urgent letter to the governor informing him of the great anxiety under which the population of Médine was living.[3] Early in April Holle reported to the governor of the preparedness of Médine to meet the threat from 'Umar, assuring the governor that 'à chaque moment à Médine il y a alerte . . . nous sommes toujours sur les armes'.[4] Thus the French had joined Dyouku Sambala in the effort to repel 'Umar's attempt to reconquer Khasso.

But 'Umar did not move directly against Médine as expected by his opponents. Instead, on leaving Diala he directed his forces against the Logo district, especially Sabousire, the headquarters of Niamody, a fervent supporter of Sambala of Médine, and therefore an enemy of the Tukulor. After Sabousire had surrendered other villages submitted without further fighting since they were taken by surprise. Thus Logo was once again brought under Tukulor control. From Logo 'Umar proceeded to the district of Natiaga, already divided into two parts, one remaining loyal to 'Umar, the other held by Semounou, supporting Dyouku Sambala. 'Umar did not have much problem in subjugating Natiaga also.[5] From all these operations it would seem that 'Umar's strategy was first to subdue the territories around Médine, then to control all the access routes and prevent the flow of trade and finally to assault Médine itself. In this way he hoped to make Dyouku Sambala and the French surrender for

1 ASAOF, 15G108/5(127), same to same, 18 Mar. 1857
2 *Ibid.*, p. 2
3 *Ibid.*, p. 4
4 ASAOF, 15G108/5(134), same to same, 8 Apr. 1857
5 ASAOF, 15G108/5(135), same to same, 14 Apr. 1857

lack of commerce and under threat of starvation.[1] But the plan did not work as he expected because he had to make a direct attack on Médine earlier than planned. The first attack on Médine took place at about 5.30 a.m. on 21 April 1857. The battle that ensued was reported to have lasted till about 11 a.m. 'Umar's forces were defeated and are said to have lost about three hundred dead.[2]

Paul Holle was sure that 'Umar would return to avenge the defeat and therefore made arrangements against another encounter. He asked that the troops, arms and ammunition at the French posts of Bakel, Galibi, Sénoudébou Diakandapé, and their neighbourhoods, be sent to Médine to reinforce the garrison there.[3]

But 'Umar must have realised the weakness of his forces when they had to fight a pitched battle against better armed anti-Tukulor fighters. Therefore, instead of launching a direct attack on Médine, and thereby becoming involved in fighting another pitched battle, he decided to use the positions of his troops around Médine to put the town under siege for some time, and confine his action to sending occasional harassing parties to shoot at French military personnel in and around the fort. Such surprise attacks were sometimes made in the night. This type of action was reported by Holle on 3 May 1857.[4]

The strategy adopted by 'Umar seems to have had the results he expected. The blockade of Médine and the surprise attacks on the fort, organised from various directions, weakened the morale of the military personnel who were only equipped to fight the war under the protection of the fort. Even more disastrous for them was the fact that their supply of ammunition was being exhausted at a time when, because of the communication problem, it was not easy for them to replenish their store. Moreover, in readiness for any possible attack, the canon had to be in use all the time. Paul Holle lamented the damage being done to the weapons in this way saying: 'Ce qui me fait le plus peine c'est le mauvais état dans lequel se trouve actuellement nos pièces de canon, car elles sont toutes démontées.'[5] To meet the emergency,

1 Tyam, *Qacida*, v. 603, p. 101
2 ASAOF, 15G108/5(138), Paul Holle à M. le Gouverneur, Médine, 21 Apr. 1857
3 *Ibid.*, p. 2
4 ASAOF, 15G108/5(142), same to same, 3 May 1857
5 *Ibid.*, p. 1

Holle asked for reinforcements from the posts at Bakel, Makhana and Sénoudébou. Stressing the need to send forces urgently, he noted that food was becoming scarce and that if the blockade were to continue much longer it would become impossible to feed the troops, especially those of them who had come from their villages to join the French forces at Médine.[1]

'Umar was apparently not pleased with results so far obtained, or probably he felt strong enough to engage in another open attack. The second pitched battle in the struggle took place on 11 May 1857, on a little island in the Senegal river. 'Umar's forces were led by Tierno Djibi, the commander of the Tukulor operations in the neighbouring district of Diomboko. The French had with them the troops of Dyouku Sambala, Bambara volunteers, and the reinforcements (regular soldiers and volunteers) from the other posts. The battle which started at about 1 o'clock in the night lasted till 10 o'clock in the morning and ended with the defeat of 'Umar's forces. The attacking Tukulor had to withdraw hurriedly, swimming across the river to their camps.[2]

In the preparation against subsequent encounters which seemed inevitable, Holle again called for more reinforcements from the other French posts. In response to his appeal a column of about six hundred men was sent from Bakel and Sénoudébou, although some of the men were reported to have deserted before the column reached Médine.[3] A third battle took place on 3 June 1857, and, as on the two previous occasions, the Médine alliance beat the army of 'Umar,[4] which lost eighty-one dead on the battlefield.[5] But the siege continued, and with the wrecking of the dispatch-boat, *Guet N'dar*, Médine was again cut off from supplies. The situation soon became so critical that Faidherbe had to lead an expedition to relieve Médine in July. He sent the first part of the rescuing force on the steam-boat *Basile*, on 2 July, and followed with eighty men on the *Podor* on the 5th. The fate of Paul Holle and his men depended on the timely arrival of this force, failing which they might be starved or forced to surrender. Faidherbe arrived at Médine on 18 July, three months and two days after the beginning of the siege. A number of local inhabi-

1 *Ibid.*, pp. 2–3
2 ASAOF, 15G108/5(149), same to same, 17 May, 1857
3 ASAOF, 15G108/5(152), same to same, 9 June 1857
4 *Ibid.*, p. 1
5 ASAOF, 15G108/1, Poste de Médine, 1853–1879

tants inside the fort had already died of starvation but enough forces survived to assist in the relief operation. 'Umar was finally defeated at Médine on 18 July 1857.[1]

The victory of the French was a mixed blessing for Dyouku Sambala and his allies. In the first place, within the context of Khasso politics, they had scored a victory over the faction led by Kartoum Sambala, and they could go ahead to strengthen their position against their opponents. Their ambition to be independent had, to a great extent, been realised. Some threat was still to be feared from the Tukulor, who were still able to act from neighbouring Ka'arta and from the relatively weaker district of Logo in Khasso; but Dyouku Sambala and his men had gained the independence they wanted, and they had the freedom to pursue their ambitions even in Khasso, though this was only under the protection of the French. So much was achieved, but at a great price. They were now dependent on the French. Moreover the siege of Médine had terrible consequences for the people of Khasso, especially for the population of Médine. Apart from those who had died in the battle, preoccupation with military activities had taken people away from their farming and other economic activities, and in consequence a terrible famine occurred which decimated the population. The misery that resulted became so acute that by the middle of 1858 the governor of Senegal was informed of the urgent need to come to the aid of Dyouku Sambala, whose people were dying daily; the shortage of grain was such that the people could not even find seeds for planting, a situation which was ominous for the future.[2]

A desire to solve the frustrating problems facing his people lay behind Dyouku Sambala's policy towards the French and the Tukulor throughout 1858. He came to rely more on the French and became more aggressive to the Tukulor because he regarded the French as the indispensable allies who would help him solve his problems, which had been caused by the Tukulor. Dyouku Sambala was also bitter against the Tukulor because he thought that while the inhabitants of Médine were dying of hunger the

1 ANSOM, in Sénégal I, 42a, L. Faidherbe à Son Altesse Impériale, Médine, 19 July 1857; Mage, *Voyage*, p. 248; Abun-Nasr, *The Tijāniyya* p. 118
2 ASAOF, 1D13/12, P. Brossards à M. le Gouverneur, Médine, 27 July 1858

Tukulor in Ka'arta were living in plenty, with reserves of food put away in barns. It was with this feeling that he sent raiding parties to the neighbouring district of Diomboko (in Ka'arta) early in 1858, and for the rest of the year he continually pressed the French for an expedition against Koniakary as a demonstration of their support for him against the Tukulor. He hoped that the success of such an expedition would inspire the Khasso people and imbue them with courage to continue their struggle against the Tukulor, while those who had emigrated to Tukulor territories would find it desirable to desert 'Umar and flock back into Khasso. He believed that an expedition against Diomboko province, if successful, could help to solve the misery caused by hunger and frequent death; but his raids against Diomboko were disappointing, yielding him only eighteen captives.[1] This made him renew his appeal for aid to the French in August 1858.[2] He wanted, specifically, the French to send a gunboat to Tombokane, on the river Senegal, in the neighbourhood of which was the village of Bokhore where, he claimed, there were still many huts filled with stored grain. With the gunboat at Tombokane, he explained, his men would be able to pillage the grain stored at Bokhore, and convey it to Médine under the protection of the cannon mounted on the boat.[3]

From the above it is clear how the misery which resulted from the siege of Médine was pushing Dyouku Sambala to plan and carry out aggression against the Tukulor in Diomboko province of Ka'arta. But the French, preoccupied for the moment with 'Umar's activities in Futa Toro and the other Senegambian states, did not actively encourage him. This was to avoid dissipating their energy by confronting 'Umar on many fronts at the same time, and with scattered forces. 'Umar, for his part, had not much to fear from Dyouku Sambala as long as his lieutenant, Tierno Djibi, was in command of his forces in Diomboko.

Because of his defeat at Médine, 'Umar was confronted, more than ever before, by the danger which the French presence in Khasso represented to the security of his emergent empire. His first move was to withdraw to Sabousire, the headquarters of the Logo district which he had reconquered in April 1857, in

1 *Ibid.*, pp. 1–2
2 ASAOF, 1D13/15, same to same, 6 Aug. 1868
3 *Ibid.*, p. 1

order to consolidate his position in that part of Khasso so that he could use it as a base for further operations against the French and Dyouku Sambala. He remained at Sabousire up till August 1857,[1] using the town as a base for his military operations against pro-French forces in the Bambuk. Later in August, his forces were engaged in campaigns against Bambuk forces led by Koura.[2] One of such campaigns took place at Keniebadougou. In defending this village against the Tukulor forces, Koura had the support of the people of Kangara, Gouladougou and Diagala. This help, coupled with the fact that 'Umar's forces were handicapped by the great difficulties of communication caused by the lack of fords or bridges over the rivers, ensured victory for Koura and his forces.[3] 'Umar's need for reinforcements became more acute than ever before, and he headed for Futa Toro where he hoped to obtain support. In the meantime he marched to Dinguiray and on to Koundian, which he found completely deserted. After reoccupying it he appointed one of his military leaders, Diam, as chief in charge, with a contingent of volunteers to help guard the fortress there. He left Koundian early in January 1858.[4]

THE STRUGGLE AGAINST THE FRENCH AND THEIR ALLIES IN FUTA TORO AND NEIGHBOURING STATES, 1858–59

After his defeat at the hands of Koura in Bambuk 'Umar appears to have decided to avoid, for some time, further military encounters with his enemies, especially the French. His reoccupation of Koundian was of strategic advantage, but he was still desperately in need of reinforcements. These he had always got from his home country, Futa Toro. His movement from Koundian was obviously determined by his desire to operate next in an

1 ASAOF, 15G108/5(1), Lt Belsange à M. le Gouverneur, Médine, 3 Aug. 1857
2 One of the allies of Dyouku Sambala of Médine in Bambuk.
3 ASAOF, 15G108/5(38), Le Lieutenant du Génie . . . à M. le Gouverneur, Médine, 24 Aug. 1857; 15G108/5(11), Médine, 22 Sept. 1857
4 Tyam, *Qacida*, pp. 106–8, vv. 630–9. Until it was destroyed in February 1889, Koundian was part of Tukulor defence system, and was used to preserve Tukulor influence against the French in the Senegambia.

area where he could be sure of recruits to his fighting force, or at least command some sympathy among the population. Apparently he hoped to reach Futa Toro by way of Futa Jallon, thereby avoiding French posts where he might encounter hostilities. But the almamy of Futa Jallon, based in the neighbouring district of Timbo, was hostile to 'Umar whom he continued to see as a revolutionary whose activities were inimical to the continuance of his regime. The almamy took steps to frustrate 'Umar's plan by putting his soldiers across the frontier to prevent him from entering Futa Jallon.[1] Not having enough forces to fight in Futa Jallon 'Umar decided to approach Futa Toro by another route, and to face whatever obstacle the French might put in his way should he find it necessary to go near their posts. He probably considered this move as less dangerous than forcing his way through Futa Jallon, where he would have had to fight a major war without any hope of winning. He passed through Bondu later in January 1858 and came up against the French at Sénoudébou. There he ordered the French post to be broken down and gave the people an ultimatum to submit to him or emigrate because, according to him, the country was no longer their own since it had been taken over by the Europeans.[2] Some of the inhabitants chose to emigrate while others decided to resist him and he had to fight them into submission, setting their homes on fire. His supporters in Sénoudébou who opted to emigrate did so under the leadership of Tierno Haimout. They were given safe conduct from Bondu to the Kingui province of Ka'arta.[3] This episode was the beginning of a new struggle for influence between 'Umar and others, including the French, in the Senegambia, especially in the Futa Toro states.

After Sénoudébou 'Umar seems to have made a correct assess-

---

1 ASAOF, 15G108/6(22), Le Commandant du Poste de Médine à M. le Gouverneur, Médine, 4 Jan. 1858

2 The reference here was to the canonical injunction on Muslims to emigrate from the *dār al-harb* rather than endure the rule of unbelievers who did not operate the *sha'ria*. In Islam, Europeans, being Christians, were at best *dhimmīs*, to be tolerated, not permitted to govern.

3 Tyam, *Qacida*, pp. 109–10, vv. 645–50. Kingui province was the area around Nioro, the capital of Ka'arta. In the area, the Tukulor could resettle, relatively easily, and give protection to the new members of the group. This was probably why they were sent over such a long distance of about 100 miles from Futa Toro.

ment of the difficulties he was up against in his bid to dislodge the French and their allies from the Senegambian states. He desisted from pushing ahead towards Futa Toro immediately. Instead he decided to insure his position against French encroachment in the Upper Senegal area and Ka'arta, which he had already conquered. He was anxious to prevent the French from having easy access to Khasso where, by exploiting their control of Médine, they could do a lot of damage to his position in Ka'arta. The surest means of communication for the French in this area was by boats on the river Senegal. To keep them off the Tukulor-controlled territories, therefore, 'Umar sought to control the river by making it non-navigable. He tried to do this by causing a barrier to be built across the Senegal at Garly, near Médine. This was in April 1858.[1] If the barrier had had the desired effect the French post at Médine would have been isolated and paralysed for want of supplies. This would in turn have made it possible ultimately for 'Umar to conquer Dyouku Sambala and reinstate himself as ruler of the entire Khasso. In the period of flood, however, the barrier was so easily eroded that by August, when Faidherbe led an expedition to Bambuk, it had been washed away enough to make it possible for small boats to sail through.[2] After the construction of the barrier in April 1858, the exact movements of 'Umar are not known, but it seems clear that he was finding his way to Futa Toro. Large-scale land fighting must have been near-impossible in the intensively rainy and hot season and this may explain the relative inactivity of the opposing forces in the following three months.

The French, nevertheless, were anxious about their position in the Senegambian area and they were apprehensive of the moves being made by 'Umar to establish contact with his supporters in the states in that area. In preparation for the continuing struggle between them and the Tukulor they not only increased the supply of arms and ammunition to their posts, but they also built military camps in other areas where there had been none before. The newly installed camps were meant to be observation posts from which limited military operations could be undertaken while help was being awaited from the big forts.

---

1 ANSOM, in Sénégal I, 41a, L. Faidherbe à son Altesse Impériale le prince Napoléon, Saint-Louis, 30 Aug. 1858
2 *Ibid.*

These forts and camps were also used to cut off communication between 'Umar and his supporters, who, whenever they lost contact with their leader, could be forced to submit to the French and their allies. In general the camps were bases for troops that constituted a kind of standing army, giving assurance and protection to French allies in the various states.[1] French policy at this time was not only designed to ensure the safety of their posts and the commerce flowing into them, but was also designed to arrest the movements of 'Umar and limit his area of influence. 'Umar's own attitude to the posts at this time was determined by the fact that they were not only commercial centres, but were also garrisoned forts from which the Guidimaka and others whom he had conquered were being incited to revolt and all efforts were being made to cut off his sources of reinforcements and provision in Futa Toro and neighbouring states.[2] In the Futa Toro episode the struggle for supremacy between 'Umar and the French was fought out in all parts of the country and, as in Khasso, the Franco-Tukulor tussle became mixed up with the local politics of the area. This gave the struggle a complex character as the reasons for the participation of the indigenous populations in the struggle varied from area to area. The struggle was conducted by both military action and propaganda.

It is not known when 'Umar first arrived in Futa Toro, but he was already there by August 1858, recruiting reinforcements and encouraging his supporters to emigrate and follow him to Ka'arta.[3] Before this time, however, the propaganda carried out by the French and their allies against him was already having adverse effects on his cause. It was reported that there had been a remarkable change in the opinion of the people about him and his mission. Faidherbe reported that the majority of the Futa Toro people who had earlier supported him now felt they had misplaced their trust, adding that:

La foi dans Alhadji, dans sa mission et dans son désintéressement, a complètement disparu. Tous disent: il nous a trompés, mais tous ont plus

1 ASAOF, 1D13/76, Commandant du Camp de Mérinaghen à M. le Gouverneur, 3 Dec. 1858
2 ASAOF, 1D13/8, Camp d'Observation à M. le Gouverneur, Mérinaghen, 27 Dec. 1858
3 ASAOF, 13G23/6, M. le Gouverneur à M. le Commandant Supérieur de la Marine, Saint-Louis, 2 Sept. 1858

que jamais peur de lui parce qu' il s'est crée une puissance réele au moyen des richesses. . . . Il a de nombreux guerriers à sa solde, et grace à eux, il fait la loi à tout le monde et partout, dans ces contrées désorganisées et dépeuplées.[1]

From this it is evident that some sections of the people were becoming dismayed with 'Umar. At the beginning they had seen him only as a religious leader who was also interested in commerce. Not many people had bothered about the expansion of his community. But with time they became appalled that he had successfully used the religious appeal to build himself up as the leader of a very powerful revolution which aimed at establishing a new religious and political order. Those whose fortunes and positions depended on the continuation of the existing order naturally joined forces together to fight him.

Indeed in Futa Toro, a country for long politically divided, and where the clans had enjoyed a large measure of autonomy, 'Umar was seen by many of the chiefs as a danger to their political authority. Those chiefs who saw him as a threat to their position found him stronger than they were individually and consequently put great premium upon, and took advantage of, their alliance with the French to oppose him. Even in Toro, his home district, 'Umar was opposed by the almamy, who made it difficult for him to enter the area in spite of his admirers among the inhabitants. He could not go there for fear that the almamy would seize the occasion to lead the various groups against him.[2] His position was getting weaker daily because people would no longer rally round him as most of them, especially the chiefs, considered he had come to ruin them socially and politically.[3] With the continued growth in the strength of the pro-French groups in Futa Toro 'Umar found the situation increasingly difficult, to the extent that towards the end of 1858 he could hardly retain any longer the majority of the warriors that he had recruited earlier. Nor could his supporters emigrate with him from Futa Toro as he wanted them to do, partly because of their feeling of uncertainty about their future in Ka'arta, and partly

1 ANSOM, Sénégal I, 41a, L. Faidherbe à son Altesse Impériale le prince Napoléon, Saint-Louis, 30 Aug. 1858
2 Brigaud, *Histoire Traditionnelle du Sénégal*, p. 44
3 ANSOM, Sénégal I, 44b/553, Robin, gouverneur p.i., à son Altesse Impériale le prince chargé du ministère de l'Algérie et des colonies, Saint-Louis, 15 Oct. 1858

because of the fear that the French and the Moors might declare war on them[1] as a reprisal.

While 'Umar was still involved in the trouble in Toro, the French formed alliances with neighbouring states whose rulers were hostile to him. In pursuing this policy Faidherbe reckoned that 'Umar would attack the non-Muslim Jolof states as well as Futa Toro states like Dimar. He then proposed alliances with these states, since in any case they were likely to see alliance with the French as being in their own interest. The French used their position in the allied states, especially their posts at Diamath in Dimar and Coqui in Diambour, to prevent 'Umar from making contact with his supporters in and around the states.[2] Consequently, he found himself surrounded in Futa Toro by hostile states. The active collaboration of many Futa Toro chiefs with the French at this juncture made him lose the struggle for supremacy even in Toro, where he had the greatest number of supporters.[3]

Another Futa Toro state where the contest was very stiff was Dimar. At this time, Dimar was having its own internal political problems arising from a rivalry between two claimants to the stool. The rivals naturally found allies in 'Umar and the French respectively, thus further complicating the struggle. A section of Dimar recognised Eliman Seydou, a supporter of 'Umar, while the other accepted only the authority of one Abdul Boli, a protégé of the French. Abdul Boli had strong support in the villages of Diamath, where he was living, and Fanaye; he was also supported by other Dimar chiefs like Aliman Samba of Tiangaye and Tamsir Diabira, a religious leader of great influence.[4] As soon as it was known that 'Umar might be coming to Dimar, Abdul Boli demanded protection from his French allies. As a result the French established a camp at Fanaye,[5] with a garrison of 451 soldiers, including 164 volunteers. The troops had at their

1 ANSOM, Sénégal I, 44b/579, Robin, gouverneur p.i. à son Altesse Impériale, Saint-Louis, 15 Nov. 1858; also Sénégal I, 44b/619, Saint-Louis, 16 Dec. 1858
2 ASAOF, 13G23/6, M. le Gouverneur à M. le Commandant Supérieur de la Marine, Saint-Louis, 2 Sept. 1858
3 Brigaud, *Histoire traditionnelle du Sénégal*, p. 44
4 ASAOF, 1D13/43, Le gouverneur à M. le Commandant du Camp d'Observation à Fanaye', Camp de Fanaye, 26 Jan. 1859
5 *Ibid.*, p. 1

service sixty-six horses, one interpreter and a number of spies.[1] The governor ordered the commandant to limit himself to purely protective and defensive functions, and not to take the offensive against 'Umar or his partisans. He was enjoined to act always with the idea that the camp was in a friendly country whose independence the French had recognised and which was only being protected against an enemy, who happened to be an enemy of the French also. He was enjoined to act with circumspection and avoid wounding the feelings of the people.[2]

By establishing the camp at Fanaye the French no doubt hoped to force the pro-'Umar forces in the district into submission, but without necessarily fighting battles. They believed they could achieve their objective by maintaining, through the fortified posts, an effective barrier between 'Umar and his supporters in Dimar. In this way Eliman Seydou and his supporters would either submit to the pro-French group or fight and be defeated.

In the circumstances 'Umar could not come to Dimar, partly because of the obstacle created by the French and partly because of the difficulties he was still facing in the Toro district. Hence he sent emissaries to advise Eliman Seydou to emigrate with his supporters to Ka'arta, which was already under Tukulor control. Obviously 'Umar at this time considered the struggle in Dimar lost to the French and their allies and only wanted to salvage what he could from the situation.

The prospect of emigrating was, however, not attractive to Eliman Seydou who replied that he would accept the advice only if all other pro-'Umar leaders in other parts of Futa Toro would do the same.[3] In fact the spirits of Seydou's supporters, excepting a few of very strong religious belief, must have been damped by the suggestion that, after fighting for a cause and losing it in Dimar, they should emigrate to a distant country where resistance wars were being fought and life was therefore still in flux. Migrating to Ka'arta was synonymous with commitment to further wars to consolidate Tukulor position against the resistance groups. In contrast to this prospect was the fact that in the other areas of Futa Toro the French were offering their allies military

1 ASAOF, 1D13/47, Camp d'Observation à Fanaye, Fanaye, 28 Jan. 1859
2 ASAOF, 1D13/43 of 26 Jan. 1859, *op. cit.*
3 ASAOF, 1D13/98, Le gouverneur à M. le Commandant du Camp d'Observation à Fanaye, Camp de Fanaye, 26 Jan. 1859

protection, thereby assuring them a settled life and the realisation of their ambitions. It was therefore not surprising that most of 'Umar's supporters made their submission to the more powerful pro-French groups and opted to stay on in Futa Toro. This situation contributed to the continued weakening of 'Umar's position which eventually made him lose to the French in the struggle for supremacy in the Futa Toro states.

In his struggle for supremacy against the French in the Senegambia, 'Umar had sought to ally with the Jolof states, and in this he was partially successful. He had supporters in Walo and the Damel of Kayor was willing to collaborate with him.[1] But in the Jolof states, as in those of Futa Toro, people saw their alliance with 'Umar or the French largely as a way of solving their own internal problems. For example, the Damel of Kayor was ready to cooperate mainly because he expected 'Umar to help him in his feud against the *Buurba-Jolof*, the paramount ruler of the Jolof confederation. Similarly, the *Buurba-Jolof* adhered to the French cause to ensure his own position. 'Umar, probably with his bitter experience in Futa Toro in mind, now tried to avoid fighting the indigenous people along with the French in the Jolof states. Instead he made an effort to unite the Jolof parties on his own side. It was probably this idea that prompted him to start negotiations with the *Buurba-Jolof*, the French ally, in September 1858. He failed in the endeavour[2] and the Franco-Tukulor struggle remained interwoven with the internal problems of the Jolof.

By the end of 1858 'Umar was at N'Dioum in Kayor and the struggle for influence among the Jolof had begun.[3] 'Umar had the support of the Damel and the Muslim population of Kayor and it was feared that he would use Kayor as a base to attack the *Buurba-Jolof*. For his part the *Buurba-Jolof* organised his forces ready to resist any attack from 'Umar,[4] and the French com-

1 ASAOF, 1D13/20, Commandant, Camp d'Observation à M. le Gouverneur, 6 Jan. 1859
2 ANSOM, Sénégal I, 44b/514, Robin, gouverneur p.i. à Son Altesse Impériale chargé du ministère de l'Algérie et des Colonies, Saint-Louis, 18 Sept. 1858; ASAOF, 1D13/18, Lougades, au Camp de Dialakar à M. le gouverneur, 27 Sept. 1858
3 ASAOF, 1D13/49, Commandant du Camp à M. le Gouverneur, Camp de Fanaye, 7 Feb. 1859
4 ASAOF, 1D13/98, Camp d'Observation à M. le Gouverneur, 10 Feb. 1859

mandant had already assured him of support by establishing two temporary military camps in his territories, one at Merinaghen commanded by Captain de Pineau, the other at Dialakar under the command of Captain Blondeau.[1] Each of the two camps was manned by a company of the 'tirailleurs Sénégalais' (Senegalese sharp-shooters)[2] and twenty-five French soldiers. Furthermore the French Commandant went on a tour of Kayor visiting Tiaral, M'Birama, Roye, and Niomré in January 1859. His aim was to inspire with confidence those of the population who were against 'Umar and had come to the French for aid. In addition he wanted to impress upon the population of Niomré the advantages of allying with the French and the misfortune that could befall them if they followed their marabouts in collaborating with 'Umar.[3]

There are no records of subsequent battles between 'Umar and the French in the Jolof states, but the French were known to be active in their operations against the allies and followers of 'Umar. Among the activities of the troops in the French camps was the arbitrary detention of people identified as his partisans. This had been the practice in Futa Toro states, especially in Dimar where soldiers had imprisoned people at Rogui.[4] In Jolof the commandant of Merinaghen claimed to have detained people as prisoners on the allegation that they committed pillage. People were similarly detained and penalised at Niomré.[5] By harassing 'Umar's followers in this way the French and their allies succeeded in bringing them to submission. On the other hand 'Umar found it impossible to protect his allies and tackle

1 ANSOM, Sénégal I, 44b/514, Robin, gouverneur p.i. à Son Altesse Impériale, Saint-Louis, 18 Sept. 1858
2 The *tirailleurs Sénégalais* comprised African troops in the colony of Senegal who, in 1857, were reconstituted at Saint-Louis by Faidherbe to serve as a regular standing army trained to meet the contingencies of French policy in the colony of Senegal and in the Senegambian states. As an army unit, it originally comprised liberated slaves from Senegal and neighbouring states who were made to believe that by serving France in the army, they became *de facto* French and therefore superior to the other Africans whom they were recruited to fight.
3 ASAOF, 1D13/20, Commandant Camp d'Observation à M. le Gouverneur, 6 Jan. 1859
4 ASAOF, 1D13/82, Camp d'Observation à M. le Gouverneur, Fanaye, 24 Dec. 1858
5 ASAOF, 1D13/89, Camp d'Observation à M. le Gouverneur, Mérinaghen, 31 Jan. 1889

the French adequately. Therefore he had to submit to the inevitable defeat by the French in the Jolof states.

With their victory in Jolof the supremacy of the French and their allies over 'Umar and his followers in the Senegambian states, especially Futa Toro, was assured. Thereafter they sought to consolidate their position by signing treaties of alliance with the Futa Toro states of Toro, Dimar and Damga.[1]

THE GUÉMOU EPISODE AND UNCONCLUDED PEACE MOVES

After losing the battle for supremacy to the French in the Senegambia, 'Umar decided to return to Ka'arta, where since January 1857 his *talibés* had been administering the country and continuing the campaigns against the Bambara Massassi and other groups who were in armed resistance.[2] On his way to Ka'arta in April 1859 'Umar was reported to have attacked the French post at Matam.[3] He was probably eager to return to Ka'arta before the rainy season of 1859 began in order to avoid being stranded in the Senegambian states. At such a time the waters of the rivers would normally rise, and the French, taking advantage of the high waters, would almost surely use their control of the communication lines, especially the Senegal river, to prevent 'Umar joining his men in Ka'arta, as well as to take limited deterrent actions against his movement in the areas along the river banks. Faced with this prospect 'Umar, with such recruits as he could muster, hastened to quit Futa Toro. By June 1859 he was heading for Koniakary, and passed through the environs of Médine on the 14th and 15th. On the 15th he camped at Khoulou, apparently to take some rest and wait for the remainder of his forces to join him.[4] In 1857 he had caused a fortress to be built at the village of Guémou. He now garrisoned it in the hope that it would ensure the safety of his line of communication between Ka'arta and Futa Toro, which was still invaluable to him as a source of supply and reinforcements.

1 ASAOF, 13G23/9, Le gouverneur p.i., Pinet Laprade, à M. le Ministre, Saint-Louis, 18 June 1863
2 Mage, *Voyage*, p. 252
3 Abun-Nasr, *The Tijāniyya*, p. 118
4 ASAOF, in 15G108/7, Commandant du Médine à M. le Gouverneur, Médine, 16 June 1859

He also wanted to use it as a base for activities designed to ruin French commercial activities and the trade centred on their post at Bakel.[1] He left one of his *talibés*, Siré Adama, in command of the garrison at Guémou while he led the other troops further into Ka'arta, inspecting the fortifications already installed in various places on the way.[2] He reached Diafounou shortly before the middle of July and arrived finally at Nioro, the capital of Ka'arta, on 28 July 1859.[3]

From his action in Guémou it is evident that although 'Umar had been defeated in the Senegambia, he regarded his defeat only as a temporary setback, and did not intend to abandon his connections with, and interests in, the area. In the meantime, however, he had to face the urgent necessity to consolidate his position in Ka'arta, where resistance to his authority was becoming widespread and persistent. For example, while he was struggling for supremacy in the Senegambia in 1858–59, Guidimaka, the province that lay between Futa Toro and Ka'arta, was continually in arms against his administration in the area and frequently cut the routes linking the area with Futa Toro. Since such activities helped their cause the French naturally encouraged those involved in Guidimaka from their fortified, garrisoned post at nearby Bakel. The garrison at Guémou, 'Umar calculated, would be at hand to deal with further armed resistance in Guidimaka.

Another method open to 'Umar for combating the French was economic. In 1858 he had built a barrier across the Senegal river at Garly to cut off communication between the French and their post at Médine, from which he hoped to debar the caravans. The Guémou post was also well situated to intercept the trade of the Moors, flowing from the right bank of the Senegal, with the French at Bakel on the left bank. By making trade connections with Bakel difficult, if not impossible, 'Umar hoped to carry on the struggle against the French. If he had succeeded in holding Guémou, a principal artery of commerce would have been sealed off and in the long run, with the state of unrest in the Senegambia, French commerce would have been stifled. Even

---

1 Tyam, *Qacida*, pp. 124–5, vv. 726–7
2 *Ibid.*, pp. 125–6, vv. 731–6
3 ASAOF, in 15G108/7, Le Commt du poste de Médine à M. le Gouverneur, Médine, 12 July 1859; Tyam, *Qacida*, p. 127, v. 740

in 1858, when Guémou had not been garrisoned, French commercial activities at Bakel were already adversely affected by the
very existence of the post. To Faidherbe 'Umar's control of
Guémou was 'particulièrement gênant, parce que ce point est
sur la route des caravanes maures'.[1] The failure of the Moorish
caravans to arrive at Bakel made Faidherbe anxious, and it was
the subject of correspondence by him in September 1858 before
he left Senegal for France. On that occasion Faidherbe had
suggested destroying Guémou.[2] The interim governor later reported that the gum trade was badly affected because the
Moorish caravans, which were held up at Guémou, had still not
reached Bakel by December.[3]

At the end of the trading season of 1858–59 the fall in the
amount of gum handled at Bakel had become so great that it was
felt that urgent measures should be taken to remedy the situation.
Faidherbe summoned a meeting of the administrative council of
Senegal (*Conseil d'Administration*) on 16 September 1859. To
enlighten members of the council on the cessation of gum supply
to Bakel he also invited Maurel, N'diaye Sour, and Mamour
Tiam[4] to the meeting. These people unanimously informed the
council that the failure of the gum trade was due mainly to
'Umar's control of Guémou and that the problem had become
really acute in the commercial season just ended because the
Moorish tribe of Ouled Sidi Mahmoud had gone into alliance
with 'Umar and had therefore ceased to bring their gum to
Bakel. As a solution to the problem these representatives of
commerce recommended strongly that the complete destruction
of Guémou was of urgent necessity. It was further recommended
that to make the destruction painful and effective on 'Umar and

1 ANSOM, in Sénégal I, 41a, L. Faidherbe à Son Altesse Impériale, le
prince Napoléon, Saint-Louis, 30 Aug. 1858
2 ANSOM, in Sénégal I, 41a, Copie des Instructions adressés par M. le
gouverneur du Sénégal à M. le Commandant Supérieur de la Marine,
gouverneur p.i., Saint-Louis, 2 Sept. 1858
3 ANSOM, in Sénégal I, 44b, Le gouverneur p.i. à Son Altesse Impériale,
le prince chargé du ministère de l'Algérie et des colonies, Saint-Louis,
16 Dec. 1858
4 Messrs Maurel et Prom were among the most important French
companies in Senegal tapping the trade of the Western Sudan. They
were also an important factor in the politics of Senegal and had considerable influence in France. N'diaye Sour and Mamour Tiam were
Senegalese businessmen acting as agents of French firms at Bakel.

the inhabitants of Guémou, the attack on the village should be undertaken during the harvest season.¹ In view of the over-whelming evidence before them, and of their duty to protect French economic interests, and therefore commerce, the council decided on the destruction of Guémou as the only solution, failing which it would become necessary to withdraw from Bakel, a place described as 'très fertile, et qui promet en ce moment une abondante récolte sur laquelle alhadji compte pour revenir dans le bas du fleuve'.²

Provisions were subsequently made and instructions given to Major Faron to attack Guémou. Faron led the attack on 25 October 1859. Although the Tukulor were caught by surprise they put up a gallant fight under their leader, Sire Adama. French forces under Major Faron numbered 1,093 soldiers of various grades, but according to Paul Soleillet's less reliable account, they numbered 1,500. After a hard-fought battle the Tukulor were defeated and the fortress was destroyed.³ With the destruction of Guémou 'Umar's plan to consolidate his position in Ka'arta free from French interference was threatened, and the Tukulor in Ka'arta were once more exposed to the French menace. This came at a time when 'Umar was already on the borders on the Segu Bambara empire, which he was plan-ning to attack. He was therefore not in a position to meet the new challange. His next move seems to have been designed to conciliate the French in order to give himself some respite from hostilities from the French side so that he could concentrate upon the conquest of the Bambara Segu empire.

Earlier on, in 1856, the French had made an offer to 'Umar to negotiate peace with him on the basis of recognising his sovereignty over Ka'arta, provided he would leave the French in their position in the Senegambian region. 'Umar now revived the idea, using it as a basis on which to open negotiations. He delegated his emir in Diomboko, Tierno Musa, to represent him in the proposed negotiation with the French. His willingness to negotiate with the French was notified in a letter to the

1 ANSOM, in Sénégal IV, 45d, Conseil d'Administration – Séance du 16 Septembre, 1859
2 *Ibid.*
3 ASAOF, 1D14, Guémou – Compte rendu, p. 7; *Annales Sénégalaises 1859*, pp. 175–83, cited in a footnote by Gaden in Tyam, *Qacida*, p. 125; Soleillet, *Voyage à Segou, 1878–1879* (1897), p. 344

Commandant of Bakel in June 1860.[1] On behalf of 'Umar the writers of the letter emphasised the willingness of the Tukulor to conclude a peace agreement and said their desire was based on the fact that the Tukulor had valuable family ties with people in Koniakary and in the areas under French control. They also expressed their belief in the peaceful intentions of the French which, they claimed, inspired them to initiate the move for peace.

Tierno Musa, emir of Diomboko, followed up the offer made to the French when he met M. Cornu, the Commandant of the Bakel post, to discuss the possible basis of agreement between the two sides. M. Cornu and Tierno Musa agreed that peace should be based on the guarantee of freedom of commerce between Ka'arta and Médine, so that caravans from Nioro and other areas of Ka'arta could move into the areas under French control, especially Médine and Bakel, without fear. The two men also agreed that the people of Khasso and all other allies of the French, should move freely in Diomboko and that all kinds of raids and pillages should be forbidden on both sides. Other points mentioned included the possibility of the French getting back from Ka'arta the inhabitants of Futa Toro who had evacuated their homes during the crisis period of 1858–59.[2] The two men appeared to be convinced of the need for peace and therefore lost no time in referring the matter respectively to the governor in Saint-Louis and to 'Umar. From the preliminary discussions there can be no doubt that the French considered trade as their top priority.

The French had no means of continuing the war against the Tukulor indefinitely, especially in Ka'arta, and Faidherbe was very favourably impressed by the Tukulor offer of peace. He summoned the meeting of the administrative council on 21 August 1860 to discuss the offer. The council noted that a peace treaty with 'Umar would imply recognising his sovereignty over Ka'arta, which he had conquered, and Segu, towards which he was advancing. Faidherbe believed that if 'Umar could bring the whole of Ka'arta and Segu under one centralised government,

1 ASAOF, 15G62/7, 'Mīn 'inda Tabbū Kadi'ija mā' Nafa Salām Tamm mā' jāmi' Sulāha Kujakari 'ila Kamādau Bakkīl mā' Sulāha'ihi (marked 'Parvenu à Saint-Louis le 23 juin 1860')
2 A record of the meeting between Cornu and Tierno Musa is contained in ASAOF, 15G1/1, July 1860

the political situation in the Niger area would improve. French explorers might then be able to travel freely there. The Council believed that if 'Umar accepted Faidherbe's terms he would automatically be recognising French authority over the territory west of the Senegal river. It was calculated that since this area had many Muslims among its inhabitants, 'Umar's recognition of French rule over them would enhance the prestige of the French on that bank of the Senegal, which should be proposed as the line of demarcation between 'Umar's territories and those under the French. It was agreed that the draft treaty should include a stipulation that the captive and subject peoples resident in either of these two areas would not be forced to leave their homes against their will. Explaining the importance of this clause to the Council, Faidherbe noted that as 'Umar considered as French captives all the inhabitants of Toro, Damga, and Khasso, these being the provinces where the majority of the population was Muslim, the French position in those areas would be strengthened by such an agreement. It was decided to send an envoy to negotiate these points with 'Umar.[1]

Faidherbe informed Tierno Musa of his desire to send an envoy to 'Umar to conclude a peace treaty, and Musa expressed his delight and willingness to cooperate in ensuring the safety of such a mission, giving further assurances as to 'Umar's desire for peace with the French.[2] Tierno Musa was careful to emphasise the same point later on when it became necessary for him to urge the French to implement their decision to send these envoys to 'Umar. In his letter to the Commandant of the French post at Médine, Musa urged that the French ambassadors be sent to 'Umar, and reaffirmed his guarantee of protection to such envoys. He also remarked that since agreement had been reached between himself and the French, there had been no harm done to the French through any action of the subjects of 'Umar in Koniakary.[3] But in spite of Tierno Musa's endeavours nothing

1 ANSOM, in Sénégal IV, 45e, Conseil d'Administration du Sénégal – Séance du 21 août 1860; also see Abun-Nasr, *The Tijāniyya*, p. 120

2 ASAOF, 15G62/8, 'Min 'inda amīr al-mūminīn khālifat al-shaikh Musa b. Sā'id al-Salām al-Tamm 'ila amīr al-nasara 'inda Faidriba (i.e. Faidherbe), (marked 'Reçu à Saint-Louis, 19 Aug. 1860')

3 ASAOF, 15G62/10, 'Mīn amīr al-mūminīn al-shaikh Musa b. Sā'id al-Sālam al-Tamm 'ila 'ariwa . . . filis Ma' Kumādau' (n.d.) but marked 'Parvenu à Saint-Louis, 4 Sept. 1860'

concrete came out of the negotiation for some time, since the envoy that was promised was in fact not sent until 1863.[1]

But from 1860 onwards a *de facto* situation did arise whereby the idea of the river Senegal being the boundary line between the French in the Senegambia and the emergent Tukulor empire was more or less accepted. For all practical purposes the hegemony of the French over the territories on the left bank of the Senegal was recognised, and the Tukulor were recognised as rulers of Ka'arta and of the as yet undefined territories east of it. The immediate concern of the French was to consolidate their control over Futa Toro and the neighbouring states. It may be recalled that they had concluded treaties with some of the Futa Toro states after 'Umar had been repelled in 1859. The experience of the struggle against 'Umar's revolution had also endeared the anti-'Umar elements in this area more to their French allies. The only problem for the French remained what the defeated, discontented pro-Umar groups might do. To pacify and win over such groups, who in any case had been impressed by their relatively weak power position, the French decided to seek a reconciliation with them. Therefore in 1860 they offered to help their erstwhile opponents out of their difficulties. In this connection they distributed seeds freely to them, just as they did to their own allies. This friendly gesture led to favourable reactions from the indigenous people. This type of friendly reaction was reported by M. Braouèzec who visited Futa Toro late in 1860. He said that 'les Toucouleurs et les Soninké nous ont fait des protestations encore plus grandes de leur dévouement à la France et ils semblaient pénétrés de reconnaissance (surtout les Soninké) pour cette main qui, après les avoir chatiés, venait à leur secours en leur envoyant des sémences (arachides) pour leurs terres dévastées'.[2]

This development strengthened the French position in the Senegambia. The failure of the Tukulor to oust the French was significant for a number of reasons. It frustrated 'Umar's ambition to make the Senegambia the nucleus of his empire. Although he succeeded in maintaining Tukulor control over a few districts

---

1 This refers to the mission of A. E. Mage and Dr Quintin which was sent out in 1863, arriving in Segu in February 1864

2 Braouèzec, 'L'hydrographie du Sénégal et nos relations avec les populations riveraines', *Revue Maritime et Coloniale*, Jan.–Feb. 1861, pp. 101–14

like Logo and Natiaga (in Khasso) and Dinguiray, from 1860 onwards the river Senegal virtually represented the boundary line between the French in the Senegambia and the Tukulor empire. Later the French were to use the Senegambia as a springboard for the conquest of the Tukulor empire and the establishment of the colony known as the French Sudan.

5 Consolidation of Tukulor Control over Ka'arta and the Overthrow of Bambara Segu and the Masina Caliphate, 1859–1864

PROBLEMS OF STRATEGY

The spread of the jihād from 1852 to 1855 and the events of the period from 1857 to 1859 clearly demonstrate 'Umar's determination to constitute the Senegambia into a nucleus of his emergent empire. During the former period, not only did he conquer several of the states in the area, but he also appointed administrators to take charge of places overrun. To guarantee his conquests, he constructed a defence system centred on garrisoned fortresses (*tata* or *ribats*).[1] Also, after ensuring some control over Ka'arta, he returned to the Senegambia in 1857, primarily to combat the enemies of his revolution, reassert his authority and expand the frontiers of his nascent empire. As is shown in the last chapter, his drive for control of the Senegambia was checkmated by the combination of indigenous political and religious elites and the French, whose positions and interests the emergence of the new empire endangered. But even after 1859 the tenacity with which 'Umar held on to enclaves of territories like Logo in Khasso, Koundian and Mourgoula, among others, obviously shows his attachment to the idea of securing a base in the Senegambia.

His aspirations having been thwarted in the Senegambia, 'Umar's immediate concern seems to have been to try to salvage what was left of the empire and to expand it if possible. Hence he turned to Ka'arta which at first he tried to protect against the French by rebuilding and fortifying Guémou, and later by fighting the resistance movements in the area. In the process he waged wars against Bambara Segu and Masina, thereby expanding his empire eastwards.

The events so far described indicate that the suggestion that

---

1 For a discussion of similar establishments in the Sierra Leone area see Siddle, 'War-Towns in Sierra Leone: A Study in Social Change', *Africa*, xxxviii, 1, 1968.

'Umar never meant to conquer the Senegambian states (Saint-Martin[1] goes so far as to claim that 'Umar's relations with the French were basically pacific in intent) cannot be substantiated. It has also been suggested by Fisher[2] that since 'Umar's interest was in recruiting troops he confined his activities to encouraging emigration (*hijra*) from Ka'arta, and did not even encourage revolts against the almamies of Futa Jallon and Futa Toro; and further, that following his failure in the Senegambia between 1857 and 1859 he was in a quandary whether to adopt a western or an eastern expansion policy. These suggestions are the result of an incomplete understanding of 'Umar's movement and the various elements comprising it. It has been suggested that expansion to the west would have been a 'thoroughly orthodox' policy which 'Umar did not undertake only because he feared it would end in disaster. This misconception would be avoided if it were appreciated that 'Umar's interest in the West (Senegambia) went beyond merely getting troops. There was no question of his being in doubt over which policy to pursue in 1859. It appears clear that he conceived the Senegambia as a nucleus of his empire; but by 1859 it was also clear to him that the idea had largely miscarried. The east he had all along considered as an area for legitimate expansion and this is borne out by his movement into Ka'arta as soon as he had overrun Senegambian states between 1852 and early 1855. His next move eastwards in 1859, especially after the French had destroyed Guémou, was a normal reaction to his failure in the Senegambia, and not a decision made out of a desire to avoid a disaster. Having conquered Ka'arta 'Umar desired to hold it against resistance groups. To be free to do this he assigned his emirs to carry on negotiations for peace with the French[3] with a view to preventing further conflicts with the latter in the rear.

WAR AGAINST THE DIAWARA

When he returned to Ka'arta in 1859 'Umar found that the anti-Tukulor resistance movements were still very strong, and in consequence Tukulor control over the country remained weak.

1 Saint-Martin, 'La Volonté de paix . . .'
2 Fisher's review of Abun-Nasr, *The Tijāniyya* . . .
3 See Chapter 4, pp. 115–18 on peace moves after Guémou.

The resistance represented a serious threat that could overthrow the regime and after the Senegambian debacle 'Umar gave immediate attention to the task of consolidating his position in Ka'arta. But it soon became clear that this problem could not be treated in isolation from the general Bambara menace. Since August 1855, when the *fama* of Segu first sent troops to aid the Massassi, the two sister states of Segu and Ka'arta had persistently sustained their cooperation against 'Umar's Tukulor invaders. By 1859 the Ka'arta – Segu combine was maintaining the most dangerous anti-Tukulor war effort in the Kingui area of Ka'arta. There were also pockets of resistance mounted by the Diawara whose interests were not complementary with those of the Bambara, although they shared a common desire to overthrow the Tukulor regime. 'Umar himself commanded the Tukulor forces which left Nioro on 12 September 1859 to suppress the resistance groups in Kingui.[1] But largely because of the Bambara logistics the campaign eventually spread beyond Kingui into areas outside Ka'arta.

On his arrival in Kingui, 'Umar fought battles against the Diawara forces in the villages of Nomo, Yerere and Tourougoumbe; but although he defeated them in these places, Karunka, the chief, and other rulers of the Diawara escaped and took refuge in the Bambara empire of Segu. Instead of pursuing them 'Umar directed his operations against the Diawara in the Bakounou area, where a battle was fought in the village of Bagouéni.[2] About two months after, the Tukulor troops left Bagouéni on 6 November 1859, and made for the ponds of Goumbankou, where their need for water could be met. By this time 'Umar gave the impression that he was retracing his steps south-west towards Nioro. Karunka, the Diawara chief, was obviously deceived by 'Umar's movements; he returned to Merkoya (called Madikouya by the Tukulor)[3] in Kingui from Segu territory where he had taken refuge. The Tukulor arrived at Merkoya, to the surprise of the Diawara, and in the battle which followed the village was destroyed and the chief of Merkoya, Katili, was beheaded. Once more, however, Karunka succeeded in escaping with his belongings, and again he found refuge in Segu from where the Bambara had sent forces to help their kinsmen against the Tukulor in Ka'arta.

1 Tyam, *Qacida*, p. 128
2 *Ibid.*, pp. 128–30, vv. 744–55   3 *Ibid.*, p. 133n.

After Merkoya 'Umar had to fight the Segu forces which had reached Beledugu at this time. The Tukulor made Merkoya the base for their operations against the Bambara in Beledugu. The first battle against the Segu Bambara forces in the area took place on 8 December 1859, and the struggle dragged on until the battle against the army of Bonota, which the Tukulor won on 19 January 1860.[1] After this prolonged encounter, however, the Tukulor could not follow up their victory: they were faced with many difficulties arising from the fact that they lacked water and food, and many people, especially women and children, were dying of hunger and thirst. They therefore withdrew to Merkoya from where 'Umar sent one of his *talibés*, Abdul Salam, to Nioro in order to bring food for the soldiers, as well as reinforcements with which to continue the fight against Segu forces. The Tukulor stayed on at Merkoya until 3 April.[2]

While his troops were camping in Merkoya, 'Umar continued to make plans for further encounters in what was becoming a war against the Bambara Kingdom of Segu. He had lost twelve of his important *talibés* and military leaders in the Beledugu campaigns which ended in January, 1860; but he seemed determined to finish with the enemy forces in Beledugu before launching any direct attack on Segu state itself. While awaiting reinforcements from Nioro, he continued to use the available forces to conduct limited operations in Beledugu. Thus in Februrary and March 1860 he was at Amady-koy, trying to defeat the attacking Bambara forces.[3] It is not known how the battle in Beledugu ended; but it is apparent that 'Umar won because, by 3 April 1860, it had become possible for the Tukulor to leave Merkoya with a view to launching a direct offensive against the Bambara empire of Segu.[4]

In this offensive the Tukulor first marched on the Kanyaga province, where Danfa, the headquarters, was captured on 19 April. Dombi, the chief of the village, was beheaded with all the men captured with him. While still campaigning in this area 'Umar received reinforcements from Ka'arta; Alawon Kowria,

1 ASAOF, 1D13/42, Le Commt de Médine. à Monsieur le Gouverneur, Médine, 20 Jan. 1860; Tyam, *Qacida*, pp. 133–4, vv. 772, 776–81
2 Tyam, *Qacida*, p. 135, v. 785
3 ASAOF, in 15G108/8, Le Commt de Médine à Monsieur le Gouverneur, Médine, 21 Feb. 1860; also 15G108/8 of 21 Mar. 1860
4 Tyam, *Qacida*, p. 137

chief of Dyawambe in Ka'arta, led his army to serve 'Umar in Segu. This chief was said to have made his submission to 'Umar at Kouloumi in 1855.[1] With this addition to his strength 'Umar was able to continue the war against the Bambara in Kanyaga province until about 19 May 1860, when he led his forces out of Danfa and continued the march towards Nyamina.

While still on their way towards Nyamina the Tukulor had a serious battle with the troops sent by Ali, the *fama* of Segu, under the leadership of Badyi. Badyi's men were routed on 22 May 1860 and the Tukulor were able to continue their march the next day.[2] They arrived at Nyamina on 25 May 1860, and camped there, intending to use it as a base for the operations against Segu. But because it was in the dry season they had great difficulties with finding enough water. The need for reinforcements was even more urgently felt because they could continue their campaigns only if they could increase their strength. 'Umar realised this and sent to Ka'arta for troops. Some nomadic Fulani from southern Ka'arta were reported to have arrived at Nyamina, where their offer to be converted was accepted and they were absorbed into the army. During the month of May it was also reported that a large number of *talibés* left Nioro with their troops to join 'Umar in the Segu campaign.[3]

Having received reinforcements, 'Umar embarked on the execution of his plans of attack on Segu, using Nyamina as a base for operations directed against various districts of the country. Karunka, the Diawara chief who had escaped from Kingui, was at the time in the region of Nyamina. 'Umar sent a column, led by Ado Aliyu, against Karunka, who was killed in battle on 31 May 1860.[4] According to Maurice Delafosse, however, it was Alfa 'Umar who was sent against Karunka, and the latter was killed at the village of Sana.[5] 'Umar sent another column against Barasso (or Barso), one of the Diawara chiefs and a lieutenant of Karunka. Barasso was defeated by the contingent led by

1 *Ibid.*, p. 137n, and vv. 794–9
2 *Ibid.*, pp. 138–9, vv. 800–7
3 ASAOF, in 15G108–8, Le Commt de Médine à M. le Gouverneur, Médine, 21 May 1860; also Tyam, *Qacida*, pp. 140–1, vv. 810–20
4 Tyam, *Qacida*, pp. 141–2, vv. 820–1. In his footnote Gaden states that Karunka was killed on 31 May 1859. This should however be 31 May 1860, a date that follows from the chronology of events.
5 Delafosse, *Traditions historiques et légendaires du Soudan Occidental* (traduites d'un manuscrit arabe inédit) (1913), p. 83

Ardo Hamadi Fayol.[1] After the Diawara refugees had been defeated 'Umar felt free to move his army in an offensive further into Segu, but still using Nyamina as a base of operations.

From Nyamina 'Umar sent about six thousand soldiers against the Segu army at Ouitala (Witala), a village very near Segu.[2] In these operations Alfa 'Umar was responsible for bringing necessary supplies to the troops, and he served as a liaison between the army and the military base at Nyamina. The battle against Segu forces led by Tata at Ouitala lasted three days, and was very bloody. The Segu forces were defeated and put to flight. Following this victory 'Umar distributed about two hundred of Ali's horses to units of his army,[3] and the Tukulor withdrew to their base at Nyamina.

From Nyamina 'Umar sent to Nioro for reinforcements to enable him continue the war against Segu. While awaiting their arrival the food shortage became acute, and the Tukulor troops moved their camp to the abandoned village of Tamana,[4] which they reached on 27 August 1860, leaving a strong garrison at Nyamina. The Tukulor could not sustain themselves on the provisions available in Tamana for longer than one week, after which they had to move on until they reached the village of Ouitala on 5 September.[5]

Ouitala had been fortified, but with the use of the cannon[6] at their disposal, the Tukulor put the village under siege. Battle began on 5 September, but the fighting did not end until the 13th when the village had been destroyed. The Tukulor army on this occasion was estimated at about 15,000 men. Both sides lost heavily, with many of the Bambara soldiers fleeing and being

1 Tyam, *Qacida*, p. 142, v. 822, cf. Delafosse, *Traditions historiques*, pp. 81, 83
2 Ouitala (pronounced Witala) was situated at a distance of about 47 kilometres from Segu-Sikoro.
3 Delafosse, *Traditions historiques*, p. 83; Tyam, *Qacida*, pp. 143–4
4 Tamana was, like Nyamina, a village in the neighbourhood of Bamako.
5 Mage, *Voyage*, p. 257; Tyam, *Qacida*, pp. 144–5, vv. 835–45
6 The two cannon were taken by the Tukulor during their struggle against the French for the control of the Senegambian states between 1858 and 1859. The cannon were found abandoned by the French after a battle at the village of Ndioum in the Ferlo area of Jolof in February 1858. Samba N'diaye who had lived for about twenty years at Saint-Louis, Senegal, had learnt how to operate cannon and it was he who made it possible for the Tukulor to use them to advantage, cf. Tyam, *Qacida*, p. 144

pursued in various directions. According to Mage, the Tukulor lost as many as three hundred men in the initial stages of the fight. In addition they lost their cannon, the search for which was conducted by Samba N'diaye, leading thirty Wolof troops, of whom seven were fatally wounded. Mage notes that the battle of Ouitala was regarded as the most bloody that the Tukulor at Segu remembered at the time of his visit. After the victory of the Tukulor, however, several of the Bambara offered themselves for conversion, and were admitted by 'Umar, who, in this way, increased his military strength.[1]

OCCUPATION OF SANSANDING

With the capture of Ouitala 'Umar was in control of a part of Segu; and he proceeded to make arrangements to bring under his control those areas of the country which he had not yet conquered. One of the most important of such areas was Sansanding, near Segu. From Ouitala, 'Umar sent one of his *talibés*, Abd al-Qadir, to inform one Koro-Mama of his ('Umar's) intention to come to Sansanding.[2] Koro-Mama wrote, inviting 'Umar to come without further delay and 'Umar left Ouitala on 13 October 1860, arriving at Sansanding on the 15th. The village surrendered without fighting and 'Umar took control, camping his forces there.[3]

'Umar obviously wanted to extend the area under his control to Sansanding, but it is curious how he set about it. Sansanding was inhabited by Muslims and was under a Muslim ruler. There

1 Tyam, *Qacida*, pp. 146–50; Mage, *Voyage*, p. 257
2 Sansanding (or Sansani) was, and is still, situated on the river Niger a short distance away from Segu. It was in 1860 inhabited mainly by Soninke merchants who were mostly Muslims. Koro-Mama was the head of the Couma family which had founded Sansanding and ruled it for a long time. A little while before the coming of 'Umar, however, Koro-Mama's family had lost power to another Soninke family, the Cissé, who were apparently related to the Cissé dynasty in Masina. The ruler of Sansanding at this time was Lamine Cissé and not Koro-Mama, 'Umar's collaborator, cf. Mage, *Voyage*, p. 258.
3 Mage, *Voyage*, pp. 258–9; Tyam, *Qacida*, pp. 151–5, vv. 874–900; in Sissoko, 'Chroniques . . .' (3e cahier), p. 132, it is stated that 'Umar left Ouitala for Sansanding after staying for a lunar month; other accounts, especially Mage's, indicate that he stayed for a shorter period.

is no evidence that he had any correspondence with Lamine Cissé, who was then ruling. Instead he chose as his collaborator, Koro-Mama, a disgruntled person who was doing everything possible to regain the power from which his family had been ousted.[1] 'Umar's action could be seen as an intervention in the internal politics of Sansanding against the ruling family. This was reminiscent of his tactics earlier in Khasso and other Senegambian states. He won control of Sansanding because the ruling chief could not afford the necessary force to fight him.

An important reason for 'Umar's success in Segu territories generally, up to and including Sansanding, was the fact that the Bambara Segu forces had so far not been fully pitched against the Tukulor. As has been pointed out in chapter 1, relations between Bambara Segu and the Caliphate of Masina had been bad, marked mainly by wars resulting from the desire of Masina to Islamise and bring Segu under its political authority. This state of war had existed since the founding of Masina in 1818 and was still continuing when 'Umar carried his campaigns into Segu territories. So far, both Segu and Masina had fought jointly against the Tukulor only in 1857[2] in Ka'arta, where their interests had been threatened by 'Umar's campaigns. Thereafter, Segu and Masina never confronted 'Umar with a combined force because their interests were distinct and conflicting.

But with the capture of Sansanding the danger which 'Umar represented to both Segu and Masina was becoming more real and disturbing to their rulers. 'Umar had still not conquered Segu-Sikoro, the headquarters of the Segu Bambara state, but it was becoming clear that he would succeed in doing this if he was not opposed with greater force and determination than had been the case hitherto. Masina had been fighting Segu in order to put it under its regime; but this ambition, and the efforts made so far to realise it, would be thwarted if 'Umar conquered the state. On the other hand, the independence which the Bambara rulers had been fighting Masina to retain would also be lost in the event of a Tukulor conquest. Both Aḥmadu b. Aḥmadu of Masina and Ali Diara of Segu appeared to have realised that if they did not settle their own problems they stood in danger of losing to the Tukulor the causes for which they had been fighting.

1 Mage, *Voyage*, p. 258
2 Sissoko, 'Chroniques . . .' (2e cahier), p. 8

'MASINA-SEGU ENTENTE' AND THE FALL OF
BAMBARA SEGU 'EMPIRE'

In face of the Tukulor threat to its interests, Masina changed its traditional policy of hostility to Segu to one of conciliation, with the object of presenting a common front against the invader. It is not known for certain when Aḥmadu b. Aḥmadu began negotiating, but by late 1860, when 'Umar had already made incursions into Segu territories, some agreement had been reached between the two. In a monograph prepared in 1893 Bellat[1] stated that the initiative for an entente came from Masina the idea being suggested to Aḥmadu b. Aḥmadu by one of his army leaders, al-ḥājj Sa'id. Aḥmadu b. Aḥmadu sent one of his lieutenants, al-ḥājj Aliyu, to negotiate with Ali Diara, *fama* of Segu, on the possibility of the latter submitting to, or at least cooperating with, Masina. If 'Umar was allowed to pursue his campaigns, it was suggested, he would end by annexing not only Segu but all other adjacent territories. Surely the Bambara would prefer domination by their neighbour, Aḥmadu b. Aḥmadu to that of an unknown but dangerous marabout, 'Umar? It was emphasised that if Segu submitted to Masina, a Muslim power and therefore fighting for the same cause as 'Umar, the latter would withdraw. To ensure acceptance of this proposal Aḥmadu b. Aḥmadu encamped his troops at Samanadougou, opposite Segu-Sikoro. Ali Diara, under psychological rather than physical attack, accepted the terms put forward by Masina.[2]

This understanding was reached ostensibly in order to arrest the progress being made by 'Umar in his empire-building. But for Masina the entente was important for another reason. So far, the wars fought by Masina against Segu had failed to achieve the objective of making the latter submit to the former. By the entente with Segu, its submission appeared to have been achieved by negotiation, in which 'Umar had been used as a factor. Masina's objective was to Islamise and rule Segu, which they would defend against external forces. 'Umar was seen as a threat to the possibility of Masina's hegemony over Segu and for this reason, Masina was prepared to fight the Tukulor, as they had

1 ASAOF, 1G84, Renseignements historiques sur le Sansanding, Capitaine Bellat (Sansanding, Mar.–Apr. 1893), p. 119
2 *Ibid.*, pp. 120–1

done to protect their interests in Ka'arta when 'Umar attacked villages which had earlier been conquered and colonised by Masina forces commanded by Ahmadu Sala Modi.[1]

Ali Diara probably saw submission to Masina as the lesser of two evils. 'Umar was an external foe whose might, judging from the result of his campaigns, appeared formidable. Ali Diara obviously regarded his action as a way of freeing his country from the Tukulor threat, while at the same time gaining a respite from hostilities against Masina, in the hope that if it became necessary to fight again in the future, Segu would have recouped its forces and would be in a better position to defend itself.[2] Aḥmadu b. Aḥmadu tried to use the new relationship to promote the Islamisation of Segu, and sent marabouts to teach the Bambara the Islamic way of life. Among these marabouts was one Ahmadu Moye Doulde.[3] Masina was still pursuing its policy of Islamisation in Segu when 'Umar annexed Nyamina and was establishing control over Sansanding.

'Umar intended to use Sansanding as a base for his campaigns to subjugate Segu, which, as stated, had now surrendered to Masina. As a Muslim, Aḥmadu b. Aḥmadu considered his control over Segu as bringing the latter into the *dār al-Islam*. He was therefore determined to expel 'Umar and his Tukulor army from Segu territory, where he saw them as aggressors. In pursuance of this policy he wrote to 'Umar, claiming that Segu was under his rule, and had accepted Islam. He requested that 'Umar should withdraw from Sansanding, which was Segu territory, and return to Nioro, his capital in Ka'arta. Aḥmadu b. Aḥmadu emphasised that Masina, ruler of Segu, was an Islamic state, and that any attack on it would be an impious act. 'Umar was said to have replied that Segu was a pagan state and therefore subject to a jihād. He ignored the claim of Masina to sovereignty over Segu but, curiously, he proposed that Aḥmadu b. Aḥmadu should join him in a common effort to conquer the country and

1 'Umar had defeated Masina forces at Kassakare in Ka'arta. See monograph compiled by Underberg on Segu: ASAOF, 1G122/1, Underberg (Segou-Sikoro, 10 Oct. 1890), p. 22; also, Mage, *Voyage*, p. 245
2 ASAOF, 1G301/1, Sénégambie-Niger-Cercle du Bandiagara, 15 Oct. 1903, p. 5
3 ASAOF, 1G184, Capitaine Bellat, Renseignements historiques . . ., p. 122.

share the territory and the booty later on. 'Umar maintained that he was at war with Segu because the latter had attacked him in Ka'arta and that having pursued its forces from Merkoya to Sansanding, he could no longer withdraw from the campaigns against it. In his reply 'Umar charged Aḥmadu b. Aḥmadu himself with having committed aggression against him in the Bakhounou province of Ka'arta, and claimed that, in that way, he had conducted himself like an unbeliever. As stated earlier, Masina's intervention in Ka'arta had been to protect areas conquered by her forces, presumably in the wars fought earlier against Segu in the border areas with Ka'arta. Aḥmadu b. Aḥmadu replied by issuing an ultimatum asking 'Umar to quit Sansanding or face war. Since 'Umar was determined to attack Segu, and was only waiting for reinforcements from Ka'arta before beginning the campaigns, war became the only means of settling the problem and the two sides started preparing for it.[1]

The war which followed was fought over the possession of Segu which both sides coveted as compensation for previous exertions to spread the *dār al-Islam*. In the encounter it was 'Umar's intention to expand his empire, which was recognised by his opponents as well as by observers who were not directly involved. The Masina rulers and many of the Muslims in this part of the Western Sudan were not convinced about the religious mission which 'Umar proclaimed. Some thought that he was a fake *khālifa* and a heretic. The learned Ahmad al-Bakkāi, leader of the Bakka'iyya order in Timbuktu, for example, regarded him, like the other Tijānis, as an infidel and even considered war against him as jihād. Al-Bakkāi therefore wrote to Aḥmadu b. Aḥmadu of Masina, urging him to fight 'Umar.[2] It was true, however, that 'Umar, like the other adherents of the Tijāniyya brotherhood, believed himself superior to all other Muslims who were not Tijānī. It is debatable, however, whether rivalry between brotherhoods in questions of belief, and wars fought against fellow Muslims, no matter what brotherhood they might belong to, could be regarded as serving the cause of Islam.

One might argue that, given the existing state of hostility and

---

1 *Ibid.*, p. 123; ASAOF, 1G103/1, Notices sur les états d'Aguibu, 1896–97; Sissoko, 'Chroniques . . .' (3e cahier), p. 133; Mage, *Voyage*, pp. 258–9; Delafosse, *Haut-Sénégal-Niger*, ii, p. 316
2 BNP, MS Arabe, 5716, f. 183, cited by Abun-Nasr, *The Tijāniyya*, p. 169

the clashes which had already taken place in Ka'arta between Tukulor armies and those of Segu and Masina, 'Umar could not feel safe in Ka'arta until either a peaceful settlement had been reached over the issues involved, or he had conquered his opponents and strengthened his position by occupying Segu. Viewed this way the attack on Segu could be seen as necessitated by military and security considerations. But, as in Ka'arta, the Cissé rulers in Masina had vested interests in Segu and were bound to clash with 'Umar in attempting to protect these interests.

In the effort to dislodge 'Umar from Sansanding, Masina fought in collaboration with the army of Ali Diara (Ouitala) of Segu. But actual fighting does not seem to have begun until about February 1861,[1] four months after 'Umar and his army had set up their camp at Sansanding, although Delafosse, with J. Salenc citing him, claims that battle began in January.[2] The evidence pointing to February is to be preferred, because it comes from reports by contemporaries, and the chronicles (the *Qacida*) of Alioun Tyam, while Delafosse's was of a much later date (1912). Moreover, February fits better into the chronology of events. Between October 1860 and February 1861, 'Umar camped at Sansanding, reorganising his forces and awaiting reinforcements from Ka'arta. Masina troops under the command of Ba Lobbo, camped, together with the troops of Ali Diara of Segu, first at Koni, and later at Tio on the right bank of the river Niger, opposite Sansanding.[3]

Aḥmadu b. Aḥmadu did not appear eager to engage in battles immediately; rather than fight he devoted his effort to further Islamising Segu. From Tio he sent six envoys to Segu-Sikoro to ascertain how far the people were accepting Islam. He ordered them to break down idol temples in Segu and begin the building of mosques in their places if the Bambara had not accepted

1 ASAOF, 15G108/9, 'M. le Gouverneur du Sénégal et dépendances', Médine, 19 Feb. 1861; and 15G108/9 of 17 Mar. 1861; also Tyam. *Qacida*, p. 157

2 Delafosse, *Haut-Sénégal-Niger*, ii, p. 317; Salenc, *La Vie* . . ., p. 412, n. 4

3 Koni, no longer in existence, was a settlement located some 40 kilometres from Sansanding on the Masina side, cf. Delafosse, *Haut-Sénégal-Niger*, ii, 316. Tio is the same as the village referred to as Tien in Bellat's monograph, see ASAOF, 1G184, Renseignements historiques . . ., p. 127; Mage, *Voyage*, p. 259

Islam. Ali Diara, *fama* of Segu, cooperated by sending two men, Kardigne and Bofofana, to accompany the Masina mission and help them accomplish their tasks. The envoys visited several villages in Segu, including Kogué, Nango, Bamebougou and Banankoro. In some of the places visited mosques were erected.[1] Ahmadu b. Ahmadu probably believed that 'Umar would withdraw his forces and return to Ka'arta if faced with concrete evidence that Segu was under the control of Masina. But 'Umar did not withdraw and, with encouragement from al-Bakkāi of Timbuktu,[2] Ahmadu b. Ahmadu was strengthened in the determination to fight him. Fighting began when some five hundred Tukulor troops, finding the river fordable, crossed the Niger to attack Masina troops at Tio. The Tukulor were defeated and lost most of their men in the battle which took place on 19 February 1861.[3]

On 20 Februrary 'Umar changed his strategy and sent out his troops in contingents to surround the Masina and Segu troops in all directions. This time the Tukulor troops were commanded by Alfa 'Umar Boila and Alfa Usman. In the battle which followed the troops of Masina and Segu were defeated. The Masina forces fled eastwards towards their country, while those of Segu fled westwards towards Segu-Sikoro.

After his success in the battle of Tio, 'Umar withdrew his forces to Kerango, a nearby village on the right bank of the Niger. 'Umar's aim this time seems to have been to reorganise his troops for a concentrated attack on Segu-Sikoro. He realised, however, that without being sure of the whereabouts of Ba Lobbo and the fleeing Masina troops it would be dangerous to embark upon the projected attack on Segu because Tukulor forces could

1 ASAOF, 1G184, Renseignements historiques . . ., pp. 127–8
2 Abun-Nasr, *The Tijāniyya*, p. 169
3 Delafosse, *Haut-Sénégal-Niger*, ii, 317; Tyam, *Qacida*, pp. 156–7, vv. 908–12; Mage, *Voyage*, pp. 259–60. The author of the *Qacida* explains that this battle began through an accident, 'Umar not being ready. The defeat of the Tukulor troops is explained as a punishment which the troops received for their disobedience to 'Umar who had forbidden them to attack the Masina army. The author of the *Qacida* was obviously concerned with showing that 'Umar had divine sanction in all that he did and was therefore always successful. But the story that the disciples were disobedient is contrary to the general tone of the *Qacida* which emphasises the loyalty and obedience of the disciples to 'Umar. Mage's account is similar to that contained in the *Qacida* and apparently comes from the same source.

be attacked suddenly by the Masina forces. To prevent this he sent troops in pursuit of the fleeing Segu and Masina armies. This expedition, led by Bubakar Takko Bali, returned a short while later to announce that Ba Lobbo and the Masina army had disappeared into Masina. A reconnaissance party sent against the Segu troops, led by Alfa Tierno Boila, camped in the village of Nango and was asked to remain there by 'Umar.[1] In the meantime, 'Umar went to Sansanding for reinforcements and by 5 March 1861 he was able to lead his army from their camp at Kerango for the march on Segu-Sikoro, where they arrived on 9 March.[2]

In planning the attack on Segu-Sikoro 'Umar had ordered Alfa Usman to join the forces under the command of Alfa Tierno Boila at Nango. Ali Diara, for his part, had also re-organised his Bambara troops, which he camped at Kanankoro.[3] On 10 March 'Umar led his army into Segu-Sikoro, which he conquered without difficulty because Ali Diara had fled, taking refuge somewhere on the borders of Masina. People who were left in the capital lost no time in making their submission to 'Umar, who took possession of all the treasures accumulated in the palace of Ali Diara, the *fama*.[4] With the occupation of Segu-Sikoro, 'Umar virtually became the ruler of the Bambara Segu empire. The occupation of Segu was the culmination of his victories against the army of Tata, son of Ali Diara, at Ouitala, and at the battle of Tio, opposite Sansanding, against the combined forces of Segu and Masina.

But although 'Umar had occupied Segu-Sikoro the battle had still not been given up by his opponents, who had been re-organising their forces in an effort to regain control of the empire. The reorganised Masina army, led by Ba Lobbo, arrived at Segu on 22 March, but battle did not begin immediately. Both sides for some time contented themselves with sending harassing parties against each other until actual battle broke out on 6 April 1861. In the fight that ensued the Tukulor

---

1 ASAOF, 1G184, Bellat, Renseignements historiques . . ., p. 130
2 Tyam, *Qacida*, pp. 160–3, vv. 927–48; Mage, *Voyage*, p. 260; Delafosse, *Haut-Sénégal-Niger*, ii, 317
3 ASAOF, 1G184, Renseignements historiques . . ., p. 131
4 Mage, *Voyage*, pp. 361–2; Tyam, *Qacida*, p. 163; Monteil, *Les Bambara du Ségou et du Ka'arta* (1924), p. 100; Delafosse, *Traditions historiques . . .*, p. 83

army lost about a hundred soldiers,[1] but re-formed and succeeded in beating back the Masina troops; the latter fled and were pursued up to the village of Dyolo.[2]

With the defeat of the Masina forces the resistance against 'Umar in Segu was virtually broken. Ali Diara and the rest of his Bambara troops were no longer equal to the task of dislodging 'Umar from Segu-Sikoro, and after they had been defeated at Kogou and Touna Ali Diara fled and took refuge with Aḥmadu b. Aḥmadu in Masina. All efforts made to capture him (Ali Diara) failed.[3] 'Umar's control over Segu was assured after the flight of Ali Diara; he assembled his *talibés* and military leaders and shared out the booty of war – in gold, silver, animals, and women.[4]

The danger implied by the escape of Ali, *fama* of Segu, into Masina partly determined 'Umar's next line of action. He realised that he could not be assured in his occupation of Segu as long as Ali was still alive in the neighbouring state of Masina, and there was the possibility that he would organise new forces and lead further attacks on the Tukulor in Segu. Since he was not yet in a position to prevent such an attack, which he could have done only through an offensive war against Masina, 'Umar decided to put Segu-Sikoro and the surrounding villages in a very strong defensive position. He did this partly by repairing the fortress of the *fama* of Segu, and surrounding it with a strong garrison. He also allocated troops to his military leaders, assigning them to defensive positions in various directions.[5] He then caused Bambara religious temples to be broken down, but kept the *bori* or *boli* (the idols) with a view to using them later on in argument against Aḥmadu b. Aḥmadu, who had earlier claimed that Segu had accepted Islam.[6]

---

1 ASAOF, 1G184, Bellat, Renseignements historiques . . ., pp. 131–2; Tyam, *Qacida*, p. 167
2 Tyam, *Qacida*, pp. 167–8. Dyolo was a village on the Niger after Sansanding on the route to Masina.
3 Monteil, *Les Bambara* . . ., p. 101; Tyam, *Qacida*, p. 168; Delafosse, *Haut-Sénégal-Niger*, ii, p. 318; ASAOF, 1G184, Bellat, Renseignements historiques . . ., pp. 132–3
4 Tyam, *Qacida*, p. 169, vv. 984–5
5 *Ibid.*, pp. 169–70, vv. 986–93
6 *Ibid.*, p. 171, v. 994

THE CONQUEST OF MASINA, 1862–64

After the occupation of Segu by 'Umar some religious leaders attempted, unsuccessfully, to resolve the hostilities between him and Ahmadu b. Ahmadu. The first marabout to try a settlement was Alfa Suleyman of Hamdallahi who was the Arabic teacher of Ahmadu b. Ahmadu. Alfa Suleyman proposed a cease-fire which Ahmadu b. Ahmadu accepted, but which 'Umar rejected. In his letter to 'Umar, Alfa Suleyman expressed his desire to see a stop put to hostilities because it was undesirable and contrary to the law of Allah for two Muslims to engage in war.[1] 'Umar was said to have rejected the proposals put to him on the ground that he could not deal with the men through whom the letter had been sent. After the failure of the first mission. Ahmadu b. Ahmadu sent three of his principal chiefs with another letter for 'Umar from Alfa Suleyman. The three men sent were Modibo Ahmadi Ahmadu, Alfa Nou and Ahmadi Ali. In his letter, Alfa Suleyman informed 'Umar that Ahmadu b. Ahmadu had agreed to stop war, following his advice, and expressed the hope that 'Umar, a compatriot (Alfa Suleyman, like 'Umar, was a Tukulor from Futa), would accept his proposals and stop the war.[2]

'Umar once more rejected the proposals to stop hostilities, asserting that Ahmadu b. Ahmadu had told a lie when he claimed that Ali Diara of Segu had submitted to him and had accepted Islam. To prove his point 'Umar took the envoys round Segu to see the relics of temples which were used for the practice of indigenous religions up till the time he occupied the country. 'Umar also charged Ahmadu b. Ahmadu with keeping under his protection at Hamdallahi Ali Diara, the *fama* of Segu, who should be his ('Umar's) prisoner. 'Umar was said to have sworn never to forgive the attacks on him so far made by Ahmadu b. Ahmadu; he would renounce his decision to go on fighting Masina only after the judgment of the Prophet had been known. He then proposed that Ahmadu b. Ahmadu should choose a convenient place where they might meet, with their armies. In this place, he proposed, the two sides should submit to the judgment of a venerated marabout, and whoever was judged wrong should take the penalties.[3] Ahmadu b. Ahmadu found 'Umar's propositions

1 ASAOF, 1G184, Bellat, Renseignements historiques . . ., p. 133
2 *Ibid.*, p. 134
3 *Ibid.*, p. 135; Sissoko, 'Chroniques . . .' (3e et dernier cahier), p. 135

unacceptable; he suggested instead that the two sides should send trustworthy men to the descendants of Uthman b. Fodiye in Sokoto to present their cases and obtain judgment. 'Umar rejected the suggestion, saying he would negotiate no further except on the terms he had put forward. The alternative, he said, was to settle their differences by concluding the war.[1] Since Aḥmadu b. Aḥmadu also did not find it possible to accept the position taken by 'Umar, war between the two continued.

'Umar's charge against Aḥmadu b. Aḥmadu, to the effect that there were people in Segu who were still practising their traditional religions should be seen against the background of his rejection of Masina's claim to sovereignty over Segu. Aḥmadu b. Aḥmadu did not claim that Segu was totally Islamised. Nor could he have made such a claim, because it was a well-known fact that since its beginning in 1818 the Cissé dynasty in Masina had been at war with Segu which it wanted to conquer and Islamise. Aḥmadu b. Aḥmadu still did not consider Segu fully Islamised and this was the essence of his sending marabouts to the country to spread Islam, building mosques and breaking down shrines. So it is plain that 'Umar's charge, and the show he made of breaking shrines and exhibiting the *bori*, did not represent an antithesis to Aḥmadu b. Aḥmadu's position. The latter accepted the fact of the existence of non-Muslims in Segu, but did not see how that could be a valid reason for 'Umar waging a war against the country. Masina's case rested on the claim that Segu had since 1818 been its sphere of influence, an area which by its recent act of submission had become part of Masina. It was the act of submission itself which made possible the systematic and peaceful spread of Islam. While the process was still going on, it was unavoidable that there would be a time lag when something of the old religions – shrines and other manifestations of non-Islamic practices – would continue: hence what 'Umar saw and deprecated. But, it was argued, the existence of pockets of non-Muslims, or areas not totally absorbed into Islam, could not be a valid ground for 'Umar to wage war. Masina's attitude was that, while it was engaged in Islamising Segu, it behoved other Muslims to cooperate, not compete, in the area.

There is an obvious parallel between the 'Umar–Masina

1 ASAOF, 1G184, Bellat, Renseignements historiques..., p. 136; Sissoko, 'Chroniques . . .' (3e et dernier cahier), p. 135; Mage, *Voyage*, pp. 262–6

dispute and that between Muhammad Bello, for Sokoto, and Bornu. Both 'Umar and Aḥmadu b. Aḥmadu appear to have been knowledgeable about the Sokoto–Bornu episode as both used similar arguments as Bello and El-Kanemi once used. Thus, like Bello, 'Umar tried to justify his jihād against Segu by referring to the existence of non-Muslims and the worship by these of rocks, trees and spirits. Also like Bello, who charged the Mai of Bornu with aiding non-Muslim Hausa against the Sokoto jihād, 'Umar accused Masina of aiding non-Muslim Segu against him. But, like El-Kanemi, Aḥmadu b. Aḥmadu responded to 'Umar's charges by admitting the existence of non-believers in Segu, but rejected that this constituted a valid case of unbelief or apostasy against Masina or a justification for war against Segu. While 'Umar adopted the puritanical stance of Bello, Aḥmadu b. Aḥmadu was, like El-Kanemi, a realist. The protracted, but useless, war against Segu probably conditioned the outlook of the Cissé. As for unbelievers, apostates, lax Muslims and strict or puritanical Muslims co-existing, Aḥmadu b. Aḥmadu seems to echo El-Kanemi's retort to Bello to the effect that:

> Every country in this region contains these four types. Any one who gains control over them by aggression will eventually have the difficulty of discrimination. And whenever the difficulty of discrimination has made all injury general, then the abandonment of the unbeliever is more acceptable than the killing of the Muslim.[1]

It is of course difficult to pronounce on the doctrinal differences which separated 'Umar and Aḥmadu b. Aḥmadu. It is reasonable to assume that each trusted the validity of his stated belief, and that judgment as to right or wrong is impossible and irrelevant. But apart from doctrinal issues, it was clear that, so far as 'Umar was concerned, war had broken out in Ka'arta and the case put up by Masina could therefore be no more than a subterfuge to deprive him of what he considered a legitimate reward for the effort already put into combating Bambara Segu, as well as Masina, since the first encounters in Ka'arta. On the other hand, 'Umar's conquests and annexations of parts of Ka'arta and Segu violated the interests of Masina in those areas. Therefore the Cissé of Masina had concrete political reasons to oppose the spread of 'Umar's revolution.

1 Brenner, 'The Shehus of Kukawa: a history of the El-Kanemi dynasty of Bornu' (unpublished Ph.D. thesis, 1968)

Against this background it is difficult to imagine that either party took the negotiations to stop hostilities seriously. So much is evident from the impossible conditions imposed by 'Umar. It is also probable that Aḥmadu b. Aḥmadu engaged in the negotiations only to gain time to organise his forces for the continuation of war.

Negotiations having broken down, preparations for war were geared up by both sides. On 3 April 1862 'Umar put Modi Muhammad at the head of a contingent which was sent to camp at Diba. 'Umar himself remained at Segu, recruiting more troops, which he later led to join those already camped at Diba. This was on 10 April. 'Umar's army remained in their camp at Diba up till 28 April, when they left for Galo; and from Galo they crossed the river on the 29th, marching into Masina territory.[1] According to the account of Abdoulaye Ali, the march of the Tukulor army from Segu to Masina territory took seventeen days. This is very close to the account of the *Qacida*,[2] and seems reliable.

The first battle between 'Umar's forces and Masina took place at Koningo, where the Masina side was led by Ba Lobbo. The Tukulor were victorious and Ba Lobbo hurried away to inform Aḥmadu b. Aḥmadu who was camping at Djenne at the time. The fleeing contingent under Ba Lobbo was hotly pursued by the Tukulor until they reached the village of Poromani. At Poromani 'Umar encountered another section of the Masina army under the command of Ibrahim b. Hamma Malik. The encounter lasted two days, with the Tukulor scoring another victory.[3] 'Umar marched his forces against those of Aḥmadu b. Aḥmadu at Djenne, but on their way the Tukulor met the Masina army at Tyayawal (or Thiayewal). In the battle which took place at Tyayawal, 'Umar's army suffered considerable losses, including the loss of some of its best *sofas*, like Kouroubatou Dembele. 'Umar, however, won in the end and, by losing at Tyayawal, Aḥmadu b. Aḥmadu lost control of Djenne, which, because of its strategic position, represented the key to the

1 Tyam, *Qacida*, pp. 175–6, vv. 1018–24
2 *Ibid.*, pp. 175–6; Sissoko, 'Chroniques . . .' (3e et dernier cahier), p. 136
3 Sissoko, 'Chroniques . . .' (3e et dernier cahier), pp. 136–7; Tyam, *Qacida*, pp. 176–7, vv. 1024–8

military and political power of Masina.[1] After Tyayawal Aḥmadu withdrew into Hamdallahi to prepare for further fighting.

In his bid to conquer the army of Masina at Hamdallahi, 'Umar found himself in fortunate circumstances. For instance, Ahmad Samfoulde, who had been a chief at Hamdallahi since the days of Ahmadu Shaikh, father of Aḥmadu b. Aḥmadu, deserted the Masina forces to join the Tukulor. Of his usefulness to the Tukulor it was recorded that 'il donna au cheikh les plus précieux renseignements'.[2] Because of the services of Ahmad Samfoulde the Tukulor found it easy to move about freely in an otherwise strange environment. But the greatest luck for the Tukulor came from the decision of Aḥmadu b. Aḥmadu not to fight immediate battles against them, but rather to put them under siege and starve them to surrender. After the battle of Tyayawal the Tukulor had run out of ammunition, especially bullets; and although they could easily have succumbed to an attack at such a time, the Masina army, having been defeated several times, was probably too weak to fight. 'Umar seized the occasion to put his blacksmiths to work, and in five days enough bullets were available to make it possible to continue the combat.[3] In the night of 11 May, 'Umar decided to take the offensive against the Masina army at Hamdallahi. He reached Hamdallahi on 16 May, and in the campaigns which followed, Aḥmadu b. Aḥmadu made fruitless efforts to regain control of the situation. After several battles, the situation became critical for Aḥmadu b. Aḥmadu, who had been wounded, and he took flight. He was later caught and put to death at Mopti by the Tukulor towards the end of June 1862. The rest of the Masina army made their submission to 'Umar.[4]

'Umar was able to defeat Aḥmadu b. Aḥmadu at Hamdallahi for a number of reasons. Firstly, Aḥmadu, as already noted, committed a tactical error after Djenne. Secondly, there were deserters from the Masina side who did a good deal of harm to

1 Ba, 'Archives Africaines: le dernier carré Toucouleur – Récit historique', *Afrique en Marche*, no. 3 (1957), p. 13; Tyam, *Qacida*, p. 178; Sissoko, 'Chroniques . . .' (3e et dernier cahier), p. 137
2 Tyam, *Qacida*, p. 178, v. 1035
3 Mage, *Voyage*, p. 265; Delafosse, *Haut-Sénégal-Niger*, ii, p. 318
4 Mage, *Voyage*, p. 265; Sissoko, 'Chroniques . . .' (3e et dernier cahier), p. 137; Delafosse, *Haut-Sénégal-Niger*, ii, 320; Tyam, *Qacida*, pp. 179–180, vv. 1036–46

the Masina cause. Thirdly, Tukulor success against Hamdallahi could be explained in terms of the fact that the town was largely unprotected, as was the case with other towns of similar importance, by any fortifications, or *tatas*, and had been abandoned by its inhabitants. Mage describes Hamdallahi as 'une immense ville sans fortifications que sa population avait abandonnée'.[1] With the capture of Hamdallahi Masina passed under Tukulor control.

Compared with Ka'arta and Segu, or even some of the smaller states in the Senegambia, Masina fell as a relatively easy prey. The whole campaign lasted barely three months. This rapid collapse cannot be explained solely by reference to logistics and strategy. 'Umar and his men would, of course, explain the episode as indeed all others, in terms of the divine sanction and guidance bestowed on the movement. But the Cissé also believed that their activities since their first jihād and the establishment of their dynasty in 1818 were divinely inspired and right. One cannot validly judge these professions of belief. It appears clear, however, that the whole episode was affected by the deep-seated political disunity which existed among members of the Cissé dynasty. Dissension had arisen from a succession dispute within the Caliphate when Ahmadu Shaikh named his son, Ahmadu b. Ahmadu, his successor in violation of the legitimate expectation of his brothers to succeed him. Ahmadu Shaikh, to ensure his son's succession, had adopted a subterfuge to eliminate his brothers from the competition for the throne. He had abdicated his right to rule to his son who thereby became ruler while he, the father, was still alive; and his brothers, Ba Lobbo and Abdul Salam, had no choice but to accept the rule of their nephew, Ahmadu b. Ahmadu. For as long as Ahmadu Shaikh lived, the disappointed brothers tolerated the situation, and by the time Ahmadu Shaikh died, the position of Ahmadu b. Ahmadu had become so strong that it was futile for the disappointed uncles to try to challenge him. They therefore continued to serve him, but with concealed bitterness and resentment.

This was the situation when 'Umar launched his campaign against the country. The disappointed elements saw 'Umar's invasion as an occasion to overthrow their nephew and gain what they considered their legitimate positions. Mage attributed the performance of Ba Lobbo and Abdul Salam in the wars against

1 Mage, *Voyage*, p. 267

the Tukulor to their expectation that once Aḥmadu b. Aḥmadu, their nephew, had been removed, they would be able to make their peace with 'Umar, whom they expected to restore them to their rightful position. According to Mage, one might interpret the flight by Ba Lobbo and his troops after only one encounter against the Tukulor at Tyayawal in this light. Mage feels certain that this hope accounted also for the immediate submission of Ba Lobbo and Abdul Salam at Hamdallahi.[1] Thus the invasion succeeded partly because it was used as an occasion for, and fused with, a palace revolution aimed at overthrowing the Shaikh.

'Umar did not, however, remain assured in his conquest of Masina for long, because by early 1863, it had become clear to those of the Cissé rulers who had condoned it that they could not thus achieve their objective. 'Umar brought his son, Ahmadu, from Segu to Masina with the intention of installing him as ruler over the country. Ba Lobbo and Abdul Salam, especially, saw their hope shattered by this move and therefore resolved to bring down the new regime.

In planning their struggle against the Tukulor, they solicited and obtained the support of Sidi Ahmad al-Bakkāi of Timbuktu. But 'Umar caught them in the plot through the disclosure made to him by Modibo Dauda, a former pupil of Sidi Ahmad al-Bakkāi, who was at the time one of his *talibés*. He arrested Ba Lobbo and Abdul Salam, and put them in prison while he continued his campaigns against Timbuktu. In May 1863, however, Ba Lobbo and Abdul Salam managed to escape from their detention to continue to organise the rebellion against 'Umar.[2] In attempting to deal firmly with the rebellion 'Umar put to death all members of the families of Ba Lobbo and Abdul Salam who were under his custody at Hamdallahi, as well as the ousted *fama* of Segu, Ali Diara. But instead of stopping the rebellion as it was hoped, this drastic step became, as in Ka'arta earlier on, the signal for widespread anti-Tukulor risings.[3]

Open fighting began early in May 1863 and lasted for nine months. The anti-Tukulor campaigns were led jointly by Ba Lobbo and Abdul Salam and Shaikh Sidi al-Bakkāi of Timbuktu.

1 *Ibid.*, p. 269
2 *Ibid.*, pp. 269–70; Delafosse, *Haut-Sénégal-Niger*, ii, p. 322
3 Mage, *Voyage*, p. 274; Delafosse, *Haut-Sénégal-Niger*, ii, p. 322

The Timbuktu troops operating against the Tukulor in Masina were led by N'Tieni who fought battles in Guimba. While the wars were raging in Masina communications with Segu were cut, and this made it nearly impossible for 'Umar to receive help from his son there. But in spite of the difficulties with which he had to cope, up to February 1864 'Umar made every possible effort to reconquer Masina. His last battle is believed to have taken place in the night of 6–7 February. In this battle 'Umar had been pursued from Hamdallahi until he reached the Bandiagara cliffs at Deguembere where he entered the cave of N'Goro. Masina forces were said to have been told of his whereabouts by a woman, and to prevent him from escaping, the Masina soldiers set the whole area on fire. 'Umar was caught in this fire and he was burnt to death on 12 February 1864.[1] Among those who died with him were two of his sons, Makki and Mahi, and some of his military leaders, including Muhammad Sire, Ahmadu Musa, Bubakar Bambi and Seidi Keika.[2]

With 'Umar's death, the task of reconquering Masina devolved upon Tijāni, his nephew and close aide in all the work of empire-building. Tijāni achieved victories over the combined forces of Masina and Timbuktu after a few months of struggle. His task was made less difficult by the dissension among his opponents – the Cissé and the ex-Fulani rulers of Masina whom the former had ousted. Rivalry for leadership among the descendants of the Cissé dynasty weakened discipline in their army, and this was said to have led to the victory of Tijāni over them in the district of Bourgou. Dissension also existed among the Timbuktu allies of Masina. This found expression in the decision of a section of Timbuktu, led by Ahmed b. Sidi-el-Mokhtar, to ally with 'Umar

1 Salenc, 'La Vie . . .', p. 417; Tyam, *Qacida*, pp. 195–7, vv. 1115–24; ASAOF, 1G301/1, 'Sénégambie-Niger-Cercle du Bandiagara' (Bandiagara, 15 Oct. 1903), pp. 6–7; Delafosse, *Haut-Sénégal-Niger*, ii, p. 323; Delafosse, *Traditions historiques* . . ., p. 86. In these latter works Maurice Delafosse erroneously claims that the rebellion against 'Umar began in September 1863 and that 'Umar died in September 1864. This evidence conflicts with what we have in chronicles compiled by eye-witnesses and participants in the events, as well as in monographs compiled a short while after by French administrators. Moreover, it contradicts the chronology of events.
2 Oral evidence collected at Segu in May 1965; also Tyam, *Qacida*, pp. 197–8, vv. 1125–9

against the pro-Cissé and majority group, led by al-Bakkāi.[1] The last phases of the war against the Tukulor in Masina was led, for the Timbuktu side, by Abiddin. In spite of the force at the disposal of the latter, however, he was defeated by Tijāni who had the support of anti-Abiddin groups from Timbuktu. Collaboration with the dissident groups in Timbuktu accounted for the victory scored by Tijāni in the Diaka areas in particular.[2] With the re-establishment of Tukulor authority under Tijāni in Masina, the Tukulor, had succeeded in establishing a vast empire extending from the borders of the Senegal river in the west to Masina in the east.

Among the factors which contributed to the success of the Tukulor in establishing their authority over this vast area of land were the nature of politics in the various states existing in pre-Tukulor times, the geographical nature of the area, and the fact that the Tukulor had the advantage of possessing, for the greater part of the time, superior arms and ammunition. As has been pointed out, an important factor that contributed to the success of the revolution in the Senegambian states was the political instability that plagued most of those states, and which 'Umar carefully exploited to his own advantage. 'Umar's success in the wars against Segu could be explained by the fact that Segu and Masina were at the time still involved in a prolonged war which had begun with the founding of the Cissé dynasty in Masina. Both Segu and Masina later realised that, for their mutual advantage, they had to come together against the Tukulor; but by the time this was done 'Umar had already conquered much of Segu territory and had occupied strategic and important positions from which to continue the war.

Even when Segu and Masina agreed to pool their resources against 'Umar, the dissension among the rulers of Masina made some of the army leaders fight halfheartedly. Ba Lobbo and Abdul Salam saw in the coming of the Tukulor a way of achieving their political ambition, and they therefore hastened to make their submission even when they were still in a position to continue the war. Again, 'Umar had established himself and had taken

1 ASAOF, in 1G83, Le Lieutenant de Vaisseau Caron à M. le chef de bataillon, M. le Commandant de Cercle, A bord du 'Niger'; Manambougou, 31 Oct. 1887, pp. 20–1; Salenc, 'La Vie . . .', p. 416

2 ASAOF, 1G83, Le Lieutenant de Vaisseau, Caron à M. le chef de bataillon . . ., Manambougou, 31 Oct. 1887, p. 21

control of the country before the people saw how mistaken they had been in their expectations. Thereafter the resistance they put up was brilliant and it resulted in the death of 'Umar; but since the people were not politically united, Tijāni, continuing the effort to reconquer Masina, still found enough room to manoeuvre and conquer both the Cissé and the al-Bakkāi forces. In most of the states conquered by 'Umar, political instability which resulted from divisions in the states rendered them easy victims.

The savannah nature of the area made military campaigns fairly easy for the invading Tukulor. The only exception was perhaps in certain sections of the Senegambian region which was forested and mountainous. There military campaigning was necessarily tardy and prolonged. In contrast, the area from Ka-'arta to Masina was for the most part open savannah and scrub-land, with large tracts of land separating villages which were far apart. In these areas it was easy for the Tukulor army, especially the cavalry contingents, to move quickly from one place to the other. In the villages houses were built together only by members of the same extended family, whose groups of houses were usually some distance from those belonging to other family groupings in the village. A common feature of the houses was that the roof was mostly of grass materials. In the dry season especially these houses, like the grassland surrounding them, were easily sus-ceptible to burning either through accident or by the deliberate action of an enemy. The Tukulor employed burning in their wars against their enemies. Very often they would set fire to villages, and while these were burning they would wait in ambush to attack and kill villagers who were attempting to escape. Burning as a part of warfare was, in the circumstance, a monopoly of the invading Tukulor, who kept moving from place to place, taking refuge in the mountains if need be. The villages could not employ burning as a weapon because they would only have been destroying themselves in the process, since it was they who had the farms and houses that would be destroyed. This means of mass destruction was often employed by the Tukulor army to force their enemies to submit.

Another factor which has been pointed out as having contri-buted to the success of the Tukulor was the fact that they pos-sessed, for the greater part of the time, superior arms and ammunition which they had bought from the French posts in the

Senegambian region and from traders dealing with the British factories in the Gambia and Sierra Leone. But equally important as the possession of these arms was the fact that 'Umar had a number of men who had had some training in Saint-Louis,[1] Senegal, in the making and use of these weapons. Among them the most notable was Samba N'diaye, who had lived for long in Saint-Louis and was a sort of 'engineer' to the Tukulor army. Such people made it possible for the Tukulor to use the two cannon which had been abandoned by a French officer during the campaigns in the Senegambian states in 1858–59. These cannon were later used to advantage against enemy states. It was the smiths among the Tukulor forces who, from time to time, continued to make more arms and ammunition for the use of the army when they were far away in Segu and Masina, and cut off from their source of supply in Senegal and Sierra Leone. As we have seen, in May 1863 for instance, after the battle of Tyayawal 'Umar was able to continue the war against the Fulani army of Aḥmadu b. Aḥmadu only after his smiths had worked continuously for about five days to provide bullets and other types of ammunition for the army.

In the last analysis, 'Umar's own merits must be mentioned as having contributed to the success of his empire-building efforts. He was a first-rate military leader and tactician and, as witnessed by many reports by the French officers who had to deal with him, he had great intelligence. He knew how to keep his men together through religious teaching and by satisfying their material needs through the distribution of booty. The account in the *Qacida* clearly demonstrates the religious zeal, and even fanaticism, of his army and adherents. These believed that he possessed extraordinary powers, and the miracles which he performed from time to time obviously confirmed their trust in the divine nature of his revolution. They were loyal and devoted to his person and

1 One of such men, Samba Ndiaye, has already been noted in relation to the use of two cannon by the Tukulor army. Others included those who had trained as carpenters, masons and smiths. These were generally responsible for building Tukulor fortresses and for making the 10,000 bullets a day, during the battle for Masina. They also turned Tukulor taxes in saltpetre and charcoal into the manufacture of local gunpowder, see Mage, *Voyage*, pp. 297–8; Hargreaves, 'The Tukulor empire of Segou and its relations with the French', *Boston University Papers on African History*, ii (1966), p. 134; July, *The Origins of Modern African Thought* (1968).

leadership. Moreover, 'Umar fully understood the psychology of his men – especially the Tukulor *talibés* – and he exploited their characteristics to make both his army and administrative system viable organs of the revolution. This approach involved compromise and arrangements that would not please purists who saw themselves as fighting to establish an ideal Islamic state. Nevertheless it was an approach that 'Umar obviously recognised to be necessary for the success and survival of the revolution. By assigning territories to some of his *talibés* and slaves to govern 'Umar infused in his followers the hope not only that they would be well off materially, but also that they could become politically important as rulers of some portions of the emergent empire. In this way he was able to hold round him a group of people who were always ready to fight the war as if they were fighting for themselves, and this spirit accounted for the success of the Tukulor.

Lastly, once the Senegambian episode was over, and some equilibrium was established in his relations with the French, especially with the 1860 entente, 'Umar was free from any threat from the French and was therefore able to deploy his talents, unhindered, against Segu and Masina. Indeed, from 1860 onwards the French even wanted him to succeed in the hope that the economic expansion of the Senegal colony into the Western Sudan would be better assured if the whole area could be governed by someone of 'Umar's calibre whom they thought would provide the political stability so essential to commercial expansion.

6 The Administration and Politics of the Tukulor Empire, 1864–1870

It has been said that attachment to the Tijāniyya provided the bond of unity within the community that created and administered the Tukulor empire.[1] But this can only be part of the explanation. A full study of the administration and politics of the empire has to proceed from an appreciation of the constant interaction of Islamic and pre-Islamic concepts of government and society. The task of reproducing an ideal Islamic society and government has never been realised. First, the concept of the ideal has always varied with the many Shaikhs who tried to translate it into reality. More important, however, has been the fact that the attempts to achieve the declared objective invariably involved violent revolutions. Revolutions are complex mass movements, always incorporating elements and ideas that share varying degrees of relationships, or none at all, with those that started them rolling in the first place. But since these were usually an inseparable part of the tools being used for achieving the declared objectives of the initiators of the revolutions, they have to be taken into consideration and they very often determine the end-product of the revolutions. As in similar revolutions elsewhere, the idea of re-creating a pure Islamic society and state should be seen mainly as a catalyst that triggered off a chain of actions and reactions. The degree to which it is retained at the end was a factor of the interaction of the diverse elements in the movements.

The interaction of Islamic and pre-Islamic concepts was a feature of the revolution that produced the empire, and it was dominant in the life of the state till its end.[2] 'Umar's strength

1 Fisher, review of Abun-Nasr, *The Tijāniyya, Bull. SOAS*, xxx, 1, 1967; Willis, 'Jihād fī sabīl Allah . . .'
2 See Ọlọruntimẹhin, 'The interactions of Islamic and Pre-Islamic Concepts'.

derived partly from his understanding of his men, who were
protagonists of different and often conflicting ideas, and from
his ability to accommodate all, by compromising when approp-
riate, in order to keep all under his leadership. He demonstrated
ability to exploit and galvanise all the strands in the revolution
towards creating a large empire. The Islamic and pre- or non-
Islamic elements were sometimes complementary and this made
it relatively easy for him to keep all together. The earliest
manifestation of the accommodation of traditional and Islamic
elements and ideas was in the jihād army which was formed,
organised and commanded largely according to current ideas
and practices in Futa Toro.[1] For this reason the army acquired
the federal character of the Futa Toro political system. Also,
in terms of leadership, the army was made up mainly of *toroBé*
elements, who were the elite corps from among whom Futa Toro
got most of its military, political and religious leaders. A careful
look at the political administration of the empire will indicate
that in terms of number and significance of positions held, as well
as of their own social status, they were dominant.

From its beginnings to the end the Tukulor state experienced
the effects of the dichotomy which existed between those of its
leaders who were eager to re-create society according to the
supposedly pure form of Islam and those who, though they took
Islam seriously, saw in the empire an expansion of the Futa Toro
political and social systems. For the latter group there was no
contradiction between Islam and the system in Futa Toro. It
would appear that this group dominated the administration and
politics of the empire from the beginning. As already evident
from the administration which 'Umar established early in 1857,
eight of the ten persons appointed as emirs (amīrs) were *toroBé*
aristocrats who combined their rule with that of army commanders.[2] This was to be the pattern followed in the administration
of the whole empire. All along, however, there is evidence that
some attempt was made to conduct the affairs of the state along
broader Islamic lines. An example was 'Umar's appointment
of a distinguished ex-slave, Mustafa, to a key political post at
Nioro.

Apart from the conflict between the Islamic and traditional
ideas and elements in the revolution, other important factors

1 See Chapter 2 for the organisation of the army.
2 See Chapter 3 for the example of 'Umar's administration of Ka'arta.

which influenced the type of constitution which was evolved for the empire included the security problems which plagued the state from the beginning, the sheer size of the empire, and the inadequacy of the communication network at its service.

Before he died in February 1864 'Umar had led the Tukulor to establish a vast empire which covered the former states of Ka'arta, Segu and Masina, together with outposts in the Sene-gambia. By 1864 the new rulers of the emergent empire were still facing enormous difficulties, and the need to overcome these difficulties seems to have dictated, at least in part, the form of the early administration which was evolved under 'Umar for the government of the empire. At the time of 'Umar's death, the hold of the Tukulor conquerors over the empire was still weak. Their greatest problem was how to suppress the resistance movements which were being mounted in various parts of the empire with a view to overthrowing the newly established Tukulor regime. 'Umar himself died in battle fighting to suppress one such resistance movement in Masina in February 1864. It must have been clear to him that, as long as the resistance to his regime remained unsuppressed, his Tukulor regime would remain in-secure and liable to overthrow any time. In his first attempts at governing, he seems to have been imbued with, and guided by, a determination to hold together, under his control, the recently conquered territories. From its structure and personnel it is fairly obvious that his administration was security-oriented.

The vastness of the empire meant that it would be difficult to rule it through a centralised form of government. Because means of communication within the empire were poor and uncertain, contact between one part of the empire and the others was often difficult and took a long time to make. The circumstances in which 'Umar and his team found themselves were such that urgent decisions, often of a military nature, had frequently to be taken in several parts of the empire. An administrative system which relied on a central authority for all important decisions would not serve the needs of the regime, and would be difficult to work. 'Umar's recognition of this fact seems to have been responsible for the decentralised system of administration he introduced.

The military nature of the administration was emphasised by its organisation, and especially the personnel recruited to run it. 'Umar did not start with an overall plan; each step he took to administer the country seems to have been dictated by the needs of the moment and of the particular area. He made plans to govern each territory as soon as it was conquered, and because there was always need to fight more battles in order to secure any conquest made, he often chose his administrators from among his followers who had distinguished themselves as military leaders. The few exceptions to this practice were in Dinguiray, where Abibu, 'Umar's second son, was appointed emir,[1] and Segu, where his first son, Ahmadu, later succeeded him. But even in such cases he always maintained garrisons under able military leaders who often took part in administration. In Koundian, for instance, he maintained a garrison under the command of one Badara Tunkara,[2] whose duty it was to help maintain the Tukulor regime in the Bafoulabe area. In general the military leaders were also the political and religious aristocracy and 'Umar had no difficulty in using them in his administration. In 1857, after the conquest of Ka'arta, he had divided the country into units over which he placed military leaders as administrators under the general leadership of Alfa 'Umar, based at Nioro. But towards the end of 1859, when he was to embark on the conquest of Segu, he needed the services of Alfa 'Umar, whom he took with him to Segu. He then left the overall control of Ka'arta to Mustafa, a military leader of slave origin;[3] the other areas continued to be governed by military leaders like Assa-Mady, who for some time ruled the Diomboko district.[4]

The military nature of 'Umar's administration came out more clearly in the governmental arrangements which he made after the conquest of the Bambara Segu empire. He had taken with him from Ka'arta some of the military leaders ruling there in order that they might help him conquer Segu. As soon as the conquest had been achieved, he hastened to send them back to Ka'arta so that they could strengthen the security of that area. Some of the leaders would have preferred to stay with him at Segu, but he would not let them. For instance, he sent back one Alfa Ahmadu who had wanted to stay with him at Segu because, as he argued, if Alfa Ahmadu were allowed to stay on, the other

1 ASAOF, in 1G32, Relation du voyage par Mage: Notes diverses, vol. i, 1866, p. 9
2 Mage, *Voyage*, p. 154
3 *Ibid.*, p. 130; Soleillet, *Voyage à Ségou 1878–1879* (1887), p. 366
4 Soleillet, *Voyage à Ségou*, p. 365

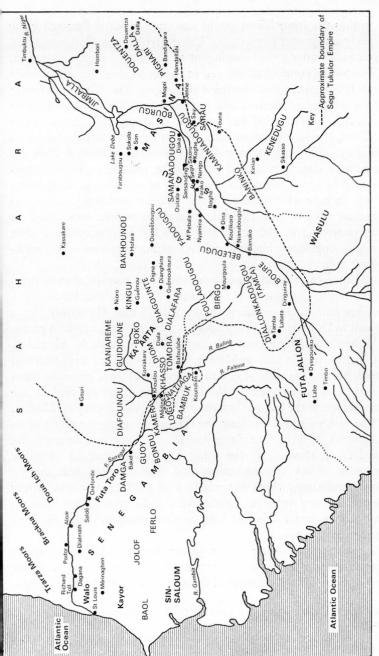

The Segu Tukulor Empire

contingents from Nioro would also wish to stay.[1] Regarding the newly conquered Segu state, 'Umar divided it up into units and put each under a clan contingent of his army for administration. The *toroBé* contingent was put in charge of Kogué district, while the Irlabé contingent occupied Babougou. The N'Guénar group took charge of Banankoro, at the same time as the Bosséia contingent controlled the area of Waourago-M'Bebala. Segu-Sikoro, the headquarters, was put under the control of soldiers of Futa Jallon origin, as well as of Bambara recruits.[2] Thus the administration established in Segu in 1862 was obviously designed to satisfy the needs of an army of occupation. This seems to be in tune with the need of the Tukulor to insure their regime against revolts and Bambara resistance movements aimed at overthrowing it. Before he left Segu for Masina in April 1862 'Umar appointed his first son, Ahmadu, to represent his authority there.[3]

'Umar conquered Masina in 1863 and remained in control there up to the time of his death in February 1864. He sent one of his *talibés* and military chiefs, Alfa 'Umar Haoussidji, from Segu to Dinguiray to bring his sons – Hadi, Muhammad Aguibu, Muhammad Mahim and Muhammad b. Mustafa b. Ahmad b. Usman – to join him in Masina.[4] These remained with him and took part in the wars of conquest against Masina. Some of them died with him in 1864. He died without having broken the resistance to the establishment of his Tukulor regime in Masina. The task of re-establishing the Tukulor regime devolved upon Ahmadu Tijāni, 'Umar's nephew, who later reconquered the Fulani of Masina. By the time of 'Umar's death in 1864 the picture of his administration that had emerged was one of decentralisation which depended for its working mainly on strong local military leaders, vested with wide powers to rule the territories under them as long as they recognised the Shaikh's sovereign powers.

For the functioning of this system 'Umar had made adequate provisions in terms of military installations and finance. As far as revenue for the running of the administration went he made it

1 Sissoko, 'Chroniques . . .' (3e et dernier cahier), p. 135
2 *Ibid.*
3 ASAOF, in 1G32, Relation du voyage par Mage: Notes diverses, vol. i, 1866, p. 12; Mage, *Voyage*, p. 264
4 Sissoko. 'Chroniques . . .', (3e et dernier cahier), p. 135

possible for the various units to remain almost completely independent of one another. He did this through maintaining treasuries at places like Dinguiray, Dabatu, Nioro, and Segu. In each case, the treasury was under the control, and served the needs, of the emir in charge of the area. For instance, the treasury at Nioro was controlled by Mustafa, who was emir till about 1870.

'Umar maintained garrisoned fortresses at such places as Koundian (in the Bambuk), Mourgoula (in the area of Kita), Koniakary, Sabousire (in Khasso), Nioro and Segu.[1] These garrisoned fortresses were often sited in areas of strategic importance from where the empire could be defended against external dangers. For example, Mourgoula and Koundian, situated between Bafoulabe and the river Niger, were defence points against external threats on the Senegambian side, especially against the French menace. Each of these fortresses, as in the case of the treasuries, was under the control of the emir in charge of the particular area, who often used the garrison to defend the territory under his rule without necessarily referring to 'Umar. While not fighting any wars, the garrisons saw to the security of their part of the empire by watching out against any outbreak of resistance from the conquered people. According to the evidence of Borgnis Desbordes, a French military officer who visited some of these forts between 1882 and 1883, the garrisons were always 'en garde contre toute velleité de résistance'.[2]

Thus supplied with the necessary tools, the emirs were able to administer the territories under them with considerable autonomy while 'Umar, the head of the empire, was far away in Masina and could not have exercised much direct control over them even if he had been willing to. That the administration was running well without direct control from 'Umar was evident from the way the various territorial units of Segu were ruled on such occasions as Ahmadu, 'Umar's son and representative at Segu, was called to Bandiagara in Masina. But it was essentially a military administration, a superstructure to intimidate the people into submission. By 1864 little had been done to affect traditional life at local or village level because the new regime

1 Gallieni, *Voyage au Soudan français* (*Haut-Niger et Pays de Ségou*) *1879–1881* (1885), pp. 449, 553, 557.
2 ASAOF, 1D69, 'Rapport sur la Campagne de 1882–1883 dans le Soudan', B. Desbordes, Bamako, 16 Feb. 1883, pp. 69–70.

lacked the personnel, as well as the time, to influence societies which for much of the time were still in armed resistance.

While 'Umar lived the empire held together, partly because the system met the contingencies of the time, partly because the material resources were sufficient to maintain it; but equally important was his leadership. In spite of the decentralised nature of the administration 'Umar was able to hold his empire together largely because of his personal qualities. He enjoyed high prestige and a good deal of confidence among his followers on account of his religious learning and his ability as a military and political leader. Much of the devotion he received came from the fact that his administration satisfied the ambitions of those who had followed him and taken part in his wars of conquest in the hope of material gain. Some of these followers not only became rich with booty, but also received political power as near-independent territorial rulers. Gallieni was probably correct in his assessment when after discussing with various officials of the Tukulor regime in Segu, he concluded that 'Umar had held the empire together 'par son prestige religieux et son habileté d'entrainer à sa suite les nombreuses populations éléctrisées par sa parole prophétique et attirées autour de lui par l'appat d'un butin considérable'.[1] Moreover 'Umar was regarded both by his followers and by his enemies as a military leader of outstanding powers. By maintaining strong garrisoned fortresses in well-chosen strategic points he managed to instil fear into the hearts of the recently conquered people. The system he had evolved owed much to his personality and the ideas associated with it, hence his death left a great vacuum and the unity of his empire died with him.

Since he died early, it is not possible to tell what form of administration he would have installed had the empire become firmly established. But what had emerged gave considerable initiative and power to provincial rulers and must have appeared right to the administrators and the *talibés*. It was reminiscent of the system of government they knew and cherished back home in Futa Toro, where the almamy was often only a figurehead and real power belonged to powerful clan or lineage group leaders.[2] 'Umar, to the administrators and *talibés*, was obviously seen as occupying much the same position of an elected Futa Toro

1 ASAOF, 1G50/34, 'Gallieni à M. le Gouverneur', Nango, 11 Oct. 1880
2 See Chapter 1.

almamy – a *primus inter pares*, who, though respected, was expected to be weak. After 'Umar's death the effort to get a successor resulted in crisis, partly because the most obvious candidate, Ahmadu, showed centralising tendencies which the Tukulor aristocracy found to be both strange and ruinous to their own political and economic interests.

The succession issue was bedevilled by another problem which related to the conflicting attitudes of the learned men as to the right rule for the *jama'a* to follow. Some preferred the rule that the Caliph should be elected from among the best men in the community. But there were those who accepted that 'Umar, the first Caliph, could have appointed his successor in exercise of his *baraka*. This group saw nothing wrong in the claim that Ahmadu had been appointed. The former group, however, tended to ignore Ahmadu's claims in favour of election, which was the Futa Toro practice in the choice of almamies.[1]

'Umar died at a time when the achievements of the Tukulor revolution were threatened more than ever before. He died fighting for the very existence of the regime in Masina, and with his death the situation became gloomy for the Tukulor who were, for some time, leaderless as the question of his successor remained unsolved. In the Masina section of the empire, however, the immediate task of re-establishing the Tukulor regime was performed by Ahmadu Tijani who reconquered the Masina Fulani. But while the succession question still remained to be solved, news of 'Umar's death was kept secret. Although he died in February 1864 his death was not officially announced by Ahmadu, his first son ruling at Segu, until towards the end of 1865.[2] This delay was apparently intended to give enough time to settle the succession question. There is no conclusive evidence to indicate that 'Umar had chosen any of his sons or followers as his successor and none of the Tukulor leaders seems to have acquired enough status to make himself acceptable to the others. In the competition to fill the vacuum, the succession problem

---

1 Apart from being the method of choosing the almamies of Futa Toro, election was also the means adopted in choosing the successors to the caliphate of Sokoto since the death of the founder, Uthman b. Fodiye. The attempt to bypass the processes of election caused trouble not just among the Tukulor but also earlier on among the Cissé of Masina. Cf. Chapter 4 on the effects of succession disputes among the Cissé on 'Umar's campaign in Masina.

2 Delafosse, *Haut-Sénégal-Niger*, ii, p. 331

caused a split in the Tukulor hierarchy, and the feuds which resulted from the split weakened the regime and contributed to the fact that their grip over the areas under their control remained fragile and ineffective.

Ahmadu asserted that he had the right to succeed his father, and that he had in fact been designated as successor by 'Umar himself. The *Qacida* records that 'Umar had in January 1860 at Merkoya in Beledugu appointed Ahmadu as his successor. It further states that before 'Umar left Segu in 1862 for the campaigns in Masina he invested Ahmadu with powers as his successor and that all of 'Umar's disciples who were present on the occasion swore allegiance to Ahmadu. The author of the *Qacida* also reports that 'Umar had called Ahmadu to Hamdallahi (in Masina) in 1863, mainly to instal him as his successor, and that the installation, at which 'Umar invested Ahmadu with full powers in the presence of all his *talibés*, did take place.[1] The *Qacida* thus gives the story of Ahmadu's appointment as having taken place on three different occasions, apparently in order to emphasise that he had been invested with the leadership of all parts of the empire. The first indication of Ahmadu's appointment was said to have taken place at Merkoya, after the conquest of Ka'arta had been completed and before 'Umar set out on the Segu campaigns. This story seems to be meant to convey the idea that 'Umar conferred the powers to rule Ka'arta on Ahmadu at this point. The story of the installation ceremonies which took place at Segu and Hamdallahi was similarly meant to convey the idea that 'Umar transferred his power over each of the territories to Ahmadu as soon as the conquest was completed. With Hamdallahi the transfer of the whole empire would then have been completed.

If 'Umar arranged so much ceremony in appointing Ahmadu it would be strange that those *talibés* who should know did not appear to know, and that Ahmadu had to delay the announcement of his father's death for so long during the struggle for the succession. On this point the account of the *Qacida* must be regarded with caution. It is essentially an official chronicle compiled by someone who spent much of his adult life in the service of 'Umar and later in the court of Ahmadu in Segu. It was written for Ahmadu, and could be said to contain the 'official'

1 Tyam, *Qacida*, p. 135, v. 784; p. 175, vv. 1018–19; pp. 187–8, vv. 1080–1082

version of the account of what happened. It is possible that the author of the *Qacida* was concerned with justifying the position of his master, Ahmadu. The latter's claim was not supported by his brothers and the *talibés* who were ruling outside Segu. Ahmadu Tijāni, with the support of the *talibés* in Masina, established his own administration over Masina after he had reconquered it. As far as is known Ahmadu Tijani, in fact, governed Masina independently of Ahmadu from 1864 onwards. Ahmadu succeeded in making good his claim over Segu (the former Bambara Segu empire); but his brothers and the *talibés* who were governing in faraway places like Dinguiray and in Ka'arta did not recognise his claim to supremacy, and ignored him. For some of them his claim was dangerous and should be opposed because it threatened the positions they had acquired under 'Umar. But for as long as Ahmadu stayed in faraway Segu, there was no threat of an immediate open clash between him and the rulers of Ka'arta and other states. In addition each ruler was faced with resistance from recently conquered peoples, and the efforts to suppress them took much of their time and energy for some time.

Ahmadu, however, continued to prepare himself for the struggle to extend his authority over Ka'arta against the rulers who opposed him there. Confrontation between Ahmadu and the coalition led by two of his half-brothers, Abibu and Moktar, did not take place until 1870, when the first attempt was made to settle the question of sovereignty and supremacy. The struggle which began in 1870 dragged on for several years, and until the issues in the civil wars which ensued had been resolved in Ahmadu's favour, the area which was effectively under his authority was limited to Segu. From 1864 to 1870, therefore, the Tukulor empire was administered as three large units, Segu, Masina and Ka'arta, each with its own peculiarities, but all sharing broad common features deriving from the fact that they were all under Muslim rulers of Tukulor origin.

AHMADU'S ADMINISTRATION OF SEGU

'Umar had left Ahmadu at the head of the administration of Segu when he left for the campaigns in Masina in 1862, apparently because he placed confidence in him. But Ahmadu was at this time largely inexperienced in the art of government. It may be, however, that by assigning him to Segu, 'Umar intended to give him some experience in governing under his own general guidance and with the support and advice of the *talibés* and military leaders left in command of the area. While 'Umar lived all went well enough, but after his death it devolved upon Ahmadu to conserve intact the empire that had just been founded. The problems facing his administration were still largely the same as those which 'Umar had attempted to solve. The recently conquered peoples (the Bambara in the case of Segu) were still in armed resistance.[1] In several areas of Segu, especially Sansanding and Kogué, the Bambara were in arms against Ahmadu's administration. The Tukulor at his disposal for the purposes of administration were the same people who had been appointed by his father, had been continually engaged in warfare for almost fifteen years, and had distinguished themselves as military leaders. Ahmadu was relatively inexperienced. Since the situation in which he was to govern was still much the same as it had been in the time of his father, the type of leadership provided by the latter was logically still required. Ahmadu was incapable of giving this leadership since he had not got the experience of organisation nor the foresight which the difficult task required. Also, he lacked the charisma and prestige of his father. Moreover, at the beginning of his administration, he did not appear adventurous enough to be able to give effective leadership.[2] These shortcomings were, in part, responsible for some of his initial difficulties with both the Tukulor and the Bambara. But he had good qualities which helped him after the initial problems had been overcome.

According to the evidence of those who knew him personally, Ahmadu was very intelligent and enlightened. He had an inquisitive mind and often sought information about events in foreign countries.[3] He was reputed to be calm and calculating, but he suffered from indecision.[4] He had the advantage, however, of having around him enlightened men of great experience who could advise him. Mage met some of these men, such as Samba

1 Ọlọruntimẹhin, 'Resistance movements in the Tukulor empire'
2 Pietri, *Les Français au Niger* (1885), pp. 98–101
3 Mage, *Voyage*, p. 213
4 *Ibid.*, p. 214; ASAOF, in 1G46, Soleillet à M. le Gouverneur du Sénégal . . ., Saint-Louis, 2 Apr. 1879; also Soleillet's report in 1G46 of 15 Oct. 1876, pp. 31–3

N'diaye, Sherif Muhammad (a widely-travelled Arab) and Sidi Abdullahi, a Moor from Tichit.[1] Ahmadu used some of these men in the administration of his state.

In the government of Segu, Ahmadu seems to have established an informal supreme council to advise him. This council comprised the *Keletigui* (the chief of the army), Tierno Alassane, Tierno Abdul Qadri, Seydou Djelia (Ahmadu's secretary) Muhammad Djelia, Aissata, Ouelibo Ba and Samba N'diaye.[2] The main duty of this council appears to have been to advise Ahmadu on broad questions of policy. At the lower level Ahmadu divided Segu into territorial units and appointed an official (an emir) in charge of each. People thus appointed were all resident at Segu where they were answerable to Ahmadu on questions affecting the areas under their control. Each district head therefore had to maintain a representative in his district to keep him informed of events in his area. From the reports of these representatives, each district head would decide what issues were important enough to be brought to Ahmadu's notice. If Ahmadu decided to submit such an issue to his council for discussion, the district head concerned was often called to attend the particular meeting of the council.[3] District heads were invited to attend council meetings only when affairs of their respective districts were to be discussed. The keeping of district heads at the headquarters was practised both by Ahmadu at Segu and Tijani at Bandiagara.[4] It is not known why they did this, but a probable reason could be that the loyalty of these officials, mostly Tukulor *talibés*, was in doubt, and it was considered necessary to keep them under surveillance at headquarters and thereby prevent them from becoming too strong and dangerous.

In the political organisation of the state, Ahmadu seems to have adopted the administrative divisions which had existed under the Bambara rulers. This was partly because the Tukulor lacked the personnel and time to effect a complete overhaul of the

1 Mage, *Voyage*, pp. 226–7
2 ASAOF, 15G76/3, 'Voyage de Demba Samba Chef Surveillant des postes et télégraphes à Nioro' (n.d., 1887?); 15G76/2, Le Lt.-Colonel Gallieni, Commandant Supérieur du Soudan français à Cheik Ahmadou', Kayes, 6 Feb. 1887; 1G320/1, Notice sur le cercle du Ségou, Le Commandant du Cercle, Ségou, 1 Mar. 1904, pp. 15–16
3 ASAOF, 1G50/24, Notes by Gallieni, dated Nango, 2 Sept. 1880
4 ASAOF, 1G320/1, Notice sur le cercle du Ségou – Le Commandant du Cercle, Ségou, 1 Mar. 1904, p. 15

organisation, and in the areas which had still not submitted to Tukulor rule, introducing changes was out of the question. In areas which had submitted, and were effectively under the Tukulor regime, Ahmadu often confirmed the conquered Bambara chiefs in their traditional positions as rulers of their people. The only difference in the position of such chiefs was that while in the past they had held their positions as of right according to tradition, they now held office because of their loyalty to the Tukulor regime. Ahmadu encouraged the founding of Tukulor villages as colonies among the predominantly Bambara populations. These colonies were used to watch for signs of insurrection. Some essential features of Tukulor provincial administration under Ahmadu in Segu were described in a report of an investigation carried out in Segu by the French administration and published in 1904:

> Les Toucouleurs n'apportèrent aucune modification dans l'organisation politique et administrative du royaume. Tous les cantons furent conservés. Mais comme la plupart de leurs chefs avaient suivi la fortune des Diaras et avaient abandonné leur fonctions, il fallut les remplacer. Leurs successeurs furent choisis dans la famille des anciens chefs, parmi les hommes favorables au nouveau régime. Cependant pour éviter toute insurrection, d'importants villages toucouleurs furent crées à côté des principales agglomérations Bambaras, notamment à Bambougou, Kogué, M'Péba, Dongasso, et Banankoro. . . .[1]

Such administrative units as existed seem to have followed the natural geographical divisions created by the rivers Niger and the Bani which also served as boundaries between territorial units. Among units which bordered on the Niger and the Bani were those with headquarters in Segu-Sikoro, the unit comprising villages on the left bank of the Niger, especially N'To, Farako and Niempena, the unit comprising villages situated on the right bank of the Bani, bordering on Jenne in Masina, and the unit with centre at Bamako.[2] In addition to these large units, there were a number of independent villages whose chiefs were supervised directly from Segu-Sikoro, the headquarters. Such were the villages of Banamba, Baroueli, Belekou, and Fabougou.[3]

1 *Ibid.*, pp. 15–16
2 ASAOF, 1G125/1, Notice géographique sur le cercle de Ségou – Le Capitaine, Commandant du cercle, Segou, 29 July 1895
3 ASAOF, 1G320/2, Notice sur le cercle de Ségou – Le Commandant du cercle, Segou, 1 Mar. 1904, pp. 38–41

Where district heads were appointed, they were responsible for the administration of villages within their districts. The administration of a village under direct Tukulor rule[1] comprised the village head or chief, a *qādī* (judge), and a tax collector.[2] In several parts of the Segu state, however, the Tukulor did not really succeed in establishing any effective administration. In Beledugu, for instance, Ahmadu did not succeed in breaking the Bambara resistance, and could therefore not have established effective administration in such areas, which remained unabsorbed parts of the empire.[3]

While the superstructure of Tukulor administration existed, as has been described, the local administration of unsubjugated areas remained what it had been under the old Bambara Segu empire. Each village was administered by a *dougoutigui* (a town or village chief) who was by custom chosen from among the elders of the family of the original founders of the village. Under the Bambara empire each village belonged to a *kafo* (an administrative unit comprising a group of villages in the same area). The number of villages in a *kafo* varied from place to place, depending largely on how many villages were geographically contiguous and willing to come together. At the head of each *kafo* was usually the chief of the most important village or someone from the oldest and most important family in the area. The relationship between the head chief of the *kafo* (*kafotigui*) and the chiefs of the villages was governed by old usages and traditions reminiscent of the administration of the Bambara Segu empire, which put emphasis on cooperation. Each *kafotigui* was responsible to the *fama* (the Bambara king at Segu) for the affairs of his *kafo*, especially on political, administrative and judicial matters.[4]

Under the Tukulor administration, however, the *kafos* became units of resistance, and were used as political and military

1 It appears clear that Ahmadu did not succeed in introducing a uniform system of administration into all areas which submitted to Tukulor rule. As has been pointed out several villages were left to be governed largely by their traditional Bambara chiefs who had been largely non-Muslims. The system being described here applied only in areas under the administration of Muslim, Tukulor or of Islamised Bambara.
2 ASAOF, 15G50/22, Gallieni's notes dated Nango, 21 Aug. 1880
3 Oloruntimẹhin, 'Resistance movements in the Tukulor empire'
4 ASAOF, 1G195/9, Notice générale sur le Soudan, Lt Sagols, May 1897, pp. 35–6; 1G87/2, pp. 33–4

confederations which gave members 'une force telle que les conquérants ne purent arriver à les soumettre'.[1] Examples of *kafos* which were used in this way were Touba, Merkoya (or Mercoia), Damfa, and Koumi. In the latter place, for example, up till the time of the French conquest, Diocé, the *kafotigui*, was still considered by all in the *kafo* as the military chief around whom all others would group whenever any external danger menaced them. It was around the Koumi chief that the Beledugu Bambara had fought successfully against the Tukulor.[2] In unsubdued areas like the Beledugu, the influence of the Tukulor was felt only through the garrisoned posts which 'Umar had built, and during military expeditions made under Ahmadu in a bid to break their resistance.

MASINA UNDER TIJĀNI

It is difficult to determine the exact boundaries of Masina within the Tukulor empire, and especially in relation to the Segu state under Ahmadu. This, according to Bardot, is because Masina had never really been held together as an entity.[3] Before the establishment of the Cissé dynasty in 1818 part of Masina had been in vassallage to the Bambara Segu empire, and the conquest of Masina by the Cissé had thereafter led to protracted wars between the latter and Bambara Segu. These wars had left the exact boundaries between Segu and Masina ill-defined since border areas often came under the rule of one or the other, depending on the fortunes of war. With the Tukulor conquest of the two states, the problem would have disappeared but for the fact that after the death of 'Umar, rulership of Masina and Segu fell into different hands again. In relation to the Tukulor administration in general, one could say that the resistance wars which they had to face most of the time made it difficult to delimit with exactitude the areas that were effectively held by them since it was possible for the administration not to have effective hold, at one time or the other, upon areas that had once been conquered by 'Umar and which therefore could, in

1 ASAOF, 1G195/9, Notice générale . . ., May 1897, p. 35
2 *Ibid.*, p. 24
3 ASAOF, 1G158/1, Notice ethnographique et géographique sur le Macina, E. Bardot, Mar. 1892, p. 3

theory or nominally, be regarded as part of the empire. As Caron noted during his visit to Masina in 1887: 'Si Tidiani possède un vaste territoire, son autorité n'est pas établie sur tous les habitants qui supportent plus ou moins bien le joug.'[1]

After the reconquest of Masina in 1864 Ahmadu Tijani took over control of the administration. He had his capital at Bandiagara, a town which had the advantage of natural defence features. In the administration of Masina Ahmadu Tijani, like Ahmadu at Segu, had a group of intimate advisers who constituted a kind of privy council, and were constantly with him at Bandiagara. These intimate advisers were mainly from among Tukulor *talibés* who had been with 'Umar since the beginning of the revolution and the establishment of the empire. Some of these men were emirs in charge of the administration of provinces.[2] He governed through having full consultation with his advisers because, as he was reported to have said, he was not a king but just a disciple carrying out the will of Allah.[3] He was not a despot, but a Muslim doing the will of Allah for his community. The statement attributed to Ahmadu Tijani illustrates how astute he was as a ruler. He based his claim to authority on his position as the religious leader of his people, and in a Muslim community such as he had around him at Bandiagara, this gave him more powers than he would have had if he had claimed to be king. In spite of the divine sanction which he thus claimed for his authority he did not rule autocratically, but by fully consulting with his advisers. In this way he gained their confidence and could be sure of their loyalty. Existing independently of the group of intimate advisers was an assembly comprising influential persons like provincial rulers and religious leaders. This council often advised Tijani on the administration and politics of the state. It also served as a court of appeal in judicial cases.[4]

Ahmadu Tijani divided the country into large units for the purposes of administration. These units were not uniform in size or population. The guiding principle in the administrative set-up seems to have been to put together groups that were

1 ASAOF, 1G83/2, Caron à M. le Commandant des Cercles, A bord du 'Niger', Rade de Manambougou, 31 Oct. 1887
2 ASAOF, 1G195/9, Notice générale . . ., May 1897, p. 58
3 ASAOF, 1G83/2, Caron à M. le Commandant des Cercles, Oct. 1887, p. 13
4 ASAOF, 1G195/9, May, 1897, p. 59

closest to one another and linked by common interests. Also, from Bardot's description of the system in Masina,[1] it is clear that the administrative set-up derived in part from the history of the country and its geography. The country had been inhabited by various enthnic groups at different points of time, and each had had its own distinct system of administration. The Habes,[2] for example, especially under the vassallage of the Bambara Segu, had maintained a system closely related to that of the Bambara Segu empire. When the Fulani Cissé dynasty was established in 1818, the leaders set up a superstructure of administration according to their own idea of Islamic government, at the same time as they adopted what was useful from the old Habe system. With the Tukulor conquest all the new rulers led by Ahmadu Tijani could do for a start was to adopt the system inherited from the ousted Cissé dynasty, the only change being in personnel. It is not surprising, therefore, that the system of provincial adminis-tration had vestiges of the old in it. In appointing officials to take charge of the administrative units, Ahmadu Tijani selected people mostly from among his Tukulor following, especially from among the leading *talibés* of al-hajj 'Umar. Like Ahmadu in Segu, how-ever, he also appointed some of the officials of the Cissé dynasty who had demonstrated their loyalty and devotion to his regime.[3] On appointment each provincial ruler or emir received a letter of investiture which specified, among other things, the amount of tax payable to the central treasury at Bandiagara from his particular area.[4]

It appears that Tukulor provincial rulers had a higher status and carried out greater responsibilities than their non-Tukulor counterparts. This difference in status can be seen in the func-tioning of the provincial system of administration. In the case of Tukulor appointees the provincial ruler himself stayed at Band-iagara as one of the intimate advisers of Ahmadu Tijani. To represent him in his province, the Tukulor official usually ap-pointed a representative based in the headquarters of his province. The representative would then carry on the routine admin-

1 ASAOF, 1G158/1, 'Notice ethnographique . . .', Mar. 1892
2 A Muslim Fulani word for describing other peoples who were non-Muslim and non-Fulani.
3 ASAOF, 1G195/9, 'Notice générale . . .', May 1897, pp. 57–8; 1G83/2, Caron à M. le Commandant des Cercles, Oct. 1887, p. 21
4 ASAOF, 1G195/9, Notice générale . . ., May 1897, p. 58

istration of the province, having the final word in matters that were not very important, but always referring important and serious questions to the provincial ruler in Bandiagara. This was much the same system as Ahmadu operated in the Segu section of the empire. On the other hand, where the provincial rulers were not Tukulor, especially where they were from among the traditional rulers, they often remained in their provinces, administering the places directly.[1]

Sometimes some of the administrative units were large enough to be subdivided into what might be called 'districts'. Wherever districts existed, district heads were appointed responsible to the official of the unit within which the districts were situated. Direct Tukulor administration hardly ever went below this level.[2] As under Ahmadu in Segu, the administration of other areas that were not completely subjugated remained in the hands of families which had been ruling in pre-Tukulor times and the administration remained as it had been in the traditional system. But also, even in areas that had submitted to Tukulor rule, Ahmadu Tijani still made use of people from among the traditional rulers. In this way the Tukulor administration in Masina seems to have tried to absorb the conquered Habe chiefs into their administration. Al-hajj 'Umar appears to have set the example when, on taking over Hamdallahi, he set free the Habe rulers who had been kept prisoners by the Cissé dynasty.[3] It was convenient for Ahmadu Tijani to follow this example and use the Habes in his administration because in any case he could not have found the necessary personnel from among the Tukulor alone. Also this practice was obviously a useful device for winning the support and loyalty of the various non-Fulani peoples against the recently ousted Cissé rulers who had been their masters since 1818. The Tukulor, in effect, tried to pose as liberators of the Habes and in this way secure their alliance against the Cissé.

In many cases Ahmadu Tijani allowed the Habe chiefs to return to their traditional posts, especially at the village level. In this way he gave them an interest in defending the regime against the Cissé. He also linked the many Habe chiefs to his central administration by calling on the principal ones among

1 *Ibid.*, pp. 58–9
2 ASAOF, 1G158/1, Notice ethnographique . . ., Mar. 1892, p. 19
3 ASAOF, 1G301/2, 'Organisation Politique, administrative et judiciaire indigène' (n.d.), p. 1

them to act as intermediaries between him and the other chiefs. At first one of the principal Habe chiefs who acted as intermediary, and who was very influential with Ahmadu Tijani, was Sanande Sana, the chief in charge of Tinta Borkio. After his death, Gogouna, chief of Ouassabari, north-east of Bandiagara, came into prominence.[1] In some places also Ahmadu Tijani kept in touch with the Habe chiefs through Tukulor provincial administrators. Ahmadu Tijani's success in making the Habes an integral part of his administration was a contrast to the failure of Ahmadu in Segu who could not reconcile the Bambara to his administration, but relied heavily on his *sofas*, who could be described as Bambara mercenaries recruited into the Tukulor army. Ahmadu Tijani's administration was similar to that of Ahmadu's Segu, however, in his almost complete alienation of the recently ousted Cissé rulers.[2] In Segu there was no such group as the Habe to be won over to the Tukulor in a common hostility against members of the ousted Bambara political class. The Bambara dynasty was older, indigenous, and inseparable from the generality of the population of the state. Unlike the Cissé in Masina, the Bambara political class did not represent an imperial superstructure against which the other elements in the society could easily be pitched. The Cissé dynasty, dating only from 1818, was too recent and had not had enough time to become fully integrated with the conquered population. Hence, the surviving dichotomy and hostility between it and the Habe, which Ahmadu Tijani exploited to stabilise his Tukulor regime.

In Ka'arta, the administration remained largely what 'Umar had made it until Ahmadu was able to gain control over the area after the series of civil wars which began in 1870. Mustafa, the ex-slave, continued to rule Nioro, while 'Umar's sons, Abibu and Moktar, continued to rule in Dinguiray and Koniakary respectively. One of the major tasks which Ahmadu set himself between 1864 and 1870 was to prepare himself for the struggle to extend his authority effectively to cover Ka'arta and Dinguiray. In his efforts to secure for himself the supreme position which 'Umar had occupied within the empire, however, Ahmadu ran into constant trouble with Tukulor rulers in these areas, especially his half brothers Abibu and Moktar. The struggle for leadership was not resolved until after the civil wars which took

1 *Ibid.*, p. 2   2 *Ibid.*, p. 3

place between 1870 and 1874 had ended favourably for Ahmadu. While the struggle lasted the empire was saved for the Tukulor between 1864 and 1870 largely because of the absence of external danger such as the French had represented between 1857 and 1860.[1] What also helped to keep the empire together was that although, as has been shown, between 1864 and 1870 it was governed largely as three independent units, certain factors helped to maintain a sense of unity among them. One such factor was the allegiance which all paid to 'Umar as the spiritual leader and founder of the empire. The division of the empire into three units resulted from the succession struggle; but while the Tukulor could not agree on a new leader to replace 'Umar, each of the participants in the struggle, even while governing the territory under him independently, did not regard himself as independent, or as ruling a territory that had an existence apart from the Tukulor empire in general. None considered himself a dissident. Each based his claim to rule upon the authority which was often alleged to have been conferred by 'Umar, the Shaikh himself, and to him loyalty was still pledged.

One consequence of this situation was that those of the Tukulor leaders who were not directly involved in the leadership tussle could always move freely from one part of the empire to the other, and settle anywhere they liked. As will be pointed out, a common tactic employed by all involved in the succession struggle was to secure the support of as many as possible of such leaders, especially the *talibés*, the original principal followers of 'Umar, who could claim, because of their closeness to him, that they knew what he said or did.[2] The picture was sometimes confused by the role of some of these *talibés*, whose actions were often guided mainly by what they considered to be their own interests. Another factor giving uniformity, and even some unity, to the Tukulor empire in this period was the fact that the units had certain administrative practices in common. These were, for example, the roles of various classes of society in government, and the working of the judicial, defence and revenue systems.

GOVERNMENT AND SOCIETY

(*a*) The *talibés* were the original followers of 'Umar most of whom had come with him from Toro and other areas of Futa

1 See Chapter 8   2 See Chapter 7

Toro as well as Futa Jallon and Bondu. The group later included people from other parts of the Western Sudan, including Masina and Segu. What distinguished the *talibés* as a class was the fact that they were learned and were often regarded as religious leaders by the Islamic community. They were also often leaders of clans or lineages. Because of their early association with 'Umar in the work of establishing the empire they acquired considerable importance and constituted the aristocracy, performing both civil and military duties in the empire. The intimate advisers who featured in the administrations of Ahmadu and Ahmadu Tijani, in Segu and Masina respectively, came from among the *talibés*, who also provided the governors of most of the provinces and other territorial units. For instance, Tierno Mussa whom 'Umar appointed in charge of Koniakary emirate in Ka'arta was a *talibé*.[1] In Masina, Ahmadu Tijani was on good terms with his *talibés*. They gave him their loyalty and he often took their advice. The same could be said of the early Segu administration of Ahmadu before discontent reduced the amount of support he enjoyed; even in moments of crisis, however, Ahmadu had the services and support of such prominent *talibés* as Seydou Djelia, Abdullahi Djelia, Ahmadu 'Umar Eliman, Ahmadu Aissata, Samba N'diaye, Ali Dia and others.[2]

The *talibés* were also important for their leadership role in commanding the Tukulor elements in the armies, which constituted the core of the military strength of the empire. Major Gallieni, who was on a mission to the empire in 1880–81 testified to this, stating that the corps of the army led by the *talibés* 'constitutent le noyau le plus sérieux des armées toucouleures et ont une réputation de bravoure très grande dans le Soudan occidental'.[3] Also as part of their active military duties, the *talibés* were in charge of the Sultan's guard, known at Segu as *Diomfoutou*.[4]

The privileges which the *talibés* enjoyed were commensurate with the importance of the duties they performed. They were exempt from the payment of taxes, and they had easy access to

1 ASAOF, in 1G46, Soleillet à M. le Gouverneur, Saint-Louis, 5 Apr. 1879; 1G50/34, Gallieni à M. le Gouverneur, Nango, 11 Oct. 1880, p. 7
2 ASAOF, 1G158/1, 'Notice ethnographique . . .', Mar. 1892, pp. 22–3
3 Gallieni, *Voyage au Soudan Français* . . ., p. 609
4 *Ibid.*

Ahmadu and other rulers.[1] Some of them, as has been stated, were provincial governors. Since they constituted the aristocracy of the empire, they were actively involved in its politics, and the stand taken by some of them was important in determining which side won in disputes. Between 1864 and 1870 Ahmadu could make his authority felt only within the Segu section of the empire mainly because his opponents in the other parts, especially Abibu and Moktar, had the support of many of the *talibés*, and the strength deriving from this support in military and religious circles made it impossible for Ahmadu to break their resistance. Even after Ahmadu had succeeded in extending the area under his authority after the civil war of 1870–74, he still had problems arising partly from the alienation of the *talibés*. From 1884 to 1891 Ahmadu had to leave his capital in Segu for Nioro in Ka'arta mainly to be able to contain the *talibés* whom he feared might collaborate with his adversaries to overthrow his authority in that part of the empire.[2]

The alienation of many of the *talibés* from Ahmadu after 1870 seems to have stemmed from their discontentment with their economic situation. Many of the Tukulor *talibés* had left their homes in the Futas to join in the campaigns of 'Umar in the hope that they would get some material gains. During the wars to establish the empire they had had to rely principally on the pillage for their subsistence. 'Umar had been generous in distributing this, so that under him, and while the war lasted, all went well. But with the establishment of the empire, and Ahmadu in control, trouble began. The *talibés* had hoped that they would have their shares of the treasures accumulated during the wars. But Ahmadu, who at first controlled only Segu, instead of distributing the treasures, guarded them for state services. He argued that the jihād had not been completed; that there were still unbelievers to be fought, and that, therefore, the treasures could not be shared because they were still needed for fighting further wars.[3]

Between 1864 and 1870 Ahmadu was faced with many problems. He had to govern the state under him at Segu, and to be

1 ASAOF, in 1G46, Soleillet à M. le Gouverneur, Saint-Louis, 3 Apr. 1879; 1G50/34, Gallieni à M. le Governeur, Nango, 11 Oct. 1880, p. 6
2 See Chapter 8.
3 ASAOF, 1G209/1, 'Notice historique du royaume et du cercle de Ségou' (n.d.), pp. 9–10

able to rule, he had to fight to subdue Bambara resistance movements. At the same time he was preparing, militarily and otherwise, to assert his authority against his halfbrothers and some
ruling *talibés*, who would not recognise his authority in Ka'arta
and adjacent territories. Because of all these involvements
Ahmadu really needed all the material resources at his disposal,
especially as the administration was not sure of any other source
of revenue.

Obviously this type of argument could not have been taken
well by the *talibés* who were in economic difficulties, far away
from home, and only trying to make new homes after many
years of wars. The *talibés* round Ahmadu in Segu could not take
kindly to the situation because it was evident that their counterparts in Masina and Ka'arta were enjoying better fortunes since
they were having a greater share of the political offices and
wealth in land and other forms of property accumulated in those
places. The rulers in Masina and the provinces of Ka'arta on the
other hand were eager to preserve their independence against
Ahmadu, who was laying claim to the supreme position previously occupied by his father, 'Umar. To succeed in their struggle
against Ahmadu, they needed the support of the *talibés* in their
areas. A way of gaining this support was by satisfying their
economic needs. This they did by the disbursement of largesses
from the treasuries under their control, and having done this,
they gave the *talibés* social security and an economic interest in
defending their position against Ahmadu. The *talibés* in Segu
considered the opponents of Ahmadu in other parts of the empire
more generous, and those in these other areas considered it
inviting hardship to allow Ahmadu to rule. Consequently the
difficulties which Ahmadu had in his dealings with the *talibés*
arose partly from the difficult economic situation, and partly
from the strains and stresses arising from the manoeuvres of the
leadership dispute. This is evident from the frequent accusations
of avarice, lack of generosity, and being generally difficult, that
were often made against Ahmadu.[1] These charges were mainly
economic in origin, but their political effects were expressed in
the preference of the *talibés* to leave Segu and reside in such
places as Nioro and Bandiagara because they preferred the Tuku-

1 Mage, *Voyage, passim*; ASAOF, 1G50/34, Gallieni, 11 Oct. 1880,
p. 7

lor rulers in those places. By the 1880s large numbers of them had moved to various parts of Ka'arta; they were in support of Ahmadu's relatives who were his political rivals – men like Muntaga and Aguibu.[1] The rather strained relationship between Ahmadu and the *talibés*[2] was partly responsible for the greater reliance which Ahmadu placed upon his *sofas* as an arm of his administration.

(*b*) The *sofas* constituted the soldiery in the Bambara Segu empire. With the establishment of Tukulor rule many of the *sofas* changed their loyalty, accepted the new regime and continued to serve in the Tukulor army. In numerical terms, the *sofas* constituted the bulk of the army of the Tukulor, especially in the Segu section of the empire. They had the characteristics of mercenaries who would fight anywhere provided they were paid. They were used mainly by Ahmadu, and very often against Bambara resistance movements in various parts of Segu.[3] Ahmadu also relied on them as a force to maintain his position against the Tukulor aristocracy. Later on, however, the word *sofa* was used to describe all non-Tukulor elements within the army, especially in Segu and Ka'arta. Thus among the non-Bambara *sofa* leaders were people like Sidoloki Diallo from Birgo in the Senegal area, Demba Dango, a Wolof and Arsegue, Ali Heri and Abdul Babani from the Hausa country.[4]

The *sofas* were at first confined to purely military functions but Ahmadu later brought some of their leaders into civil administration as a way of reducing the influence of the *talibés*. He appointed some of the *sofa* leaders as provincial governors. For instance, the almamy of Mourgoula up to 1880 was a *sofa*,[5] and Ahmadu, on taking over the administration of Masina in

1 ASAOF, 1G209/1, 'Notice historique du royaume . . .'; 1G50/34, Gallieni, 11 Oct. 1880, pp. 7–8
2 As has been pointed out Ahmadu made use of some *talibés* as his intimate advisers and in his provincial administration. Those so employed were often devoted to him; but because of their devotion they were suspect to the other *talibés* who regarded them as belonging to the favoured group and therefore as accomplices.
3 ASAOF, 1G50/34, Gallieni, 11 Oct. 1880, p. 8; 1G158/1, 'Notice ethnographique . . .', Mar. 1892, p. 23
4 ASAOF, 1G158/1, 'Notice ethnographique . . .', p. 23
5 ASAOF, 1G50/34, Gallieni, 11 Oct. 1880, p. 7

1891, appointed Alfa Mussa, a *sofa* chief, in charge of the important Djenne province.[1] With the increasing prominence of the *sofas* in Ahmadu's administration the *talibés*' resentment against him increased and relationship between the *sofas* and the *talibés* was often strained.[2]

(c) The *Habes*, as a group, were important only in Masina, where Ahmadu Tijani gained their support by treating them kindly and by integrating their chiefs into his administration. By giving them a new and higher status in society than they had had under the Cissé dynasty, Ahmadu Tijani tied the fortunes of the Habes to those of his regime, and they therefore had interest in defending the regime against the Cissé as well as any external body that might threaten it. Explaining the attachment of the Habes to the regime of Ahmadu Tijani, and the Tukulor in general, it is said that: 'Habitués à se voir piller et vendus comme esclaves, ils se voyaient, du jour au lendemain, traités comme des gens libres. Tidiani leur donnait des chevaux, les emmenait dans les expéditions et faisait largement leur part du butin.'[3]

Because of their role in the civil administration of Masina the Habes were important in its politics. But they were the more important because they constituted the core of the army of Ahmadu Tijani. With time they too became aware of the power they could wield in the struggle between the Tukulor and the resisting Fulani descendants of the Cissé. While Ahmadu Tijani lived the Habes were always on his side. But after his death Habe chiefs increased their influence and acquired the right to participate in deciding which of the Tukulor should rule. For instance, the Habes were instrumental in getting Ahmadu Tijani's cousin, Sa'id b. Tamsir, elected as his successor.[4] It was also the support of the Habe chiefs which made it possible for Muniru to succeed to power in Masina much against the will of Ahmadu who had tried to influence some Tukulor *talibés* against him.[5] It was largely because they were dissatisfied under Muniru that it was possible

1 ASAOF, 1G158/1, Notice ethnographique . . ., Mar. 1892, p. 22
2 ASAOF, 1G209/1, Notice historique du royaume . . . (n.d.)
3 ASAOF, 1D137, 2e Partie/iii, (7), 'Séjour à Mopti' (n.d.), p. 403
4 *Ibid.*, p. 404
5 *Ibid.*, pp. 404–5; ASAOF, 1G158/1, 'Notice ethnographique . . .', Mar. 1892; 1G301/1, 'Sénégambie-Niger-Cercle du Bandiagara', Bandiagara, 15 Oct. 1903

for Ahmadu to secure the latter's abdication in 1891.[1] By 1892, the Habes had become so important in the politics of Masina that Bardot, leading the French investigating team, advised that they were the most important factor to be reckoned with if the French ever hoped to conquer Masina. Bardot concluded his report by saying that: 'C'est donc avec les Habes que se fera la conquête du Macina et il ne faudra pas négliger leur concours dans l'organisation de la nouvelle conquête. Il sera plus utile, et plus indispensable que celui des Peulhs ou des Bambaras.'[2]

JUDICIARY

The administration of justice was very much the same in all parts of the empire. In areas which had been brought under direct Tukulor administration, justice was administered according to Islamic traditions. In such places persons learned in the Qur'ān and conversant with the Islamic laws were appointed as *qādī* (judge) to administer justice. But as in the other aspects of civil administration, where the Tukulor had allowed indigenous systems of administration to remain, or where they had failed to subjugate the people, justice was administered according to the traditions of the people concerned. An examination of the system in Masina, typical of the practice in the other parts of the empire, will show in some detail the administration of justice in the Tukulor empire. Masina is used as an example because it was ruled by both Ahmadu Tijani and Ahmadu, the head of the empire.

In general, two systems of judiciary existed – one for the Muslims[3] and the other for the non-Muslim areas. For the Muslims each village had its own *qādī*, who had competence only

1 ASAOF, 1G158/1, 'Notice ethnographique . . .', Mar. 1892, p. 2; 1D137, 2e Partie/iii, (7), pp. 404–6
2 ASAOF, 1G158/1, 'Notice ethnographique . . .', Mar. 1892, p. 2
3 It need not be assumed that justice was administered by the Tukulor in all areas that were Muslim. There were Muslim areas which had adopted Islamic juridical procedures even before the advent of the Tukulor conquerors. Such areas often continued to use Muslim institutions in their administration even when they remained actively opposed to the Tukulor regime. Examples of such areas were Timbuktu under the al-Bakkai family, the Cissé-dominated areas in Masina and Sansanding.

over civil cases. All criminal cases were normally tried at the court in the district headquarters. More serious criminal cases, such as murder or any act involving the letting of blood, could in the first instance be tried in the court of the provincial governor. In practice, since Tukulor provincial governors were often at the capital, such cases were tried only at Bandiagara. Appeals could be brought from the village to the district headquarters, and from the latter to Bandiagara, the highest court of appeal.[1] This was usually the court constituted by Ahmadu Tijani, and later on by Ahmadu, his intimate advisers and the provincial governors resident in Bandiagara. Thus the structure of the judiciary consisted of at least four layers: the court constituted by the village *qādī*, that at the district headquarters, that of the provincial governors,[2] and the final court of appeal sitting at Bandiagara.[3] In areas under the direct administration of Bandiagara, cases were brought before the *qādī* of Bandiagara from where appeal could be taken to the court of Tijani and his notables. Among the *qādīs* who had served at Bandiagara were Tierno Aimoutou Ba, Tapsiru, Ahmadu M'Peredio and al-ḥājj Dongo.[4]

In discharging their duty the judges used as their books of reference the Maliki code, especially as set out in the *Risala* of al-Qairawānī. Judges do not appear to have been appointed as fulltime officials. In addition to their judicial function they were expected to read and explain the Qur'ān to those who came to them for instruction. Judges in Bandiagara, for instance, often met in Ahmadu Tijani's palace to study the Qur'ān together.[5] There does not seem to have been any fixed payment for *qādīs*. Such payments as they had were irregular, coming mainly from their part of fines inflicted on offenders. It is reported, for

1 ASAOF, 1G305/2 (2e section), Sénégambie-Niger-Cercle du Djenné, 1903–1904, p. 6; 1G301/3, Organisation politique, administrative et judiciaire indigène . . ., p. 5
2 This seems to have been limited to such provinces as Jenne whose governors were *sofa* chiefs and, being non-Tukulor, were resident in their provinces. Such courts also existed in Ka'arta and adjacent territories where, because of the great distance separating them from Segu, Tukulor provincial governors had to stay in their provinces, visiting Segu periodically instead of residing there.
3 ASAOF, 1G305/2 (2e section), pp. 6–7
4 ASAOF, 1G301/3, Organisation politique, administrative . . ., pp. 5–6
5 *Ibid.*, p. 6

example, that in the area of Jenne the *qāḍī* was the recipient of half of all fines collected from court proceedings. To ensure enough funds for themselves it is claimed that in punishing offenders, *qāḍīs* made excessive, almost exclusive, use of fines as a form of punishment. Hence it is reported: 'Toutes les peines de l'emprisonnement ou corporelles n'étaient infligées qu'aux malheureux, tandis que les riches étaient condamnés à des fortes amendes. Le kadi y trouvait son bénéfice.'[1] Judges often assured themselves of funds from this source, and because they were a part of the administration, they were often also maintained out of state revenue.

However, from the evidence available it seems that justice was fairly dispensed under the Tukulor. This was so even when persons involved included high ranking officials, such as provincial governors. Fairness was made possible because both Ahmadu Tijani and Ahmadu entertained cases brought by private persons even against the provincial governors. Ahmadu, for instance, where necessary, would not hesitate to give judgment in favour of a private citizen against a provincial governor. Such a case was brought by one Kassim, who complained that Muhammad Muntaga[2] wrongly deprived him of his captive. In his judgment Ahmadu ordered that Muhammad Muntaga should, without fail, return the captive to Kassim.[3] Ahmadu also inspired confidence in his provincial officials by sometimes referring cases brought to him back to the governor from whose province such cases had been brought. Cases thus referred were usually those not involving the governors themselves.[4] This appears to be a reflection of the classical *Naẓr al-maẓālim* system of justice.[5]

The administration of justice in the non-Muslim areas of the empire must have varied from place to place, but the Habe example in Masina will be dealt with here because some evidence is available on it. In some areas the Habes had judges who, by imitation, were called *qāḍī*, but their functions were limited to

1 ASAOF, 1G305/2 (2e section), p. 7
2 He was the *Wazīr* (senior governor) in charge of Ka'arta and a brother of Ahmadu, the *amīr al-mūminīn*.
3 ASAOF, in 15G76/5, 2nd enclosure, Traduction des lettres d'Ahmadou trouvées à Nioro – No. 15 à Mountaga (n.d.)
4 *Ibid.*, No. 6
5 See Levy, *The Social Structure of Islam*, pp. 332, 334, 348–51

petty cases tried according to the customs of the people.[1] More seriously involved in the administration of justice were, in addition to the traditional chiefs, judges called *Hogon* and *Lagam*. The Hogon was said to be the chief-priest of one of the deities. The Hogon's primary duty was to lead in religious ceremonies, and to assist him in his judicial functions, an assistant called *Kediou* was appointed. Both the Hogon and the Lagam had competence to judge serious cases, civil or criminal. The Habe judges were said to have been paid from court proceeds, especially from property confiscated from condemned witches and wizards, or arms, objects or animals which were thought to have been used in committing murder or in inflicting wounds on someone.[2]

REVENUE: TAXES

A good part of the revenue of the Tukulor empire came from taxes collected from the people. These taxes were of different kinds. There was, for instance, the ordinary tax payable by all taxable adults, in addition to which there were special taxes like the *Diaka*, probably a corruption of *zakat*; the *Moudou*, *Kharāj* and *Oussourou*, *'Ushr*, each payable only by special categories of people. The *Diaka* was one-tenth of the harvest and other categories of property paid only by Muslims. Non-Muslims were exempt from the payment of this tax.[3] The *Moudou* was the grains (rice or millet) given voluntarily by each good Muslim to the district chief to dispose of as he pleased. It was a kind of religious contribution. The chief often took one-fifth of the contribution, and the rest he distributed to the poor.[4] *Oussourou* was the name given by the Tukulor to the tax paid by the caravan traders in various parts of the empire. It comprised one-tenth of the total value of the merchandise and a piece of guinea

1 ASAOF, 1G301/1, Organisation politique, administrative . . ., p. 5
2 *Ibid.*; also ASAOF, 1G195/9, Notice générale . . . May, 1897, p. 59
3 ASAOF, 1G305/2 (2e section), p. 4
4 *Ibid. Muddu* is a measure, but it was probably used here by the Tukulor to mean *Zakat*, the payment of which is canonically enjoined. *Zakat* represents alms which, from the Muslim point of view, are expiatory donations rigidly ordained by the religion, and fixed in proportions relative to the nature and quantity of the property. See Ruxton, *Maliki Law* (1916), p. 31

cloth on each captive employed by the caravans. In addition to *Oussourou*, all cattle owners had to pay one from every thirty beasts they possessed, and one sheep out of every forty, to the governor each year.[1] *Kharāj* was a land tax, payable by non-Tukulor, especially the conquered non-Muslim people.[2] Hence, the exaction of the *Kharāj* from the inhabitants of Guimbala area in Masina was explained as a step taken 'en punition de sa soumission tardive'.[3]

The governor or district head in charge of a particular territorial unit was usually informed of the amount of tax expected from the area by the central administration. The amount thus levied was then shared out over the component villages in the area by the governor. For the purpose of collecting taxes, tax collectors based at fixed posts were often chosen by the central administration. Tax collectors were mostly Tukulor; but there were areas where the indigenous rulers were allowed to collect taxes and submit the proceeds later. These were in areas where the rulers had demonstrated their trustworthiness.[4] The arrangement described relates to the collection of ordinary taxes.

The ordinary taxes were usually submitted through the district head of the area to the central treasury. This was when the collection was not done by a Tukulor tax collector. For his labour in collecting and transporting it, the district head usually received one-fifth of the tax. After the rest had been submitted, one-third used to be sent to the provincial governor, one-third distributed to the village heads, the central authority retaining the remaining third.[5] It was in this way that taxes were used for financing the administration of the state. Again, as with the judicial system, the Tukulor seem to have followed the classical Islamic rules relating to the collection and administration of taxes.[6]

1 ASAOF, 1G305/2 (2e section), p. 5
2 Ruxton, *Maliki Law*, p. 83
3 ASAOF, 1G301/3, Organisation politique, administrative . . . , p. 4
4 *Ibid.*, p. 3; 1G305/2 (2e section), pp. 2–3
5 ASAOF, 1G305/2 (2e section), p. 3
6 See Levy, *The Social Structure of Islam* for a description of *Kharāj*, pp. 13, 24, 58, 309–24; *'Ushr*, pp. 304, 309, 314f; *Zakāt*, pp. 58, 154, 249f, 309, 494 and *Jizya*, pp. 3–4, 12–13, 15f, 23, 58 and 254; also Khadduri, *War and Peace in the Law of Islam* for *jizya*, pp. 145, 184, 189, 191–2, 273; *Kharāj*, pp. 126 and 189

7 Power Struggles and Civil Wars in the Tukulor Empire, 1870–1879

In the bid to establish himself as the supreme authority in the Tukulor empire, Ahmadu had adopted the title of *amīr al-muminīn*.[1] But to be accepted as such, he still had to overcome opposition from his brothers, those who did not consider his claim as legitimate, as well as from those *talibés* who had been ruling independently since the death of 'Umar. It was Ahmadu's determination to surmount the opposition to his claim to supremacy that led to civil wars in the empire in 1870. Up to 1870 both Masina and Ka'arta had remained independent of him, largely because he was not in a position to enforce his will. He chose to subdue Ka'arta first, apparently because there, unlike in Masina, authority was diffused and power was held by several persons who had been appointed to their posts by his father. He probably realised that much as these rulers might oppose the idea of his becoming supreme, they were not necessarily doing so for the same reasons, nor with the same amount of determination. Each *talibé* or member of the aristocracy had his own particular or group interests to protect, not just against the centralising Ahmadu, but often also against the other *talibés*. And since nobody occupied the pre-eminent position which Ahmadu Tijani had established for himself in Masina, it was not immediately clear what alternative the Tukulor rulers in Ka'arta would have in place of Ahmadu. Occupying the most strategic, and probably the most important, post at Nioro was Mustafa. However, he was a liberated captive who, even if he had entertained the idea, seems to have realised that it would be futile for him to put up any strong opposition to Ahmadu, the eldest of 'Umar's sons, or put up a claim to leadership over the other sons of 'Umar and the *talibés* in Ka'arta. Ahmadu tackled Ka'arta first partly also because he reckoned that the resistance to his authority in the

1 Abun-Nasr, *The Tijāniyya*, pp. 129–30, 132

area would be weaker than it would be in Masina; the possibility
of a concerted movement against him was not likely in Ka'arta
whereas it was a certainty in Masina. He probably calculated that
after he had brought Ka'arta under his control, he would be in a
stronger position to tackle the Masina problem.

Before he moved to Ka'arta, however, a movement against him
was already under way under the leadership of Abibu and Moktar,
two of his half-brothers. Both were sons of Aissatu, a Sokoto
princess whom 'Umar had married during his stay there, in
contrast to Ahmadu who was born of an ex-slave, Fatma.[1]
Abibu had been appointed by 'Umar to take charge of Dinguiray,
the first territory to be conquered by the jihād army. Soon after,
Moktar was appointed to rule a section of Diomboko province.[2]
Abibu was reputed to be courageous and generous. He enjoyed a
good reputation and prestige among the *talibés*; he could be
haughty and sometimes violent, but because of his generosity and
the open way in which he received newcomers, he was generally
admired and accepted as a leader. Moreover, he was highly
intelligent. Moktar, his younger brother, was remarkable for his
frankness, and straightforward dealings, attributes which recommended him to many of the *talibés*. The two brothers were bound
together by an extremely deep affection which they do not seem
to have had for other people.[3] On the other hand, as far as the
talibés in Ka'arta and adjacent territories were concerned, the
unfavourable reputation which Ahmadu had acquired with the
talibés in Segu was a disadvantage in the impending struggle. This
did not necessarily mean that all the *talibés* who were not in
favour of Ahmadu were therefore ready at all costs to back up
Abibu and Moktar. In their opposition to Ahmadu, Abibu and
Moktar, together with their following, did not hide their desire to
take control of Nioro, the capital of Ka'arta, where Mustafa was
in charge. While Mustafa would not, on his own, fight against
Abibu and Moktar over Nioro, he informed Ahmadu of the plans
of his half-brothers; Ahmadu therefore hastened to Nioro to
forestall them.[4] He arrived there at the end of 1869, to assert his

1 Pietri, *Les Français au Niger* (1885), p. 102
2 ASAOF, 15G109/1 (107), Le Commandant du Cercle de Médine à
  Monsieur le gouverneur du Sénégal, Médine, 11 June 1870; also
  15G109/1 (157) of 8 Nov. 1870
3 Pietri, *Les Français au Niger*, p. 104
4 Soleillet, *Voyage à Ségou*, p. 375

authority over Ka'arta.[1] It seems likely that it was at this time that he took the title of *amir al-muminin* at a public ceremony said to have been attended by a sharif from Morocco. The Alawite sharifian dynasty in Morocco claimed descent from the Prophet.[2] The presence of a member of the dynasty at the ceremony at which an *amir al-muminin* was being proclaimed must have added an aura of dignity and legitimacy, which could strengthen Ahmadu's position with the *'ulāma'* class. His original claim was that his father, through an exercise of the *baraka* with which he was endowed, had appointed him a caliph. The Nioro ceremony was obviously meant to dramatise the divine sanction of his claim. It is not clear whether the sharif was specially sent from Morocco or whether he was just passing through that part of the Tukulor empire at the time.

Using Nioro as a base, Ahmadu took steps to counter Abibu and Moktar's move against him in other parts of Ka'arta. He had brought with him from Segu an army of about 16,000 men, and he was said to have spent the early part of 1870 recruiting an additional 2,000 men from various parts of Ka'arta.[3] The concern with building up a large army indicates the seriousness of the situation which he was facing. It was only after he had arrived at Nioro that he realised that opposition to his claims was not limited to Abibu and Moktar; but that his other half-brothers like Muniru, Ahmidu and Dari, though not all necessarily supporting Abibu's movement, were also opposed to his claim to supremacy and wanted to rule their various areas independently.[4] Abibu and Moktar also had a larger following than Ahmadu had expected.

In his bid to control Ka'arta independently of Ahmadu, it was reported that Abibu claimed 'avoir une lettre de son père qui lui

1 ANSOM, in Sénégal I, 58a, Valière à Monsieur le Ministre de la Marine, Saint-Louis 24 Sept. 1874; Abun-Nasr, *The Tijāniyya*, p. 132
2 The Alawite dynasty was founded in Morocco in 1660. Members of the dynasty adopted the title 'Sharif' to emphasise their claim to be descendants of the Prophet. The founder of the dynasty, Moulay Rachid, was one of the descendants of Hassan, son of 'Ali, cousin of the Prophet and the fourth Caliph. The name of the dynasty, 'Alawi', came from this connection. See Cornevin, *Histoire de l'Afrique des origines à nos jours* (1964), p. 213
3 ASAOF, 15G109/1 (157), Le Commandant de Médine à M. le Gouverneur du Sénégal et dépendances', Médine, 8 Nov. 1870
4 *Ibid.*, p. 2

donne Nioro',[1] thus basing his claim on the authority of his father, which was also the basis of Ahmadu's claim. We do not know how valid Abibu's claim was. The important thing, however, was that he and his supporters were prepared to fight to make it a reality. A situation was thus created in which the *talibés* could intervene to influence settlement one way or the other. The desire to control Nioro was based on strategic considerations. After the destruction of Guémou, the biggest and most important garrisoned fortress, on which the Tukulor defences in Ka'arta largely depended, was at Nioro. Once control over Nioro was secured the task of controlling Ka'arta would have been comparatively easy.

While Ahmadu was building up his army in Nioro, Abibu and Moktar pushed ahead with their plans in other parts of Ka'arta. Abibu had secured the support of most of the *talibés* who were with him in Dinguiray, and having secured his position there, he moved across to Koniakary to join his brother, who had been in control of Diomboko province.[2] As part of their plan to march on Nioro, Moktar later moved some soldiers to Guidioume, a village situated between Koniakary, headquarters of Diomboko, and Nioro.[3]

Although Ahmadu had been building up his army for the struggle against Abibu and his supporters, who were advancing towards Nioro, he did not feel strong enough to take any immediate military action against his opponents and he therefore waited until towards the end of 1870. There were two main reasons for this. The first was that he was faced with an armed resistance which the Bambara had mounted at Guémoukoura as part of their general resistance movement against the Tukulor regime. It was quite certain that the Bambara were eager to exploit the internal political problems of the Tukulor to achieve their objective, which was to regain their independence. Ahmadu could not disregard the Bambara threat to deal with the internal struggle against Abibu without exposing his army to defeat at the hands of the Bambara, although he was reported to be 'très

1 *Ibid.*, p. 3
2 ASAOF, 15G109/1 (107), Le Commandant du Cercle de Médine à M. le gouverneur du Sénégal et dépendances, 11 June 1870
3 ASAOF, 15G/109/1 (116), Le Commandant de Médine à M. le gouverneur du Sénégal et dépendances, Médine, 14 July 1870; also 15G109/1 (157), 8 Nov. 1870. p. 3

occupé a surveiller ses frères qui . . . l'inquiètent sans cesse'.[1] On the other hand he could not have moved against the Bambara without fearing that he might lose ground to his Tukulor rivals. This consideration probably made him decide to remain at Nioro, where his forces were concentrated and where his defences were assured against attacks, instead of taking the offensive against any of his adversaries. An additional reason for delaying military action was that the rainy season usually began about the end of May. To have attempted to fight during this period would have raised insuperable problems.

Realising how difficult the situation was, Ahmadu attempted to settle with his rivals without recourse to armed conflict. He did this apparently to enable him to concentrate his forces against the Bambara resistance without at the same time leaving Abibu in a stronger position. He could do this by using the Tukulor chiefs and *talibés*, whom he had assembled at Nioro to effect a settlement of the dispute between him and his brothers, especially Abibu. In pursuance of this idea, he sent envoys to Koniakary to summon Abibu to Nioro, if necessary by force. The latter, on receiving the message, replied through the envoys, that he was ill at the moment and unable to move but that he would come as soon as he was fit to travel.[2]

It was believed at the time that Abibu was only temporising in the hope that Ahmadu would soon be leaving Nioro for Segu and that as soon as he had left, Abibu would be able to use the opportunity to establish himself as the ruler of Ka'arta. Ahmadu's message could be seen as an invitation to surrender. This Abibu had no intention of doing. Because of lack of understanding and a common basis for negotiation, this attempt to settle the dispute failed, and since it became clear that a settlement would not be reached without fighting Ahmadu spent what time he still had increasing his military strength. Thus in October 1870 he sent to Saint-Louis, Senegal, for the purchase of 1,500 guns and a quantity of ammunition.[3]

1 ASAOF, 15G109/1 (114), Le Commandant du Cercle de Médine à M. le gouverneur du Sénégal, Médine, 26 June 1870. See also Qlqrunti-mẹhin, 'Resistance movements . . .' for examples of the politics of the resistance movements, in particular the interrelationship between them and intra-Tukulor problems.

2 ASAOF, 15G109/1 (116), Le Commandant du Cercle de Médine à M. le gouverneur, Médine, 14 July 1870

3 ASAOF, 15G109/1 (157) same to same, 8 Nov. 1870

While preparations for a civil war were being made the two principals took care to cultivate friendly relations with the French. They seem to have been competing with each other in assuring the French of their friendly dispositions. On the side of Ahmadu, a Moroccan sharif even intervened to show that he and Ahmadu were both friends of the French. The sharif was at the time staying as a guest of Ahmadu at Nioro, and was probably the same man who had witnessed the ceremony at which the latter took the title of *amīr al-muminīn*. The sharif, it was reported, wrote to the French Commandant at Médine, promising to visit him before long. The Commandant also reported that; 'Je reçois à chaque instant des messages d'Amadou Sékou, de Moktar et des autres fils d'Allagui qui m'assurent de leur amitié.'[1]

One could explain the action of the Tukulor in professing their friendship to the French in terms of their desire to keep out the French from the internal affairs of the empire and prevent them from directly intervening on the side of one or the other party to the struggle. In addition both sides wanted a sure market from which arms and ammunition could be obtained, and this depended largely on the French, who could open or close their arms market at will. It was, for example, from French-controlled markets at Saint Louis that Ahmadu ordered the 1,500 guns mentioned above.

To the French the political situation in the Tukulor empire was welcome. They could get the maximum political and commercial advantages by exploiting the weakness of the Tukulor regime. They could help to keep the regime weak by ensuring the prolongation of the struggle for power by supplying arms and ammunition to both sides. At the time of the Franco-Prussian war, it would have been difficult, if not impossible, for the French to intervene in foreign wars the result of which was not easy to foresee. Since 1860 their immediate concern had been to establish a firmer control over the Senegambian states free from complications which Tukulor interests in the area involved. Now the internal political problems of the Tukulor empire were such that they were left with free hands to pursue their objectives. The only other obstacle they had in the Senegambia were the British who occupied Gambia, and they were now free to continue negotiations which they had opened for a possible exchange of territories.[2]

1 *Ibid.*
2 See Hargreaves, *Prelude to the Partition of West Africa* (1966), for an

By November 1870 the struggle for power among the Tukulor had taken the form of armed conflict. The first effort by Abibu and his supporters to march on Nioro had been made with the attack on the village of Kaniari and neighbouring villages on the Koniakary–Nioro route. This attack was not successful and Abibu and his men had to return to Koniakary. Meantime Ahmadu was mobilising his forces to move on Koniakary, where he hoped to be able to use the arms and ammunition which he had just bought from Saint-Louis.[1] By the beginning of December Ahmadu was reported to be moving his forces from Nioro to take control of the fortified village of Guémou, and there were rumours that Abibu and Moktar would submit to him.[2]

We have no information on the fighting which took place between the forces of Ahmadu and those of Abibu and Moktar. What is known is that before the end of January 1871 Ahmadu had defeated his rivals. In his report the Commandant of the Médine post told the governor of Senegal that Ahmadu had sent his secretary, accompanied by one Muli Hamed, to give him the news of his victory and to thank him (and through him, the governor) for the help rendered to him during the struggle. The Commandant was informed that Moktar had been arrested and chained, and was to be taken to Segu; Ahmadu had, however, not been able to do anything with Abibu who was described as 'le plus turbulent de tous'.[3] With Abibu still at large and active, it was obvious that the victory scored by Ahmadu was at best temporary and indecisive. The arrest of Moktar was not necessarily going to help Ahmadu in tackling the problems that lay ahead. Abibu continued to be active, and his supporters, especially among the *talibés*, were not yet discouraged in the struggle against Ahmadu.

---

account of the Anglo-French negotiations on the French proposals for the exchange of Gambia for other territories in West Africa.

1 ASAOF, 15G109/1 (162), Le Commandant du Cercle de Médine à M. le gouverneur du Sénégal . . ., Médine, 19 Nov. 1870. This letter also contains the information that Ahmadu's men arrived at Médine on 19 November, 1870 to carry the guns and ammunition which had been delivered at the French post there. The consignment had been kept in the house of Moumar Diak, a trading agent of the French company of Maurel et Prom, pending the arrival of Ahmadu's men.

2 ASAOF, 15G109/1 (164), Le Commandant du Cercle de Médine à M. le gouverneur, Médine, 11 Dec. 1870

3 ASAOF, 15G109/ (164), same to same, 25 Jan. 1871

Many of the *talibés*, even in Nioro, disagreed with Ahmadu's handling of the situation and because of their disagreement with him, many of the Tukulor notables from the provinces of Diomboko, Moktar's emirate, and Nioro decided to withdraw their support. Many of them decided to quit the Tukulor empire and return to their original homes in Futa Toro. As a result there occurred a mass movement of the Tukulor from Nioro and Diomboko back to Futa and this weakened the morale and the effectiveness of Ahmadu's army. It also weakened his political position. He had hoped that, with victory in the struggle against his brothers, he would be free to march on and destroy the Bambara resistance movements, particularly the build-up at Guémoukoura. But those who decided to forsake his regime were the most important for the organisation and operation of his army – they were those 'sur lesquels il comptait comme devant être le meilleur noyau de son armée'.[1] The army, having lost its leadership in this way, became subject to other weakening influences. There was, for example, discontent among the Bambara *sofas* who could not see that they had anything to gain in fighting for Ahmadu against other Tukulor or against Bambara resistance movements. The immediate effect of the situation was the thwarting of Ahmadu's plans against the Bambara, in particular the siege being maintained at Guémoukoura.[2] Also, since the notables withdrew as a result of their opposition to him, it is reasonable to assume that they were potentially dangerous to his regime, especially as possible allies for any anti-Ahmadu group that might arise.

Ahmadu attempted to solve his immediate problems by suspending his plans to fight against the Bambara who pitched their camps at Guémoukoura. He devoted his energy to reorganising and increasing his army, but even in this he was faced with great difficulties. Among those of the Tukulor notables who were still around him, the imprisonment of Moktar and the execution of some of the principal supporters of Abibu and Moktar was regarded as outrageous. The action soon became a source of embarrassment to him in his relationship with some of his brothers and *talibés*, who were now refusing to cooperate with him.[3] For example, Aguibu, generally considered as next in rank

1 ASAOF, 15G109/1 (184), same to same, 12 Mar. 1871 2 *Ibid.*
3 ASAOF, 15G109/3 (240), same to same, 21 Nov. 1871: 'L'emprisonnement de deux de ses frères depuis huit mois et l'éxécution de leurs

to Ahmadu,[1] and whom the latter had put in charge of the administration of Segu while leaving for Nioro to fight the movement led
by Abibu and Moktar, refused to respond to a request for a
contingent of soldiers. There were suspicions at Nioro that
Aguibu might be trying to declare himself independent,[2] and
fears of a successful coup made Ahmadu uneasy and eager to
return to Segu. This eagerness explains in part some of the steps
that he took to settle the struggle with Abibu.

The attitude of the *talibés* and other notables is understandable
if one contrasts their position in the traditional Tukulor government system in Futa Toro with what would be their position in
the centralised system which Ahmadu was trying to establish. In
the former Ahmadu would have been at best a *primus inter pares*,
and subject to the control of the *talibés*, especially those of them
who were lineage group leaders. In contrast to this position,
Ahmadu was now making effort to establish himself as a supreme
powerful head, whose authority would be based on a strong,
standing, professional army, comprising largely the Bambara
sofas. The *talibés* could well foresee that if Ahmadu succeeded
their own positions would be those of servants rather than associ-
ates. Apparently to make it impossible to evolve this seeming
Caesarism, many decided to withdraw from Ahmadu's army, the
main instrument relied upon for effecting the change. Moreover,
some of them must have been sincerely convinced that 'Umar
himself, whose administration seems to have confirmed the idea
of 'the just system', never intended that Ahmadu should do this.

The greater part of 1872 was spent by Ahmadu in an effort to
break the movement that was still being led against him by Abibu.
He also continued to plan towards the suppression of the Bambara resistance movements, which, if unsuppressed, might constitute a barrier between Segu and Ka'arta. Abibu, for his part,
continued to reorganise his forces against the inevitable final test
of strength against Ahmadu. In this bid, he had the support of
Tukulor notables from Futa Toro and of the almamy of Futa
Jallon. It is not clear how the latter came into the alliance against
Ahmadu, although it is to be expected that Tukulor notables who

---

principaux partisans, qui vient d'avoir lieu, lui créent de grandes
difficultés.'
1 Oral evidence collected at Segu, 1965
2 ASAOF, 15G109/3 (240), Le Commandant de Médine à M. le gouverneur, 21 Nov. 1871

had left Nioro and Diomboko in protest against the policy of Ahmadu would join forces against him. By January 1872 Abibu, with the help of his allies, had built up a considerable army. Troops estimated at about 10,000 strong were reported to have reached Koundian on their way to Ka'arta where they expected to fight against the forces of Ahmadu. The troops were from both Futa Toro and Futa Jallon. The Futa Jallon contingent was led by Souri, the almamy of Futa Jallon, and Seydou (Sa'id), a brother of Moktar.[1]

Apart from this large-scale military build-up the struggle against Ahmadu also took the form of organised rebellions mounted against his regime in several areas of Ka'arta. Areas where there were rebellions included Diomboko where Moktar had been ruling, Tomora and even Kingui province (with Nioro as capital).[2] For the greater part of the period before the rainy season began in 1872 Ahmadu could do no more than fight to suppress these rebellions while at the same time keeping an eye upon the Bambara resistance movements.

In the struggle for power between Ahmadu and Abibu the French as in 1870–71, remained uncommitted to either side. Their main interest was to see commerce continue to flourish in their various trading posts, particularly at Médine and Bakel. Hitherto the political trouble in the Tukulor empire had been beneficial to French economic interests, as they had been able to sell arms and other goods to all concerned. In 1872, however, the situation in the Tukulor empire gave rise to anxiety because the raids on trade routes being carried out by anti-Ahmadu forces were having adverse effects on French commerce. At the beginning of the rebellions of 1872 in Ka'arta it was reported that the only damage done to French commerce was in relation to the trade in grain 'apporté prèsque éxclusivement par les Toucouleurs'.[3] It was regretted that the caravan routes in Diomboko were almost completely closed, but that the Moorish caravans were still able to bring their goods to the posts after paying the necessary duties

1 ASAOF, 15G109/4 (242), same to same, 6 Jan. 1872
2 *Ibid.*, also correspondence from same to same contained in 15G109/4 (243), Médine, 3 Feb. 1872; 15G109/4 (244), Médine, 16 Feb. 1872; and 15G109/4 (246), Médine, 26 Mar. 1872
3 ASAOF, 15G109/4 (242), Le Commandant de Médine à M. le gouverneur, 6 Jan. 1872.

in Diomboko.[1] As the rebellions continued and pillaging of caravans increased the damage to commercial interests became more grievous, but even then the French avoided all direct interference in the internal problems of the Tukulor, though they made efforts to limit the rebellions and their effects on trade. Thus when it was rumoured that Sambala, their ally at Médine, was aiding the Tomora people in their raids on Diomboko, the French took immediate preventive action. Reporting to the governor, the Commandant of Médine noted:

> Le premier but à atteindre est la neutralité complète du Khasso. Nous avons le droit de l'éxiger d'après le traité passé avec Sambala par lequel il s'engage à proteger notre commerce. . . . L'importance de cette affaire est toute commerciale; j'aurai donc soin de consulter les traitants et toutes mes mesures seront prises de concert avec eux.[2]

The representatives of French commercial interests in Médine, led by the commandant, accordingly brought pressure on Sambala to desist from aiding the raids in Diomboko, and in his letter to the governor of Senegal on the issue, Sambala claimed that he was not in any way connected with the rebellions and raids in Ka'arta.[3] The governor, apparently not satisfied, wrote to Sambala on 8 May 1872 on the bad effects the rebellions were having on French trade, pointing out that his action was inconsistent with the treaty of 30 September 1855 which had been concluded with the French. The governor pointed out: 'Il y avait, en effet, lieu de craindre que ces pillages amenassent un résultat fâcheux pour notre commerce avec Ka'arta; en empêchant les petites caravanes de venir à l'escale par la crainte d'être attaquées en route.'[4] From this it is clear that the preoccupation of the French at this time was to protect their commercial interests in the Tukulor empire, and as long as such interests were protected, who won in the struggle between Ahmadu and Abibu was not important. They were, however, eager to limit the area covered by the rebellions so that peace could be re-established early enough for trade to recover.

With the French abstaining from direct intervention the Tukulor continued their struggle for power and by June 1872

1 *Ibid.*
2 ASAOF, 15G109/4 (244), same to same, Bakel, 16 Feb. 1872
3 ASAOF, 15G109/4 (247), Sambala à M. le gouverneur, Médine, 6 Apr. 1872
4 ANSOM, in Sénégal I, 56d, 'Moniteur de la Flotte', Paris, 15 May 1872

when the rains had begun, a temporary end had been brought to the rebellions, and the trade routes were once more open for the caravans. This made it possible for the Moors to bring their gum for sale at the French trading posts at Médine and French commerce enjoyed another period of boom. According to Valière, the governor of Senegal, by August 1872 the volume of the gum trade for that season had already exceeded the total for that of the previous year. The governor explained that this was due to the cessation of hostilities in Ka'arta, and hoped that peace would continue within the Tukulor empire.[1]

The cessation of hostilities came with the beginning of the rainy season during which hardly any fighting could be done as the rivers would be flooded. It was also the time when people could usefully engage in their agricultural work. But Ahmadu was also eager to end his involvements in Ka'arta for another reason. He was disquietened by reports of events in Segu where, he feared, Aguibu was plotting to overthrow his authority and assume control. He was anxious to return there to establish himself before the situation became impossible. By June 1872 he was reported to be building up his army for a march on Segu 'pour remplacer sous son autorité ce pays qui profitait de la guerre du Ka'arta pour chercher à recouvrer son indépendance.'[2]

But as long as Abibu remained armed and determined to continue the struggle Ahmadu would not dare to leave Ka'arta. Because of lack of co-operation from the Tukulor notables it was clear that any idea of ending the war through immediate military action was out of the question. Since Ahmadu found it imperative to make an early return to Segu, he had to resort to negotiations with Abibu with a view to ending the struggle. Peace in Ka'arta, he must have calculated, would give him a free hand to deal with Aguibu in Segu.

In the negotiations for peace, Moktar, whom Ahmadu had imprisoned since early in 1871, and Fatma, Ahmadu's mother, who had been put at Dinguiray by 'Umar and was now in Abibu's custody, became useful pawns. Ahmadu wanted his mother with him at Segu and in 1871 he had made an unsuccessful military effort to secure her release.[3] Abibu thereafter de-

1 ASAOF, 13G23/16, Situation générale de la Colonie, 12 Aug. 1872
2 ANSOM, in Sénégal I, 56d, 'Moniteur de la flotte', Paris, 15 June 1872
3 ASAOF, 15G109/3 (216), M. le Directeur des affaires politiques à

manded, as a condition for releasing Ahmadu's mother, the release of Moktar, his brother. Abibu also insisted that on his release, Moktar should be reappointed ruler in charge of Diomboko.

To have reinstated Moktar in his post at Diomboko would have meant a confirmation of the position of the forces opposed to him under the leadership of Abibu. Ahmadu did not like this and he thought of breaking the resistance of Abibu through military expeditions against Diomboko, Futa Toro and Dinguiray. The Tukulor notables in Nioro, however, refused to cooperate, claiming that they were tired of wars. It was of course not in the interest of the Nioro notables to help Ahmadu to become as strong as he wanted, but rather to prevent his effort at establishing a centralised, patrimonial political system. Faced with opposition Ahmadu gave up the idea of a new campaign and concentrated his efforts on ensuring the effective administration of Nioro, and assuring himself of the loyalty of the *talibés* there.[1]

For some time he continued to build up his army at Nioro, with a view to using it, if necessary, to effect his return to Segu. But his earlier plan to send expeditions against Dinguiray and Futa Toro was having adverse repercussions. The French saw this plan as dangerous because if Ahmadu succeeded in controlling the two banks of the Senegal, French commercial interests would be completely dependent on his whims and caprices. A way of preventing Ahmadu from achieving this objective was to stop the sale of arms to him, and to this end the French reached some understanding with Bubakar Sa'ada, the almamy of Bondu, who agreed to stop all caravans coming from the Gambia and carrying arms towards Ka'arta.[2] They also placed an embargo on sales of arms by the French merchants to Ahmadu.[3]

With the opposition of the Nioro *talibés* and the reaction of the French, Ahmadu found it impossible to prosecute any of his plans. He remained virtually immobilised at Nioro until January 1873 when pressure was brought on him to release Moktar, before the *talibés* would agree to furnish him with an army and accompany

---

Saint-Louis, Médine, 24 June 1871; 15G109/3 (222), M. le Directeur des affaires politiques à Saint-Louis, Médine, 20 July 1871

1 ASAOF, 1G109/4 (250), Le Commandant de Médine à M. le gouverneur, Médine, 26 June 1872; also same to same in 15G109/4 (251), Médine, 1 Aug. 1872.

2 ASAOF, 1G109/4 (251), same to same, 1 Aug. 1872

3 ASAOF, 15G109/4 (257), same to same, 15 Nov. 1872

him to Segu.[1] It was apparently because he found himself in an impasse that Ahmadu agreed to release Moktar and return him to his post in Diomboko in exchange for his mother, whom Abibu agreed to release from Dinguiray.[2]

Thus ended what was to be only the first phase of the struggle between Ahmadu and Abibu in Ka'arta. The struggle had lasted over two years at the end of which Ahmadu gained no more than the effective control of Kingui province (Nioro) and Abibu and Moktar remained very much in the same position that they had been before the outbreak of hostilities in 1870.

Ahmadu had to go back to Segu to establish his authority against any possible rival such as Aguibu. Before leaving, however, he put Muhammad Muntaga, one of his brothers, in charge of Nioro, and took with him Mustafa who had ruled the place till his arrival at Nioro in 1869. By March 1873 Ahmadu had left Ka'arta with such army as he was able to collect and was heading for Segu.[3]

Though an agreement had been reached in this way, it was quite clear to both sides that a final settlement had only been postponed. Both sides therefore spent the rainy season in preparations for a war that appeared inevitable before any conclusive settlement could be reached. In this phase of the struggle, the principal characters were still Ahmadu, Abibu and Moktar; but in place of Mustafa we now have Muntaga. Ahmadu had appointed Muntaga in charge of Nioro in the hope that he would serve as a counterpoise to the influence of Abibu and Moktar. Being, like them, a son of 'Umar it was expected that he would enjoy more support and prestige among the *talibés* than Mustafa, the ex-slave, had had. As a son of 'Umar he was expected to be more personally involved in the politics of the empire and to have his own interests to protect against the ambition of the other two brothers. It was probably because he believed that Muntaga nursed some hatred and envy against Abibu and Moktar that Ahmadu had appointed him to Nioro, hoping that he would always remain loyal to him against them. On the other hand, it was believed that Muntaga distrusted Ahmadu, and only submitted to his authority with reluctance and impatience. It was believed

1 ASAOF, 15G109/5 (259), same to same, 21 Jan. 1873
2 Pietri, *Les Français au Niger*, pp. 102–6
3 ASAOF, 15G109/5 (261), Le Commandant de Médine à M. le gouverneur, Médine, 24 Mar. 1873

191

that he was not pleased with owing his position to Ahmadu and that he believed that he ought to have been in a position of power as of right.¹ It was therefore difficult to predict what role he would play in the impending clashes, the more so as he did not declare support for either side while both were preparing.

In preparation for war, Abibu intercepted and appropriated by force the tributes being carried from the various emirates to Ahmadu at Segu. In addition, he dispossessed and drove out the *talibés* who were still loyal to Ahmadu in Dinguiray. Moktar, once restored to Diomboko, continued his collaboration with Abibu. He also persecuted Ahmadu's supporters in Diomboko. Some of the pro-Ahmadu *talibés* in Diomboko had attempted to resist his authority by controlling a few villages against his will. Moktar acted vigorously and fiercely to suppress their revolt until the defeated partisans of Ahmadu emigrated, and he regained firm control of the situation. These measures which amounted to a declaration of war on Ahmadu took place in June 1873.²

Abibu chose June to begin hostilities because it was the beginning of the rainy season during which the rivers were usually flooded and difficult to cross. The Niger in particular usually overflowed its banks and the torrents often became so rapid that it would be extremely difficult for an army to use the river for passage. From the military point of view, therefore, Segu was usually virtually cut off from Ka'arta during the rainy season.³ With Ahmadu virtually confined to Segu, his rivals expected that they would find it easy to control Ka'arta.

Having established firm control over Diomboko, the supporters of Abibu and Moktar in Nioro put pressure on Muntaga to support them. Muntaga realised that Abibu and Moktar were already in a strong position in the struggle, and though he did not like them enough to be a willing collaborator he did not want to be openly against them. But even though he felt constrained to cooperate with them, he did not want to do so openly because although Abibu was already marching his army from Dinguiray, he had not yet made juncture with Moktar, and news reaching him indicated that Ahmadu was sparing no pains in his effort to move his forces to Ka'arta. Muntaga's aim seems to have been to guarantee his own position no matter who won. If Ahmadu was

1 Pietri, *Les Français au Niger*, pp. 106–9
2 *Ibid.*, pp. 110, 112
3 *Ibid.*, p. 111

successfully cut off in Segu then it was certain that Abibu and Moktar would win and it would be in Muntaga's interest to collaborate with them. Conversely, if Ahmadu reached Ka'arta early enough with his army Muntaga would support him and still keep his position at Nioro. While Abibu and Moktar appeared to be in a stronger position, however, Muntaga continued to send them reinforcements.[1]

Ahmadu too was busy with preparations during the rainy season. More than ever before, he was generous to the *talibés* and made every effort to get their unflinching loyalty. He also continued to build up his forces. His army succeeded in crossing the river Niger at Fogni on 15 December 1873, arriving at Nioro towards the end of the month.[2] The wars which were fought as part of the struggle for Ka'arta between Ahmadu and his brothers took place in the dry season of 1874.

With the arrival of Ahmadu at Nioro, Muntaga quickly changed course, deserting Abibu and Moktar with whom he had hitherto collaborated hesitantly. The military support which, henceforth, he gave to Ahmadu contributed to the success of the latter against his brothers and rivals. The wars ended with the defeat and arrest of Abibu and Moktar, and consequently with Ahmadu establishing his authority over Ka'arta.[3]

However, even after his victory many of the *talibés* in Nioro did not support Ahmadu as he had hoped; he found that they were largely unenthusiastic, some even hostile, with many of them refusing to follow him to Segu as he demanded. Many of them sincerely could not see anything wrong in the action of Abibu and Moktar. They were convinced that 'Umar never intended that Ahmadu should reign supreme. According to the evidence of Samba Ndiaye, one of Ahmadu's close aides who informed Soleillet on the events in the country, some of the *talibés* saw the problem as one of whether or not Abibu and Moktar should have a share in the heritage of their father. They were convinced that the brothers were entitled to their own part of the heritage and so could not see why Ahmadu should put them in chains like criminals. The *talibés* argued that if 'Umar had not meant that each of his sons should have control of parts of the empire, he

1 *Ibid.*, pp. 112–13
2 *Ibid.*, pp. 113–14
3 See *ibid.*, pp. 115–24 for details of the manoeuvres and battles between Ahmadu on the one hand and Abibu and Moktar on the other.

would not have built treasuries in the headquarters of each province. They saw the measures taken by Ahmadu only as an expression of his excessive desire for power, and a wish to establish an autocracy.[1] It was not only the *talibés* who had always been in Nioro and who had demonstrated loyalty to Abibu and Moktar who opposed Ahmadu; there were also some from Segu who demonstrated their opposition.

It would appear that the *talibés* from Segu had their own grievances against Ahmadu because of the latter's reliance upon his *sofas*, the Bambara recruits who formed the majority of his army. They accused him of wanting to carry everything with him to Segu 'où, l'un de ces jours, tu te feras adorer par le kafir, comme une idole'.[2] The reference to 'kafir' (unbelievers) worshipping him was an expression of what the *talibés* thought of the relationship between the *sofas*, mostly of Bambara, non-Muslim origin, and Ahmadu. Many of the *talibés* had often shown dislike for the prominent positions occupied by some *sofa* chiefs in Ahmadu's administration, which they could contrast with the situation under other Tukulor rulers like Ahmadu Tijani in Masina and Abibu and Moktar, in Dinguiray and Diomboko respectively. Many of the *talibés* from both Nioro and Segu opted to stay in various parts of Ka'arta, where they were nearer to their original homes in Futa Toro rather than follow Ahmadu to Segu. He appealed to them in vain that they should come with him to Segu and help in suppressing the resistance of the 'unbelievers' at Sandanding. With the refusal of Ahmadu to release Abibu and Moktar, many of the *talibés* could no longer support him 'parce que l'émir leur paraissait devenir trop autoritaire'.[3]

Ahmadu of course relied upon his Bambara *sofas* to maintain his position and centralise the administration of the empire. The Tukulor aristocracy did not like his objective nor the instruments he was using to achieve it. Hence the complaint against the *sofas* and the refusal to be moved by Ahmadu's religious appeal.

ADMINISTRATIVE REORGANISATION OF THE EMPIRE

In spite of discontent against his regime from many members of the aristocracy Ahmadu took advantage of the opportunity created

1 Soleillet, *Voyage à Ségou 1878–1879*, pp. 375–7
2 *Ibid.*, p. 377
3 *Ibid.*, p. 378

by his victory to strengthen his position and assume greater control of the empire. Up till 1873 he had been master over the Segu section only, but with the defeat of Abibu and Moktar early in 1874, he became also master over Ka'arta. The only part of the empire now outside his control was Masina, where the position of Ahmadu Tijani remained strong and unchallengeable. Ahmadu consolidated his position by reorganising the administration of Ka'arta. He divided it into emirates and appointed those who were loyal to him as emirs, including Muhammad Muntaga, who was put in charge of Nioro, and made to represent the supreme authority of Ahmadu in Ka'arta. Notable among the other emirs, who were made responsible to Muntaga, were Seydou (Sa'īd), Bassiru, Daye, Daha, Nuru and Ahmadu Moktar. A condition of their appointment was that they would all come to Segu once a year for one of the principal Muslim festivals.[1] This was apparently to create opportunity for consultation.

At the end of the civil wars in Ka'arta in 1874 the Tukulor empire had two principal figures at the head of its administration: Ahmadu in Segu and Ka'arta, and Ahmadu Tijani in Masina. Ahmadu did not take kindly to the independence of Masina within the Tukulor empire, and he would have liked to put it under his direct control as he had succeeded in doing in Ka'arta. Nevertheless faced with internal problems in Segu and Ka'arta, he had meanwhile to reconcile himself to the fact that Ahmadu Tijani's position in Masina was impregnable. The latter had seized the occasion of the struggle in Ka'arta to further strengthen his own position. Victory in Ka'arta did not therefore necessarily put Ahmadu in any stronger position in relation to Masina. Three years after he had established control over Ka'arta, he had still not contained the opposition to his regime well enough to be able to tackle Masina, where Ahmadu Tijani was reported as profiting 'habilement des dissensions qui survivent entre les vainqueurs après les succes'.[2]

Although no open clashes are known to have occurred between Ahmadu and Tijani, the relationship between them remained

1 Oral evidence collected at Segu 1965; also ASAOF, 1G63/2, Notice sur El Hadj Omar, Saint-Louis, 25 May 1878; Soleillet, *Voyage à Ségou 1878–1879*, pp. 379–84
2 ANSOM, in Sénégal I, 61C, G. Brière de l'Isle, Gouverneur du Sénégal, à M. le Ministre de la Marine et des Colonies, Saint-Louis, 22 Aug. 1877

strained, and fraught with mutual suspicion. In 1878 the relationship was bad enough for Ahmadu to suspect that Tijani might
ally with foreigners against him. He forbade Soleillet, a French
commercial agent on a mission to the Tukulor empire, to go to
Masina, on the grounds that the roads were unsafe. Soleillet
however reported that from the evidence available at Segu, the
main reason for Ahmadu's action was that he feared a possible
alliance between the French and Ahmadu Tijani.[1] The existence
of Masina as an independent unit continued until 1891, long after
Ahmadu Tijani had died and only because the Tukulor demonstrated group solidarity to accommodate Ahmadu, whom the
French soldiers had chased out of Nioro.

Although Masina remained independent of him, Ahmadu's victory in Ka'arta seems to have strengthened his position in Segu
where he had feared his regime threatened. On his return in 1874,
Ahmadu settled amicably with Aguibu, who had been ruling Segu
while he was fighting in Ka'arta, and other people whom he had
feared to be planning to overthrow him. But although the country
was reported peaceful after the settlement,[2] Ahmadu did not trust
Aguibu. According to the information given to the commandant
of Médine by Bassiru, the newly appointed emir of Diomboko,
Ahmadu was keeping Aguibu under watch at Segu, and would
not send him out as emir for fear that he might declare his
independence.[3]

In the Ka'arta section of the empire the newly appointed emirs
appeared to have the situation under control, but the anti-
Ahmadu groups continued to express their discontent by
occasional acts of violence. Evidence of cooperation among the
emirs exists, but among the emirs and some lesser officials there
were men whose attitude to the problems of the empire ranged
from sheer indifference to virtual rebellion. By about August 1874
rebellion broke out in Diafounou against the authority of Nuru,
the newly appointed emir. In an effort to suppress the rebellion
which was becoming difficult for Nuru to control, Bassiru, the

1 Explorations dans le royaume de Ségou – Conférence faite pour M.
   Soleillet le 26 mai 1879, *Bulletin de la Société des Etudes Coloniales et
   Maritimes*, May 1879, p. 133
2 ASAOF, 15G109/6 (281), Le Commandant de Médine à M. le gouverneur, Médine, 28 Mar. 1874; same to same in 15G109/6 (283), Médine,
   23 Apr. 1874 for much the same information.
3 ASAOF, 15G109/6 (288), Le Commandant de Médine à M. le gouverneur, Médine, 28 June 1874

emir of Diomboko, sent a contingent of troops to Diafounou. Bassiru's contingent was commanded by Assa Madi, one-time interim ruler of Diomboko. Others who aided Nuru to suppress the rebellion included Bassiru's brother Mourtada, Dahe the emir of Diala, and the ruler of Logo in Khasso.[1] The war in Diafounou continued until the end of October when the Tukulor forces succeeded in breaking the rebellion. The menace had been so serious that Nuru decided to build a fortress at Tambakhara, his headquarters, to cater for the future defences of the empire in the area.[2] The action of Bassiru and others in this case typified co-operation among Tukulor rulers in Ka'arta.

One has no evidence to indicate the attitude of Muhammad Muntaga to the Diafounou episode. But one could make some deductions from the fact that the aid to Nuru was initiated and coordinated by Bassiru and not by Muntaga, who was regarded as the head of the Ka'arta section and representative of Ahmadu's authority. That he let leadership of the Tukulor slip to Bassiru on this issue might have been evidence of his indifference. But it could also have been that Muntaga himself was at the time involved in quelling rebellion. There is evidence that Diavoye, a former chief of Tomora where Abibu and Moktar had found support in 1873, was still leading a rebellion against Ahmadu's regime in the Nioro area in December 1874.[3]

There were clear cases among Tukulor officials of lack of cooperation with, and even rebellion against, the regime headed by Ahmadu. An example was the case of Moriba Safere, district head of Saro, who refused to obey Bassiru, his emir, especially when the latter asked him to furnish a contingent of troops to be sent against the rebellion in Diafounou. Moriba Safere was so difficult in his attitude that Ahmadu had to intervene to settle the feud between him and Bassiru,[4] but this intervention did not prevent war from breaking out between the two in 1876. Moriba Safere had the support of the almamy of Timbo in Futa Jallon while Bassiru had the support of Logo and some other Tukulor emirates.[5] Faced with greater forces from Diomboko Moriba

1 ASAOF, in 15G109/6 (6), 'Copie du Régistre Politique – mois de Septembre 1874, Médine'.
2 *Ibid.* Nov. 1874
3 *Ibid.*, Dec. 1874
4 *Ibid.*, and 15G109/6 (b), Oct. 1874
5 ASAOF, 15G110/1 (327), Le Commandant du Poste à M. le gouver-

Safere, rather than submit, escaped and found refuge apparently among the resistance groups in Diafounou.[1] This evidence of Tukulor rulers fighting each other indicates the weakness of the administration in Ka'arta. Again, we do not as yet have evidence to show the attitude of Muhammad Muntaga on this issue, but one would have expected him to intervene in the affair instead of leaving it to Ahmadu to settle from Segu.

Perhaps the greatest weakness of Ahmadu's administration arose from the lack of adequate communication between Segu, the capital, and outlying districts like Ka'arta. Lack of communication made it difficult, and sometimes impossible, for Ahmadu to control, or at least supervise the activities of his emirs. The empire was plagued by resistance movements organised by the various subject groups, particularly the Bambara. Each Tukulor ruler found the task of suppressing such movements a difficult and absorbing job, and it was often imperative for each governor to deploy his forces for the maintenance of security within his own district or province, and to take less interest in events in other parts of the empire. In some cases the resistance movements created effective barriers between the different areas of the empire. For example, the armed resistance of the Bambara in Beledugu virtually cut away communications between Segu and Masina as it was difficult to cross Beledugu without massive military expeditions.[2]

Given the situation it was easy for an ambitious provincial ruler to attempt to become independent of Ahmadu. On their appointment, in order to make consultation and deliberation possible, Ahmadu had instructed his emirs to come to Segu once a year to celebrate one of the principal Muslim festivals. But apart from Bassiru and Nuru,[3] the emirs generally did not obey this instruction. In July 1877, for example, Ahmadu invited Muntaga and Bassiru to Segu to celebrate the *Id-el-Kabir* (*tabaski*) festival, and it was generally believed that he wanted to

---

neur, Médine, 25 Jan. 1876, also same to same in 15G110/1 (328), Médine, 10 Mar. 1876; 15G110/1 (331), June 1876; and 15G110/1 (333), Médine, 4 July 1876

1 ASAOF, 15G110/1 (334), Le Commandant du Poste à M. le gouverneur, Médine, 7 Sept. 1876.
2 Archinard, *Rapport Militaire . . . 1888–1889*
3 Oral evidence collected at Segu, 1965

use the occasion to discuss with his brothers the problems of the empire;[1] neither attended.

It is not known why Muntaga did not go. Bassiru was said to have sent a message explaining that he had to stay at Koniakary to be near enough to settle the problem coming up at Logo.[2] This reason was genuine,[3] but Muntaga appears to have stayed away out of habit. The situation was conducive to the development of separatist feelings among the Tukulor rulers, and those who were ambitious did not lose the opportunity to rule as if they were heading separate states. Thus by 1880 it was already reported that Muhammad Muntaga, Daye and Muniru were not on good terms with Ahmadu and were ruling their areas without any reference to him.[4]

Muntaga, apart from his personal ambitions, constituted a focus of other discontented forces. In any case, Ahmadu seems to have envisaged trouble in that quarter and went ahead to build his own forces against a possible struggle. As part of his efforts to win over the *talibés*, in November 1878 he arranged marriages between several of them and some of his own relatives. Paul Soleillet, who was at Segu at the time, reported marriages between Ahmadu's relatives and Ahmadu Souliman Diom, Amedeki, Mahmadou Tierno, Mamadou Baba, Mamadou Boubakar, Samba Lili, Ahmadu L'Amin, and Bouiel, all but one of whom were *talibés* from Nioro, explaining: 'L'émir espère, par ces mariages, les détacher de Moult Aga [*sic*] et les fixer auprès de lui. Ils sont d'ailleurs tenus d'avoir une maison à Sikoro, les soeurs de l'émir ne devant pas quitter la ville.'[5]

All these preparations clearly indicated that trouble existed within the empire. Ahmadu himself told Bubakar b. Alfa Saʿīd, one of his supporters at Nioro, how widespread the discontent might be, and that there were plotters against his regime, not only

1 ASAOF, 15G111/1 (18) Le Commandant du Poste de Médine à M. le gouverneur . . ., Médine, 13 July 1877
2 ASAOF, 15G111/1 (32), Le Commandant de Médine à M. le gouverneur, Médine, 30 Oct. 1877
3 Another conflict, again involving the French and the Tukulor, broke out between Sambala of Médine and the Khasso provinces of Logo and Natiaga in 1877. The conflict was halted only after the French had broken Sabousire, headquarters of Logo, in 1878.
4 ASAOF, in 15G111/1, M. le Dr Bayol à M. le Commandant Supérieur, Bakel, 12 June 1880
5 Soleillet, *Voyage à Ségou 1878–1879*, p. 437

at Nioro but even in Segu.[1] Clearly he was convinced of the possibility of struggle between him and Muntaga. The struggle, leading to civil war, did not come until 1884.[2]

The French maintained a neutral stand while the civil wars were being fought in the Ka'arta section of the Tukulor empire between 1873 and 1874. This was because, unlike in 1872 when Ahmadu's action was seen as damaging to French commercial interests, they did not for the moment feel that the situation represented any threat to their commerce. It may be recalled that in 1872 Ahmadu, in his bid to crush Abibu's movement, had planned to send military expeditions against Dinguiray and the Futa Toro. The French saw the move as detrimental to their interests and they therefore took steps to stop the supply of arms to him not only from Senegal but also from the Gambia. By this move the position of Ahmadu in the struggle for supremacy was made difficult, and he had to withdraw to Segu without achieving his mission. In the process he seems to have realised that it was unrealistic to pursue policies, or adopt tactics, that would alienate the French while he was faced with internal problems of the empire. During the struggle against Abibu and Moktar, therefore, he took steps to restore friendly relations between him and the French. He appeased the French by easing the conditions under which they traded with the Tukulor empire. This was done partly by reopening the caravan routes linking the French posts to the Ka'arta section of the empire. Those routes had been closed during the wars of 1870–72. In addition Ahmadu waived the payment to the Tukulor administration of duties normally chargeable on the merchandise of the Moors trading with the French. He sent an envoy to the French commandant of Médine in February 1873 to inform him that the newly appointed interim ruler of Diomboko, Assa Madi, had been instructed to refund duties already paid by the French agents at Médine. Ahmadu informed the commandant that the only condition for the refund would be the presentation of a note from the commandant by any of the agents concerned. The commandant reported that the promise given by Ahmadu was being fulfilled, and mentioned specifically

1 ASAOF, 15G76/5 (2) Traduction des lettres d'Ahmadou trouvées à Nioro – no. 11, à Bubakar ben Alfa Seidou (n.d.)
2 See Chapter 8 below.

the case of one Ibrahim Gouya who had fifty guinea pieces refunded to him.[1]

With these concessions granted to them the French saw their commercial interests protected. They now regarded Ahmadu's administration as friendly and saw no reasons for continuing with the strained relations of 1872 which had been marked by the French embargo on arms and ammunitions to Ahmadu. Indeed by March 1873 the commandant of Médine was able to report on French relations with Ahmadu's regime, saying: 'Les relations que j'ai pu établir avec lui sont très amicales.'[2] This change to friendly relations came, happily enough for Ahmadu, at a time when the political situation in the Tukulor empire was precarious and the struggle for supremacy in Ka'arta had just been halted temporarily. With the friendly relations restored between him and the French, Ahmadu was able to tackle his internal problems as they arose with the assurance that the French would remain neutral if not really helpful. Partly, it was the attitude of the French which made it possible for him to tackle and defeat his rivals, Abibu and Moktar, in 1873–74.

The French at this time were preoccupied with the expansion of commerce, and in relation to the Western Sudan they were eager to monopolise the commerce of the Senegambian region, the control of which was regarded as vital to the control of the commerce with the Tukulor empire. When the politics of the Tukulor empire threatened their position in the Senegambian area, as in 1872, they reacted in an unfriendly manner. But when, as was the case from 1873, Tukulor politics left them a free hand to work out their policy, they reciprocated with friendship, caring less which of the contestants was in control.

The only other competitors against the French in the Senegambian region were the British who occupied the Gambia. The French continued to bring pressure on the British to cede the Gambia to them. This was because they thought that the control of the Gambia would give them the monopoly of the commerce of the Senegambian area. The importance of this monopoly was seen in relation to the Western Sudan (really the Tukulor empire) whose economy could thereby be controlled without any

1 ASAOF, 15G109/5 (260), Le Commandant de Médine à M. le gouverneur, Médine, 28 Feb. 1873
2 ASAOF, 15G109/5 (261) same to same, 24 Mar. 1873

recourse to arms. The governor of Senegal pointed out in 1872 the importance which his administration attached to the possession of the Gambia, saying: 'Nous ne pourrons nous dissimuler que le gouvernement de la colonie ne sera le souverain dispensateur des événements du Soudan que lorsqu' il possédera la Gambie.'[1] It was this desire to control the economy of the Tukulor empire by establishing themselves exclusively in the Senegambian region which made the French push ahead negotiations with the British Government.[2]

While these negotiations were going on, and the Tukulor were preoccupied with their civil wars and their aftermath, the French geared up their efforts to turn the Tukulor empire into their commercial sphere of influence. Each officer sent out into the field was told to make the development of French commerce his primary duty and each officer, especially the commandants of posts, made every effort to let his actions be guided by the needs of French commercial interests. Commercial interests exerted considerable influence on French overseas policy at this period, and their opinion was often considered important in evaluating the work of officers in the field. Conscious of this, officers usually did their best to be on good terms with the commercial groups. An example was the commandant of Médine who in 1874 was given a certificate of competence and good conduct by the French commercial agents at Médine. In a certificate signed by forty-three traders ('traitants'), the governor of Senegal was told that the commandant, Monsieur Bourillet 'a fidèlement et dignement remplit la mission qui lui a été confiée'.[3]

The French commercial houses had considerable influence in this period on the direction of French external relations. Their major interest in Africa appears to have been the development and control of the commerce of the Sahara region and the Western Sudan, where they were eager to eliminate the British presence which was considered an obstacle to the development of French interests. France already had colonies in Algeria and Senegal, and it was thought that it would be in her best interest

1 ANSOM, in Sénégal I, 56a, V. Valière, Gouverneur du Sénégal et dépendances à M. le Ministre de la Marine et des Colonies, Saint-Louis, 15 June 1872
2 Hargreaves, *Prelude to the Partition* . . . for a survey of these negotiations.
3 ASAOF, in 15G109/6, Certificat, Médine, 10 June 1874

to use these two places as bases for the expansion of commerce with the Sahara and the Western Sudan. Moreover, the Sahara was considered a vital link between Algeria and Senegal. It was to exploit the possibility of using the Sahara in this way that Paul Soleillet was sent out on an exploratory mission in 1874 by 'la Société de Geographie de Lyon'. It was while carrying out this mission that he reached In-Salah on 6 March 1874.[1]

Adopting Soleillet's report the Avignon Chamber of Commerce argued that the Sahara had not been directing its commerce to Algeria, partly because of the hostility of the population towards the French. They explained that the hostility arose originally from the French occupation of Algeria during which the Muslim fanatics withdrew into the Sahara. Lack of commercial relations between Algeria and the Sahara was also explained as due to the lack of French trading posts in the Sahara. The Chamber of Commerce then claimed that the establishment of French consulates or agents to take care of French nationals, protect French commerce and safeguard French influence in the Sahara and the Sudan was imperative.[2] The Chamber proposed a programme that needed a good deal of political action and commitment and which could therefore be embarked on only by the state. The Chamber recognised that the state would have to be committed but they also argued that

> C'est de cette manière seulement que nous attirerons à nous le commerce du Sahara. Jusqu' ici cette déviation du commerce a profité à l'Angleterre; et cependant, au dire de M. Soleillet, et d'après l'allemand Gerald Rolffs, . . . les produits français sont plus appréciés dans le Sahara que les produits Anglais.[3]

This episode was typical of the efforts which the commercial interests in France were making to influence the direction of French external relations. The mission of 1874 carried out by Soleillet was important as a prelude to that which he later carried out to Segu in 1878–79. It kindled interest in the idea of linking Algeria with Senegal through the Sudan (meaning the Tukulor empire), especially by way of Timbuktu. The idea behind all these missions was to ensure for the French the monopoly of commerce of the Western Sudan, from which they hoped to

1 *Voyage d'Alger à Saint-Louis du Sénégal par Tombouctou (Conférence du M. Paul Soleillet)* (1875), p. 31

2 *Ibid.*, p. 12

3 *Ibid.*, p. 13

exclude all other European powers. They were convinced this could be achieved through diplomacy alone, and without attempting a military conquest. In all these movements, the commercial interests took the initiative and got the government to orientate its policy accordingly. Because of the influence of the commercial interests on the formulation of external policy, the French were extremely reluctant to get involved in the internal affairs of the Tukulor, especially when the internal situation could not be said to be having bad effects on French commerce.

Thus although the civil wars which ended with the victory of Ahmadu in 1874 left over some disturbing effects on Tukulor politics, the French did not seek to interfere in the internal problems of the empire. Rather, because the Tukulor did not interfere with their commerce, they sought to strengthen the friendly relations already existing between them. In 1874, for example, M. Valière, the governor of Senegal, seized the occasion of the visit to Saint Louis of one Tambo, said to be an envoy of Ahmadu, to propose a new treaty to the Tukulor ruler. He sent a draft treaty to Ahmadu, and although no reply came from the latter, another effort was made in 1875 to get him to agree to another treaty, the draft of which was sent through a messenger.[1]

The French concern for commerce was also evident in their reaction to the civil wars which were fought between Moriba Safere of Sero and Bassiru of Diomboko in 1876. In these wars Sambala of Médine, an ally of the French, had aided Moriba Safere because of his hatred of the Tukulor regime. The French felt the detrimental effects of the wars on their commerce, but rather than interfere directly in the internal problems of the Tukulor, they decided to limit the extent of the wars by bringing

1 ASAOF, 13G23/17, Notes sur la situation générale de la colonie laissées à mon successeur, Valière, Saint-Louis, 20 May 1876; Hargreaves, 'The Tokolor empire of Segou and its relations with the French', pp. 135/6; Saint-Martin, 'Les relations diplomatiques entre la France et l'empire Toucouleur de 1860 à 1887', *Bull. IFAN*, B. xxvii, 1965, esp. pp. 192–6. Saint-Martin's version of Valière's relations with the Tukulor conveys the wrong impression that a treaty was indeed concluded between the two. Kanya-Forstner echoes this error when he says 'This agreement also remained unratified . . .', see Kanya-Forstner, *The Conquest of the Western Sudan: A Study in French Military Imperialism* (1969), p. 50. Contrary to what Saint-Martin and Kanya-Forstner claim, the negotiations initiated by Valière were in fact abortive.

pressure to bear on Sambala, their ally, to stop all cooperation with either of the warring parties. Valière, the governor of Senegal, wrote to Sambala disapproving of his action and warning him against further intervention in the affairs of the Tukulor.[1]

The French attitude was dictated partly by the fact that they could not afford the means required to meet the consequences of military involvement but more important was the fact that they were reluctant to do anything that would spoil the good relations which had hitherto ensured for them profitable commercial activities. The wars in Ka'arta, as long as they were limited to the right bank of the Senegal and none of the French allies and states in the Senegambian valley was involved, could have favourable effects on French commerce. The French made profits from the sale of arms and ammunition to the warring parties. Bassiru, for example, bought large quantities of arms from the French between December 1875 and April 1876.[2]

THE LOGO PROBLEM AND THE WORSENING OF
FRANCO-TUKULOR RELATIONS, 1870-79

With the protraction of the Diomboko-Sero conflict the wars were becoming ruinous in their effects on French commercial interests, and the French were getting increasingly anxious that the states in the Senegambian area, where they were trying to maintain complete control, should not become involved. Logo, one of the regions of Khasso, was, however, actively aiding Bassiru, emir of Diomboko, in his war against Sero. Niamody, the ruler of Logo, sent an army to help Diomboko. The French saw this action as undermining their position economically and politically. They therefore made efforts to induce Logo to abandon the Tukulor cause and accept protection from the French. In this attempt the French had sent a mission, headed by one M. Simon, to hold talks with Niamody in 1875.[3] But in spite of the

1 ASAOF, 15G110/2 (74), Le Gouverneur à M. le Commandant du Poste de Médine, Saint-Louis, 2 May 1876
2 ASAOF, 15G110/2 (7), Copie du Régistre Journal – mois de Janvier, 1876, Médine, 31 Jan. 1876; 15G110/2 (9) 'Copie du Régistre Journal mois d'Avril, 1876', Médine, 30 Apr. 1876
3 ASAOF, 15G110/1 (328), Poste de Médine à M. le gouverneur, Médine, 10 Mar. 1876, p. 1

assurances reportedly given by Niamody to the contrary, Logo continued its military aid to Bassiru, the Tukulor ruler of Diomboko. Just as they had stopped Sambala of Médine from aiding Moriba Safere of Sero on the grounds that such aid would prolong the war which the French considered detrimental to their commerce, the French were also decided to stop Niamody from further helping Diomboko. To achieve their objective they sought to bind Niamody by an undertaking allegedly given to M. Simons in 1875 to the effect that he would renounce the Tukulor and ally with the French. By sending an army to Diomboko, Niamody, it was claimed, was violating not only the undertaking said to have been given in 1875, but also the treaty of 30 September 1855 between the French and the Khasso confederation, to which Niamody allegedly belonged. Under this convention, it was claimed, the Khasso chiefs had engaged themselves not to send any army across one bank of the river Senegal to the other. Niamody, however, rejected the French claim on the ground that he was not a party to the 1855 convention and that his own interests demanded that he should continue his association with the Tukulor.[1]

Niamody's claim that Logo was not included in the 1855 convention, if understood to mean that Logo was not bound by it, was right. At the time that Sambala of Médine and other Khasso chiefs concluded the convention with Faidherbe, the French governor of Senegal, Khasso had been conquered by 'Umar and the Khasso signatories were all subject to him. The signing of the convention was an act of rebellion aimed at regaining their independence. Only Sambala and his allies succeeded in maintaining a *de facto* independence under French military protection. It will be remembered that Logo, Natiaga and other Khasso districts were reconquered by 'Umar early in 1857, and Logo, especially under the leadership of Niamody, had since remained loyal to the Tukulor rule.[2] Relations between Logo and Sambala

1 *Ibid.*, p. 3
2 Against this background, it is wrong to write as Kanya-Forstner does of the Tukulor in Ka'arta 'beginning to expand into Logo and Bambuk on the French side of the river' in 1876 (*The Conquest of the Western Sudan*, p. 56). Hargreaves, in an earlier work, makes a similar mistake when he speaks of Niamody as someone who 'had disavowed Sambala's authority, and allowed the Tokolors to build a fort at Sabousire . . .' ('The Tokolor empire of Segou and its relations with the French', p. 137)

of Médine, the French ally, had also continued to be bad. The French were eager to strengthen their position in the Senegambian states, and therefore that of their ally, Sambala. But the French attempt to forcefully detach Logo from the Tukulor regime, using the 1855 convention as a base, was a violation of Tukulor sovereignty in the area, and was certain to provoke hostility. As Niamody pointed out, his interests demanded that he should continue to collaborate with the Tukulor. Such interests included the continued protection by the Tukulor against Sambala of Médine and allies, protected by the French, in the struggle for supremacy in Khasso. In a way the Franco-Tukulor struggle in Khasso, which culminated in the siege of Médine (1857), was once more being reopened as part of the general struggle for the control of the Senegambian region.

The French officers on the spot believed that the elimination of Tukulor influence from the whole of the Senegambian states was a necessity if they (the French) were to enjoy a monopoly of the commerce of the area, and to be in a position effectively to forestall moves by the British to share in it. In the absence of any other policy from the home government, French policy towards the Tukulor in the Senegambian states, and especially in Khasso, continued to be guided by what the local officers interpreted to be in the interest of French commerce, the protection of which was their main assignment. They were the more impressed by the British threat to the French position in the Senegambian states and in relation to the trade emanating from the Tukulor empire when in May 1876 the government of the British colony of Gambia wrote to Ahmadu, the Tukulor ruler, informing him of a proposed British trade mission to his empire. The aim of the mission, it was explained, was to open up the trade of the Tukulor empire to the British and to promote Anglo-Segu friendship. The mission led by the governor of the Gambia, H. I. M. Cooper, was to travel to Segu through the Senegambian states of Walo and Khasso, and later cross to the Ka'arta section of the empire.[1] It was feared that the British might succeed in penetrating the empire if pro-Tukulor, but anti-French, states like Logo and Natiaga in the Senegambia collaborated with them and provided a base for operating in the Tukulor empire. To prevent such a situation from arising, the French intensified their

1 ANSOM, in Sénégal III, 10 bis, H. I. M. Cooper to Amade Seyhou, King of Segou-Sekoror, Bathurst, 13 May 1876

effort to strengthen the position of their ally, Sambala of Médine, and detach Logo from its Tukulor connection. It was apparent, however, that the French policy would lead to hostilities not only between the Khasso groups (Sambala and Niamody of Logo), but also between the French and the Tukulor empire.

Before the two sides engaged in battles, however, the French government had formulated a definite policy for the guidance of the governor of Senegal in his relations with the Segu Tukulor empire. According to the home government's policy, the officers were required to develop the market in raw materials which were needed by French industrial manufacturers, and for the supplying of French manufactured goods to the Africans. The governor was instructed that French policy 'doit être essentiellement pacifique et ne viser à aucune extension de territoire qui entretiendrait l'agitation dans la zone où s'approvisionnent nos marchés, et nous obligérait à des sacrifices constamment renouvéllés d'homme et d'argent'.[1]

According to the instruction of the minister, French commercial interests in the Senegambian states demanded a peaceful policy. In terms of the Logo crisis this implied a peaceful settlement that would exclude military involvements. This policy was the opposite of the view of the local officers on the spot who had been inducing the French authorities to go to war against Logo as a means of protecting French commerce. But the home government was not only convinced that French commerce would be best protected by pursuing a peaceful policy: a peaceful approach was in fact a necessity for the success of French overseas policy at this time. France was just recovering from the disastrous effects of the Franco-Prussian war, and more than anything else, she was concerned with re-establishing her position in Europe. For the realisation of this objective, all available resources were needed. As the minister pointed out to the governor of Senegal:

La France s'efforce, en ce moment, de concentrer ses forces et ses ressources dans le but de reconquérir la situation qu'une guerre malheureuse lui a fait perdre en Europe; elle ne peut s'épandre au dehors, prendre d'engagements onéreux, inscrire à son budget des dépenses qui réduiraient ses moyens de défense.[2]

1 ANSOM, in Sénégal I, 61a, Instruction remise à Monsieur le Cl. Brière de l'Isle, Gouverneur du Sénégal, par le Ministre, Paris, 19 July 1876
2 *Ibid.*

It is clear from the minister's instruction that the French government did not consider that it was in a position to furnish either the men or the materials for pursuing an aggressive policy in Senegal and the Western Sudan. The minister told the governor not to embark on expeditions except 'dans des cas exceptionnels alors que la sécurité de nos comptoirs l'éxigéra'.[1]

Although the desire of the home government to avoid war or any other form of military involvement in the Senegal and the Tukulor empire was very clear from the minister's instruction, the governor of Senegal and his men in Khasso appeared to be determined to force the hands of the ministry to adopt their own aggressive and expansionist policy under the guise of protecting French commerce and trading posts. To achieve their objective, they continually portrayed Tukulor action in Logo as ruinous to French commerce in the Senegambia and Tukulor empire. Thus on 9 June 1877 the commandant of Médine reported to the governor of Senegal that it would be necessary for Sambala and his allies to make a decided effort, once for all, to get rid of Niamody and his chiefs in Logo because Niamody 'est l'ami intime des Toucouleurs et qu'à un moment donné, il peut nous faire beaucoup de mal'.[2]

Apart from the uneasy relations that had existed between Niamody on the one hand and Sambala of Médine and allies on the other (in which the French had been involved as allies of the latter) the French local officers also saw Niamody as a danger to French political and commercial interests. The commandant of Médine for example had reported that 'il y a un homme dans le haut fleuve qui gêne beaucoup, même sur le point de vue commercial, c'est toujours Niamody, chef du Logo'.[3] For the commandant of Médine, as for most of the other French service men in the area, politics and commerce were inseparable. Thus in July the commandant of Médine again reported on Niamody claiming that 'Sur le point de vue politique, Niamody, dans le Logo, persiste dans sa défense de laisser passer sur son territoire les gens de Tombo [*sic*] qui se rendre [*sic*] a Médine'.[4]

1 *Ibid.*

2 ASAOF, 15G111/1 (17), Le Commandant du Poste de Médine à M. le gouverneur', Médine, 10 July 1877

3 ASAOF, 15G111/1 (15), Le Commandant de Médine à M. le gouverneur, Médine, 9 June 1877

4 ASAOF, 15G111/1 (17), Le Commandant du Poste de Médine, 10 July 1877

At this time the almamy of Futa Jallon, based at Timbo, had been sending help to his ally, Moriba Safere of Sero, in the latter's war against Bassiru. Niamody was not only the ruler of Logo, which was a Tukulor dependency, he was also an ally of Bassiru and an active participant in his wars against Sero. Consequently Niamody could not let Futa Jallon send reinforcements through his territory to strengthen the enemies of the Tukulor regime in Ka'arta. Hence the charge that he was not letting Timbo people pass through his territory to Médine. The Commandant of Médine also alleged in his report that the relationship between Logo *per se* and Timbo had for long been hostile. The reason for the alleged hostility was not stated. What is clear is that at this time Niamody would not let Timbo trading caravans pass through his territory to reach the French post at Médine. The French desire for uninterrupted commerce in the Senegambian area was thus being frustrated, and the commandant of Médine considered the situation intolerable.

The instruction which the commandant was expected to carry out was, however, that he should never do anything that would put the French in an embarrassing situation in their relations with the Tukulor empire or any of the other smaller states. He was enjoined to work always to bring about peace among such Khasso chiefs as were in conflict, and that Sambala of Médine should be specifically forbidden to go to war with his neighbours. But in his hostility to Logo, the commandant of Médine sought to bring the French government to the side of Sambala in hostility to Niamody. He portrayed Sambala as the champion of French commerce which Niamody was trying to ruin in the area. Sambala's hostility to Niamody was given out as having arisen from the former's desire to protect French commerce, so he was really fighting the French cause. He was reported as promising to remain peaceful as long as Niamody allowed the caravans from Timbo to reach the French post at Médine and it was said that he would fight only if Niamody prevented the Timbo people from reaching Médine. As a token of his desire for a peaceful settlement, the commandant reported, Sambala was eagerly awaiting the arrival of the French governor to settle the trouble between him and Niamody.[1] It was in this way that the commandant of the Médine post attempted to induce the French authorities in Senegal to wage war against Logo, either as allies of Sambala of

1 *Ibid.*, pp. 2 and 3

Médine or as an independent action of their own taken in the interest of French commerce. Given the attitude of the French officers and commercial agents around him, Sambala naturally felt encouraged in his hostility to Niamody. The relations between the two continued to worsen until by August 1877, the two sides had armed and were ready to go to war against each other.[1]

As a result of the report of the commandant of Médine on the situation in Khasso, the governor of Senegal gave instructions that Sambala of Médine should be allowed to go to war against Niamody of Logo if he wanted to do so.[2]

Meanwhile there had been a change of command at Médine. Assessing the situation, the new commandant of Médine, M. Boye, recommended that it was best to avoid war. Boye told the governor that he was reliably informed that Bassiru, the emir of Diomboko, had instructed Niamody not to initiate hostilities against Sambala, but rather to remain armed at home. Niamody was naturally assured of Tukulor help in case of attack from Sambala of Médine. Boye recommended that in the situation in which the two sides were armed in readiness for war, it would be better to work to prevent the actual outbreak of war. He informed the governor that he came to this conclusion after he had had a meeting with the business interests and the trading community in Khasso. These had told him that if war broke out between Sambala and Niamody, there would be little or no trade for them in the following year, and in that case it would serve no useful purpose for them to continue to stay at Médine. Boye asked for a new approach to the solution of the Khasso problem in view of the apprehension expressed by the commercial interests. He suggested that a solution might be to appeal to Ahmadu to order Bassiru to ask Niamody to move to the right bank of the Senegal where he would be in Tukulor territory. If the governor approved of the suggestion, he (Boye) would be ready to go to Segu to negotiate with Ahmadu. He mentioned that one of the Médine traders, Moumar Diak, who enjoyed considerable influence there, was ready to lead him to Ahmadu.[3]

It is clear from the above that even the seemingly peaceful

1 ASAOF, 15G111/1 (24), Le Commandant de Médine à M. le gouverneur, Médine, 3 Sept. 1877
2 ASAOF, 15G111/1 (26), Le Commandant du Cercle de Médine à M. le gouverneur, Médine, 30 Sept. 1877
3 *Ibid.*, pp. 2–3

approach being advocated by Boye was aimed at giving the French absolute control of the Senegambia. His suggestion that Niamody should move to the right bank of the Senegal implied that the Tukulor and their allies should evacuate Khasso in order that Sambala, the French ally, could feel safe. Boye, acting under pressure from the French commercial interests, probably did not think of the implications of his suggestion at the time. He found himself in a situation that had become critical and complicated before he became commandant, and, contrary to the wishes of his predecessor, he wanted to solve the problem by peaceful means.

In this endeavour he achieved some temporary success. He was able to persuade the governor of Senegal to abandon his hostile attitude for a while. The governor authorised him to do all he could to effect a peaceful settlement between Sambala and Niamody.[1] The governor having thus modified his attitude, Boye spent the month of October 1877 negotiating for peace. At first he invited Niamody to Médine for a settlement. The latter refused the invitation on the ground that it would be dangerous for him to leave his capital, Sabousire, at a time when Sambala's army was already alerted for an attack on Logo at any moment. To allay Niamody's fears, Boye went to Sabousire to negotiate with him. Niamody was reported to be in favour of a peaceful solution, but would not commit himself to any solution so long as Sambala was armed and still nursed the idea of attacking Logo.[2] Though he did not succeed fully with Niamody, Boye continued his efforts to secure a peaceful settlement.

He wrote to the governor of Senegal, suggesting that since Bassiru, the emir of Diomboko, to whom Niamody was responsible, had not gone to Segu for the *Tabaski*, but had stayed on at Koniakary to see to the settlement of the Logo affair, he, Boye, could go with him to Segu in order to settle the Logo problem with Ahmadu, the head of the Tukulor empire.[3] While awaiting further instructions from the governor, Boye made approaches to Bassiru, 'songeant combien la politique de conciliation est urgente dans un pays qui, comme Médine, est privé de toute communication à partir de cette époque de l'année'.[4]

1 ASAOF, 15GIII/1 (30), Le Commandant de Médine à M. le gouverneur, Médine, 31 Oct. 1877
2 *Ibid.*
3 ASAOF, 15GIII/1 (32), same to same, Médine, 31 Oct. 1877
4 ASAOF, 15GIII/1 (34), same to same, 4 Nov. 1877

Though Bassiru was favourable to the idea of a peaceful solution, Boye could not achieve peace because Sambala, encouraged by the governor's original support for war, was bent on fighting. To Boye's suggestion that he should stay his plans to attack Logo until the governor's reply had been received, Sambala replied that he would no longer wait because the governor himself had authorised him to go ahead. He would march on Logo and test whether the Tukulor were in fact in a position to support Niamody militarily. Faced with Sambala's attitude Boye wrote to the governor, expressing the fear that if Sambala went into Logo, his forces might be repulsed and the war carried into Médine. He pointed out that such a situation would not be in the interest of the French.[1] Apparently, Sambala believed that because of the internal situation in the Tukulor empire, the rulers would not be able to send forces to aid Logo. But a day after his decision to wage war, a column of about 1,500 Tukulor troops moved into Logo to aid Niamody. This frightened Sambala and he was again willing to listen to suggestions from Boye, who advised that settlement of the conflict should be left to the governor and Ahmadu. Sambala then suspended his activities mainly because he was convinced that he needed more forces to be able to tackle Logo, which was being actively supported by Bassiru.[2]

In reporting on the latest developments in the Logo conflict, Boye informed the governor how he had prevailed on Sambala not to fight. He then emphasised that the state of war which had prevailed in Khasso was already having adverse consequences on French commercial interests in the Senegambia. He reported that all the caravans intending to trade with the French at Médine had been arrested and detained at Koniakary by Bassiru, the Tukulor emir of Diomboko. As a result of Bassiru's action, trade between the Tukulor empire and the French at Médine had stopped completely for about a month. He indicated that both Ahmadu and Bassiru were still favourable to the idea of a negotiated solution, and therefore the situation could still be ameliorated. He then asked the governor for directives.[3]

The governor's reply was virtually a renunciation of any peaceful solution. He rebuked Boye for having stopped Sambala from

1 *Ibid.*
2 ASAOF, 15G111/1 (36), same to same, 5 Nov. 1877
3 Same to same in 15G111/1 (37), Médine, 16 Nov. 1877

going to war on the strength of assurances of peace from the Tukulor. Brière de l'Isle, the governor, maintained that all the Tukulor wanted was to gain time to organise against the French in Logo. He maintained that by stopping Sambala from going to war, Boye had merely played into the hands of the enemies of the French, and worse still, that Boye's action would only lead to Ahmadu assuming the role of arbiter in Logo, which should be avoided at any cost. The governor pointed out that Boye's fears of the consequences that might arise from a war between Médine and Logo, two indigenous states which were used to fighting each other, were totally unjustified. He emphasised that if it ever happened that Sambala's forces were repulsed and the war reached Médine, the post was fortified and armed enough to meet any threat. He told Boye that all he would need to do would be to stay in the fort with the French soldiers and fight against the enemy only when he came near. He pointed out that this was the example of Paul Holle,[1] which, if followed, would be found to be an adequate means of destroying the opposing forces.[2] This directive made war inevitable.

Bassiru had earlier in the month written to warn that the French should leave Niamody alone and that should the latter be attacked he would send forces to aid him. In his reply to Bassiru's warning, Brière de l'Isle instructed Boye to tell Bassiru that Logo was a part of the Khasso confederation, which was under the French protection, and that Niamody should submit to Sambala, the head of the confederation or leave Logo for the Tukulor territory on the right bank of the Senegal. This, Boye was instructed to tell Bassiru, was the only condition for peace between the French and the Tukulor.[3]

Implicit in this ultimatum was the claim of French sovereignty over the Senegambia, as well as the idea that the river Senegal in this part formed the boundary between the Tukulor Segu empire and the area under French authority. This claim was clearly unacceptable to the Tukulor who were also determined to fight, if necessary, to maintain their position in Khasso and the Senegambia generally.

1 Paul Holle, a mulatto, was the Commander of the French forces against 'Umar's Tukulor forces in the siege of Médine, 1857
2 ASAOF, 15G111/1 (19), Brière de l'Isle, le Gouverneur, à M. le Commandant de Médine, Saint-Louis, 20 Nov. 1877
3 Same to same in 15G111/4 (20), Saint-Louis, 3 Dec. 1877

War broke out between Sambala and Niamody in November 1877. Bubakar Sa'ada, the almamy of Bondu, allied with Niamody and the Tukulor, contrary to the expectation of Sambala and the French that he would ally with them.[1] The first efforts of Sambala's forces were devoted to destroying crops on farms in the border villages of Logo. On 6 December 1877 Sambala's forces claimed to have burnt down three small villages – Farakotossou, Marene Toure and Lakafia – before withdrawing from Logo to camp at Lotou and Kounda on the frontier.[2]

In his letter to Boye, Brière de l'Isle had instructed him to give protection to the French post as well as Sambala's *tata* (fortress) at Médine. He was also to encourage and support Sambala in the wars against Logo. On Boye's report of 29 November 1877 to the effect that Sambala's forces were destroying crops on Logo farms, Brière de l'Isle gave his approval saying: 'Cette manière d'agir est de bonne guerre, le ravage des récoltes et l'enlèvement des troupeaux sont les moyens habituels de repression du fort contre le faible dans toutes les guerres des peuplades de l'Afrique entre elles.'[3] Having promoted the war, Brière de l'Isle in this way continued to manage it on behalf of the French, but without any reference to superior authorities in France.[4] But his military resources to help Sambala against Logo were limited, and because of active Tukulor support for the latter, the war continued to drag on much longer than Brière de l'Isle had expected.

Brière de l'Isle authorised this campaign because he hoped that Sambala could be used to subjugate Logo, and that with its submission, French political and commercial influence would spread over a wider area. His plan was to complete the war while

---

1 ASAOF, 15G111/1 (38), Le Commandant de Médine à M. le gouverneur, Médine, 29 Nov. 1877
2 *Ibid.*; also 15G111/1 (41), Guerbaek, le Sergent du poste à M. le gouverneur, Médine, 18 Dec. 1877
3 ASAOF, 15G111/4 (20), Le Gouverneur du Sénégal à M. le Commandant de Médine, Saint-Louis, 3 Dec. 1877
4 The ministerial instructions cited earlier on pp. 208–9 (contained in ANSOM, Sénégal I, 61a, dated 19 July 1876) and the course of events stated above both prove that Brière de l'Isle took the ultimate responsibility for the war in Logo. This is contrary to Hargreave's suggestion that 'in 1878, he secured authority for a show of force in support of France's one loyal dependent in the Upper River . . .' ('The Tokolor empire of Segou and its relations with the French', p. 136). Brière had in fact caused the war to start earlier on in 1877

the waters were still high and before the middle of the dry season. For some months after the end of the rainy season, the river Senegal would be in flood and would, therefore, still be a barrier separating Khasso from Diomboko, and it would be difficult for Tukulor soldiers to cross the river to give aid to Niamody in Logo. Given French support, it was calculated, Sambala's forces would win easily and quickly and the French would reap all the advantages they hoped for.

But it turned out that Niamody and his Tukulor aides were stronger than expected, and as the war dragged on the prospect of victory for Sambala's forces became remote. It was feared that since the floods were subsiding, fordable points would soon form on the river Senegal and Tukulor troops could then cross to reach Logo where they could defeat Sambala's forces and their French allies. If this happened the French would be in an embarrassing position, in addition to missing all the advantages they had hoped to gain. Arguing in this way, Brière de l'Isle instructed the commandant of Médine to tell Sambala that he had to finish with Logo quickly, and that:

> Je ne lui ai donné l'autorisation de faire rentrer le chef du Logo dans le devoir qu'à la condition qu'il en aurait fini avec lui avant la baisse des eaux; qu'il ne doit pas laisser le temps aux gués de se former pour donner passage aux Toucouleurs sur les points supérieurs du fleuve, sous peine de se mettre dans une situation fâcheuse. . . .[1]
>
> La lutte, si elle se prolongeait, aurait pour effet probable de nuire au commerce de l'escale et ne répondrait plus du tout au but que je me suis proposé en autorisant Samballa à agir contre le Logo.[1]

By this time, as is clear from the governor's letter, the situation was becoming critical for the French. To give up the struggle would not necessarily repair the damage already done to their relations with the Tukulor empire. The prolongation of the war could lead to a Tukulor victory which would put the French and their allies in Khasso in a worse situation than they had been before. To continue the war was therefore becoming a necessity, but to do this more effort was needed than Sambala was capable of dispensing. To avoid failure, it was becoming inevitable that the French should intervene to fight the war directly. The fears expressed by Brière de l'Isle seemed confirmed when on 14

1 ASAOF, 15G111/4 (4), Le Gouverneur du Sénégal à M. le Commt de Médine, Saint-Louis, 15 Feb. 1878

February 1878, the Tukulor succeeded in getting about 220 troops over to Logo. This was reported to the governor of Senegal by the French commandant at Bakel.[1]

To avert danger Boye, the commandant at Médine, again made moves to negotiate peace with Bassiru and Niamody,[2] but apparently he did not stay long enough at Médine for anything to come of his negotiations. The new commandant at Médine, M. Wyts, obviously following the approach of Boye, claimed that peace was the only way of protecting French interests, and asked for permission to negotiate between Sambala and Niamody. This request was refused by his superior local officer, the commandant at Bakel.[3] In another letter Soyers, the commandant of the Bakel *cercle*, accused Wyts of not following his instructions. He claimed that by going to Sabousire to hold talks with Niamody, Wyts had compromised French prestige and interests.[4]

Wyts had in fact arranged a truce between Sambala and Niamody on 18 March 1878 and at this time was awaiting a directive from the governor that would enable him to settle the Logo problem on the basis of a definitive treaty.[5] All hopes for a peaceful solution were shattered, however, when Brière de l'Isle sent a telegram, ordering Wyts to cause the war to be started again in order to secure the submission of Logo. Wyts, in his reply claimed that war had in fact reopened before the governor's telegram reached Médine.[6] By giving orders that war should be resumed the governor let slip an opportunity to end the Logo situation on a peaceful note and showed his preference for a solution based on conquest.

To enable them to effect the conquest of Logo Soyers and Brière de l'Isle made the French government believe that what was happening in Logo was an insurrection of a district against

1 ASAOF, 15G111/4 (9), Brière de l'Isle, le Gouverneur à M. le Commt du Poste de Médine, Saint-Louis, 19 Mar. 1878

2 ASAOF, in 15G64, M. Boye à M. le Commandant du Cercle du Bakel, Médine, 22 Mar. 1878

3 ASAOF, 15G111/4 (4), M. Soyer à M. le Commt du Poste de Médine, Bakel, 1 Apr. 1878

4 ASAOF, 15G111/4 (10), Soyer, Commt du Cercle de Bakel à M. le Commt du poste de Médine, Bakel, 30 Apr. 1878

5 ASAOF, 15G111/2 Bulletin Agricole, Commercial et Politique, Médine, mois de Mars, 31 Mar. 1878

6 ASAOF, 15G111/2 (31), Wyts, le Commt de Médine à M. le gouverneur . . ., Médine, 23 Apr. 1878

the authority of Sambala, the French ally and head of the Khasso confederation. It was reported that in the interest of French commerce it was necessary to suppress the insurrection and that, so far, the war had proved detrimental to commerce in the Senegambia until the French participated in arranging peace in Khasso. It was further reported that, as a result of the temporary peace achieved, some trade was being carried on at Médine. The ministry was, however, informed that there was fear that rather than submit, Logo would soon reopen war with every assurance of military aid from Bassiru, the Tukulor emir of neighbouring Diomboko. In that case, it was pointed out, victory over Logo would not be possible until perhaps about six months later in November 1878.[1]

This false picture of the situation was obviously given to Paris in order to force the hands of the home government to adopt a policy which in effect contradicted the ministerial instruction of 1876 on French policy in the Senegambia and towards the Tukulor empire. The picture was also meant to keep the home government uninformed about the actual role of the governor and his staff in promoting war in Khasso. Brière de l'Isle and his aides sought to convince the ministry that, in keeping with its instructions, their preoccupation had been the protection of French commercial interests. Niamody of Logo was painted as the obstacle. It was claimed that the clash between Niamody and Sambala had arisen over the latter's desire to protect French commercial interests, and that Niamody was receiving aid from the Tukulor rulers, who were said to be eager to renew their imperial ambitions in the Senegambia. All this was to make the home government accept the necessity of fighting to suppress Logo in order not only to protect their commerce but also to combat the Tukulor, who had been their rivals since the time of 'Umar and the siege of Médine.

In conformity with this approach it was reported to Paris that:

Bassirou et Mountaga ont profité des dissensions survenues entre le Logo et le Khasso pour se meler à la lutte et assurer leur influence dans ce pays, Il est donc logique de soutenir Sambala, roi du Khasso, lorsque ce dernier essaie d'arracher le Logo à l'influence des frères d'Ahmadou. Le Khasso est la première barrière à opposer aux projets ambitieux des

1 ASAOF, 13G24/421, Situation Politique – A Monsieur le Ministre, Saint-Louis, 21 Apr. 1878, in 15G64, Le Commandant du cercle de Bakel à M. le Commandant du poste de Médine, Bakel, 5 May 1878

Al Hadjistes et Sambala doit être soutenu par tous les moyens possibles afin de l'opposer aux chefs du Kaarta.[1]

In short the report emphasised that the Tukulor, using Ka'arta as a base, were again in armed opposition to the French presence in the Senegambia as they had been between 1855 and 1859, that Khasso was the major barrier, and that it was therefore logical, in the French interest to support Sambala.

In his pressure on the home government to support war against Logo, Brière de l'Isle continually harped on the theme of Tukulor hostility to the French in the Senegambia. He gave the impression that the main Tukulor ambition was to eliminate the French from the Senegambia and that their involvement in Khasso was only incidental. He emphasised that 'leur but est de nous isoler à Médine et cette tendance d'intéret vient se joindre à leurs sentiments de rancune contre Sambala, le seul chef du haut pays que le grand prophète n'avaient pu réduire, grace à l'héroique défense du fort de Médine en 1857'.[2]

Having thus depicted the Tukulor as the enemies of the French Brière de l'Isle concluded that not to act against them in Logo 'serait laisser accumuler l'orage, encourager même sa formation que de rester spectateurs impossibles de retour des la puissance du grand prophète'.[3] The French government were told in effect that the alternative to a policy of war was to keep watching, passively the re-establishment of Tukulor power in the Senegambia and the elimination of French interests.

Having asked for military intervention in such strong terms, Brière de l'Isle did not wait for a reply from the home government before writing to Sambala and his allies to reassure them of the determination of the French government to continue to support them. The new commandant of Médine, Chevrier, was instructed to induce, and actually succeeded in inducing, Sambala and his allies to resume war against Niamody and the Tukulor in Logo.[4] But although the French succeeded in pushing Sambala and his men to resume the attack, it was feared that the

1 ASAOF, 1G63/2, Notice sur El Hadj Omar, Saint-Louis, 25 May 1878, p. 7
2 ANSOM, in Sénégal I, 61c, G. Brière de l'Isle, Gouverneur du Sénégal à M. le Ministre de la Marine et des Colonies, Saint-Louis, 5 June 1878
3 *Ibid.*
4 ASAOF, 13G24/592, Situation Politique – A Monsieur le Ministre, Saint-Louis, 7 July 1878

hope of success was remote partly because the war was already having ruinous effects on the Khasso population. The governor of Senegal argued with the ministry that since the war began in November 1877, the Khassonkés had not been able to cultivate their land and consequently were suffering from a terrible famine. The only way to achieve success against Logo, it was pointed out, was by open French armed intervention as requested in the letter of 5 June 1878. If Sambala did not win, it was claimed, the French would suffer loss of prestige, and to avoid this direct French military intervention was indispensable.[1]

Apparently to make the French government believe that military intervention would lead to an easy victory, Brière de l'Isle informed the ministry that Ahmadu had written to say that in the meantime he had forbidden Bassiru to send troops to Logo. In spite of this attitude on the part of Ahmadu, it was pointed out, the French would still need to go to war because although Ahmadu had forbidden his emir from going to war, he was not necessarily thereby conceding to the French any right to be in Logo nor was he admitting the river Senegal as a boundary between the Segu Tukulor empire and what Brière de l'Isle called the French states. He reported that:

> Malgré toutes ses belles paroles, Amadou dit dans sa lettre qu'il ne reconnait point la rive droite du fleuve comme limites de ses états et des nôtres, qu'aucun écrit n'a fixé de limites entre lui et les français et que s'il y'avait un traité à faire à ce sujet, tous les pays de l'ouest jusqu'au Taro [*sic*][2] devraient être compris dans son territoire.[3]

Brière de l'Isle argued that this claim to sovereignty over the Senegambia allegedly made by Ahmadu was a proof of the need for French intervention in Logo, as he had emphasised in his letter of 5 June 1878. According to him, this alleged declaration also proved 'd'une façon éclatante combien il est indispensable que nous sommes décidés à faire respecter les traités, même par la force si cela est nécessaire'[4] It is clear that his strategy was to impress upon the ministry that it was imperative to fight at the

---

1 *Ibid.*, p. 2
2 The reference here is probably to Toro, the home district of the Tukulor leader.
3 ASAOF, 13G24/592, Situation Politique – Monsieur le Ministre, Saint-Louis, 7 July 1878
4 *Ibid.*, pp. 2–3

same time as he assured them that it would be easy to win the war. While the French government was being pressured in this way, the war was dragging on with varying fortunes for the two sides.

Before August Sambala was already finding it difficult to continue the war and the prospect that he might surrender frightened Brière de l'Isle into sending an urgent letter to Paris, stressing that Sambala's situation in relation to Logo was worsening from day to day. He then repeated his earlier requests for military intervention, claiming that 'la néccessité de notre intervention ressort de plus en plus de la situation actuelle'.[1]

We do not have evidence to show that the French government gave authority to the governor to use French forces against Niamody. Brière de l'Isle had, however, all along been giving military support to Sambala – he had at least ordered that the fort and garrison at Médine be used to protect Sambala against attacks from Logo – and all he wanted was to legitimise his action and have authority for intervention on a larger scale. By the middle of September, he had sent troops to fight on the side of Sambala. These troops arrived at Médine on 19 September, and marched against Logo, unannounced, on the 22nd. The Logo army, caught unawares, was defeated and the people took flight in various directions.[2] Sabousire, the headquarters of Logo, was destroyed and Niamody was killed, probably when he was attempting to cross the river Senegal to Diomboko.[3] On the French side about fourteen soldiers were killed and buried at the French posts at Dagana and Richard Toll; there were also fifty wounded.[4] As a result of the operations in Logo many of the inhabitants emigrated into Diomboko to seek refuge under Bassiru,[5] and the French put Logo under military occupation.[6]

Officially, Brière de l'Isle explained the invasion of Logo as a measure against Niamody and his men who 'osaient contester nos

1 ASAOF, 13G24/658, Brière de l'Isle, le Gouverneur du Sénégal à Son Excellence M. le Ministre, Saint-Louis, 7 Aug. 1878
2 ASAOF, 15G111/2 (31), Le Commt de Médine, 19 Oct. 1878
3 *Ibid.*, p. 3; 1D37/6 (2), Expédition dans le Ht. Fleuve, colonne de Sabousiré, 1878
4 ASAOF, 1D37/4 (11) and 1D37/7, 8, Expédition dans le Ht. Fleuve – colonne du Sabousiré 1878
5 ASAOF, 15G111/3 (1), Le Commt de Médine à M. le Gouverneur, Médine, 26 Jan. 1879
6 ASAOF, 15G111/2 (31), same to same 19 Oct. 1878

droits et menacer notre établissemment dans le haut Sénégal'.[1] This explanation was obviously given to justify an action which was really a calculated aggression, within the terms of the ministerial instruction of 1876 which gave permission for military expeditions only on rare occasions when French commercial interests, especially the trading posts, might be in danger. But although Brière de l'Isle succeeded in breaking Niamody, the French did not thereafter necessarily feel safer in Khasso. Badon, the brother of Niamody, was permitted to return to Sabousire and rebuild the town on the condition that he would be loyal to the French.[2] Badon, however, remained loyal to the Tukulor instead. Some years after, he was reported to be hostile to the French,[3] and since the latter could not continue to maintain forces in Logo indefinitely it became obvious that they would lose their hold on the district. All the French gained out of this expensive aggression was the consolidation of their position in relation to Sambala and his men, who had always been their allies in any case. With this faction of Khasso, a treaty was concluded in the name of the governor of Senegal on 26 September 1878. The treaty expressed the gratitude of Sambala and his men to the French for their support and promised to protect French commercial and political interests in Khasso.[4]

On the other hand, the invasion of Logo was regarded by the Tukulor rulers as an act of hostility committed by the French against them. According to Soleillet, who was on a mission to Segu shortly after the episode, the Tukulor rulers considered the invasion as an unprovoked attack on their territory. Segu was not planning any immediate retaliatory expedition against the French, but it was made clear that normal relations with the French would be impossible until after Brière de l'Isle, the governor of Senegal, was removed.[5] Thus the Logo affair upset the delicate equilibrium which had sustained Franco-Tukulor relations. In

1 ASAOF, 1D37/6 (2), Expédition dans le Ht. Fleuve – colonne du Sabousiré 1878
2 ASAOF, 15G111/3 (3), Le Commt de Médine à M. le Gouverneur, Médine, 17 Sept. 1878
3 ASAOF, 15G112/1 (39), Le Commt de Médine à M. le Commandant Supérieur du Haut Fleuve, Médine, 6 Mar. 1880; 15G83/7(2), Combes à M. le Gouverneur, 3 Oct. 1884; 15G83/7 (6), Combes à M. le Gouverneur, Kayes, 27 Nov. 1884
4 ASAOF, 15G1/5, Traité, Médine, 26 Sept. 1878
5 Soleillet, *Voyage à Ségou 1878–1879*, pp. 430–2

effect the invasion of Sabousire ruined such good relations as had existed between the French and the Segu empire and made normal relations impossible for some time. This accounted in part for the difficulty which Paul Soleillet had with the Segu rulers over a proposed treaty of commerce.[1] The French commercial interests protested against the invasion of Logo because its effects were ruinous to their trade. They were particularly concerned that trade with the Tukulor empire would cease for some time and that 'le Logo, qui était un pays riche et prospère, est complètement ruiné'.[2]

SUMMARY

From the above it is clear that the period 1870–78 was one of strain for the Tukulor empire. Internally it ran the risk of being dismembered as a result of the civil wars that marked the intra-Tukulor struggle for power. The political problem was solved temporarily with the victory of Ahmadu over his half-brothers in Ka'arta. The Tukulor were able to find their own solution to the problem of power partly because they were free from external intervention. External intervention was averted partly by the care which all sides to the power struggle took not to do anything that would make the French support one side against the other. Also because of the Franco-Prussian war and the ruinous consequences it had upon France, the French were really not in a position to meet the cost of involvement in the political problems of the Tukulor. Their main concern at this time was the peaceful expansion of commerce through which they hoped France would find means of recovering her losses in the war. They found the situation in the Tukulor empire favourable to the growth of their trade, especially the trade in arms and ammunition, and so they did not find any need for intervening either to ensure a quick end to the wars or to help one side win against the other.

Ahmadu's victory did not, however, represent a final solution of the power struggle in the Tukulor empire. Unreconciled groups continued to show their resentment to the regime through rebellions and acts of sabotage. This situation was typified by the civil wars between Bassiru, Tukulor emir at Diomboko, and

1 *Ibid.*, p. 431
2 *Ibid.*, pp. 430 n1

Moriba Safere of the district of Sero in Kaʻarta. The rebellions, and the widespread Bambara resistance movements which were active in their anti-Tukulor struggles, had disastrous effects on commercial activities, the preoccupation of the French at this time. To protect their trade interests in the Tukulor empire, the French made efforts to limit the wars to the empire by preventing their ally, Sambala of Médine, from intervening one way or the other in the affairs of the Tukulor in Kaʻarta. By keeping Sambala out of the affairs of the Tukulor in Kaʻarta, the French succeeded for some time in limiting the wars and rebellions to the left bank of the Senegal.

Niamody of Logo, a Tukulor dependency in Khasso, however, continued to give military aid to the Tukulor in Kaʻarta. In this way, the impact of the situation in Kaʻarta reached the Senegambia, an area where the French were trying to maintain a monopoly of commercial and political control. To promote their own security in the area the French made efforts to detach Niamody of Logo from his Tukulor connection and persuade him to serve the French interest. This was, however, impossible because of the politics of Khasso which posed Niamody of Logo as a bitter rival of Sambala of Médine, the French ally and enemy of the Tukulor. It was the attempt of French officers to enforce their own solution that resulted in the civil wars in Logo between 1877 and 1878. Brière de l'Isle regarded Logo as the strategic key to the Senegambia, and decided to fight to control it in spite of official policy. The war was fought as a Franco-Tukulor contest for influence and supremacy in the Senegambia, a revival of the 1857–59 episode. The French got a temporary satisfaction from their victory in Logo but at the expense of the good relations that had existed between them and the Tukulor.

8 The Tukulor Empire and French Penetration, 1880–1887

We are concerned in this chapter with the nature of French penetration into the Tukulor empire. This could be divided into two phases: the period of peaceful penetration marked by a conscious desire to preserve the delicate equilibrium which came into existence after the Guémou episode, and the era of aggression which was initiated by Governor Brière de l'Isle. The year 1876, the beginning of Brière de l'Isle's governorship, represents a line of separation between the two phases. Brière de l'Isle's contribution to French penetration has been discussed in the last chapter. By and large those who succeeded him built upon his achievements so that there was a continuity between his period and the period from 1880 to 1887 which is the main focus of this chapter. In dealing with French penetration and the internal problems of the Tukulor empire from 1880 to 1887, a brief background survey of Franco-Tukulor relations from 1860 to 1879 will be given as an introduction.

FRANCO-TUKULOR RELATIONS TO 1879

As has been explained earlier, after the Franco-Tukulor struggle for the control of the Senegambia from 1857 to 1859, the two sides came to cherish a desire for peaceful relations. This desire was exemplified in the peace moves which were made in 1860. Although no definitive peace treaty emerged from the Franco-Tukulor discussions,[1] the desire to end or at least suspend wars

1 Some authors have suggested erroneously that a treaty was concluded in 1860 between the French and the Tukulor. See for example, Saint-Martin, 'Les relations diplomatiques entre la France et l'empire toucouleur de 1860 à 1887', *Bull. IFAN*, B, xxvii, 1 and 2, 1965, pp. 185–6; Kanya-Forstner, *The Conquest of the Western Sudan*, p. 42

led both the Tukulor and the French to accept, albeit tentatively, the outcome of the 1857–59 wars as a *de facto* situation. In particular it was generally conceded that the river Senegal henceforth represented a divide between their respective spheres of influence or authority. The exception to this was the existence of pockets of Tukulor-dominated territories in the Senegambia such as Logo in Khasso, Koundian in Bambuk and the emirate of Dinguiray on the borders of Futa Jallon. The situation represented a delicate equilibrium which, though it was not satisfactory to both sides, nevertheless was a reality which the two sides had to reckon with to sustain their relations until 1876. From 1860 onwards the French concentrated attention on developing and expanding their commerce with the Western Sudan. This new orientation was partly influenced by the commercial groups who found war ruinous to their interests and would therefore, no longer support any policy that would involve further wars. Rather than antagonise the Tukulor the French soon began to see a viable, strong Tukulor empire as a desirable situation which would help the development of French commerce in the area by guaranteeing a stable political base. In any case the French at this time lacked the resources to prosecute an aggressive policy. On their own side, the Tukulor wanted a cessation of hostility so as to be able to concentrate on their campaigns against the resistance in Ka'arta and to spread the jihād to Segu and Masina. In the circumstances peace between the French and the Tukulor was something of a necessity.

It was to build upon the understanding which the 1860 peace moves promoted and to establish friendly relations with the Tukulor that the French sent out a diplomatic mission to Segu late in 1863. The mission, comprising a marine lieutenant, Eugene Mage, and Dr Quintin left Saint Louis, Senegal, late in 1863 and reached Segu on 28 February 1864.[1] In addition to promoting peaceful political relations the mission was to seek commercial concessions from the Tukulor. Negotiations between Mage and the Tukulor rulers continued intermittently until 1866 when a treaty was concluded.

In spite of discrepancies between the French and Arabic versions,[2] this treaty was clear on the main point which Mage had

1 Mage, *Voyage*, p. 167
2 ASAOF, 1G32, Notes diverses, vol. i, 1866 – Relation du Voyage par Mage, 21 June 1866; ANSOM, in Sénégal III, 9; Mage I, Note sur le

been asked to negotiate with the Tukulor ruler. Faidherbe, the governor who sent out the mission, had wanted Ahmadu to guarantee to the French the right to establish fortified posts along the river Niger. This was rejected as it aimed at commercial monopoly and had political undertones which were unacceptable to the Tukulor. Ahmadu, however, promised protection to French persons and their commerce, on condition that a ten per cent duty was paid on the merchandise being traded within the Tukulor empire. In return Tukulor subjects would have freedom of movement in areas like Saint-Louis and the Senegambian states which were under French influence. As Yves Saint-Martin rightly points out,[1] this last clause implied an acceptance and recognition by the French of Tukulor suzerainty over the Western Sudan.

In his own report Mage emphasised that it was best for the French to cultivate, and base their relations on, friendship with the Tukulor empire, although he also indicated the possibility of an alternative policy which was to conquer and dominate the empire.[2]

The mission of Mage did not achieve its main objective and the treaty did not represent much of an advance on the existing level of relations. Nevertheless, the treaty represented an affirmation of the desire for peace and friendly relations which had been demonstrated since 1860. Indeed, for several years it remained the basis of French relations with the Tukulor empire, even though the French were disappointed with it and did not ratify it. The alternative policy of conquest and domination through military means, which Mage indicated in his report, was impracticable and was hardly thought of for at least a decade after 1866. The reasons for the attachment to peaceful and friendly relations were partly the fact that the pushful Faidherbe had left the colony of Senegal for Algeria, and partly because the commercial interest, supported by the home government, would not support any policy involving the use of force. Indeed the home government made it clear that it would not increase the colonial force nor support any policy that would involve the use of more force than

voyage d'explorations de MM. Mage et Quintin dans l'Afrique occidentale de 1863 à 1866, Paris, 21 July 1866; also Saint-Martin, 'Les relations diplomatiques . . .', pp. 188/91

1 Saint-Martin, 'Les relations diplomatiques . . ., p. 191
2 Mage, *Voyage*, pp. 662–3

was available in the colony itself. The governor of Senegal in 1867 informed his subordinate officers of the policy of the home government saying:

> Son Excellence le ministre de la marine et des colonies, dans sa dernière dépêche, m'informe qu'il lui est absolument impossible d'augmenter les forces militaires et navales de la colonie, et il m'invite formellement à ne pas engager mes moyens d'action sans une nécessité absolue pour quelque opération que ce soit qui serait de nature à créer des besoin auxquels ces forces ne pouraient suffire. . . .[1]

The governor then reserved to himself the authority to decide what expeditions, if any, should be embarked on in Senegal or in the Western Sudan. Because of the opposition of the commercial interests, and the involvement of France in the disastrous Franco-Prussian war and its aftermath, a policy based on force in relation to the Tukulor empire was ruled out for several years.

The Tukulor rulers themselves, preoccupied with their internal squabbles for power, remained friendly, but always insisted that the French should observe the treaty of 1866. In a letter in 1867, for instance, the provincial governor of Nioro, Mustafa, claimed that the Tukulor had remained loyal to the treaty and asked the governor of Senegal to suppress the brigandage being committed by some Bambara under the protection of the French.[2] Ahmadu himself not only maintained friendly relations with the French, but he also tried to use the existing friendly relations to strengthen his position within the Tukulor empire. He wanted the French to supply him with arms and ammunition, especially cannon, which would be useful in his wars, and asked persistently for those which Faidherbe had promised him at the time of Mage's visit.[3] Ahmadu realised the superiority of cannon over the other types of arms available to the Tukulor: this had been demonstrated since his father made use of two cannon in his wars. The French realised what Ahmadu wanted, and though they were unwilling to meet his demands they did not totally reject them. Instead, they supplied him with cannon that were too heavy to be of use to

1 ASAOF, 13G33/3 (No. 77, Circulaire-I-23), Gouvernement du Sénégal, Saint-Louis, 10 June 1867
2 ASAOF, in 15G63, Min Mustafa 'amilu al-Shaikh 'Umar bilādat Nuru 'ila Sultanu 'Indar, marked 'Reçu le 6 Septembre 1867'
3 Mage, *Voyage*, p. 559; Saint-Martin, 'L'artillerie d'El Hadj Omar et d'Ahmadu', *Bull. IFAN*, B, xxvii, 1965, pp. 506–72

him. In a letter to the governor of Senegal in 1869, Ahmadu complained that the cannon left at Bakel for him were too heavy for his beasts to carry, and that since they would be difficult to use, he was returning them to the governor.[1]

Ahmadu's desire to acquire more arms was dictated by the fact that he was at the time intensifying his efforts to suppress the resistance posed by his brothers – Abibu and Moktar – to his claim to supremacy in the empire. In 1869 he had taken the title '*amir al-mūminīn* to emphasise that he was the head of the empire.[2] The French would not actively help to build up Ahmadu's power against his rivals. Rather they maintained friendly relations towards all the power cliques in the Tukulor empire, and thus left the contestants to dissipate their energy and neutralise one another in the protracted struggle that followed. Thus they studiedly remained uninvolved in any direct way in the affairs of the Tukulor even when the latter were engaged in a ruinous power struggle from 1870–76. The main reason for the French attitude was the fact that the Franco-Prussian War had had debilitating effects on the French nation whose government thereafter concentrated on regaining its pre-1870 power and prestige in Europe. The need to recover from the war dictated the concentration of attention on commerce which could contribute to the rehabilitation of the French economy and the re-emergence of France as one of the great European powers. It was against this background that both the French and the Tukulor consciously tried to maintain good relations between them up to 1876.

The French maintained this posture until Brière initiated a new era of aggression and expansion under the guise that he was protecting French commercial interests and guaranteeing the security of French establishments in the Senegambia. He found the avenue for his expansionist policy in the crisis in Khasso between the French protégé, Sambala of Médine, and the Tukulor dependency of Logo. Brière manipulated the crisis until he had a chance to mobilise French forces to destroy the headquarters of Logo, justifying his action by arguing the need to support the French ally who alone guaranteed French presence in the area. Although Brière achieved his objective by cleverly deceiving the French government and ignoring the opinions of some of his own

1 ASAOF, 1G32/3, no. 35 'Rapports avec Ahmadou et son vassal Mohammed Bassirou de la région de Nioro, 1866–1869'
2 See Abun-Nasr, *The Tijāniyya*, pp. 129–30

assistants on the spot, his action disrupted the delicate equilibrium which had sustained Franco-Tukulor relations since 1860.

As has been pointed out in the last chapter, the French invasion of Logo led to the worsening of relations between the French and the Tukulor empire. One of the results of the bad relations was Soleillet's failure to obtain the commercial treaty which he had set out to conclude with the Segu rulers in 1878. The impact of Tukulor reaction was felt particularly by the French commercial interests represented by Soleillet. They saw their trade with the Tukulor empire diminish in volume and value. This had led to the protest of the commercial groups against Brière de l'Isle, whose unilateral action in ordering the invasion of Logo was making things difficult for all concerned. It soon became clear to the French that their loss, in terms of commercial and political relations with the Tukulor empire, was making it possible for their rivals, the British, to strengthen their own position in relation to the same empire. Failure to take action, the French realised, would only lead to a British victory in the struggle for the control of the commerce of the Tukulor empire. This fear of British competition served as an excuse for Brière de l'Isle to embark upon expansionist activities, even when these ran counter to French official policy as enunciated by the Ministry of Marine and Colonies in Paris.[1] Arguing the need to guarantee the security of the French against the Tukulor and the British competitors, Brière de l'Isle initiated the expansion programme which his successors were to use in forcing the hands of the French government into the conquest of the Tukulor empire.

THE GALLIENI MISSION AND ANGLO-FRENCH RIVALRY 1880–81

As a reaction to the French invasion of Logo in 1878, the Tukulor leaders demonstrated their desire to establish relations with the British. The first indication of their willingness to welcome the British, who had earlier indicated their desire to establish relations with them,[2] was given to Paul Soleillet during his visit to

1 See Kanya-Forstner, *The Conquest of the Western Sudan*, chapters 3–5 for a discussion of French official policy in this period.
2 ANSOM, in Sénégal III, 10 bis, H. I. M. Cooper to Amade Seyhou, King of Segou-Sikoro, Bathurst, Gambia, 13 May 1876

Segu in 1878. He was told by Seydou (Sa'īd) Djelia, one of the intimate advisers of Ahmadu, the Tukulor ruler, that the Tukulor wanted to establish relations with the British. Djelia explained that the Tukulor could not accept the French idea that they should deal with them to the exclusion of the British. Rather they would deal with the British as well.[1] With this attitude on the part of the Tukulor, it was easy for relations between them and the British to develop. In a report, Gallieni claimed that Cooper from the British Colony of Gambia visited Segu in 1876, travelling across the Senegambian states of Bondu and Khasso.[2] Since we have no confirmation from other sources this statement by Gallieni should be taken with a good deal of reservation.

From Gallieni's report it would seem that Cooper was able to establish a basis for sustaining relations between the British and the Tukulor. He seems, for instance, to have found agents who were willing to promote British interests in the various sections of the Tukulor empire. Gallieni mentioned the case of a trader, Abibou, who, though pretending to be concerned only with trade, was in fact a political agent of the British, for whom he was said to have carried out political missions in Bondu and Khasso in 1878. In that year, he was said to have visited both the almamy of Bondu, Bubakar Sa'ada, and Sambala of Médine, the French ally in Khasso. Gallieni believed that Abibou's mission in 1878 was to organise an anti-French alliance in the Senegambia.[3] By 1880 Bubakar Sa'ada of Bondu was also still being suspected by the French of being in some secret political relations with the British.[4] From all indications it appeared to the French that British political influence in and around the Tukulor empire was increasing to the detriment of the French.

On the commercial side the French found the growth of British interests equally, if not more, disturbing. Tukulor reaction to the French invasion of Logo seems to have taken the form of a

1 Soleillet, *Voyage à Ségou 1878–1879*, p. 443
2 ASAOF, 1G50/25, 'Gallieni à Monsieur le Gouverneur', Nango, 10 Sept. 1880
3 *Ibid.*, p. 2
4 *Ibid.* The suspicion might have come from the fact that Bubakar Sa'ada had supported Niamody and the Tukulor against Sambala and the French during the invasion of Logo in 1878. Bubakar Sa'ada's action was a disappointment to the French who had expected him to ally with them rather than with Niamody and the Tukulor.

determination to reduce their commercial relations with the French, if such relations could not be totally eliminated. In pursuance of this policy, the Tukulor seem to have diverted trading activities away from the French trading posts, and to have concentrated mainly on trading with the British. It was reported that it was particularly noticeable that caravans from Segu, Nioro, Jenne and other principal commercial centres in the Tukulor empire always ignored French trading posts like Médine and Bakel to go to the British colonies of the Gambia and Sierra Leone to sell their merchandise, as well as to buy British manufactured goods.

Early in 1879 a party of over one thousand traders from Segu visited Sierra Leone.[1] This was evidence of the increased commercial relations between the Tukulor empire and the British in Sierra Leone. There was also a suspicion of British ambition to encircle the French in the Senegambia by uniting the Gambia to Sierra Leone through acquiring a sphere of influence in the interior. It was believed that it was in pursuance of this idea that messengers were sent from Sierra Leone to Timbo in the Futa Jallon in 1879.[2]

As a result of the switch in the direction of Tukulor trading activities, the volume of British trade with the empire was by 1880 said to be enormous. It was reported that by 1880 most of the European goods found in the Upper Senegal area, among the Bambara of Beledugu and the Tukulor on the Niger, were mostly of British origins. This was the case particularly with clothing materials and arms and ammunition. The British were said to be gaining ground daily in their commercial activities in the area from Futa Jallon to the right bank of the Niger, an area which they 'inundated' with their trading posts. The progress being made in this area by the British at the expense of the French was said to be not only commercial but also political.[3]

Although the initiative for encouraging British trade with the Tukulor empire was that of the Aborigines Department of the Sierra Leone Government, the French ascribed it to the big commercial houses in Sierra Leone and the Gambia; they alleged that official action only followed to back up the commercial

1 Fyfe, *A History of Sierra Leone* (1962), p. 414
2 *Ibid.*, p. 427
3 ASAOF, 1G50/25, 'Gallieni à M. le Gouverneur', Nango, 10 Sept. 1880, pp. 3-4

interests and to enter into more formal political relations with the Tukulor.[1] An example of official political action taken by the British in their relations with the Tukulor empire was the Cooper mission in 1876.

In his report, Gallieni alleged that Cooper wrote to the rulers of Bondu and Khasso in 1876 at the same time as he had written to Ahmadu. Cooper was said to have proposed to Ahmadu that the British colonial government should construct a commercial route to link the Gambia with the Segu Tukulor empire. The proposed route was to pass through Bambuk into Ka'arta from where it would lead to Segu. Nothing seems to have come of this project. Later on, however, one Dr Ross (an obvious reference to Governor Rowe) from the British colony of Sierra Leone was said to have pursued the same subject on behalf of the British colonial administration. In 1880, it was claimed, Dr Ross wrote to Ahmadu, indicating British interest in the building of a trade route that would, from Sierra Leone, follow the valley of the Scarcies through the Tukulor territory of Dinguiray to the Niger, and following the right bank of the Niger to Segu-Sikoro, the capital of the Tukulor empire. Dr Ross also informed Ahmadu of the plan to send a British mission to Segu to conclude a political and commercial convention with the Tukulor ruler himself. Of Tukulor reactions to the British moves, it was reported that Ahmadu himself was convinced that the British proposals would be advantageous to his empire, and that he was well-disposed to the idea of allowing British commercial installations along the right bank of the Niger.[2]

1 *Ibid.*, p. 4
2 *Ibid.*, pp. 5–8. Information related here on British relations with the Tukulor empire was said to have been given to Gallieni's interpreter at Segu in 1880 by Ahmadu himself. Gallieni was able to confirm his interpreter's report from his own interviews with Seydou Djelia, one of Ahmadu's principal advisers: see ASAOF, 1G50/25, Gallieni à M. le Gouverneur', Nango, 10 Sept. 1880, p. 7. While it may be true that British interests and influence were growing in the Tukulor empire, it is necessary to take Gallieni's evidence with some reserve as he may have exaggerated the volume of British activities in his report with the intention of forcing the French authorities to adopt a more forceful policy in their relations with the Tukulor empire. Like all French officials in the Senegal area, Gallieni was eager to see the British eliminated, especially from the commerce of the Tukulor empire which, since the time of Faidherbe, had been regarded as a vast hinterland that should serve the needs of French commercial establishments in Senegal. See Hargreaves,

It is against this background of developing rivalry that French activities should be understood. The French had always regarded the British as unwelcome rivals in the Senegambia, and this evidence of the increasing activities of the British, not only in the Senegambia but also in the Tukulor empire, goaded them into adopting a policy calculated to eliminate British competition and guarantee to themselves exclusive control of the Tukulor empire.

The new policy adopted towards the Tukulor empire in 1879–1880 was formulated under Brière de l'Isle, then governor of Senegal. The renewed effort of Brière de l'Isle and his men to pursue a vigorous expansionist policy in relation to the Tukulor empire came at an opportune moment when they could expect to have encouragement and support from their home government. Towards the end of 1878, the struggle for power between the monarchists and republicans was settled. With the resignation of MacMahon and the accession to power of Jules Grévy on 30 January 1879, the republicans gained ascendancy over the monarchists and the political problem which had nearly paralysed the last regime in France was settled. The significance of this in the colonial field was that new men like Jules Ferry, Admiral Jauréguiberry and M. de Freycinet, who believed in the expansion of the French Empire, came into office and substituted action towards expansion for the inactivity, characterised as 'la prudence passive', of the last regime.[1] The new regime was still concerned with the French position in relation to other European powers, but they were also eager to promote the expansion of French empire. They therefore gave the necessary support to, or at least condoned the actions of, energetic colonial agents like Brière de l'Isle.

Brière de l'Isle's policy aimed at the eventual inclusion of the Tukulor empire within the French colonial system. At the beginning it found expression in the idea of linking the Senegal with the Tukulor empire by a rail line. This policy grew out of two considerations. The first was really a part of the Faidherbian idea that the Western Sudan was a vast hinterland that should be exploited to strengthen the economic interests of the French

---

Prelude to the Partition of Africa, p. 255 and *passim* for a survey of Anglo-French rivalry in the Senegambia up to 1883.

1 Hardy, *Histoire de la Colonisation française* (1928), p. 229; Trammond and Reussner, *Eléments d'histoire maritime et coloniale contemporaine: 1815–1914* (1947), p. 383

colony of Senegal. The railway project was conceived as a means of increasing the economic activities of the Western Sudan in general so that it could compensate rapidly for the cost that its conquest would involve. By 1879 Brière de l'Isle and his officers believed that the eventual conquest of the Tukulor empire was inevitable. The second justification for the railway project was that it would be used to bar the British from any access to the Tukulor empire and assure exclusive possession and exploitation of the area by the French. It was maintained by the French authorities that 'il fallait couper au plus tôt à nos rivaux l'accès du Haut-Niger pour nous assurer la possession éxclusive de cette grande route de l'Afrique intérieure'.[1]

For the execution of this project, the French government created 'Le commandement du Haut Fleuve' in 1879,[2] and Captain J. S. Gallieni was appointed to head the mission ('Mission du Haut Niger') which would survey the territories along the river Niger and determine the feasibility of the project. The mission headed by Gallieni was to examine both physical and political problems. It included Lieut. Vallière, M. Pietri and Dr Tautin, and left Saint Louis on 30 January 1880.[3] Before it left Gallieni had already made certain suggestions on what should be done by the French government in relation to the Tukulor empire. From these suggestions it is possible to see the aggressive manner in which Gallieni and his men meant to carry out their mission.

In November 1879 Gallieni had suggested the establishment of new posts at Bafoulabe, Fangalla and Kita. The creation of posts was meant to serve important commercial and political objectives in French relations with the Tukulor empire. The new posts were meant to signify new boundary claims which the French could assert against the Tukulor empire. Gallieni explained that he recommended the siting of a post at Bafoulabe because this would be strategically useful in any French bid to reverse the idea contained in the treaty concluded with Ahmadu by Mage on the boundary question. He claimed that the treaty gave the idea that the river Senegal formed the line of demarcation between the

1 Legendre, *La Conquête de la France Africaine* (n.d.), p. 75
2 The French Parliament approved the study of plans for a Senegal–Niger railway in 1879. See Hargreaves, 'The Tokolor empire of Segou and its relations with the French', p. 138
3 Legendre, *La Conquête de la France Africaine*, p. 76; Hargreaves, *Prelude to the Partition*, pp. 256–65

Tukulor empire and the French possessions in the Senegambia.[1] Bafoulabe, sited at the confluence of the rivers Bakhoy and Bafing, was strategically placed to serve as a base for French operations against the Tukulor empire. Gallieni pointed out that the building of posts, especially at Bafoulabe, should be regarded only as a stage in the process of taking over the Tukulor empire without having to resort to fighting an immediate open war. Bafoulabe, he further recommended was a convenient, advantageous point from which revolts against the Tukulor empire could be encouraged and used as a means of breaking the empire. He observed that anti-Tukulor resistance groups, like the Bambara and the Malinke, would be encouraged to receive the French among them, suggesting that they would cooperate with the French, whom they would see as protectors against the Tukulor regime. On the commercial side, Gallieni claimed that the proposed posts could be used to exclude the British from the commercial activities of the Tukulor empire over which the French would then establish a monopoly.[2]

Brière de l'Isle, the unrelenting promoter of French imperial expansion, must have been delighted to find such a willing agent as Gallieni. In his enthusiasm to realise his ambition, he equipped and sent out the Gallieni mission on 30 January 1880, even before the French parliament had voted the relevant grants for the prosecution of the survey mission. Also between them, the governor and Gallieni extended the scope of the mission from one charged with making feasibility surveys to one tackling large political issues.

What Gallieni failed to recommend was how to realise his grand ideas without provoking the Tukulor rulers into hostility against the French. Yet when he set out on his mission on 30 January 1880 it was with the ambition of realising the objectives set out in his memorandum on the establishment of posts.

Gallieni left Saint Louis armed with a letter from the governor,

1 This idea of an accepted boundary was obviously Gallieni's creation. The Tukulor certainly did not accept it since they controlled Dinguiray and Logo and had allies in Futa Toro, all in the Senegambia. The struggle in Khasso, which led to the French invasion of Logo in 1878, was significant in showing the determination of the Tukulor to fight to maintain themselves and their allies in the Senegambian states.
2 ASAOF, 1G50/11, Note relative à l'emplacement et à l'établissement d'un poste à Bafoulabé, Gallieni, Saint-Louis, 20 Nov. 1879

Brière de l'Isle, to Ahmadu, assuring him of the French desire to continue friendly relations with the Tukulor empire. Brière claimed that the greatest testimony of the French desire for friendly relations was the fact that for the previous fifteen years after the visit of Mage and Quintin peace had been maintained between the French and the Tukulor. Gallieni, he said, was sent to strengthen the friendship already existing between the French and the Tukulor. What the French now wanted, he emphasised, was the development and extension of commerce, as well as a guarantee for its protection. He asked Ahmadu to agree to the signing of the treaty which Gallieni would be presenting to him as a mark of his friendly disposition towards the French.[1] Though he was armed with a letter which assured Ahmadu of the desire of the French for friendly relations, Gallieni and his men carried out their mission in an impetuous way that could only have made the Tukulor ruler hostile to the French cause.

Instead of going direct to Segu to negotiate with Ahmadu, Gallieni and his men addressed themselves to the task of finding allies among the anti-Tukulor Bambara populations in the region between Upper Senegal and Bamako on the Niger. It was for this reason that Gallieni and his men avoided the more direct and secure route to Segu through Ka'arta. Instead they chose to explore the route from Bafoulabe by the way of Kita to Bamako. Gallieni himself explained that his mission chose the latter route because 'elle savait qu'elle trouverait sur la ligne Bafoulabé-Kita-Bammako une série d'États hostiles aux Toucouleurs et auprès desquels elle se présenterait avec des hommes importants parents rapprochés des chefs de ces contrées'.[2] He also explained that his mission explored this route because they were sure that they would find allies among the people who would see the French as protectors against their Tukulor enemies. Bamako, he claimed, was not only a commercial centre; it was also a strong political base from which operations against the Segu Tukulor empire could be directed. It was therefore necessary for the French to link their posts with Bamako, and it was this consideration that made the mission head for Bamako.[3]

1 ASAOF, 1G52/5, Le Gouverneur à Ahmadou, Sultan de Ségou, Saint-Louis, 29 Jan. 1880
2 ASAOF, 1G50/20, Gallieni, le chef de la mission du Haut-Niger, à M. le Gouverneur, Nango, 7 July 1880, p. 4
3 *Ibid.*, p. 3

Gallieni and his men thought of exploiting the anti-Tukulor feelings of the Bambara in Fouladougou and Beledugu to achieve their objectives. The mission failed in this largely because though it was true that the Bambara wanted help against the Tukulor regime, they would not accept the offer made by Gallieni's mission because they could not trust the French. In many places the Bambara suspected the French of some undisclosed diabolical design against them. They knew that Gallieni and his men were heading for Segu where they would enter into relations with Ahmadu, the head of the Tukulor empire. The Bambara believed that the French were friends of the Tukulor, and that they had come into the Beledugu in order to survey the Bambara territory with a view to helping the Tukulor against them. To the claims of Gallieni's mission that they were their friends and ready to collaborate with them against the Tukulor, the Bambara reacted by regarding the Frenchmen as deceitful and dangerous persons who should be exterminated. Gallieni reported that in many places the Bambara sincerely believed that it was necessary to exterminate 'les blancs qui venaient dans le Bélédougou pour tromper les habitants et aider les Toucouleurs à les subjuguer'.[1]

Gallieni's mission failed to win the support of the Bambara because it fell victim to its own designs. The Bambara considered the French as their enemies and were therefore hostile to the mission, which was pillaged at Dio on 11 May 1880.[2] This attack marked the end and the failure of the mission among the Bambara of Beledugu. The failure of the Beledugu mission marked a setback to the Brière de l'Isle–Gallieni project to expand French colonial empire under the guise of dealing with the Tukulor empire and the British, and emphasised the need for a new approach to French relations with the Tukulor empire and the problem of British competition. The Dio incident made the French realise that they could not possibly encounter both the British and the Tukulor at the same time; they therefore decided to tackle the British first. They realised that to be able to exclude the British from the Niger and the Tukulor empire, they would need the cooperation of the Tukulor rulers, and in August 1880[3]

---

1 Gallieni, *Voyage au Soudan Français* (*Haut-Niger et Pays de Ségou*), *1879–1881* (1885), p. 211

2 Legendre, *La Conquête de la France Africaine*, p. 77

3 ASAOF, 1G50/24, Gallieni à M. le Gouverneur, Nango, 2 Sept. 1880,

Gallieni was instructed to proceed from Bamako to Segu to negotiate a treaty with Ahmadu.

In his second letter to Ahmadu, Brière de l'Isle explained that a letter had earlier been written to him to assure him of the French desire to strengthen their friendly relations with the Tukulor empire. The letter he had written earlier was lost during the Dio incident,[1] and the purpose of the second letter was to reiterate the points already made in the lost letter. Ahmadu was told that the purpose of Gallieni's mission was to strengthen the commercial links between the French and the Tukulor by the conclusion of a treaty.[2]

The treaty which Gallieni set out to negotiate with Ahmadu was meant to guarantee to the French several privileges among which were the exclusive right to trade with and establish posts in all parts of the Tukulor empire, and the exclusive right for the navigation of, and the establishment of French stations on, the Niger.[3] If these privileges were granted, it was calculated that it would be easy for the French to eliminate the British in the competition for the commerce of the Western Sudan in general.

Gallieni set out for Segu with the idea that, if given sufficient inducements, Ahmadu would readily sign such a treaty. He soon realised how wrong he was from the attitude of the Tukulor ruler to his mission. Ahmadu forbade Gallieni to reach Segu, giving strict orders that he and his men be kept at Nango, a village about forty kilometres away. They remained at Nango for several months without being granted an audience by Ahmadu.[4]

Gallieni explained that the hostile reception accorded his mission was due partly to the British who had, through their agents from Sierra Leone and the Gambia, informed Ahmadu

p. 25; 1G351/4, Monographie du cercle de Ségou, L'Administrateur, Ségou, 8 Feb. 1921, p. 3

1 This refers to the letter already cited. ASAOF, 1G52/5, Le Gouverneur à Ahmadou, Sultan de Ségou, Saint-Louis, 29 Jan. 1880

2 ASAOF, 1G52/25, same to same, 19 July 1880

3 ASAOF, 1G50/35, Gallieni à M. le Gouverneur, Nango, 25 Oct. 1880

4 Legendre, *La Conquête de la France Africaine*, p. 78; ASAOF, 1G50/24, Gallieni à M. le Gouverneur, Nango, 2 Sept. 1880, p. 4; 15G76/1 Le Gouverneur au chef des croyants Ahmadou El-Kebir-Mouduy, Sultan de Ségou, Saint-Louis, 2 Dec. 1880; 1G351/5, Monographie du cercle de Ségou', L'Administrateur, Ségou, 8 Feb. 1921; ANSOM, in Sénégal III, 10 bis, Capitaine Gallieni au Gouverneur, Saint-Louis, Nango, 25 Oct. 1880

that his mission was in the Tukulor empire to do the exploratory work necessary for the eventual conquest of the Tukulor by the French. Among the British agents who were alleged to be responsible for the sinister reputation which the French had acquired before the arrival of the mission, Gallieni mentioned Abdul Bubakar,[1] presumably the almamy of Bondu who had been reported earlier on to be an ally of the British and the Tukulor. According to oral tradition at Segu the explanation of Ahmadu's action was that by refusing to see Gallieni and his men, he was only acting according to the prophecy of, and instructions given by, 'Umar. According to the Segu tradition, 'Umar had predicted that various French missions would come to Segu but that only the first of them, which happened to be that of Mage and Quintin, would be peaceful and should be received by Ahmadu; the others, after Mage's, would come with hostile intentions and should be refused entry into Segu, the capital of the Segu Tukulor empire. This was why, according to the story, Ahmadu confined Gallieni at Nango and gave him no audience.[2] Both explanations shed some light on the attitude of the Tukulor ruler; but they do not tell the whole story. Gallieni himself gave the remaining, and probably the most important, explanations for Tukulor action in some of his correspondences.

He reported that Seydou Djelia, one of Ahmadu's principal advisers, told him the reasons for his confinement to Nango. First among the reasons given was the non-fulfilment by the French of the terms contained in the treaty concluded with Mage in 1866. For instance, the French had up till 1880 not supplied the Tukulor with cannon as promised by the governor of the Senegal during Mage's visit to Segu. The treaty was also not observed in relation to the agreement on the freedom of movement for Tukulor caravans in the Senegambia. Secondly, the French were accused of aiding Moriba, a dissident subject of the Tukulor in Ka'arta,[3] and of providing asylum for his men in territories under French protection. A third reason grouped together a number of important and recent events all of which incensed the Tukulor

---

1 ANSOM, in Sénégal III, 10 bis, Gallieni au Gouverneur, Saint-Louis, Nango, 25 Oct. 1880; ASAOF, 1G50/41, same to same, le 28 Dec. 1880
2 Oral evidence at Segu, May 1965
3 This refers to the role of the French ally, Sambala, in the civil wars between Bassiru, the Tukulor emir of Diomboko and Moriba Safere, district ruler of Sero. See Chapter 7 above.

against the French. These included the invasion of Logo and the construction of a French post at Bafoulabe.[1] Both acts were interpreted as a violation of the territorial rights of the Tukulor. Lastly there was the conduct of Gallieni's mission among the Beledugu Bambara shortly before the mission set out for Segu. Gallieni reported the complaint of the Tukulor against the association of his mission with the Bambara who were still in resistance against the Tukulor regime, and claimed that Seydou Djelia told him that:

> Enfin, pour venir nous trouver, vous avez passé chez nos ennemis·
> Malgré la défense du roi de Ségou, vous avez passé chez ses sujets
> révoltés; vous avez beaucoup parlé sur votre route, dans le Fouladougou
> à Kita, à Bammako. Il y a la dedans une obscurité profonde que nous
> n'avons pas encore percée.[2]

It is clear from this passage that Gallieni's conduct among the Bambara of Beledugu had greatly compromised his mission, and had earned it a bad reputation before it reached Segu. The Tukulor were determined to deal with Gallieni and let his mission leave Nango only after they had been satisfied about the reasons for its recent activities in Beledugu. Gallieni himself admitted indulging in anti-Tukulor activities, but claimed, falsely, that he did so in order to dispel the distrust of the Bambara towards him and his men.[3]

Given this hostile and unpromising beginning, and especially the suspicion that pervaded the relationship between the Tukulor officials and Gallieni, it is not surprising that the mission failed. The mission remained at Nango from August 1880 until March 1881, when it was allowed to leave the Tukulor empire. Gallieni spent the period of his stay at Nango in protracted negotiations which led to the conclusion of a treaty which not only fell short of the expectations of the French, but was in fact unusable. The treaty, concluded on 3 November 1880, provided, among other things, for the protection on a reciprocal basis, of Tukulor subjects and French protected persons engaged in trade in the Senegambia and within the Tukulor empire. The Tukulor ruler also promised to encourage trade between his empire and the French posts. The

1 The Bafoulabe post was built in 1879. See Trammond and Reussner, *Eléments d'histoire maritime . . .*, p. 383
2 ANSOM, in Sénégal III, 10 bis, Procès Verbal de la 1er Séance – 31 Oct. (1880), 3 h. du Soir.
3 Gallieni, *Voyage*, p. 209

treaty categorically rejected the French request for permission to build posts along the Niger and other parts of the Tukulor empire for commercial and other purposes. In return for the facilities granted them, the French promised to supply some quantity of arms and ammunition to the Tukulor, in addition to paying them royalties on articles traded within the empire.[1] The treaty did not guarantee to the French the privileges which they had sought in order to exclude the British from the trade of the area, nor enable them to prepare for the eventual liquidation of the Tukulor regime.

Apart from their failure to negotiate what they set out to obtain, the treaty could not be used to exploit the limited possibilities it offered for the development of French interests. This was partly because the document itself was of doubtful validity. Gallieni, who wrote the French text, seems to have written as many versions of it as he pleased on several occasions. The result was that several inconsistencies and variations exist in the various copies of the treaty submitted to the French government.[2] In addition to internal inconsistency in copies of the French text, which Ahmadu did not sign, there was the more serious case of differences between Ahmadu's Arabic copy and his interpretation of the treaty on the one hand, and the French text on the other.

One important clause stipulated by Ahmadu in the letter he attached to the treaty, and which is not contained in any version of the French text, is the statement that the first condition to be fulfilled before he could enter into relations with the French

1 ANSOM, in Sénégal III, 10 bis/C., Traité d'amitié et de commerce conclu avec l'Empire du Ségou entre G. Brière de l'Isle, gouverneur du Sénégal et le Sultan Ahmadou (n.d.); in Sénégal III, 10 bis, Télégramme, Capitaine Gallieni au Gouverneur, Nango, 9 Mar. 1881; ASAOF, 1G57/44, Télégramme Confidentielle, Gallieni à Gouverneur, Saint-Louis, Nango, 9 Mar. 1881

2 Variations exist in the text of the treaty as recorded in the following documents: ANSOM, in Sénégal III, 10 bis Télégramme, Capitaine Gallieni au Gouverneur, Nango, 9 Mar. 1881; in Sénégal III 10 bis/23, Traité d'amitié et de commerce conclu avec l'Empire du Ségou' (n.d.). An obvious inconsistency between these two documents is the name of the signatory for the French side. In the first Gallieni signed on behalf of Brière de l'Isle, and in the second he signed on behalf of Valière. More serious, however, is the internal variation between the two copies; they also vary from the text of the treaty contained in ASAOF, 1G57/44, Télégramme Confidentielle, Gallieni à Gouverneur, Saint-Louis, Nango, 9 Mar. 1881

would be the destruction of the French posts at Bafoulabe and Kita.[1] The implication of this demand was clear to the French authorities. Ahmadu was claiming sovereignty over the Senegambia and indicated that he regarded French activities, especially the building of forts, in this area as incursions on Tukulor territories. A testimony to the correctness of this interpretation of Ahmadu's demand was the action that he took immediately after he had made it. Gallieni reported that Ahmadu gave orders to Tukulor rulers, especially those in Ka'arta and the Senegambia, to prevent the French from penetrating up to the Niger. He gave orders particularly to his representative at Mourgoula (in Fouladougou, also sometimes called Birgo) to cut all communication between Kita and the Mandingo states in Senegambia.[2] It was clear to the French that to accede to this clause by accepting the treaty would imply the total abandonment of all they had achieved in terms of territorial control in the Senegambia. The treaty was, if only for this reason, unacceptable to them.

But it was also unacceptable because it contained clauses which required the French to supply Ahmadu with cannon and other arms and a large quantity of ammunition. Ahmadu made this demand mainly to be able to increase the strength and effectiveness of his army. He needed a strong army to be able to combat intra-Tukulor rivalry for power which was undermining his own position, and to suppress the various anti-Tukulor resistance movements in several parts of the empire. If the French supplied him with sufficient weapons, there was the possibility that he would use them to establish himself as the supreme power in a united Tukulor empire. This would be ominous for the future of French interests in the area. To realise their ambition, the French would prefer a weak, divided Tukulor empire. It was also feared that any weapons supplied to Ahmadu might be used against the French, since he had made it clear that he considered the French to be encroaching upon Tukulor territories. For these various reasons, the French government refused to ratify the treaty.[3]

1 ASAOF, 13G25/1, Le Gouverneur du Sénégal à M. le Ministre de la Marine et des Colonies, Saint-Louis, 24 May 1881
2 ASAOF, 1G57/39, Gallieni au Colonel, Niagassola, 2 Apr. 1881
3 ANSOM, Sénégal III, 10 bis/107, Note pour le Ministre par le Conseiller d'Etat, Directeur des Colonies, Paris, 15 June 1881; in Sénégal IV, 75(a), 'Ministre de la Marine et des colonies – Note',

With the treaty unratified and unusable, Gallieni's mission achieved practically nothing of importance. He himself claimed that the treaty of Nango represented for the French great progress towards penetrating the centre of Africa because it gave the French protectorate rights over the Niger from its sources to Timbuktu. He also made the claim that the treaty would lead to the increase in, and development of, French influence and commerce in the territories bordering the Niger in the Sudan, which area, he claimed, henceforth belonged to the French.[1] On the basis of the facts that we have, the claims made by Gallieni are both unjustifiable and unfounded.

From the point of view of the colonial ministry in Paris the failure of Gallieni mission was regrettable for another reason – that the mission itself represented an act of insubordination against ministerial instructions by the governor of Senegal. Brière de l'Isle had been used to flouting ministerial orders by exploiting loopholes in his instructions to carry out his own programme. He did this with the war in Khasso from 1876 to 1878, justifying his action on the grounds that it was necessary for the security of French commercial and political interests. Once again, he had extended the permission to engage in an exploratory mission to translate his own ideas about French political expansion into reality by sending out the Gallieni mission even before parliament voted the funds for the survey work it had authorised. Brière de l'Isle used to get away with his tactics of confronting the ministry with a *fait accompli*, especially when Admiral Jauréguiberry, a former governor of Senegal and supporter of French expansion overseas, was the minister. But Jauréguiberry's successor, Rear-Admiral Cloué, would not tolerate such an act of defiance from a junior officer. Consequently, he wrote to Brière de l'Isle, charging him with responsibility for the misfortunes of the Gallieni mission and the difficulties encountered in the Kita area by the Upper Senegal High Command mission. Admiral Cloué's despatch to Brière de l'Isle in February 1881 included these condemnatory statements: 'Vous ne vous êtes jamais préoccupé du programme énoncé dans les instructions que j'ai données . . . vous avez vu dans mes instructions un paragraphe,

---

Paris, 11 Mar. 1882; De Card, *Les Traités de Protectorat conclus par la France en Afrique 1870–1895* (1897), p. 137

1 Gallieni, *Voyage*, p. 407

qui, pris isolément, répondait à vos idées et vous avez negligé tous les autres.'[1]

In spite of the annoyance of the minister over Brière de l'Isle's act of defiance, the ministry had no doubt about the need to continue to maintain the French presence in the Western Sudan. But because of the failure of the Gallieni mission and the ineptitude with which it was conceived and carried out, it became urgent to repair the damage done to Franco-Tukulor relations. The failure of the mission was seen as a temporary setback, and it was decided to lay the foundation for further negotiations. Consequently, while rejecting Gallieni's treaty, the French government sent gifts to Ahmadu and paid him royalties on French merchandise traded in the Tukulor empire as stipulated in the treaty.[2] In taking this step, the French calculated that they would be able to reopen negotiations which they hoped would lead to the conclusion of a convention that would conform more to French interests. It was also calculated that the measure would facilitate the operations of the French colonial officers in the Western Sudan.[3] The activities of the French officers under Borgnis Desbordes[4] were sometimes overtly anti-Tukulor; but in sending gifts to Ahmadu, the ministry hoped to be able to convince him about the peaceful intentions of the French government towards his empire and it was believed that 'on évitera ainsi une rupture brusque qui pourrait être très préjudiciable à nos intérets sur le Niger'.[5]

While the French government made efforts in this way to protect French interests in and around the Tukulor empire, the penetration of the Tukulor empire via the Niger was being intensified by the mission led by Colonel Borgnis Desbordes.

1 N'Diaye, 'La colonie du Sénégal au temps de Brière de l'Isle (1876–1881)', *Bull. IFAN*, B, xxx, 2, 1968, pp. 463–512, esp. pp. 495–6
2 ANSOM, Sénégal III, 10 bis/III, Rapport au Ministre – achat des cadeaux pour le Sultan Ahmadou, Paris, 18 June 1881
3 While Gallieni was being detained at Nango the project for the linking of Upper Senegal with the Niger was being vigorously executed under the command of a determined marine officer, Gustave Borgnis-Desbordes.
4 See pp. 246ff. for information on Desbordes and his activities.
5 ANSOM, Sénégal III, bis/107, Note pour le Ministre par le Conseiller d'Etat, Directeur des Colonies, Paris, 15 June 1881

THE CONSTRUCTION OF THE KITA-BAMAKO ROUTE AND
THE FRENCH ESTABLISHMENT AT BAMAKO, 1881–83

Borgnis Desbordes was chosen to lead the French exploratory mission to the Niger after Gallieni had gone on his mission to Segu. Borgnis Desbordes continued the exploratory work begun by Gallieni with enthusiasm, and the French government seemed determined to give energetic support to the project which was considered as very important for the expansion of French commerce. In support of the mission the Natioual Assembly voted a sum of 1,300,000 francs to the Ministry for the Marine and Colonies on 2 August 1880. This grant was for the creation of new fortified posts and for financing research parties in the region between the Upper Senegal and the Niger. In pursuance of this objective, a decree was issued on 6 September 1880, authorising the creation of the 'Upper Senegal High Command' ('le commandement du Haut-Senegal'). Borgnis Desbordes was subsequently appointed to carry out the project. He was instructed to carry out the building of new posts, particularly at Fangalla, Gouniakori and Kita. He was also to direct studies in the Upper Senegal region, and particularly between Bafoulabe and the Niger, examining the possibility of establishing a rail-line that would link Médine, the point at which the Senegal ceased to be navigable, to Bamako, Manabougou or Dina on the Niger.[1]

The idea behind this project was to ensure for the French a continuous line of communication between their colony of Senegal and the Tukulor empire through the river Niger. They would be able to exploit this area, to the exclusion of the British and other nations, for the development and expansion of French commerce. The points chosen for the construction of the posts, especially Kita, were supposed to be strategic points from which commerce could be effectively tapped to the exclusion of the British, but without any need for the use of force. The French authorities believed that they could control the commerce of the Tukulor empire peacefully through the use of protected trading posts established along the rivers Senegal and Niger.

1 ANSOM, in Sénégal IV, 73, Instructions pour le Commandant Supérieur dans le haut Sénégal, Paris, 4 Oct. 1880; ASAOF, 1G61/28, Instructions pour le commandant Supérieur dans le haut Sénégal par le Vice-Amiral, Ministre de la Marine et des Colonies, Paris, 4 Oct. 1880

In the interpretation and working of this policy, the French government in Paris often differed from their representatives in Senegal. Sometimes the differences in interpretation resulted in contradictory instructions being given to the men executing the project on the Niger. This, coupled with the fact that the leader of the mission, Borgnis Desbordes, sometimes carried out his instructions in a way to satisfy his own urge for forceful action which often contradicted official policy, accounted for the seemingly clumsy character of the enterprise.

This was in a way a reflection of the working of the government in Paris. As has been pointed out, the government was generally in favour of French overseas expansion, particularly in the commercial field. But the government was also eager to re-establish the French position in Europe by maintaining friendly relations with the other powers. This concern for her position in Europe made it impossible for France to pursue a bold, consistently forward colonial policy since she had to consider the susceptibilities of the other powers. In the Western Sudan, for instance, while France was eager to eliminate the British from the competition for the commerce of the Tukulor empire, she could not afford a policy that could be regarded as openly aggressive for fear of British reaction in Europe. Because of these considerations, therefore, the regime's colonial enterprises were carried out at a time when the government was only groping for a workable policy. Hardy gives a graphic picture of the tentative nature of the regime's policy when he says: 'En réalité, il a, durant quatre années à peu près, tatonné, fait l'apprentissage du pouvoir, hésité souvent, dans le détail de sa politique coloniale, entre sa volonté d'expansion et ses principes de paix européenne.'[1]

The situation was made worse by the lack of continuity in the direction of the colonial ministry. Direction of colonial affairs was exercised by many people, none of whom stayed for long in office. The Waddington ministry constituted by Jules Grévy, was replaced by that of Freycinet, which was also soon replaced by that of Jules Ferry. The latter exercised power for seven months before he was succeeded by Gambetta who remained only seventy-seven days in office. Then came Freycinet's new ministry presided over by Duclerc, which resigned in January 1883.[2]

The situation was such as to give strong characters in the

1 Hardy, *Histoire de la Colonisation*, p. 229
2 *Ibid.*, pp. 229–30

colonies the opportunity to influence the execution of policy according to their own interpretations. Brière de l'Isle and the newly-appointed supreme commandant of the Niger project, Borgnis Desbordes, were such strong characters who wanted the French penetration of the Tukulor empire pursued in a determined, forceful manner. They often came into conflict with the government in Paris whose ministers could not always support the measures taken in Senegal, nor justify such measures to the National Assembly which had the power of the purse. At this time, whenever conflict concerning the policy in Senegal arose between Paris and the colonial administration, the views of Paris prevailed only for a while, at best forcing a temporary modification of colonial enterprises.

In relation to the Niger mission, the first conflict between Paris and Brière de l'Isle arose from the instructions which the latter gave to Borgnis Desbordes. Among other things, Brière de l'Isle instructed Desbordes to use the forces at his disposal to punish the Bambara of Beledugu who had pillaged the convoy led by Gallieni in May 1880.[1] In effect Desbordes was asked to use the forces at his disposal as an expeditionary column forcefully to break through the barrier which the Bambara constituted between Upper Senegal and Bamako.

Having thus ordered attack on the Bambara of Beledugu, Brière de l'Isle wrote to Ahmadu, explaining that the Bambara had attacked Gallieni's convoy because they knew that the French were friends of the Tukulor. He then informed Ahmadu of the determination of the French government to punish the Bambara in Beledugu and Bamako for their action. It was for this purpose, he declared, that Borgnis Desbordes had been sent with an army that would be based at Kita.[2]

Brière de l'Isle sent this message to Ahmadu in the hope that the latter would be delighted with the proposed expedition against his enemies, the Bambara. It could also have been planned as a way of getting Gallieni out of Ahmadu's clutches.

Desbordes, contemptuous of the African, was enthusiastic about the idea of waging a military expedition against the Bam-

1 ANSOM, in Sénégal IV, 73, Instructions remises à M. le chef d'escadron d'artillerie de la marine, Borgnis-Desbordes, Commt Supr. dans le haut-fleuve, Saint-Louis, 23 Nov. 1880
2 ASAOF, 15G76/1, Le Gouverneur au chef des croyants Ahmadou . . ., Saint-Louis, 2 Dec. 1880

bara. He was eager for action and would have waged war against the Bambara but for the timely intervention of Paris. He had in fact issued an ultimatum to the Bambara to break down their forts and fortifications at Goubanko, Dio and Bamako as the only condition for beginning any negotiation between them and himself. Failing this, he declared, he would attack them.[1]

In a memorandum from the ministry, however, it was pointed out to Brière de l'Isle that his instructions to Desbordes amounted to a reversal of the official policy. It was pointed out that the money voted for the mission was for the creation of posts and the peaceful occupation of the country, and not, as it was being used by Brière de l'Isle, to cover the cost of any expeditionary column against the people. It was pointed out that the French government intended to achieve its objective of spreading French influence by peaceful means and that the operations embarked upon by Brière de l'Isle and Desbordes 'engageraient très gravement la responsabilité du ministre vis-à-vis du Parlement'.[2] The minister for Colonies, Admiral Cloué, wrote to Brière de l'Isle, expressing his disapproval of the measures being taken against the Bambara, especially the reprisals being pursued by Desbordes. The minister emphasised that 'notre tâche est de créer des relations pacifiques avec les populations et de préparer du terrain pour notre commerce dans le pays compris entre Médine et Ségou-Sikoro'.[3]

In view of the minister's letter, Brière de l'Isle cancelled his former instructions to Borgnis Desbordes, explaining wrongly, that the ministry had changed its policy.[4] Henceforth, the mission had to achieve its goal without recourse to force. Desbordes was advised to send treaty-making missions to the Mandingo territories, especially Bouré and Dinguiray, and to the territories bordering on the river Niger. The aim of the missions would be to find allies among non-Tukulor populations who were hostile to the Tukulor regime. Brière de l'Isle claimed that this approach

1 ASAOF, 15G57/22, B. Desbordes, le Lt-Col., Commandant Supérieur du Haut-Fleuve à M. le Capitaine Marchi, 25 Jan. 1881
2 ANSOM, in Sénégal IV, 73, Monsieur le Ministre – Au sujet des Instructions donnés par le Gouverneur du Sénégal au Commandant Supérieur du Haut-Fleuve, Paris, 3 Dec. 1880
3 ANSOM, in Sénégal IV, 73, 'Monsieur le Ministre à M. le Gouverneur du Sénégal', Paris, 4 Jan. 1881
4 ANSOM, in Sénégal IV, 73 bis, 'Borgnis-Desbordes: Rapport sur la Campagne 1880–1881 dans le Soudan', pp. 79–81

coincided with that recommended by Gallieni, who had emphasised the need to find allies against the Tukulor. He also maintained that such an approach was a necessity because 'les
tendances du Département, poussé par l'opinion de la chambre des
députés, sont d'agir pacifiquement nonobstant l'agression de
Dio'.[1]

Desbordes had to carry out his mission according to his new
instructions; but he continued to show his preference for a more
forceful approach by advocating a complete break with the
Tukulor empire and the declaration of French protectorates in
the Mandingo states in the Upper Senegal. He claimed that it was
necessary to break relations with the Tukulor because they had
continued to be obstacles in his way and, from his experience with
them, he was convinced that no good and durable result could be
achieved by the French until the Tukulor influence had been
completely removed.[2]

For Desbordes good and durable achievements consisted of the
complete takeover of the Tukulor empire. He used the British
presence and the threat it represented to French interests to
emphasise the importance and inevitability of the measures he
recommended. He stressed that if the French failed to declare
the states adjoining the Tukulor empire as their protectorate, the
British would do so, with disastrous consequences to French
interests in the Tukulor empire. In that case, the French would
only have succeeded, at great cost in men and money, in creating
a blind alley between Bafoulabe and Kita, an area which would
consequently remain not only costly to maintain but also unpro-
ductive, since all the produce of the Niger area and the Mandingo
states, particularly Bouré, would be diverted to Sierra Leone.[3]
Again in May, while pressing the need to adopt the measures he
advocated during the forthcoming 1881–82 campaign, Desbordes
repeated virtually the same arguments.[4]

The French government, however, seemed reluctant to get
involved in commitments of a military and political nature in the

1 ASAOF, 3B98/2, Correspondence avec le Commandant Supérieur dans
  le haut-fleuve, année 1881, par M. le Gouverneur du Sénégal, Brière de
  l'Isle, 2 Feb. 1881
2 ASAOF, 15G1/599, Le Lt-Col., Commandant Supérieur du Haut-
  Fleuve à M. le Gouverneur, 30 Mar. 1881, pp. 2–4
3 *Ibid.*, p. 4
4 ASAOF. 1G15/898, Le Commandant de la Marine à M. le Gouverneur,
  17 May 1881

Western Sudan. They continued to indicate, by the measures taken, that their priority was for the peaceful development and expansion of commerce. Thus, by a decree issued on 14 November 1881, the administration of colonies was made the responsibility of the ministry of commerce, though defence of the colonies remained the responsibility of the ministry for the marine.[1] This arrangement seems to indicate the preponderant importance which the government attached to commerce in their overseas policy of the time.

It was against this background of continual conflict of ideas between the home government and the colonial officers in Senegal that Desbordes carried out the mission of 1880–81. Briefly, the achievement of the mission included the construction of a route linking Bafoulabe to Kita, the building and garrisoning of a fort at Kita and the construction of 121 kilometres of telegraphic line between Bafoulabe and Toukolo. Other assignments carried out by Desbordes's mission included the drawing up, after a topographic study, of a map of the country between Médine and Kita, and the building of commercial provisions stores and rest houses at such places as Solinta, Badumbe, Toukolo and Goniokory. Desbordes also mentioned the conclusion of treaties with Mandingo states in places like Baguakadougou, Gadougou, Bouré, Kamera and Bamako.[2]

The treaties spoken of could not, of course, have been valid documents since they were concluded with subject peoples under Tukulor rule. They were, however, important to the extent that their conclusion represented an improvement in the relations between the French and the various people who, during Gallieni's visit, had been distrustful of, and hostile to, the French. The strategy of wooing the Bambara and other non-Tukulor peoples on the basis of a common hostility to the Tukulor regime appeared to be yielding fruits.

The plan for the campaign of 1881–82 was very much the continuation of what was begun in 1880–81. Emphasis was laid, as in the previous year, on the continuation of the construction of a route leading to Bamako and the building of posts along it.[3]

1 ASAOF, 13G25/4, Le Ministre de la Marine à M. le Gouverneur du Sénégal et dépendances, Paris, 4 Dec. 1881
2 ASAOF, 1D64, 'Rapport sur la Campagne 1881–1882 dans le Soudan', Borgnis Desbordes (n.d.), pp. 1–2
3 *Ibid.*, pp. 3–4

Official policy also continued to emphasise the need to carry out the mission in a peaceful manner. Officially France wanted to achieve its objectives without breaking off friendly relations with the Tukulor empire.[1]

The 1881–82 mission did not achieve the results envisaged for various reasons. First, there was an unexpected change in the direction of the route being built. The aim of the mission had been to construct the route through Beledugu to Bamako, but a deviation from the original plan had to be made at Badumbe.[2] Secondly, there were problems connected with the insufficiency of the naval materials made available to the mission, lateness in sending much-needed provisions from France and the fact that many of the personnel of the mission suffered from yellow fever.[3] The Tukulor had also begun to react against French penetration. The most effective reaction which disturbed the mission was the closing of the caravan routes which linked Ka'arta to French posts in the Upper Senegal. By sealing off the routes the Tukulor made it difficult, and sometimes impossible, for the French to continue their commercial activities in the region, and even to get food and other provisions for sustaining the personnel of the mission. Pro-Tukulor people in the Senegambia also began to refuse offers of employment in the construction work of the mission, and even among those already employed incidents of desertion increased.[4]

For the 1882–83 campaign the target aimed at was the definite establishment of the French on the Niger at Bamako. A fort was to be built there, and a garrison comprising two companies of *tirailleurs Sénégalais* and half a company of the Spahi – 'un peloton de spahis' – was to be maintained.[5] The provision made for the maintenance of garrisions seems to imply that the ministry was tending towards the policy advocated by Brière de

1 ASAOF, 3B98/9(17), Instructions pour M. le Lt-Col. Bourdiaux, Commandant Supérieur, Vallon, Saint-Louis, 26 July 1882
2 ASAOF, 1D64, 'Rapport sur la Campagne 1881–1882 dans le Soudan', p. 107
3 *Ibid.*, pp. 8–22
4 ASAOF, 3B98–9(17), Instructions pour M. le Lt-Col. Bourdiaux, Commandant Supérieur, Vallon, Saint-Louis, 26 July 1882
5 ANSOM, in Sénégal I, 99, Instructions sur les opérations au délà de Kita pendant la campagne 1882/83 par le Ministre de la Marine et des Colonies, Paris, août 1882; in Sénégal I, 99a, Rapport au Ministre au sujet de la campagne 1882–1883 sur le Niger, Paris, 30 Aug. 1882

l'Isle and Borgnis Desbordes both of whom, as governor of Senegal and supreme commandant of the Niger mission respectively, had been responsible for launching the programme of French expansion in the Western Sudan.

But the governor of Senegal at this time was M. Vallon. He with Lt-Col. Bourdiaux as the new supreme commandant in place of Desbordes, who had been recalled to France, was directing French enterprises on the Niger along the peaceful lines originally advocated by the home government. Vallon was soon to prove unsympathetic towards, and unprepared for, the new forceful approach which the policy required. The ministry probably found it necessary to make changes in the personnel of the mission as it decided to reappoint Desbordes as supreme commandant for another period of service.

With the adoption by the ministry of a forceful approach, it seems logical that someone like Desbordes who believed in such a policy should be put in charge of the operations. But Vallon did not agree to the programme for the campaign of 1882–83, and was certainly against the reappointment of Desbordes. His objection to the 1882–83 programme was clear from the letter he wrote to Lt-Col. Bourdiaux about it, in which he refused all responsibility for the execution of the project, apparently because he did not believe in its feasibility. He said: 'Je refuse formellement au ministre d'assumer la responsabilité de son éxécution quand nous pouvons à peine assurer notre action jusqu'à Kita'.[1] Vallon also made his objections known to Borgnis Desbordes after the latter had taken over command of the project. He told him that he was not consulted by the ministry over the preparation of the 1882–83 plan, and would have nothing to do with it. He therefore told Desbordes that he would be completely independent of him, the governor, in the discharge of his duties. He regarded the mission as a special responsibility given by the ministry to Desbordes for the execution of which the latter would not be in any way answerable to, or dependent on him, the governor.[2]

Consistent with this declaration Vallon steadfastly refused to give any help to Desbordes, even when the latter asked him specially for military assistance. As part of his explanations for

[1] ASAOF, 3B98/50, A. M. le Commandant Supérieur, Vallon, Saint-Louis, 20 Sept. 1882
[2] ASAOF, 3B98/69, A. M. le Lt-Col. Borgnis-Desbordes, Vallon, Saint-Louis, 18 Oct. 1882

refusing to cooperate, Vallon maintained that having ignored his advice in the formulation of a programme, the ministry should find means of executing it.[1] He also explained that to give aid to Desbordes would be to expose the colony of Senegal to external attacks in an attempt to assume a strange responsibility for a programme which had been launched without due considerations for its feasibility.[2]

Given the pronounced clash of ideas between Paris and the governor of Senegal, and the complete lack of cooperation between the governor and the commandant, not much in the way of concrete results could be expected from the 1882–83 mission. The two men were separated by fundamental differences of outlook. It soon became clear to the ministry that one of the two would have to go before any progress could be achieved in the attempt to penetrate the Tukulor empire. Borgnis Desbordes was for a forceful, determined approach to the solution of the problem and this accorded with the new thinking of the ministry at the time. It is in this light that one should see the ministry's retention of Desbordes and the appointment of a new governor to replace Vallon. A new governor for Senegal and dependencies, René Servatius, was appointed by a decree of 26 October 1882 and assumed office on 15 November.[3]

The appointment of a new governor marked the determination of the French government to push the project begun in 1880 to a successful end. Informing Desbordes of his appointment and assumption of office, the new governor proclaimed absolute confidence in the success of the Niger mission. He assured Desbordes of his cooperation, and expressed confidence in his ability. He said with some rhetorical effect that with cooperation, the two of them would work for France and for the spread of civilisation: 'Unissons nos efforts, nous travaillons pour la France, pour la République et pour la civilisation.' With this note of assurance he asked Desbordes to formulate as early as possible all his requests for the 1883–84 campaign so that these could be forwarded to Paris without delay.[4]

The new governor was expressing the thinking of the home

1 ASAOF, 3B98/70, same, 19 Oct. 1882
2 ASAOF, 3B98/71, same, 23 Oct. 1882
3 ASAOF, 3B98/51, 'Colonel Desbordes', René Servatius, Saint-Louis, 20 Nov. 1882
4 *Ibid.*

government in his assurance to Desbordes. The latter, a consistent advocate of the use of force, went ahead to employ the forces at his disposal to break Tukulor obstacles in his way. In December 1882 he committed the first direct attack on the Tukulor empire by forcing the evacuation of Tukulor chiefs from Mourgoula, the headquarters of the Birgo district in the Mandingo areas between Upper Senegal and the Niger. Mourgoula was a stronghold of the Tukulor in an area that was generally hostile to the Tukulor regime, the almamy was one of the Tukulor provincial chiefs who, according to Gallieni, had been instructed by Ahmadu to prevent the French from reaching the river Niger.[1] Desbordes complained frequently against the activities of the Tukulor in Mourgoula which he considered to be prejudicial to French interests in the area. He complained that Mourgoula, situated between Kita and the rest of the Mandingo states, was a living evidence of the military strength of the Tukulor, and its existence symbolised the weakness of the French *vis-à-vis* the Tukulor, the fear of whom was preventing would-be French allies from coming to them. In this vein Desbordes reported on Mourgoula saying: 'Elle était pour nos alliés le signe évident de notre faiblesse; elle empêchait de venir a nous tous ceux qu'effrayait encore la puissance d'Ahmadou.'[2]

He considered the breaking of Mourgoula inevitable if the French were to achieve their objective of penetrating the Tukulor empire via the Niger, and attacked on 22 December 1882 with two companies of 250 and 106 troops each. He realised that he would not be able to break the fortress, even with these forces, if he were to attack the town directly. He therefore camped four hundred metres away and sent to invite the almamy, Abdallah, and his chiefs for discussion. Abdallah and his chiefs arrived undefended, only to find themselves treacherously surrounded by troops, arrested and expelled under armed escort to Ka'arta. Later on, Desbordes took control of Mourgoula, destroyed the fortress and installed a puppet of the French as almamy in January 1883. Desbordes reported that the main operation against

1 This information was given by Gallieni as part of his report on the treaty of Nango (3 Nov. 1880). It was to indicate the difference between Ahmadu's and French interpretations of the treaty and to emphasise the determination of the Tukulor regime to oppose French penetration of their territory.
2 ASAOF, 1D69, Rapport sur la Campagne de 1882–1883 dans le Soudan par B. Desbordes, Bamako, 20 Mar. 1883, p. 73

Mourgoula lasted from 19 to 28 December 1882. The destruction of this fortress weakened Tukulor political influence in the Mandingo country, and worse still, by isolating and exposing the fortress at Koundian[1] it created a weak spot in the Tukulor defence system.

The new governor, René Servatius, endorsed Desbordes's action and assured him of the determination of the French government to give active support to the Niger project. He also authorised the use of force to break resistance movements opposing the French programme. Said he in a telegram: 'Brisez les, vous êtes là pour cela. Vous serez soutenu par moi, par le ministre et par le parlement. Faites des éxécutions. Chassez sans pitié les paresseux et les incapables.'[2] When he was later informed of the evacuation of Mourgoula, he sent congratulatory messages to Desbordes, and promised to report the good news to Paris.[3]

With such cooperation and encouragement, Desbordes pressed on and reached Bamako on 1 February 1883. He started negotiations with the Bambara chief of Bamako and his brother Titi, who was so powerful as to be called 'le véritable chef'. Titi and the other Bambara chiefs assured Desbordes of their willingness to cooperate with the French against the Tukulor. They also gave their consent to the building of a fort. Desbordes supervised the building of the fort which was completed in March 1883.[4]

Desbordes soon discovered, however, that though the people generally were united against the Tukulor regime, they were divided broadly into two groups on other matters. The two main groups were the non-Muslim Bambara and the Muslim Moorish populations. The Bambara welcomed the French as allies against the Tukulor, but only the show of force made the Moors accept the French presence as a *fait accompli*. The Moors, who were also the commercial class in Bamako, preferred to ally with a Muslim power against the Tukulor. For this reason they were reported to have made advances to Samori Ture,[5] whom they would have

1 *Ibid.*, pp. 74–86
2 ASAOF, 3B98/7, Télégramme Colonel, René Servatius, 26 Jan. 1883
3 ASAOF, 3B98/11, Télégramme, 30 Jan. 1883; 3B98/13, Télégramme, 5 Feb. 1883
4 ASAOF, 1G69, Rapport sur la Campagne de 1882–1883 dans le Soudan par Borgnis-Desbordes, Bamako, 25 Mar. 1883, ch. v, p. 118
5 Samori Ture was the ruler of the Mandingo state of Wasulu. He was at this time still involved in the campaigns which the founding of his empire entailed.

preferred to have as their ruler. Desbordes also claimed that the Moors of Bamako had furnished contingents for Samori's army. He had to negotiate with them for almost a month before they reconciled themselves to the French presence.[1]

With the establishment of the fort at Bamako, the target for the 1882–83 mission had been achieved. Desbordes was, however, not very enthusiastic about the achievement. He expressed fear that Samori might attack the French on the Niger, especially at Bamako, and that since one must regard the Moorish acceptance of the French as nominal, there was the danger of Samori finding in them allies against the French. In that case, the French might be evacuated from Bamako. It was therefore to guarantee the French position that Desbordes took the offensive against forces of Samori under the command of Fabou, one of his army leaders. Desbordes pursued Samori's soldiers, who were at the time at various posts near the Niger, chasing them from near Bamako to Bankoumana from where they crossed to Kangaba on the right bank of the Niger. The encounter, which lasted from 2 to 4 April, seems not to have been serious. All that Desbordes and his men achieved was to frighten away, temporarily, Samori's soldiers. Boilève, a member of the 1882–83 mission, noted that the French forces were already too weak to be able to do much more. He reported that Samori's men in fact came back during the rainy season to reoccupy their posts at Kangaba and Déguélla on the left bank, and Faraba on the right bank, of the Niger.[2]

It is not known whether Samori really represented a threat to the French at this time or whether the operations against his troops were started by Desbordes as a way of satisfying his enthusiasm for the forceful expansion of French influence. If the latter was the case, the story of the alliance of the Bamako Moors with Samori should be seen as having been put up to explain his hostility to the emergent state of Wasulu.

The French government continued to emphasise commercial expansion as their main target and did not seem to be ready for the kind of military and political involvement being pursued by Desbordes. The administrative arrangement made for the mission in Upper Senegal and the Niger showed the way the French

1 ASOF, 1D69, Rapport sur la campagne de 1882–1883 dans le Soudan par B. Desbordes, Bamako, 25 Mar. 1883, ch. v, pp. 118–20

2 *Ibid.*, p. 120; ASAOF, 1D75, Campagne 1883–1884 dans le Soudan, Boilève, Saint-Louis, 8 Aug. 1884, ch. ii, p. 51.

government was thinking. In February 1883 the government charged the director of the railway project with overall control of the personnel of the whole mission, specifically including military workers. The reason for this was that the government considered the railway project to be the main task of the mission, and the director of the railway project the most important of the officials. The measure was taken because 'là où est la responsabilité là doit être le commandement'.[1]

This represented a step forward in a process which began in December 1881 when the civil administration of the colonies was placed under the control of the ministry of commerce. It seems that an effort was being made, for once, to resolve a dilemma by which the French government, though concerned primarily with the expansion of commerce, had, since the Logo affair (1876–78), been committed on several occasions to adopting military and political enterprises it did not originally plan for, but into which it was dragged because it employed for the execution of its policies men whose background and training fitted them mainly for forceful, military approach to the solution of problems.

One could say also that at the end of the 1882–83 campaign the need to employ force had become less obvious than before. Not only had the route to link Upper Senegal with the Niger been traced, but posts had been built in several places along it. In addition to posts already in existence in places like Bakel, Kayes, Médine and Bafoulabe, other forts had been erected at Badumbe, Toukolo, Koundou and Bamako.[2] These posts were linked by a telegraphic line.[3] In effect, all the background work had been done to make possible the peaceful exploitation of the commerce of the area. The French had also succeeded in gaining the confidence of the Bambara, and had nothing to fear from their side. The Bambara cooperated with the French because they saw them as allies in their struggle against the Tukulor regime.

Moreover, in relation to the Tukulor empire, the French had nothing to fear for the moment. The Tukulor were involved in debilitating internal wranglings and could not, in the meantime, resist the French penetration. At the end of the 1883–84 campaign

---

1 ASAOF, 3B98/16, Le Gouverneur à M. le Commandant Supérieur, Saint-Louis, 7 Feb. 1883
2 ASAOF, 1D69, 'Rapport sur la campagne de 1882–1883, dans le Soudan par B. Desbordes', ch. viii, Tableau A, p. 327
3 *Ibid.*, Tableau c, Service Télégraphique, p. 332

it was reported that Ahmadu had not fought against the French penetration. He had not even protested against such obvious outrages against his empire, as the evacuation of Mourgoula and the establishment of fortified posts along the Niger up to Bamako much as these acts represented a diminution of his power and authority. The inaction of Ahmadu *vis-à-vis* the French was explained as due to his preoccupation with the internal problems of his empire, particularly with the power struggle between him and Muhammad Muntaga, who, since 1874 had been ruling at Nioro in Ka'arta. Boilève reported that 'pour le moment, il me semble surtout préoccupé par l'attitude de son frère Montaga [*sic*], roi du Ka'arta'.[1] Ahmadu was apparently already preparing for the civil war that resulted from the power struggle between him and Muntaga in 1884.

THE MUNTAGA REVOLT AND POWER STRUGGLE IN THE TUKULOR EMPIRE

Ahmadu had appointed Muhammad Muntaga to take charge of Ka'arta after the civil wars of 1870–74. Then he had thought that Muntaga's appointment would be a guarantee of his own authority and supremacy in Ka'arta. He had hoped that because of his jealousy of, and opposition to, Abibu and Moktar, who had just been defeated, Muntaga would always remain loyal to him as the head of the empire. Muntaga, though opposed to Abibu and Moktar, was, however, no less ambitious than these men. His manoeuvres during the civil wars of 1870–74 clearly indicated that he had fought on the side of Ahmadu not because he believed in or subscribed to his claims to supreme position within the empire. Nor did he support him because he liked him better than the other two brothers. His action was guided mainly by his calculations of which side would provide him with the better opportunity to satisfy his ambition. At the moment of choice, Ahmadu appeared the stronger side, and also the man through whom he was more likely to get as much position and power as he desired.[2]

1 ANSOM, in Sénégal IV, 79 bis, Campagne 1883–1884 dans le Soudan, Chapitre II par Boilève', Saint-Louis, 8 Aug. 1884; ASAOF, 1D75, Campagne 1883–84 dans le Soudan, Boilève, Saint-Louis, 8 Aug. 1884, p. 57
2 See Chapter 7, pp. 191ff.; also Pietri, *Les Français au Niger*, pp. 112–24 for the role of Muntaga in the civil wars of 1870–74 in Ka'arta.

With the elimination of Abibu and Moktar, and his own appointment to Nioro, the most powerful post in Ka'arta, Muntaga was on his way to getting as much power as he wanted. But he did not like being subordinate to Ahmadu. Therefore, after having consolidated his position, he sought to make himself autonomous in Ka'arta. In an attempt to achieve this objective he ran into trouble with Ahmadu who had some loyal followers at Nioro and other centres in Ka'arta. The first evidence that the relationship between Ahmadu and Muntaga had become strained was reported by the middle of 1880, just about the time that Gallieni was setting out for Segu on his treaty-making mission. At that time it was being said openly at Nioro and all over Ka'arta that Muntaga and several of his chiefs had accused Ahmadu of having attempted to assassinate them. It was claimed that a conspiracy to effect the assassination had just been foiled. The chiefs were reported to have sworn their allegiance and loyalty to Muntaga, and to have declared their support for him against Ahmadu. This information is contained in the entry made on 28 June 1880 in the register of the French post at Médine.[1]

Because of the division among the *talibés* in Nioro, however, Muntaga had to pursue his ambition cautiously. Some of the *talibés* were still loyal to Ahmadu and Muntaga needed time to persuade them to switch their loyalty to him or, if necessary. to fight to overcome their opposition. By 1882 his determination to break with Ahmadu became clearly evident. He began to look for allies among his brothers and *talibés* outside Ka'arta. It was in this connection that he sent his cousin and confidant, Seydou Makola, to Dinguiray in July 1882 to try to win over Aguibu[2] to his side. Earlier, Muntaga was reported to have expelled from Nioro those of the chiefs who showed themselves to be on the side of Ahmadu. He had also been keeping to himself nearly all the

---

1 ASAOF, 15G112/2, Copie du Régistre Journal du Commandant du Poste – mois de juin, Médine, 1 July 1880; 1G52/34, 'Depêche télégraphique, Commandant Médine à Commandant Supérieur, Bakel', 27 June 1880

2 Aguibu was a son of 'Umar who at this time was emir of Dinguiray. He was in charge of the administration of Segu from 1870 to 1873 when Ahmadu was away in Ka'arta fighting the civil war against Abibu and Moktar. He was, during the period of his regency suspected of ambition to seize power from Ahmadu. His relationship with Ahmadu was not known to be good at this time.

taxes and tribute collected in Ka'arta.[1] In December 1882, Desbordes, leading the French mission, reported Muntaga's independent attitude and his attempts to disregard the authority of Ahmadu. He had then exploited this tendency for his purpose. Hence, when he sacked the almamy of Mourgoula and his chiefs, he wrote to Muntaga, assuring him of the French desire to be friendly with him, and declared that the French were opposed only to Ahmadu. Desbordes, who had sent Dr Bayol to Muntaga to conclude a treaty, even wrongly thought that Muntaga would want a French alliance against Ahmadu.[2]

In his search for allies, Muntaga enlisted not only such of his half-brothers in Ka'arta as Ahmidu, Muniru, and Daha (all emirs and district heads), but also the support and encouragement of Ahmadu Tijāni of Masina. The latter kept Muntaga informed of Ahmadu's manoeuvres against him. In 1883, for instance, he was reported to have sent messengers to Muntaga to warn him to be on his guard against Ahmadu. The information about the role of Ahmadu Tijāni reached Boilève through his spy at Nioro ('mon espion de Nioro').[3] By 1883 it was widely known that an understanding existed between Muntaga, Aguibu and Ahmadu Tijani against Ahmadu.[4] All the time, Ahmadu himself was busy organising his forces and finding support among the *talibés* in Segu and Ka'arta. He also sent as far away as Futa Toro, Bambuk and Bondu to find recruits for the army which he intended to use in Ka'arta against the forces of Muntaga and his allies.

By mid-January 1884 Ahmadu was already on his way from Segu to Ka'arta. He camped for some time at Nyamina on the Niger, apparently to recruit reinforcements and give the troops some rest before continuing the long march to Ka'arta to quell Muntaga's rebellion. It was at Nyamina that he announced to his troops that they were going to Nioro. Before then many people had believed that his army was to be used against the Bambara resistance movement in Beledugu.[5] The civil war which resulted

1 ASAOF, 13G25/8, Le Gouverneur du Sénégal à M. le Ministre de la Marine et des Colonies, Saint-Louis, Sept. 1882
2 ANSOM, in Sénégal I, 99b, B. Desbordes à M. le Gouverneur du Sénégal et dépendances, Marc de Dalaba, 24 Dec. 1882
3 ANSOM, in Sénégal IV, 79b, Boilève, Le Commt Supérieur du Haut-Sénégal à M. le Gouverneur du Sénégal', Kayes, 13 Oct. 1883
4 ISH 1E/4, Extrait du journal du Poste, Bamako, 16 Nov. 1883
5 ISH 1E/3, Fort de Bammako, Extraits du journal, 15 Jan. 1884; also 1E/9 of 18 Jan. 1884

from the power-struggle between Ahmadu and Muntaga dragged on from early 1884 till nearly the end of 1885. While in Ka'arta, Ahmadu's son, Madani, ruled Segu on his behalf. The war lasted for so long partly because of the mode of fighting which was adopted.

Ahmadu, realising that his army was not strong enough to face Muntaga's in a pitched battle, decided to avoid direct confrontation, especially early in the struggle. Rather than attempt to force a quick decisive action, Ahmadu used his army to blockade the routes leading to Nioro from Segu and the Senegambia. This was to make it difficult, if not impossible, for Muntaga to receive reinforcements from his allies. The blockade gradually weakened Muntaga's men who were confined to Nioro and a few other places.[1] Muntaga became so desperate that he looked for reinforcements even from among the Bambara, who had their own resistance struggle to fight against the Tukulor as a group. Ahmadu for his part continued to seek aid from the Senegambia. But the French made it practically impossible for reinforcements to reach either side, and also placed an embargo on sales of arms to the Tukulor.

The French saw the revolt of Muntaga as creating a situation that was favourable to the promotion of their policy in the Western Sudan. The Tukulor would not have the time nor the means to oppose French penetration as long as they were preoccupied with their internal wars. The ease with which the French had pushed up to Bamako without resistance from the Tukulor between 1882 and 1883 had proved this. The French therefore tried to ensure that the internal struggle would continue as long as possible. To do this, Combes, the supreme commandant in charge of the 1883–84 French mission, gave orders to the commandants of the French posts along the Senegal and the Niger to prevent reinforcements going to either Ahmadu or Muntaga from crossing the rivers to Tulukor territories. In this way the French maintained an effective barrier between Ka'arta and the Senegambia. Even if the Bambara had been willing to take advantage of the situation in Ka'arta to weaken the Tukulor regime by allying with Muntaga against Ahmadu, they could not do this because Combes and his men persuaded Bambara chiefs not to intervene

1 ASAOF, 13G25/17, Le Gouverneur du Sénégal à M. le Ministre; Saint-Louis, 12 Aug. 1884

in Tukulor affairs.[1] In these circumstances, the Tukulor continued the civil war in various parts of Ka'arta for a long time without any definite result.

The civil war ended with the victory of Ahmadu over Muntaga who was killed during the invasion and destruction of the fortications at Nioro about September 1885. Muntaga's forces disbanded after his death.[2] But as in the 1870–74 encounter with Abibu and Moktar, Ahmadu's victory over Muntaga, and the latter's death, did not necessarily give him a firm control over Ka'arta. For the moment he had succeeded in disorganising his opponents; but they were as yet neither reconciled to him nor completely defeated. One of Muntaga's steadiest supporters, Daha, emir of Farabougou, escaped from the battle at Nioro back to his district. Two of Muntaga's younger brothers, who were also emirs, Ahmidu and Muniru, found asylum for a while at the French post at Kita and later at Bamako. Under the protection of the French in the posts, they eventually found their way to Masina where they were sure of protection from Ahmadu Tijani.[3] With these men at large Ahmadu recognised that his own position in Ka'arta was still precarious as he could be attacked from any direction at any time. He made efforts to capture some of them, but without success. For example, he sent a cavalry corps into Farabougou in pursuit of Daha, but Daha could not be found. Other opponents of Ahmadu remained active against him. Some even unsuccessfully solicited French help.[4]

Given the insecurity of his position in Ka'arta, Ahmadu found it unsafe to return to Segu. He was not sure of the loyalty of the Tukulor chiefs in Ka'arta, whilst he knew that to leave for Segu might be to cut his own throat. But apart from the lack of control over the political situation, he faced more menacing problems. The Bambara, especially in Beledugu, had taken advantage of the confusion in the Tukulor state to intensify their resistance, and

1 *Ibid.*, pp. 2–3
2 ASAOF, 1D79/113, Le Commandant supérieur p. i. à M. le Gouverneur du Sénégal, Kayes, 27 Sept. 1885
3 ASAOF, 1D79/110, Le Commandant Supérieur p. i. à M. le Gouverneur . . ., Kayes, 3 Nov. 1885
4 ANSOM, in Sénégal IV, 84b, Copie pour le Ministre des depêches du Commandant des cercles à Commandant Supérieur, Bakel, 11 Nov. 1885; in Sénégal IV, 84b. Confidentielle – Le Lt-Col. Commandant Supérieur du Haut-Sénégal et dépendances, Kayes, 20 Dec. 1885

they succeeded in forming themselves into virtually independent enclaves, cutting nearly all communications between Segu and Ka'arta. For Ahmadu to be able to go back to Segu, he would need a strong army to break through the barrier created by the Bambara. Such an army was not forthcoming since the majority of the *talibés* in Nioro would not cooperate either in recruiting forces or in following him to Segu. Moreover, with the death of Mustafa, the first emir of Nioro and one of Ahmadu's ablest army leaders, the Tukulor troops in Segu were dispirited and ill-organised. Mustafa died at a time when the army had to face the onslaught of the Bambara, who, in their anti-Tukulor campaigns, were almost at Segu, the capital.[1]

The Bambara menace, coupled with the unsettled political problem of the Tukulor, was disconcerting enough to Ahmadu. But the situation was to be further complicated by the arrival in the Senegambia of a marabout, Mahmadu Lamine. Mahmadu Lamine was born at Goundiourou,[2] a village near Médine in Khasso. He had returned to Segu in 1878 after many years of pilgrimage during which he acquired a reputation for learning and piety. His reputation was such that by about 1880 he was reported to have got a large and growing group of followers at Segu, and his popularity was already giving Ahmadu some concern,[3] especially since Lamine was friendly with Ahmadu Tijani of Masina.[4] It was said that Ahmadu had confined Mahmadu Lamine to Segu. But while Ahmadu was still embroiled in the Ka'arta war, Lamine took the opportunity to leave Segu at the end of May 1885. He was reported to have passed through Bamako on 1 June 1885, heading for Goundiourou[5] where he arrived in July. He continued to tour Khasso, Bambuk and Bondu, preaching to the people and recruiting forces for a war he was planning to fight against 'unbelievers', especially at Gamou. In pursuance of this idea, he was reported to have entered into alliance with the almamy of Bondu, Bubakar Saada and Abdul Bubakar of Bambuk.

1 ASAOF, 1D79/127, Commandant Supérieur p. i. à M. le Gouverneur du Sénégal . . ., Kayes, 1 Oct. 1885
2 Frey, *Campagne dans le Haut Niger (1885–1886)* (1888), p. 250
3 ANSOM, in Sénégal I, 63a G. Brière de l'Isle, le Gouverneur du Sénégal à M. le Ministre de la Marine et des Colonies, Saint-Louis, 5 May 1880
4 Frey, *Campagne dans le Haut-Niger*, pp. 254–5
5 ISH, 1E/6, Poste de Bamako, Journal du Fort, 1 June 1885

By December 1885 his forces numbered about 250 armed men, assembled at Goundiourou.[1]

As a native of Khasso Mahmadu Lamine appears to have aimed at uniting the Khasso people in an alliance with the neighbouring states of Bondu and Bambuk, with a view to expelling the French and the Tukulor who had dominated the area since 'Umar's revolution. This plan, a sort of proto-nationalist movement against foreign domination, was bound to bring Mahmadu Lamine into conflict with Ahmadu in those former districts of Khasso under Tukulor control in Ka'arta. As will be seen later, Mahmadu Lamine's campaigns affected both the French and the Tukulor, and opposition to him was to bring them into a temporary alliance in 1887.[2] In the meantime, Lamine was another reason why Ahmadu should stay in Ka'arta.

The French had thought they could exploit the confusion in the Tukulor empire to push ahead their penetration programme; but for various reasons they found it impossible to do so.

1 ANSOM, in Sénégal IV, 84b, Confidentielle – Le Lt-Col. Commandant Supérieur du Haut Sénégal à M. le Gouverneur du Sénégal . . ., Kayes, 20 Dec. 1885
2 See B. Ọlatunji Ọlọruntimẹhin, 'Muhammad Lamine in Franco-Tukulor Relations, 1885–1887', *JHSN*, iv, 3, December 1968, pp. 375–396 for further discussion. See also Fisher, 'The early life and pilgrimage of al-Hajj al-Amīn, the Soninke (d. 1887)', *JAH*, xi, 1, 1970, pp. 51–69. Fisher's article is unnecessarily speculative in parts. An example is this unsubstantiated statement on the first page of the article: '. . . Indeed he may sincerely have sought a French alliance. The yoke from which he sought to liberate his own Soninke was not French, but Tokolor [*sic*]; and in addition, he may have been moved also by religious principles, standing in that tradition of reform in West Africa which may be traced back beyond any European penetration . . .', p. 51. Surely, there is enough in existing literature to show clearly that the Tukulor were not alone in dominating the Senegambia in this period; French imperialism was as much a reality. It is not clear whether Fisher is suggesting that Lamine as a person, or the religious principles to which he refers, preferred one imperialism (the French) to the other (the Tukulor). Jihād in West Africa has been concerned both with fighting infidels and European intrusion or imperialism. Lamine's movement was no exception since he was concerned with liberating his people from the imperial presence of both the Tukulor and the French.

FRENCH PENETRATION HALTED, 1883–87

Although this was the situation in the Tukulor empire, and in spite of the fact that Jules Ferry, Prime Minister and Minister for Foreign Affairs, was becoming an enthusiastic advocate of colonisation, the French did not make much progress between 1883 and 1885 in their bid to penetrate and establish themselves in the Tukulor empire. This was partly because both official and public opinion in France was in this period generally opposed to the continuation of the Upper Senegal–Niger enterprise. It was argued that the missions were costing too much and had yielded no profit. The idea behind the establishment of the Upper Senegal High Command in 1879 was to find a way to facilitate and increase French commercial activities in the Senegambia and the Tukulor empire. In other words, the originators of the programme conceived it as a commercial enterprise to be achieved peacefully. But as has been noted, the executors of the programme, mainly military and naval men, had involved the missions in military expeditions incurring expenditure which business-minded groups regarded as wasteful. The effort to redress the balance between commerce and the idea of conquest, which appealed to the military officers, could be seen from the control which the ministry of commerce was given over the civil administration of the colonies and the greater control which officials of the ministry were given over colonial enterprises such as the Kayes–Bamako railway project. The reluctance of the government to continue to finance the Upper Senegal–Niger enterprise as it was being run by the military was also evident during the 1883–84 campaign.

In that year, most of the orders made for supplies of concrete materials for construction work, and provisions like clothing, food and other much needed articles, were very often drastically reduced by the ministry, and there were always delays in sending the insufficient quantities of articles that they decided to send to Kayes, with the result that such articles often arrived too late to meet the immediate needs of the officers and men in the field. Not only were materials sent in insufficient quantities, they were also sometimes of poor quality, especially the food. In the report on the 1883–84 campaign, it was pointed out, among other things, that 'tous les vivres expédiés de France n'ont pas toujours été de bonne qualité. Le fait a été signalé au Département.'[1] With insufficient material and lacking adequate and proper care for the personnel of the mission, not much progress could be expected.

In 1883–84 the mission hardly did more than conserve what had been achieved up to the 1882–83 campaign. It was in fact mainly the services rendered by the commercial houses operating in the area that made even this modest record possible. Among these were the firms of Maurel et Prom (formerly known as 'Couscousserie'), based at Saint-Louis, whence their factors in the various trading posts along the Senegal were supplied, Landais et Guttin, based at Dakar, and G. Devés, based at Saint-Louis. The contributions of these firms to the promotion of the French enterprise included serving as transporters of the goods from France for the mission. Until the sending from France direct to Kayes in 1883 of two boats – *Richelieu* and *Soudan* – the commercial houses often helped in transporting the mission's civil and military personnel in boats carrying their own wares. Even in 1883 the firm of Landais et Guttin was still responsible for carrying 800 tons of coal needed for the railway project and the domestic use of the personnel. The 'factories' of these companies also served as stores for the goods and personal effects of the service men. Another way in which the companies helped was by providing goods on credit whenever the mission was short of materials and money.[2] Maintained in this way, the 1883–84 mission could certainly not have embarked on expansionist projects in an attempt to take advantage of the confused situation of the Tukulor empire and establish the French.

For the 1884–85 campaign the ministerial instructions of 4 September 1884 made it clear that the future of the French enterprises in the Western Sudan was still to be determined by the French parliament. The supreme commandant of the mission was therefore instructed not to do anything that would prejudice the decision of the parliament.[3] This of course meant that the mission should not do anything that would commit the government to further action. Although Jules Ferry was an advocate of colonial expansion, he could not carry parliament with him on the

1 ASAOF, 15G83/5, Compte-rendu sur le service administratif du Haut-Sénégal-Niger pendant l'année 1883, Saint-Louis, 31 Mar. 1884
2 *Ibid.*
3 ASAOF, 15G83/6, 'La question du Haut Fleuve devant la Chambre: Rapport du Commandant Supérieur', Kayes, 1 Nov. 1884

Sudan question. Parliament refused to grant credits for the continuation of the rail line from Kayes to Bamako.[1] Ferry came under heavy criticism over his colonial policy, which some parliamentary groups condemned as having brought France into clashes with Britain and Italy. Clemenceau claimed that Jules Ferry, through his colonial enterprises, especially in Tunisia, had 'refroidi des amitiés précieuses' and 'suscité des amitiés bein faites pour surprendre'.[2] He was accused in effect of causing France to lose the friends she had made at great cost. Some people, particularly the Revanche Party, saw Ferry's policy as leading to his participation in the Berlin West African Conference of 15 November 1884 which had been summoned by Bismarck. He was also condemned for acceding to the convention of Berlin of 26 February 1885 on colonies. By acceding to this convention, it was claimed, Ferry was dancing to Bismarck's tune and allowing France to become an instrument of German policy. The most outstanding spokesman of this group was General Boulanger, 'le général Revanche'.[3]

Faced with a barrage of criticisms and a reserved and sometimes hostile parliament that refused to grant credits for carrying out his colonial enterprises, Ferry resigned from office on 30 March 1885.[4] Given this situation in France, no forceful colonial policy could be pursued in 1884–85, and though the internal weaknesses of the Tukulor empire would have made it easy for the French to establish control there, they had no means of doing so. After Ferry, colonial activities were still pursued, but on a modest scale and with a deliberate desire to show parliament that these could be made to pay. This dictated the continued emphasis that was placed on commercial expansion as against a policy of territorial occupation.

Analysing the task of the French in the 1885–86 campaign, Galiber, the Minister for Marine and Colonies, explained that this consisted in assuring as much security as possible along the lines of posts already built up to Bamako in order to make it serviceable for the development of French commerce. He instructed the supreme commandant that there should be no question of establishing new protectorates and the idea of conquests

1 Hardy, *Histoire de la Colonisation*, p. 239
2 *Ibid.*, p. 240.
3 *Ibid.*
4 *Ibid.*

should be ruled out. He emphasised the French desire to maintain friendly relations with all the indigenous populations among whom they would be operating by scrupulously respecting their institutions, customs and religious beliefs:

> Notre unique ambition (il faut le proclamer bien haut et mettre nos actes d' accord avec nos déclarations) est d' entretenir de bonnes relations avec tous les indigènes qui nous environnent, en respectant scrupuleusement leurs institutions, leurs coutumes et leurs croyances religieuses.[1]

French policy in the Sudan was at this time designed to conserve what had been secured, and no more. It was dictated by the uncertainty that still surrounded the policy that the new parliament would adopt towards the project in Upper Senegal and the Niger. Attempts had been made to induce the previous government and parliament to continue their interests in the Western Sudan by using economic arguments. To sustain the wavering interests of parliament, the vaunted economic possibilities had to be shown concretely. Hence the emphasis in the ministerial instruction was on the development of commerce. The minister forbade the supreme commandant to get involved in expansionist policy which would necessitate any spending by the government. He explained the need for a guarded policy by referring to the attitude of the new parliament, warning that:

> il ne faut pas perdre de vue, au début de la campagne surtout, que nous sommes dans une période d'expectative que nous commande à la fois les réserves formulées à la tribune du Parlement et l' incertitude qui plane encore sur la ligne politique qu' adoptera la nouvelle chambre dans la question du Haut-Sénégal.[2]

On relations with the Tukulor empire, the minister explained that French policy was based on the necessity to avoid all complications from the Tukulor side in order to be able to pursue the French programme to increase trade without expenses. During the 1885–86 campaign, therefore, French policy consisted in conciliating Ahmadu and assuring him of their peaceful intentions and desire to be on friendly relations with him. Colonel Frey, the new supreme commandant, was instructed to open negotiations

1 ANSOM, in Sénégal IV, 84a, Confidentielle – Instructions pour la campagne 1885–1886 dans le Haut-Sénégal, Galiber, Le Ministre de la Marine et des Colonies, Paris, 23 Sept. 1885
2 *Ibid.*

with Ahmadu at Nioro as soon as he arrived at Kayes. Frey was to assure Ahmadu that rather than diminish his authority, the French establishment, as represented by the line of posts along the Senegal and Niger, would strengthen it by providing an effective barrier to any possible attack by Samori against the Tukulor empire.[1] It would also serve to strengthen the Tukulor regime because it would be used to purge the country of undesirable bands of plunderers. Colonel Frey was authorised to explore the possibility of concluding a written convention with Ahmadu.[2] In this way, it was hoped, Ahmadu would be conciliated.

No convention was in fact signed with Ahmadu; but the conciliatory policy of the French, made necessary by the attitude of parliament in Paris, suited Ahmadu very well because it gave him a much needed respite from external threats and enabled him to concentrate on the settlement of the menacing internal problems arising from the intra-Tukulor struggle for power and the resistance movements. The only point that could have brought complications between Ahmadu and the French was the latter's relations with the Bambara.

The French had secured the cooperation of the Bambara while building posts along the Niger by assuring them that they would be ready to help them against the Tukulor. While the French were eager to conciliate Ahmadu in 1885–86, they were also willing to keep the Bambara alliance. To do this, they continued secretly to sell arms and ammunition to the Bambara, while the embargo on the sale of arms to the Tukulor, imposed in 1885, continued. French action was governed by their desire to ensure that Ahmadu would not be strong enough to suppress the Bambara. If Ahmadu succeeded against the Bambara, his power to meet external threats, such as the French penetration, would increase. It was to avoid this that efforts were secretly made to aid Bambara resistance. Explaining that arms and ammunitions had been sent to be distributed to the Bambara of Beledugu, the Under-secretary at the Colonial Office, M. de la Porte, expressed the hope that with the arms, if well organised, the Beledugu Bambara would be able to continue their anti-Tukulor resistance to French advantage by keeping the Tukulor weak through con-

1 Such an attack was thought likely because of the wrong assumption that Samori and Ahmadu were hostile to each other.
2 The Minister's instructions in ANSOM, Sénégal IV, 84a of 23 Sept. 1885

tinuous fighting. In addition, the French were to try to persuade the Bambara chiefs to place themselves under French protection. If this could be done, the French hoped to be able to establish their domination eventually by merely using the Bambara against the Tukulor.[1] In his note of 5 December 1886 Freycinet, the Minister of Foreign Affairs, approved the line of action adopted by the ministry for colonies. Thus Paris modified the 1885 policy, which forbade expansionist ventures. The Foreign Office saw the establishment of the French in this part of the Sudan as essential for checking British expansion towards the Niger.[2] No doubt, this approach was preferred because it would not expose the French to direct, open hostility against the Tukulor empire and would therefore be a less costly way of conquering the latter. Indeed for advocates of an inexpensive French expansion in the Western Sudan there was encouragement to hope for success, not just because of the use to which Bambara elements could be put, but also because of the expectation, which the Abd al-Qadir's mission stimulated, that the Tukulor empire was soon to be overthrown in an army *coup d'état* being organised by a section of the Tukulor army under Bafi. A supposed envoy of the *jamā'a* of Timbuktu, Abd al-Qadir, visited France from January 1885 to February 1886 under the auspices of the ministries for colonies and external affairs. Both M. Galiber, the minister for colonies and the external affairs minister gave him an enthusiastic welcome. He had audiences with several interested bodies, including the French Geographical Society; he was received at a session of this society and later had an interview with General Louis Faidherbe, former governor of Senegal.[3] Commercial circles were enthusiastic about the expected peaceful conquest of the Sudan. The pursuit of the Abd al-Qadir offer continued to be a factor which was reckoned with, secretly, by officials in Paris until 1887 when the whole affair was discovered to be no more than a mirage.[4]

1 MAE, in *Mémoires et Documents: Afrique*, 85, Le Sous-Secrétaire d'Etat au Ministère de la Marine et des Colonies à Monsieur le Gouverneur du Sénégal, Paris, 20 Oct. 1886.
2 MAE, *Ibid.*, Freycinet à l'Amiral Aube, Paris, 5 Dec. 1886
3 *Compte Rendu des Séances de la Société de Géographie et de la Commission Centrale* (1885), pp. 1–2, 251–2
4 See Ọlọruntimẹhin 'Abd al-Qadir's Mission as a Factor in Franco-Tukulor Relations', *Acta Africana: Genève-Afrique*, vii, 2, 1968, pp. 33–50 for full treatment of this theme.

During the period 1886–87, however, the French did not really have much opportunity to work out their policy, modified as stated above. This was due partly to the diversion of attention caused by the armed conflict with Samori. Of greater and more immediate significance, however, was the rise of Mahmadu Lamine, a common enemy of the French and the Tukulor, who made cooperation with the Tukulor more important for the moment than the encouragement and exploitation of anti-Tukulor Bambara resistance movements as a means of safeguarding French interests in the Sudan.

By December 1885 Mahmadu Lamine had begun his campaign for the creation of his own state, which was to be carved out of the Senegambia. Hitherto he had devoted his time to preaching and recruiting troops in Khasso and the neighbouring states. In the process of his campaign, he attacked territories under the influence of both the French and the Tukulor, and both began to see him as a common enemy. He attacked the French post at Bakel and the surrounding villages. He also subjugated Ferlo and outlying districts of Tiali, Nieri and Gamou,[1] all areas considered by the French to be under their influence. His activities on the right bank of the Senegal were no less menacing to the Tukulor regime. There the Ka'arta districts of Guidimaka and Diafounou accepted his authority.[2] By early 1886 Mahmadu Lamine was already campaigning in Bambuk and Bondu. He had in fact conquered Boulebane, the headquarters of Bondu, whence on 23 September 1886 he directed attacks against the French post of Sénoudébou.[3] This was the situation when in October 1886 Gallieni assumed duty as supreme commandant of the 1886–87 mission.

For the French, success for Mahmadu Lamine might very well have meant the end of their influence in the Senegambia. The French authorities realised this, as is evident from the analysis of their situation which claimed that 'notre influence, notre commerce, l'éxistence même de nos comptoirs du Sénégal, étaient en question'.[4] To save the French from the ruin that Mahmadu

1 ASAOF, 1D90, Rapports du Lt-Col. Gallieni pendant la Campagne 1886–87
2 *Ibid.*
3 *Ibid.*, MAE, in *Mémoires et Documents: Afrique*, 85, Le Sous-Secrétaire d'Etat au Ministère de la Marine et des Colonies à M. le Gouverneur du Sénégal, Paris, 20 Oct. 1886
4 ASAOF, 1D90, Rapport du Lt-Col. Gallieni pendant la Campagne 1886–87, pp. 2–3

Lamine could cause them, Gallieni was instructed to fight against him during the 1886/87 campaign.[1]

In Ka'arta, Ahmadu also had to fight to dislodge Mahmadu Lamine from those areas where his men had been established. Lamine's son, Souaibou (or Soybou), had been installed chief at Gouri, headquarters of Diafounou, for example. By November 1886 Ahmadu had begun to fight to dislodge Lamine's son and supporters from Diafounou[2] and fighting was still in progress by February 1887.[3] In that month, the siege against Gouri brought success for Ahmadu's forces. Lamine's son and supporters escaped, and Diafounou submitted to the Tukulor regime.[4] Although Ahmadu succeeded in regaining control of Diafounou, Lamine's forces continued to be active in many other parts of Ka'arta. The French had been unable to dislodge him from the Senegambia, where he appeared to be increasing his popularity and strength daily.

The desire to eliminate Lamine determined, in part, the attitude of the French to the Tukulor during the 1886–87 campaign. It was recognised that cooperation with Ahmadu would hasten the defeat of Mahmadu Lamine. The French also realised that to antagonise Ahmadu was to complicate the situation for themselves. It was appreciated that a hostile Ahmadu could do a lot of damage to French interests at a time when the French were not in a position to fight back, preoccupied as they were with Mahmadu Lamine. It was therefore thought best to conciliate Ahmadu and ally with him against Mahmadu Lamine. An agreement, possibly a treaty, it was thought, would be useful for the purpose. Such an agreement, it was argued, would also be useful diplomatically in relation to the Berlin convention on colonial possessions.[5] It was to achieve these two objectives that Gallieni was authorised to negotiate a protectorate treaty with Ahmadu.

1 MAE, in *Mémoires et Documents: Afrique*, 85, Le Sous-Secrétaire d'Etat au Ministère de la Marine et des Colonies à M. le Gouverneur du Sénégal, Paris, 20 Oct. 1886
2 ANSOM, in Sénégal IV, 87b, Le Lt-Col. Gallieni à M. le Gouverneur du Sénégal, Kayes, 2 Dec. 1886
3 ANSOM, in Sénégal IV, 87b, Télégramme du Commandant Supérieur du Soudan français, 20 Feb. 1887.
4 ASAOF, 1G156/2, Notice historique sur la région du Sahel, de Lartique, 1897
5 ANSOM, in Sénégal IV, 87b, Le Lt-Col. Gallieni à M. le Gouverneur du Sénégal, Kayes, 7 Feb. 1887

During the negotiations, it was clear that the two sides were suspicious of each other, but the need for cooperation against a common enemy, Lamine, certainly made them agree on the need for the treaty, which was concluded with Gallieni through Ahmadu's representatives on 12 May 1887.[1] As both sides probably realised at the time, the treaty was important for the moment only as a symbol of their desire to cooperate against Lamine. For future relations between the two it could be said that it was useless. The treaty contained terms upon which agreement was impossible, such, for instance, as the claim that Ahmadu should put the Tukulor empire under French protectorate, a situation which the Tukulor ruler would never accept.[2]

The common threat that drew the French and the Tukulor together continued until December 1887 during which time the 1887–88 campaign had begun. Mahmadu Lamine was defeated and killed in December 1887.[3] After his liquidation, Franco-Segu relations were to take a new turn.

1 For an account of the negotiations and the terms of the treaty, see Gallieni, *Deux Campagnes au Soudan français: 1886–1888 par le Lieutenant-Colonel Gallieni* (1891), pp. 185–9
2 See Ọlọruntimẹhin 'Mohammad Lamine in Franco-Tukulor Relations . . .', p. 388ff for an analysis of the treaty of Gouri.
3 Ọlọruntimẹhin, 'Senegambia – Mahmadou Lamine', in Michael Crowder, ed., *West African Resistance. The Military Response to Colonial Occupation* (1971), pp. 80–110, for an analysis of the various elements in the Lamine movement as well as the military confrontation with the French.

9 The Fall of the Tukulor Empire, 1888–1893

Hitherto, French penetration, in spite of assurances to the contrary, was already threatening the existence of the Tukulor empire. This was because in seeking to establish themselves on the Niger, the French had made themselves the pivot around which all anti-Tukulor forces could unite. The French gave military aid to the Bambara who, as usual, were relentless in their determination to bring about the fall of the Tukulor empire. This, unfortunately for the Tukulor, was at a time when civil wars were raging in the empire, which consequently was not in a strong position to repulse external threats. The situation caused by the internal political instability and the external threat to the empire was such that, to retain his position as its head, Ahmadu had to remain in Ka'arta from 1884 onwards,[1] while Madani, his son, controlled the administration of the Segu section. No effective coordination of efforts was possible between them because of the barrier created by the Bambara. As a result, the total forces of the empire could not be deployed together and each section had to defend itself separately as the need arose.

What saved the Tukulor empire from collapse up to 1888 was lack of continuity in French colonial policy and, as has been pointed out, partly the fact that Paris was not giving enough financial support to the French effort at territorial expansion. Also there was the rise of Mahmadu Lamine. His movement threatened both the French and the Tukulor presence in the

---

1 Ahmadu had gone to Nioro in 1884 to quell a rebellion. Thereafter circumstances compelled him to stay on there even though he always wanted to go back to Segu. The suggestion by Professor Hargreaves that Ahmadu moved his headquarters from Segu to Nioro deliberately to escape 'from the immediate range of French operations' appears to miss the point; see Hargreaves, 'The Tokolor empire of Segou and its relations with the French', p. 143

Senegambia, and as both were eager to be rid of Lamine's proto-nationalist movement they realised the need for cooperation. They therefore joined forces in 1886–87 to fight him, rather than continue their hostility to each other. As soon as Lamine was defeated, however, the Franco-Tukulor hostility, shelved temporarily, was resuscitated.

Conflict arose first over the Senegambia, where Lamine had just been eliminated, but later spread to other areas. In the struggle that ensued, the French again allied with the various anti-Tukulor groups and the dissident members of the Tukulor aristocracy. Thus in the struggle that finally led to the fall of the empire there was on the one side the French at the head of a coalition which included the Bambara and other resistance movements, and on the other side Ahmadu at the head of a coalition which included external friends like Samori Ture and Ali Bouri of the Jolof. The situation was complicated by the fact that the Tukulor rulers were at the same time still involved in their struggle for power and each group within the empire took such part in the war as it judged to be in its own interests.

Lamine's still-born empire spread over Khasso, Bambuk and Bondu in the Senegambia, as well as Guidimaka and Diafounou areas of the Ka'arta section of the Tukulor empire. After his defeat competition and aggression again became the keynote in Franco-Tukulor relations. Gallieni gave priority to the re-establishment of French control and influence in the Senegambia. Apparently finding the presence of the Tukulor in the area inconvenient he took measures calculated to eliminate them. He built forts and stationed troops in several places, and sought to destroy Tukulor defences. In particular, he drove the Tukulor soldiers from their fortress at Koundian in April 1888.[1] Koundian was a strongly fortified settlement, symbolising Tukulor presence in the Bambuk. It was built by 'Umar as part of the defence system of the empire and was the residence of a Tukulor district chief.[2] The success of the French attack was significant evidence of their attempt to weaken their Tukulor rivals.

In his letter to Gallieni, Ahmadu protested vehemently against

1 ASAOF, in 15G76/2, Minā ilā hakim faransi harsu bilādati Kulūnil Galilinir (i.e. Colonel Gallieni) (marked: Nioro, no. 1, mai, 1888)
2 'Nouvelle de M. Mage', *Revue Maritime et Coloniale*, xi, Paris, 1864, p. 160

the French action, pointing out that the attack on Koundian was contrary to the provisions of the treaty of Gouri (1887).[1] Gallieni in his reply, argued that the evacuation of Koundian was not directed against the Tukulor, but towards promoting peace and stability in the area. He explained that he had ordered the evacuation of Koundian only in response to the continual complaints of the Malinke chiefs, and that the inhabitants of Koundian had put the country in a state of unrest through their marauding activities in Bambuk. He claimed that such complaints were first brought to him in 1887, but that he had then ignored them. The complaints had, however, continued till the time he ordered the evacuation. The Malinke, he claimed, were under French protection and he could not continue to ignore their complaints. He did not want to encourage the Malinke to make trouble; therefore he thought it was better to remove the source of trouble. Hence the evacuation of Koundian which, according to him, was the seat of the trouble-makers. Gallieni assured Ahmadu that notwithstanding the Koundian incident, the French still cherished and would maintain the friendly relations between them and the Tukulor.[2]

Although there must have been some banditry in Bambuk and other areas of the Senegambia after the wars against Mahmadu Lamine, Gallieni's explanation was not necessarily true. His motive in causing Koundian to be evacuated was not to avoid trouble as he claimed: it was to put the French in a stronger position so that they would be able to win in the competition for control of the Senegambia. The Tukulor chiefs were themselves not deceived by Gallieni's explanation. That they were aware of his motive was evident from the protest letter which Muhammad Aguibu, the emir of Dinguiray, wrote to him. Aguibu told Gallieni that he regarded the latter's action as having arisen from a desire to penetrate and establish French presence on Tukulor territories at all costs.[3] In spite of further assurances to the contrary,[4] the Tukulor saw the Koundian episode as a definite

1 ASAOF, in 15G76/2, Nioro, no. 1, mai 1888
2 ASAOF, in 15G76/2, Le Lt-Col. Gallieni, Commandant Supérieur du Soudan français à Ahmadou, 23 May 1888
3 ASAOF, 15G81/1 Correspondance avec Aguibu – Mohammed Aguibu ben Cheik Omar à ton ami le Colonel Gallieni, 24 June 1888
4 ASAOF 15G81/2 Correspondance avec Aguibu – Au Chef Mohamadou Haguibou ben Cheik Omar de la part du Commandant Rivière des Borderis à Kayes, 28 June 1888

indication of French threat to their empire, and they reacted accordingly. When Archinard took over control of French operations in October 1888 he reported that the Tukulor had stopped all relations with the French.[1] Ahmadu had also taken steps to send new garrisons to the evacuated fortress at Koundian.[2]

But in spite of Tukulor protests the French did not cease their offensive, though no direct attack was made again for the rest of 1888. Instead of confronting the Tukulor directly, the French adopted the method, first tried in 1880 by the Gallieni mission, of exploiting the Bambara resistance movements. However, as was found out by Desbordes at Bamako in 1883 the Bambara were themselves united only in their opposition to the Tukulor. They had their own internal differences, which sometimes prevented them from opposing the Tukulor collectively. The French realised that as long as such internal differences persisted the Bambara would be difficult to manage and would be ineffective as instruments against the Tukulor. They therefore made efforts to unite the Bambara, especially those of Segu and Beledugu. In this endeavour the internal differences of the Bambara was not the only obstacle to be surmounted. Another obstacle was the distrustful attitude of a section of the Bambara towards the French, arising from the French collaboration with Ahmadu from 1886 to December 1887.[3] The section of the Bambara led by Karamoko Diara[4] were not convinced that the French could collaborate with the Tukulor if they were sincerely against them. The distrust of the French which was manifested towards the Gallieni mission in 1880 had, for this reason, been resuscitated. These obstacles notwithstanding, efforts to unite the Bambara continued.

In their manoeuvres among the Bambara the French made use of their Bamako post as a base. From Bamako they tried to use some of the people in the resistance movement to persuade Karamoko Diara to embrace the French cause. For this, Bamako

1 Archinard, *Le Soudan français en 1888–1889: rapport militaire* (1890), p. 6
2 *Ibid.*, p. 26
3 The collaboration with the Tukulor had been necessitated by a desire to eliminate Mahmadu Lamine.
4 From the ruling family ousted by the Tukulor from the Segu Bambara empire.

chiefs, particularly Titi, the military chief, and the chiefs of Nyamina, were used. The head chief of Nyamina, Sa'id Kouro, for instance, served as an intermediary between the French and Karamoko Diara. By the end of Gallieni's mission, however, the French efforts to win over Karamoko Diara had not yet succeeded The Nyamina chief was still useful to the French in other ways. He agreed to serve the French against the Tukulor by arresting *sofas* in the Tukulor army and, when possible, killing them. While doing this he was assured of French support because, as he was told, 'Tu es un chef français'.[1]

This was the situation when Archinard arrived to take over control of French operations in October 1888. As he himself said, French official policy at this time remained what it had been since 1879 – that is, the expansion by peaceful means of French commerce and influence.[2] Archinard maintained, however, that on his arrival he found that he could not work this policy because Ahmadu, head of the Tukulor empire, and Samori at the head of the emergent Wasulu empire, were obstacles that would foil any idea of peaceful expansion. He claimed that this was the lesson that French experience in the Sudan since 1880 had taught, and insisted that the realisation of French ambitions depended upon the disappearance of Ahmadu and Samori, or at least the annihilation of their power and authority. He expressed the belief that the only reason the French officers who had served in the Western Sudan before him had not fought to achieve this end was that French forces in the area were not considered strong enough for the task involved.[3]

With this conviction Archinard began his commission with a determination to conquer not only the Tukulor empire, but also the Wasulu empire of Samori. As will be seen in this chapter, Archinard was the architect of the French conquest of the Tukulor empire. Most of the time, he acted independently of the French government in Paris. He systematically confronted the government with a series of unavoidable decisions arising out of situations which he himself had created, and the government was forced to adopt them. Thus, in spite of official policy, Archinard led the government on to the conquest of the Tukulor empire.

1 ASAOF, in 15G82, Correspondance avec Nyamina – Le Commt de Bamako à Sidi Koné, Chef de Nyamina, 12 Aug. 1888
2 Archinard, *Rapport sur la campagne 1890–1891* (n.d.), p. 179
3 *Ibid.*, pp. 179–80

Indeed the career of Archinard in the Western Sudan justifies Jean Darcy's statement, that in French colonial expansion, colonial officers were often more important than the government officials in Paris. As he claims, French colonial conquests did not result from any studied official plan but 'dans l'histoire des origines de notre empire colonial, le calcul des hommes d'état entrèrent pour beaucoup moins que le caprice d'un colon audacieux, ou l'initiative intelligente de tel officier'.[1] As will be seen, Archinard was able to conquer the Tukulor empire mainly because of his diplomatic skill and his ability to exploit, to French advantage, the existing political situation in the empire. As before, the Bambara were a key factor in this.

On his arrival in October 1888 Archinard continued the task, which Gallieni had begun, of re-establishing French influence over the Senegambia. Part of the measures he took included the establishment of new garrisoned forts, such as the one built at Koussama Kounou.[2] He also stationed troops at various places in Khasso.[3] These measures, meant to ensure French control of the Senegambia, were also rightly interpreted by the Tukulor as preparations for an attack on their empire. The Tukulor interpretation of French activities in the Senegambia was right because for Archinard, the fall of the Tukulor empire was the only worthwhile objective and all his activities were geared to this end.

Ahmadu, having sensed the danger to his regime, took precautionary measures to guard against a possible French attack and ensure control over the internal affairs of the empire. He sent troops to police the movements of the French along the river Senegal from Badumbe to Koulou.[4] He also took steps to ensure the cooperation of the outlying districts of the empire. For instance, he sent to Aguibu, the chief in charge of Dinguiray, to remind him of the difficult position of Dinguiray and how best to protect it against external threats. Dinguiray was like an enclave surrounded by the state of Futa Jallon, the Wasulu and the French in the other states of the Senegambia, especially Bambuk.

---

1 Darcy, *France et Angleterre: cent années de rivalité coloniale; Afrique* (1904), p. 222
2 The exact location is not now known, but it was presumably in Khasso.
3 ASAOF, in 15G76/3, Affaires politiques: l'espion Cheik Diko envoyé dans le Nioro et rentré à Kayes le 17 janvier, Kayes, 18 Jan. 1889
4 ASAOF, in 15G76/3, Affaires Politiques – Note, Kayes, 9 Dec. 1888

Aguibu was reported to have sent to Ahmadu to assure him that he was in full control of the situation, and to give information about the activities of Samori and the French. In addition he sent gifts of 2,000 kolanuts, three swords and four guns as a token of his loyalty.[1]

Ahmadu's reaction did not deter Archinard in his preparations against the Tukulor empire. He intensified the offensive against the Tukulor not only by continuing the military build-up in the Senegambia and reopening the negotiations for a Bambara anti-Tukulor alliance with the French, but also by attempting to set the Tukulor chiefs against one another. As has been shown, the French had provided asylum for two of Ahmadu's brothers, Muniru and Ahmidu, at the end of the Muntaga revolt in 1885. In 1887 these two were sent to Bandiagara where it was hoped that they would strengthen the anti-Ahmadu forces under Ahmadu Tijani's leadership. In 1888 Archinard continued this policy of setting the Tukulor chiefs against one another by opening negotiations with Aguibu, emir of Dinguiray, with a view to winning him over to the French, who, it was explained, were not against the Tukulor as a whole but against Ahmadu specifically. Archinard also made attempts to detach from Ahmadu the Tukulor chief of Koulou,[2] Mourtada. Pressure was brought upon Mourtada to abandon the Tukulor and support the French during his visit to the Jolof state in the latter part of 1888. Then he had been invited to go to Saint Louis where the French governor would honour him and grant him protection against Ahmadu if it was necessary to do so. Mourtada had refused the invitation claiming that, unlike Muniru and Ahmidu, he had nothing against Ahmadu, and was loyal to him. Having failed to win Mourtada over, Archinard threatened to arrest him if he went to Futa Toro, especially through the district of Damga.[3] Mourtada was apparently suspected of being on a mission to seek allies for the Tukulor against the French, and Futa Toro was the most likely place to find such allies, hence the threat of arrest if he went there. So far, it appears that Ahmadu still had the situation under control.

1 ASAOF, in 15G76/3 Affaires Politiques: l'espion Cheik Diko . . .'
2 Koulou was at this time one of the places where Ahmadu stationed troops to police French activities in Khasso and along the river Niger.
3 ASAOF, in 15G76/3, Affaires Politiques – Un Courrier Politique Ousman Dialo envoyé sur la rive droite . . ., Kayes, 24 Jan. 1889

Archinard did not stop with the formation of alliances; he took measures to weaken Tukulor strength directly. One such measure was the embargo which he placed on the sale of arms and ammunition to the Tukulors.[1] This was a veritable sign of French hostility, and obviously intended to weaken the Tukulor army. Ahmadu protested, to no avail, against the embargo, pointing out to Archinard that it was an unfriendly act contrary to the terms of the treaty he concluded with Gallieni in 1887.[2] A more direct attack on Tukulor defences, was the destruction of the fortress at Koundian.

THE DESTRUCTION OF KOUNDIAN

After Gallieni's successful attack on Koundian Tukulor forces had succeeded in driving out the French garrison and retaking possession of the fortress. It was situated in a naturally protected environment, being placed in the centre of a ring of mountains, in the Bambuk.[3] It occupied a strategic position in the Tukulor defence system, especially as far as territories in the Senegambia were concerned. It served, for instance, as a link between Ka'arta and Dinguiray, and it was partly to break this link that Archinard destroyed it. Archinard himself stated that the destruction was motivated by a desire to block all communication between Koundian and Dinguiray. It was hoped that the result would be considerable enough 'pour que l'armée d'Aguibou ou celle d'Ahmadou ne fût pas renforcée des fanatiques laissés a Koundian par El-Hadj et qui auraient eu de nouveaux motifs de haine contre nous'.[4] The destruction of Koundian, it is clear, was a continuation of an earlier practice by which the French destroyed or sought to destroy fortresses which served the Tukulor as bases for military operations. The French had been doing this whenever they felt strong enough, or wherever a convenient excuse could be found. Thus they had destroyed Tukulor fortresses at Sabousire (1879), Goubanko (1881) and Daba (1883).[5] In this way they systematically weakened Tukulor military strength.

1 ASAOF, in 15G76/2, Sultan Ahmadou au Chef des Européens, Commandant des affaires orientales, le Colonel, translator's dating: Kayes, 24 Jan. 1889
2 *Ibid.*
3 Archinard, *Le Soudan français en 1888–1889: rapport militaire*, p. 26
4 *Ibid.*, pp. 23, 26   5 *Ibid.*, p. 28

Apart from the aim of weakening the Tukulor empire with a view to an eventual French conquest, Archinard considered the destruction of Koundian as useful in the struggle for the control of the Senegambia, and also necessary if the French were to control Bambuk and be in a position to explore the gold deposits for which the country was famous. The alternative, it was said, was for the French to renounce the struggle in Bambuk and, in the process, to lose their prestige.[1]

Archinard decided on the destruction of Koundian entirely on his own. He had in fact destroyed it before he made any reference to the governor of Senegal. To destroy Koundian he launched a surprise attack. He secretly sent Captain Quiquandon at the head of an advance guard which was to police the routes leading to Koundian and cut all communications with the fortress. The advance guard, comprising forty men armed with guns, left Bafoulabe on 14 February 1889. They were later joined by about four hundred auxiliaries. They all reached Koundian on 18 February at 4 a.m. after a journey of about 100 kilometres. The fortress was immediately put under siege and a surprise attack[2] was made which lasted till 4 p.m. before the French could take Koundian. The French used not only guns, but also cannon; in all, about 474 cannon-shots were fired. With superior weapons, the fortress could have been taken much earlier but for the formidable resistance put up by the Tukulor garrison. Archinard acknowledged their dogged resistance, saying: 'Les gens de Koundian avaient bien résisté et le bombardement était prolongé.'[3]

It was after Koundian had been destroyed that Archinard wrote to the governor of Senegal to inform him of the action and the necessity for it. He sought to gain the governor's support for his action by enumerating the advantages which would derive from the destruction of Koundian. Among these was the effect that it would produce on Franco-Tukulor relations. He claimed that future relations with Ahmadu should be easier because no other fortress in the Tukulor defence system was nearly as strong as Koundian. He believed that the episode would instil terror in the minds of the Tukulor rulers who would henceforth stop their

1 ANSOM, in Sénégal IV, 92c, Commandant Supérieur à Gouverneur, Saint-Louis, Bafoulabe, 21 Feb. 1889
2 Archinard, *Le Soudan français en 1888–1889: rapport militaire*, p. 23
3 *Ibid.*, pp. 27–8

hostility towards the French: 'L'effet produit sera le terreur et remplacera l'hostilité que causait une menace dont l'effet se faisait attendre.' He was sure that neither Aguibu nor Ahmadu would move against the French after the Koundian episode. Whatever might follow from it, in any case, he argued, the destruction of Koundian was inevitable: 'De toute façon cette action s'imposerait un jour ou l'autre.'[1]

Apart from the above considerations the destruction of Koundian was also seen as a way of winning over the Bambara to an alliance with the French against the Tukulor. The French collaboration with Ahmadu in 1886–87 had made the Bambara distrustful, and all French efforts to win over the Bambara of Segu and Beledugu as allies against the Tukulor had failed. Archinard intended to reopen negotiations with the Bambara and the Koundian episode, it was hoped, should have convinced them that the French were truly anti-Tukulor and could consequently be trusted by the Bambara.

The immediate effect was, however, the worsening of relations between the French and the Tukulor. In his letter to Aguibu, Archinard attempted to remove any idea that the destruction of Koundian was an act of aggression against the Tukulor. He claimed, quite wrongly, that Koundian was no longer under Tukulor control, and that by destroying it, he had merely removed a source of trouble in the Senegambia.[2] Archinard's tactics, rather than pacifying the Tukulor as he wanted, naturally had the effect of making them see the French as deceitful invaders. Aguibu, replying to Archinard's letter, pointed out that the destruction of Koundian was an invasion of Tukulor territory. For the settlement of the problems involved he advised Archinard to address himself to Ahmadu at Nioro.[3] In his letters to Ahmadu Archinard repeated his arguments with Aguibu,[4] but Ahmadu made it clear that he considered the French as aggressors and as

1 ANSOM, in Sénégal IV, 93c, Commandant Supérieur au Gouverneur, Saint-Louis, Bafoulabe, 21 Feb. 1889
2 ASAOF, 15G81/4, Correspondance avec Aguibou – Commt Supérieur à Aguibou, Kalada, 22 Feb. 1889
3 ASAOF, 15G81/7, Correspondance avec Aguibou – Muhammad Aguibou à Commt Supérieur du Soudan français, translator's date: 10 Apr. 1889
4 ASAOF, 15G76/2(12), Commandant Supérieur Archinard à Ahmadou, Kalada, 22 Feb. 1889; 15G81/16, Commandant Supérieur à Ahmadou, Marigot du Soulounko (avant Niagassola), 23 Mar. 1889

having violated the treaty of 1887.[1] Archinard's later efforts to make Ahmadu believe that the French intentions towards the Tukulor were peaceful failed. For example, in May 1889 he tried to assure Ahmadu that the French had no territorial ambitions, and cited the fact that he had not encouraged or aided Ahmadu's rebellious subjects in Guidimaka.[2] It was obvious, however, that his manoeuvres could not succeed with the Tukulor, because he was at the same time already involved in negotiations with the Bambara.

The destruction of Koundian represented a real threat to the Tukulor empire. As a result of it, the line of communication between the main part of the empire and such outlying districts as Dinguiray was cut. Aguibu, who had only recently assured Ahmadu of his loyalty, became isolated in the midst of French posts; it would be difficult henceforth for him to give Ahmadu any effective cooperation. His isolation meant that his position had become weak and that he would be more susceptible to pressures from the French than he had been so far. At least he would be anxious for his personal safety. Apart from thus disrupting and weakening the leadership of the Tukulor empire, the loss of Koundian also meant a dislocation and weakening of Tukulor defences. The situation was made worse by the fact that the Bambara would now have the inspiration to ally with the French. In short the security problems of the empire were increasing at a time when its defence arrangements were badly disrupted and weakened. Ahmadu realised the danger in the situation and decided to act swiftly.

He had planned to react to the destruction of Koundian by leading a military operation, to be directed from the district of Koniakary against the French. The intention had been to direct attacks against the French posts of Bakel, Bafoulabe and Médine from Koniakary. He could not carry out these plans, however, for several reasons. In the first place, as a result of several years of civil war and unrest, Ka'arta was at this time suffering from a serious famine, and it would be impossible to find enough food to feed the troops if they were to go on an expedition. Secondly, he could not embark on an expedition against the French at the time

1 ASAOF, 15G81/13, Ahmadou el-Kebir El Médiniou à Archinard, translated and dated Siguiri, 9 Apr. 1889
2 ASAOF, 15G81/19C Commandant Archinard à Ahmadou, Diago, 19 May 1889

for fear that the Bambara might take advantage of the situation to attack Nioro and the neighbouring villages. It was this consideration that made the *talibés* advise Ahmadu against an expedition against the French in March 1889.

In spite of his problems Ahmadu did not renounce his plans against the French. Instead he made efforts to overcome his difficulties. To tackle the problem of food, for instance, he gave orders to the districts of Fansané and Tomora to store their grain in barns and not to sell any part under any pretext.[1] This was to ensure that food needed for the projected operations in Koniakary would not be sold to the French who had their posts near by along the Senegal. Ahmadu also began to look for allies. He sent emissaries to the Buurba Jolof, Ali Bouri, and Abdul Bubakar, the almamy of Bosséia in Futa Toro, in the hope of finding allies who would collaborate with the Tukulor and fight against the French from both the Senegambia and Ka'arta at the same time.[2] Thus Ahmadu intensified his preparations against the eventual clash with the French.

THE NYAMINA GARRISON AND THE FORMATION OF ALLIANCES

Archinard, constant in his belief that the fall of the Tukulor empire was not only necessary but inevitable, continued also to be very active in taking both defensive and offensive measures. Apart from stationing troops in several villages along the Senegal and the Niger, he sent missions to seek alliances with various Bambara chiefs in the Beledugu. For some time, however, the Bambara remained discouraging in their attitude. With rumours that Ahmadu would soon be returning from Nioro to Segu to organise Tukulor forces, the need for Bambara co-operation became more urgent, and Archinard took another step aimed at demonstrating the friendly disposition of the French to the

1 ASAOF, 15G76/3, Le Lieutenant Monziols, Commandant, le cercle de Bafoulabe, à M. le Commandant Supérieur du Soudan français, Bafoulabe, 5 Mar. 1889; 15G76/3, Affairs Politiques: l'Espion Cheik Diko . . ., Kayes, 18 Jan. 1889
2 ASAOF, 15G76/3, Renseignements fournis par le Cherif Abderaman, le 4 juin 1889 à son retour de Nioro. Abderaman, a Moor, was a secret agent of the French. He had been sent to Nioro on a political mission. He spent twenty days there before returning to Médine.

Bambara and their common hostility to the Tukulor. Early in May 1889 he built a fortified post at Nyamina, near Segu on the river Niger.[1]

This was in a sense a defensive measure taken against the Tukulor. Nyamina chiefs, it may be recalled, had since 1888, been friendly to the French and had in fact been willing agents in the latter's efforts to secure the co-operation of Segu and Beledugu Bambara. Nyamina was therefore ideal as a base for French operations at this time. Archinard feared that if he succeeded in returning to Segu, Ahmadu would certainly be in a stronger position to attack the French. If he succeeded in controlling Segu, the plan to attack the French from Koniakary would not only be carried out, but worse still from the French point of view, Ahmadu could at the same time attack the French from the Segu side. He would also be able to combat the Bambara resistance with greater determination and effect. Of the strategic position of Nyamina in the French defence against the Tukulor, Archinard stated:

> En occupant Nyamina, à deux ou trois jours de Ségou, non seulement nous tenions en quelque sorte Ahmadou qui ne peut pas rentrer chez lui sans entrer en pourparlers avec nous, mais nous pouvions, en cas d'agression du côté de Kayes, répondre immédiatement du côté de Ségou sans risquer d'être pris à revers, car nous opérions en pays ami, au milieu des Bambaras, nos alliés naturels.[2]

The only difficulty which Ahmadu had in returning to Segu was the Bambara who, through their resistance movements in Beledugu, created an effective barrier separating Ka'arta from the Segu section of the Tukulor empire. To return to Segu, Ahmadu would have to cross Beledugu, but to do so he would need to subdue the Bambara, an undertaking that would involve a huge military effort. Archinard considered Bambara collaboration as vital to his plans, and the building of the fort at Nyamina was seen as a step towards achieving it. The Bambara should be convinced of French determination to help them by the fact that the fort was garrisoned with troops from the Bamako post, and Captain Septans put in charge.[3] In this sense the occupation of Nyamina was an effective measure against the Tukulor.

1 ASAOF, 15G81/19, Commandant Archinard à Ahmadou, Diago, 19 May 1889
2 Archinard, *Le Soudan français en 1888–1889: rapport militaire*, p. 17
3 *Ibid.*, pp. 17–19

Ahmadu wrote to protest against Archinard's action at Nyamina. He pointed out that this violated the territorial rights of the Tukulor and the 1887 treaty.[1] But protests apart, Ahmadu was really not in a position to take any practical steps against the French. Beledugu remained an effective barrier, and a constant source of embarrassment to him. He remained virtually confined to Ka'arta.

His son, Al-Madani, who was ruling at Segu and therefore nearer to Nyamina, would have been better placed to act against the French. Unfortunately, however, he, like the Bambara, fell victim to Archinard's diplomacy. The Tukulor from Segu saw Archinard's action at Nyamina as directed against the Bambara. Madani saw the French as useful instruments for breaking the Bambara resistance. The Bambara also saw the French occupation of Nyamina the way Archinard wanted – an evidence of French hostility towards the Tukulor and consequently an assurance that the French could now be trusted as allies against the Tukulor empire. Reporting the attitudes of both the Bambara and the Tukulor to the occupation of Nyamina, Archinard wrote: 'A la nouvelle de l'occupation de Nyamina . . . Madani affecta de ne regarder cette occupation que comme dirigée contre les Bambaras. Les Bambaras, de leur côté, la regardèrent comme dirigée contre Madani et personne ne bougea.'[2] Having achieved this diplomatic success against both the Beledugu Bambara and the Tukulor, Archinard confidentially reopened negotiations with the ruling Diara family of the Segu Bambara.

The Segu Bambara under the leadership of the Diara family had hitherto not yielded to French pressure for an anti-Tukulor alliance. They wanted to break the Tukulor regime, but they did not necessarily think the French less evil. They were convinced that the French could not be trusted as allies because of the apparently shifty nature of the French policy which made it possible for them to associate with both the Bambara and the Tukulor simultaneously. It may be recalled that the 1888 French mission to the Segu Bambara failed largely because of lack of confidence in, and fear of, the French. Archinard was convinced that he needed the cooperation of the Segu Bambara to bring

1 ASAOF, 15G81/20, De la part du roi des Croyants à Archinard, (n.d.), May 1889?
2 Archinard, *Le Soudan français en 1888–1889: rapport militaire*, p. 19

about the fall of the Tukulor empire. He therefore determined to remove the distrust that had hitherto made cooperation impossible. With the Nyamina episode, he thought the circumstances auspicious for negotiations to be reopened with the Segu Bambara.

Archinard sent a mission to the Diara family in August 1889. The mission, led by Lt Marchand, was to negotiate an alliance with the Segu Bambara through the Diara ruling family. Negotiations were to be based on the necessity to cooperate to destroy their common enemy, the Tukulor. To ensure the continuity of friendship between the Bambara and the French after the fall of the Tukulor, the Diara family were promised reinstatement as the lawful rulers of Segu, which had been the kingdom of their predecessors up till the time of the Tukulor conquest. In return the Diara would guarantee protection for French commerce throughout their regained kingdom and as long as this was done, the French would continue to help and protect the Diara against all external threats. As proof of the French determination to wipe out the Tukulor empire, Marchand was instructed to tell the Diara, that from their post at Bamako, the French had been distributing arms and ammunition to the Beledugu Bambara who, like the Segu Bambara, were in resistance against the Tukulor. As a token of friendship towards the Bambara, Archinard sent as gifts to the Diara, '40 pièces de toile des vosges et 40 litres de tafia'.[1]

The mission left Bamako for Farako, where the Diara had had their headquarters since the Tukulor conquest of Segu on 25 August 1889.[2] In the negotiations Marchand dealt with Mari Diara, who appeared to have been forewarned about the mission.[3] The attempt to secure an alliance failed, mainly because the Segu Bambara still feared and distrusted the French. This is clear from the reported statement of the Diara family: 'Les Français font alliance avec tout le monde, sont amis avec tout le monde, même avec leurs ennemis; ils font des promesses qu'ils ne tiennent pas.'[4]

The failure of the Marchand mission demonstrates clearly the

---

1 ASAOF, 1G115/2, Instructions données à M. Marchand pour sa mission du Ségou, Le Capitaine Underberg, Bammako, 25 Aug. 1889
2 *Ibid.*, p. 8
3 ASAOF, 1G115/1, Le Sous-lieutenant Marchand à M. le Capitaine Underberg, Nyamina, 10 Sept. 1899, pp. 3, 9
4 *Ibid.*, p. 10

nature and purpose of the Bambara resistance movements.[1] The Segu Bambara were determined to overthrow the Tukulor regime and re-establish their authority and power over Segu. They welcomed external assistance; indeed, they had support from other Bambara groups and the al-Bakkāi family in Timbuktu. But they did not in the process want to replace one master by another. They rightly suspected that the French were only seeking to use them as instruments to establish their own rule in Segu. The Diara thought that to cooperate with the French would be to ruin themselves and to establish the French as successors to the Tukulor. For this reason they did not find it possible to accept the proposal for an alliance.

Archinard, however, did not give up the attempt to win the Segu Bambara to the French side. In the last phases of the negotiations, the Segu Bambara must have been affected in their attitude by the fact that other resistance groups, especially the Beledugu Bambara, had accepted the French as allies. It is not surprising, therefore, that eventually in December 1889 the French succeeded in persuading the Diara family to collaborate with them against the Tukulor. The agreement came as a pleasant surprise even to the French negotiators, and it was therefore the more valued. One of the men on the mission noted: 'Je n'ai jamais moi-même été pleinement convaincu que la mission de Farako pourrait réussir et avait réussi.'[2]

Thus by the end of the 1888–89 campaign, Archinard had succeeded in weakening the Tukulor defence, especially with the destruction of Koundian and the building of a garrisoned post at Nyamina. Also with the conclusion of the agreement with the Segu Bambara, he had succeeded in allying with the French several of the anti-Tukulor groups for a projected conquest of the Tukulor empire. Thus by the end of 1889 the stage had been set for the war against the Tukulor empire to begin at any time. Archinard, by his activities, had committed the French to war as the only means of protecting French interests in the Western Sudan. By destroying Koundian and occupying Nyamina, he had made it impossible for peaceful relations to exist between the French and the Tukulor. On the other hand the basis of agreement between him and the Bambara was the plan of war against the Tukulor. Thus at the end of 1889 it could be said that war

1 Ọlọruntimẹhin, 'Resistance movements in the Tukulor empire'.
2 ASAOF, 1G115/7, Fangali-Somba (Messe *Ke le*), 28 Jan. 1890

between the French and the Tukulor had become almost unavoidable. For this Archinard was responsible; he had not consulted the authorities in Paris, but he had also avoided large-scale military involvements that would have called for more money than was originally made available, a point on which the French government would have been sensitive. He had brought about the situation by diplomacy and a very careful exploitation of the political situation. This was why it was possible to commit the French government without its being aware of it.

Preparations for war had not been one-sided. Ahmadu himself had planned to fight the French earlier in 1889, and he had not done so only because the circumstances within the empire were not favourable. Since then he had continued his efforts to find allies among the Senegambian states against the French. Also by the end of 1889, his efforts to solve the problem of food shortage had yielded fruit. Harvest in the year had been good and the situation had improved correspondingly.[1]

With the threat of famine removed, Ahmadu could face the danger to his empire with more determination. He continued to plan for military expeditions against the French during the following dry season, that is from late 1889 to early 1890. In addition to the earlier plan to use Koniakary as a base for operations against the French posts at Médine and Bakel, Ahmadu was reported to be planning to send expeditions against the French in the Bafing valley from the Diala district of Ka'arta. It had become definite that the almamy of Bosséia in Futa Toro, Abdul Bubakar, and Badon, the chief of Logo in Khasso, were actively collaborating with him.[2] He was also reported to be acquiring large quantities of arms and ammunition. According to reports of French spies, Ahmadu had, in 1889 alone, acquired '322 fusils à pierre à un coup de traite; 600 barels de poudre de traite; 30 charges de pierres à fusils; 20 fusils à tir rapide (probablement des carabines Wenchester à répétition d'après sa description) avec des cartouches; 6 pistolets et un grand nombre de sabre'.[3] These were obviously obtained through the British since Archinard had already placed an embargo on the sale of arms and ammunition to the Tukulor empire.

1 ASAOF, in 15G76/3 Agissemements d'Ahmadou, 9 Oct. 1889
2 ASAOF, in 15G76/3, Affaires Politiques – Note, Kayes, 5 Oct. 1889
3 ASAOF, in 15G76/3, Le Capitaine, Commandant, le cercle de Médine, à M. le Commandant Supérieur, Kayes, Médine, 31 Oct. 1889

THE FALL OF THE SEGU SECTION OF THE EMPIRE

Saboné and the 'boundary problem'

When Archinard returned for the 1889–90 campaign, both the French and the Tukulor were already armed, and were still arming for war. Apparently eager for action after a period of rest in France, he created an imaginary boundary problem between the Tukulor and territories supposedly placed under French protection. In December 1889 he wrote to Ahmadu, stating that he had been informed that Tukulor chiefs in the Dianghirte district of Ka'arta had taken four thousand kilogrammes of grain from the inhabitants of Saboné[1] on the Niger. He then claimed that Saboné, like all other villages on the same bank of the Niger, belonged to the French, according to the information allegedly given him by Gallieni. Archinard asserted that the Niger had always been the boundary between the Tukulor empire and what he called French territories. He claimed that the boundary was marked by a series of French establishments, starting from Saint Louis in Senegal and including Kayes, Bafoulabe (on the Senegal), Badumbe, Saboné, Sambabougou, Dioufa and Méné-méné right into the Bambara country. He then warned the Tukulor to keep to their own side of the river. He announced his intention to send troops to protect the villages he claimed against the Tukulor if, within twenty days, Ahmadu did not reply, guaranteeing that Tukulor troops would no longer cross the Niger to visit these villages again for any purpose.[2] In plain terms, Archinard offered war as a solution if Ahmadu would not willingly surrender to these territorial claims.

Ahmadu naturally rejected such an outrageous claim and Archinard announced his decision to occupy the villages forcefully and damn the consequences.[3] In another letter Ahmadu again emphasised that Archinard's action was a violation of Tukulor territorial rights, and that he intended to deal with it

1 This was probably the tax payable to the Tukulor administration by the district.
2 ASAOF, 15G76/2(32), Le Lt-Col. Archinard, Commandant Supérieur du Soudan français, à Sultan Ahmadou, Kayes, 6 Dec. 1889
3 ASAOF, 15G76/2(34), Archinard à Ahmadou, Kayes, 28 Dec. 1889

accordingly.[1] Henceforth, a state of war existed between the French and the Tukulor.

Collapse of Segu and Ouossébougou, 1890

At the beginning of 1890 Ahmadu had concluded a reliable alliance that included Futa Jallon, Futa Toro, Wasulu and Jolof.[2] Each of these states came into the alliance in response to Ahmadu's appeal for a joint effort because each saw it as an effective way of dealing with the French threat to its own existence. For example, Samori's state of Wasulu had been under attack by the French since 1883 when Desbordes led an expedition against Samori's troops after the establishment of the French post at Bamako. By joining the coalition being formed against the French by Ahmadu, Samori certainly hoped to be better able to fight for the preservation of his state. For Ali Bouri N'Diaye, the *Buurba Jolof*, the struggle against the French had been long. After a short period of collaboration with the French to fight against Hamadou Cheikou, who attempted to conquer Jolof state in 1875, Ali Bouri had found it necessary to fight against the French in order to maintain the independence of the Jolof. Ali Bouri was a very strong Muslim who belonged to the Tijāniyya brotherhood. In his struggle against the French, he had used religious appeal to form an anti-French coalition which embraced Abdul Bubakar, almamy of Bosséia in Futa Toro, Lat Dior, the Damel of Kayor and Saer Mati, chief of the Rip and son and successor of Maba, who had earlier proclaimed a jihād in the area and had fought against the French. Ali Bouri had also entered into negotiations with Ahmadu for the formation of what was described as a 'ligue tidiane combattant avec acharnement notre influence civilisatrice'.[3]

Partly to make collaboration impossible between Ali Bouri's coalition and Ahmadu's, the French decided to create a barrier between the Senegambia and the Tukulor empire. Hence, it was decided to wage war and maintain cavalry in the Senegambian

1 ASAOF, 15G76/2(38), Mīna 'ila muqaddam 'askarihi Arsinal (i.e. Archinard), marked 'Reçu 15 Jan. 1890'
2 Ọlọruntimẹhin, 'Anti-French coalition of states and groups in the Western Sudan', *Odu*, new ser., no. 3, April, 1970
3 ANSOM, in Sénégal I, 80b, Clément Thomas, Gouverneur du Sénégal et dépendances à M. le Sous-Secrétarie d'Etat, Colonies, Saint-Louis, 30 May 1890

states of Jolof, Kayor and Futa Toro. To this end Archinard
stationed troops, as has been noted earlier, in the Senegambia,
especially along the Senegal. The French fought in Jolof particularly to remove Ali Bouri from the position of power. They had
just succeeded in doing this early in 1890[1] when war between the
French and the Tukulor was already imminent. Thus, by allying
with Ahmadu, Ali Bouri was being consistent with his policy of
opposition to French expansion. As he had just been chased out
of Jolof at this time, alliance with Ahmadu must have appeared
to him also as the only means of continuing the fight to regain his
territory.

As his contribution to the anti-French war efforts, Ali Bouri
furnished large contingents of Wolof troops and volunteers to
Ahmadu's army in Ka'arta.[2] With this addition to his forces,
Ahmadu was again in a position to fight for the survival of his
empire. But the French did not fear the collaboration between
Ahmadu and Ali Bouri so much as they feared that between
Ahmadu and Samori. Archinard was convinced that if Ahmadu
and Samori had the chance to coordinate their efforts the consequences could be disastrous. He was determined to prevent this
at all costs, and this determination really dictated his next line of
attack against the Tukulor. He was convinced that unless
Ahmadu and Samori disappeared from the scene, the French
would never achieve anything in the Western Sudan. As a
beginning of the effort to conquer Ahmadu and Samori, he convinced the governor of Senegal that an attack on Segu was
necessary.

Recommending the measure, the governor of Senegal, Clément
Thomas, asked the French government in Paris to authorise the
attack on Segu. He claimed that it was the only way of breaking
the power of the Tukulor and of Samori, and that it was a
necessary step for the realisation of French economic and political
interests in the Western Sudan. In support of his recommenda-
tion he wrote: 'Une considération domine toutes autres: nous ne
ferons rien de durable dans le Soudan tant que Ahmadou et
Samory n'aurons pas disparu.'[3] The ministry was urged to

1 *Ibid.*
2 ANSOM, in Sénégal I, 80b, Clément Thomas à M. le Sous-Secrétaire
   . . ., Saint-Louis, 31 May 1890
3 ANSOM, in Sénégal I, 80b, 'Depêche Télégraphique – Gouverneur à
   Colonies, Paris', Saint-Louis, 25 Feb. 1890

authorise an immediate attack on Segu because it was the only
way of preventing Ahmadu from reaching Segu where he would
recruit forces and be in a stronger position to collaborate with
Samori against the French. By destroying Segu, not only would
coordination between Ahmadu and Samori be made impossible,
but also the prestige enjoyed by Ahmadu in Ka'arta would be
reduced as, with the conquest of Segu, he would have lost control
of his empire. The French would then restore the Bambara to their
position of power in Segu. In this way, the continued protection
of French commercial and political interests would be guaranteed.
It was specially impressed on the ministry that the march upon
Segu should be embarked on immediately because a better
occasion for doing so might never occur. On Archinard's authority,
the governor assured Paris that sufficient troops, arms and
ammunition were already available to the mission. The Bambara,
he said, were ready to cooperate with the French, and the
operations involved would not be bloody. The governor's telegram reads:

> Moment actuel est propice; matériel et munitions sont suffisants,
> troupes prêtes; Archinard affirme action sur Ségou non meutrière.
> Après mûr examen étant donné surtout entente actuelle entre Ahmadou
> et Samory dont il importe couper communications; occasion meilleure
> ne se retrouvera pas. Veuillez autoriser avec confiance marche sur
> Ségou et programme occupation économique Soudan arreté par vous
> peut être appliqué alors avec assurance.[1]

In these terms Archinard and Clément Thomas decided upon the
invasion of Segu and made the ministry believe that such a step
was inevitable.

The ministry gave its approval for the attack and asked to be
informed of developments.[2] The ministry's position is understandable. Much as it wished to avoid conquest, it was eager to
expand French commerce. It was told that the obstacle to commercial expansion could be removed at no extra cost to the
government, and that the measure recommended was really
inevitable. The ministry had only one proposal before it and it
had to adopt it.

The ministry's approval did not mean much to Archinard, who

1 *Ibid.*
2 ANSOM, in Sénégal I, 8oc, Colonies à Gouverneur, Saint-Louis, Paris,
27 Feb. 1890

had actually mobilised his forces against Segu even before the ministry was asked for approval. Troops camped at Lontou near Médine began to march to Segu on 15 February 1890,[1] whereas the governor of Senegal did not ask the ministry for approval of the project until 25 February.

The march on Segu was undertaken at a time when Ahmadu could not leave Ka'arta to defend that part of his empire. This was partly because Beledugu still constituted an effective barrier between Ka'arta and Segu. Ahmadu also had enough on his hands meeting the French offensive along the Senegal and had no time to counter the offensive in Segu. He did not know that an attack was being planned against Segu by the French and their Bambara auxiliaries. Therefore he could neither act against them nor forewarn his son, Madani, who was ruling at Segu. The Tukulor empire was in real danger of collapsing, but without the leaders knowing it.

Archinard's army of 3,600 men reached Segu on 6 April 1890, at 5.30 a.m. when most of the inhabitants were still sleeping. The town, taken by surprise, was immediately put under siege and bombarded from all directions. After a gallant defence against an army that was better armed and better placed strategically, the Segu army surrendered and Archinard took control of Tukulor fortifications in the town. The surrender took place at 3.30 p.m. after only a few hours of fighting, but the battle had been disastrous for the Tukulor. It was reported that in the battle French artillery fired 2,776 cannon rounds and used seventy kilograms of gunpowder, in addition to using swords and other weapons.[2] The Tukulor found it impossible to continue the struggle after Archinard had taken control of their fortresses and disarmed the soldiers. Moreover, leading members of Ahmadu's family and other Tukulor chiefs were taken hostage to serve as a basis for negotiations later on with Ahmadu.[3] All this undoubtedly had a demoralising effect on the Segu Tukulor who might have been willing to continue the struggle against the invaders. With the loss of Segu the whole fabric of the Tukulor empire was shaken, and the struggle ahead was crucial for the survival of the empire.

1 ASAOF, 1D105, 'Archinard, Rapport Militaire, Campagne 1889–1890', Kayes, 13 July 1890, p. 12
2 *Ibid.*, pp. 17–18
3 *Ibid.*, p. 88

But this was not to be all. After occupying Segu Archinard led his forces into Beledugu to attack the fortress at Ouossébougou, virtually the only important symbol of Tukulor authority among the Beledugu Bambara.[1] The garrisoned fortress and the town of Ouossébougou were destroyed in a military operation between 24 and 27 April 1890.[2]

The destruction of Ouossébougou could be seen as part of Archinard's policy of weakening Tukulor defences by breaking its garrisoned forts. By this action he ensured, for instance, that the Tukulor would be defenceless against French and Bambara operations in Beledugu. He gave other reasons for destroying Ouossébougou. One of these was that it was to reassure the Bambara of French determination to cooperate with them against the Tukulor. He claimed that after the unannounced attack and destruction of Segu, the Bambara demanded the fulfilment of the French promise of aid against the Tukulor. The Bambara, he said, rightly pointed out that Ouossébougou had been the centre from which the Tukulor had made it impossible for them to be free. The destruction of Ouossébougou, he explained, was therefore necessary in order to reassure the Bambara and keep them loyal to the French alliance.[3]

The point of course was that Archinard was continuing his campaigns against the Tukulor empire without any reference to his government. He had always believed in the usefulness of the Bambara as instruments for the conquest of the Tukulor and therefore found no difficulty in explaining his unauthorised action on the grounds of the necessity to keep them loyal to the French alliance.

After the destruction of Segu Archinard had written to Ahmadu informing him of the conquest of Segu. He explained, flippantly, that his attack on Segu was the consequence of Ahmadu's refusal to recognise a frontier between the Tukulor and the French. He claimed that this refusal was typified by the fact that Ahmadu did not yield to his demands over Saboné; he also accused Ahmadu of unwillingness to permit a free flow of commerce on the Niger. The conquest of Segu was a penalty for these alleged sins.[4] In

1 *Ibid.*, p. 45
2 *Ibid.*, pp. 51–86
3 *Ibid.*, pp. 25–50
4 ASAOF, in 15G76/2, Le Lt-Col Archinard, Commandant Supérieur du Soudan français à Ahmadou, Ségou, 9 Apr. 1890

writing to Ahmadu in this way, Archinard certainly hoped to shock him with the news of the loss of his capital. He also hoped to be able to determine his next line of action from the reaction of Ahmadu.

THE CONQUEST OF KAʿARTA, JUNE 1890–JANUARY 1891

Archinard spent the greater part of the month of May trying to divide, and thereby weaken, Tukulor leadership. At the same time he encouraged the non-Tukulor populations of Kaʿarta to declare themselves independent of Ahmadu and accept the French as their saviour from Tukulor tyranny. By this method he hoped to be able to conquer the Tukulor empire without much military involvement. Archinard understood how disunited the Tukulor ruling class was and tried to exploit the disunity to incapacitate Ahmadu. He realised, for example, that much as individual Tukulor chiefs would be ready to fight to preserve their positions, they would not necessarily stake their fortunes in order to defend Ahmadu. Several of the Tukulor leaders, in fact, found Ahmadu's claim to supremacy distasteful, and would really prefer to let him fall if only to give themselves more power and importance. The constant internal struggle for power within the Tukulor empire since 1864 was indeed due to this mentality on the part of the Tukulor ruling group.

Ahmadu eventually lost grip of the situation partly because he was not leading a united people. For his own part Archinard sought to make the Tukulor feel safe in their individual positions by emphasising that he was not against them, but against Ahmadu specifically. The French, he assured them, were eager to continue on friendly relations with them, even though they were determined to remove Ahmadu. This was in essence the message he addressed to Tukulor clan leaders who were with Ahmadu in Kaʿarta in May 1890. Among the people he addressed in their capacities as heads of the various Tukulor groups were Tierno Bokar (leader of the Bosséia group), Ciré Eliman (Toro), Tierno Ibrahim Sibé (Irlabé) and Abdoulaye Ali (Lao). Most of these people were military leaders, and by trying to win them to his side Archinard hoped to incapacitate Ahmadu militarily, and thereby facilitate his conquest. He failed, however, in this particular case; the leaders concerned decided to be loyal to Ahmadu.

This information is contained in the minutes written on the letter to the leaders.[1]

Before knowing the result of the attempt to detach from Ahmadu his military leaders, Archinard had entered into correspondence with Aguibu, the emir of Dinguiray who had once been suspected of ambition and disaffection against Ahmadu. Archinard told Aguibu that he captured Segu only because Ahmadu had become impossible to deal with. He assured Aguibu, however, of the French determination to continue to be friendly with him, and hoped that he would reciprocate in the same manner.[2] Aguibu's reply, assuring Archinard of his friendship, amounted to a capitulation to the French and a desertion of the general Tukulor cause.[3] He later proved a willing collaborator in Archinard's campaigns against Ahmadu and seems to have felt happy that he was riding to power in the Tukulor empire on the back of the French and as a result of the downfall of Ahmadu, who once accused him of plotting a *coup d'état* at Segu. But ambition apart, Aguibu may have succumbed to the French because he was in a difficult situation. His territory, Dinguiray, had been cut from all effective communications with the Tukulor empire and it was at this time encircled by the French. We shall be hearing more of him as an active collaborator with Archinard in the last phases of the conquest of the Tukulor empire.

Apparently to make the subject peoples revolt, Archinard proclaimed them independent of Ahmadu and declared them French-protected groups. He declared that such Ka'arta districts as were adjacent to the French posts on the Senegal, like Guidimaka, Diomboko, Tomora and Dialafara, were henceforth under the direct control of himself, but that they would be administered each according to its traditional system of government in the pre-Tukulor era. He announced the appointment of one Abdul Cadi from Segu as chief in charge of the Ka'arta district of Diafounou. He then addressed himself to Bambara groups in Kingui (Nioro district), Bakhounou and Ka'arta-Biné. He

1 ASAOF, 15G76/2(42), Le Lt-Col. Archinard . . . à Tierno Bokar etc., 10 May, 1890
2 ASAOF, 15G81/20, Correspondance avec Aguibou: Commandant Supérieur à Aguibou, Dinguiray, Kita, 13 May 1890; see also Saint-Martin, 'Un fils d'El Hadj Omar: Aguibou, roi du Dinguiray et du Macina (1843?–1907)', *CEA*, 29, viii, 1, 1968, pp.144–78
3 ASAOF, 15G81/21, Muhammad Aguibou à Archinard, marked 'Reçu le 16 mai 1890 à Goniokori'.

declared them also independent and invited them to nominate their own rulers, whom he would accept and protect after the people's delegates had met him. The proclamation containing all these points was printed and widely distributed in the French posts and in the areas concerned.[1]

Archinard's strategy is understandable. He was seeking to win to the French side the non-Tukulor groups by offering them their independence, the thing they had been fighting for in all their resistance wars against the Tukulor. If the people were approached in this way, he reckoned that Ahmadu would certainly not have their support for his war efforts against the French; they would rather seize the occasion to fight him. In this way, Archinard planned to use them to conquer the Tukulor. He appealed to the groups individually, but at the same time, in order to ensure that he would not fail with all, even if he found difficulties in persuading some.

Apart from the fact that the political disunity within the empire made him vulnerable to external attacks, Ahmadu found the situation difficult also for a number of other reasons. One of such reasons was that his allies were not as much help as he had expected. Archinard tried to weaken his strongest ally, Samori Ture, by going into alliance with, and giving military aid to, the latter's enemy, Tiéba the ruler of Kenedugu, adjacent to Samori's Wasulu empire. In May 1890, Archinard sent one of his officers, Captain Quiquandon, with a contingent to support Tiéba in his struggle against Samori.[2] Henceforth Tiéba became a factor in Archinard's plan to conquer the Tukulor empire.

It was after Archinard had embarked on the harnessing of the various forces described above that he sent to Ahmadu, asking him to surrender to the French. On condition that he surrendered, Ahmadu was promised his life and the allocation of a village in Dinguiray, to which he could retire with some members of his family who had been taken prisoner at Segu but who would now be released to him.[3] Archinard knew, of course, that Ahmadu would not surrender. His aim was obviously to provoke him to action. Ahmadu, however, gave no reply, and by the end

1 ASAOF, in 15G76/2, Circulaire no. 42d. Circulaire affiché à Kayes et à Médine, 11 May 1890
2 Archinard, *Rapport sur la Campagne 1890–1891*, p. 79
3 ASAOF, 15G76/2(43), Commandant Supérieur à Ahmadou, 15 May 1890

of May, Archinard sent him a message which was in effect an ultimatum to surrender or be ready for war.[1]

Ahmadu was in a weak position at this time and Archinard obviously realised this before giving his ultimatum. But in spite of odds, Ahmadu himself had not been taking chances in the face of the French threat. The alliance which he had formed was being mobilised for the defence of the empire. Ahmadu now had, in addition to the Tukulor regular army, forces from his allies in Futa Toro, Bondu and also the Jolof army of Ali Bouri. He also had with him in Ka'arta the remnants of his Segu army led by his chief *sofa*, Seikolo, and Tukulor *talibés* like Ciré Eliman and Abdoulaye Djelia.[2] With these forces he was taking measures to defend the empire against the French. Early in June 1890 he sent troops to Diala, from where the French at Kayes were to be attacked. On 6 June Tukulor forces unsuccessfully attempted to reach Archinard's men at Kayes. On that day they clashed with Archinard's men at the village of Bougoura, about three kilometres from Kayes, but they were defeated.[3] But although they were defeated in the Bougoura encounter Tukulor troops were sent to garrison various places in Ka'arta, especially in Koniakary and areas that were similarly close to the French.

ATTACK ON KONIAKARY AND CAMPAIGNS IN KA'ARTA

Archinard mobilised his forces against the Tukulor in Koniakary later in June. The Tukulor had a garrisoned fort in Koniakary which they used as a converging point for Tukulor reinforcements from Futa Toro and their forces in Ka'arta. Archinard decided to break Koniakary to be safe from Tukulor menace from that side, and also as a means of cutting communication between Futa Toro and the Tukulor in Ka'arta. The French expedition against Koniakary began on 12 June and lasted till the 15th when the fortress was broken.[4] Even after Koniakary had been occupied

1 ASAOF, in 15G76/2, Le Lt-Col. Archinard . . . à Ahmadou, Kayes, 30 May 1890
2 ASAOF, 1D119/3, *Journal Officiel de la République française*, No. 276, Dimanche 11 octobre 1891, p. 4886
3 ASAOF, in 1D105, Rapport Militaire, Campagne 1889–1890, Kayes, 12 July 1890, p. 121
4 ANSOM, in Sénégal, I, 80, Depêche Télégraphique: Gouverneur Sénégal à Colonies, Paris, Saint-Louis, 29 June 1890

Archinard still sent raiding expeditions into the neighbouring districts and battles were fought in areas around Médine like Fansané and Koliguémou. These operations lasted till early June 1890.[1] After Koniakary had been occupied Archinard put Sambala, the French ally in Khasso, in charge. Sambala with his forces then manned the fortress against the Tukulor.[2]

As with the other steps hitherto taken by him, Archinard's campaigns in Koniakary resulted from his own decision taken without prior consultation with his government. He had already occupied Koniakary before Paris heard about it, apparently through the commercial agents in Senegal who were opposed to war. It was in fact the ministry that asked for information on Archinard's activities in Koniakary[3] before he, through the governor of Senegal, informed them, confronting the government with a *fait accompli*.

The occupation of Koniakary was the beginning of a protracted Franco-Tukulor war in Ka'arta. The immediate target of Tukulor war efforts in the following few months was to dislodge the French and Sambala, their ally, from Koniakary. In spite of the rainy season that posed enormous difficulties to serious campaigning, fighting continued in Koniakary and several other neighbouring places until towards the end of September 1890. In these wars Jolof forces, commanded by the Buurba Jolof, Ali Bouri, played a very important part.[4] Tukulor troops from Futa Toro also came to aid Ahmadu against the French. One of the contingents from Futa Toro was led by an influential marabout, Tierno Abou Alpha, a relation of the district chief of Sero in Ka'arta. When he was caught by the French, he was shot so that others from Futa Toro would be scared away from giving military aid to Ahmadu against the French.[5] With encouragement from allies, and in spite of all odds, the war continued with varying fortunes for both the French and the Tukulor until 22 September

1 ASAOF, in 1D105, Rapport Militaire: Campagne 1889–1890, Kayes, 12 July 1890, pp. 130–64
2 ANSOM, in Sénégal I, 80, Depêche Télégraphique: Gouverneur à Sénégal à Colonies, Paris, Saint-Louis, 29 June 1890
3 ANSOM, in Senegal I, 80c, 'Sous-Secrétaire d'Etat des Colonies à Gouverneur, Saint-Louis', Paris, 20 June 1890
4 ASAOF, in 15G86/2, 'Situation Politique – Ka'arta', 5 Sept. 1890; also the political report of 19 Sept. 1890 in 15G86/2
5 ASAOF, in 15G86/2, Rapport sur l'éxecution du marabout Tierno Abou Alpha, fusillé à Medine, le 7 septembre 1890

1890 when the Tukulor were effectively defeated at Koniakary, and Ahmadu had to withdraw with his forces back to Nioro.[1]

Ahmadu lost the struggle for Koniakary partly because the campaigns were fought during the rainy season during which communication was often difficult. He encountered enormous difficulties resulting from the fact that there were many deserters among the non-Tukulor members of his army. Some who did not desert were not much use as they did not fight with determination.[2] One must also not forget the fact that the French fought with superior weapons, including cannon. In any pitched battle the Tukulor were likely to lose. For instance, in the battle which took place at Koniakary on 11 September 1890 the French used 82 cannon shot and 3,500 gun shot against the Tukulor.[3] This was exclusive of the weapons used by volunteer forces and the Khasso army led by Sambala.

The failure of the Tukulor in Koniakary had a number of disastrous consequences for them. First, Ahmadu had to withdraw his forces to Nioro. This gave the French the opportunity and encouragement to plan further attacks on other places in Ka'arta. The Tukulor army lost several of its leaders and a considerable number of war horses, which they did not find easy to replace. Thus their fighting power in subsequent battles was reduced. With the French success, many of the inhabitants of Koniakary and other districts felt exposed to danger from the French and therefore tried to protect themselves by offering to make their submissions to the French. Archinard realised that Ahmadu was in real difficulty after the Koniakary episode, and he therefore decided to attack him as quickly as possible before he had time to reorganise his forces at Nioro.[4]

The loss of Koniakary was fatal to the cause of the Tukulor and virtually decided the subsequent events in Ka'arta. Ahmadu did his best to reorganise his forces and was still able to fight battles against the French in Ka'arta for another four months. From September 1890 to January 1891, important pitched battles were

1 ASAOF, in 15G86/2, Situation au Soudan à la date du 19 septembre, 1890 – situation politique: Ka'arta; Importance de l'échec d'Ahmadou devant la place de Koniakary, 22 Sept. 1890
2 ASAOF, in 15G86/2, Situation Politique – Ka'arta, 5 Sept. 1890
3 ASAOF, in 15G86/2, Situation au Soudan à la date du 19 septembre 1890
4 ASAOF, in 15G86/2, Situation au Soudan à la date du 30 septembre 1890, Kayes, 30 Sept. 1890

fought at Niogoméra (23 December 1890); Korriga (30 December 1890); Gouri in Diafounou (3 January 1891); and Bandiougoula (11 January 1891). The Tukulor lost in most of these battles and Ahmadu, finding it impossible to continue the defence, abandoned Ka'arta to the French and escaped to Masina with such of his chiefs as were still loyal to him. This was in January 1891.[1]

AHMADU IN MASINA

Before this time Ahmadu Tijāni, who had headed Masina since 1864, had died. The new ruler of Masina was Muniru. Muniru, it may be recalled, had collaborated with Muhammad Muntaga in the latter's rebellion against Ahmadu in 1884–85. With the defeat of Muntaga he had escaped from an almost certain death in the hands of Ahmadu by seeking asylum in the French posts. He arrived in Masina in 1887, about the time when Tijani died. Thereafter Muniru successfully got himself elected as the ruler of Masina, a much stronger position than he had ever occupied before. In this position he continued his hostility to Ahmadu. At first, he was not going to let Ahmadu enter Masina and even after he had yielded to pressures from the *talibés* and Ahmadu came in, he wanted to keep him at a distance from Bandiagara, so that his own position might be safe. To Muniru and his supporters, the fall of Segu and Ka'arta represented Ahmadu's own personal misfortune which they had no obligation to repair.

However, Muniru, to maintain his authority, had made his alliances among the Tukulor and Habe aristocracy in a way that alienated some of the powerful groups. These groups saw the arrival of Ahmadu as an opportunity to wreak vengeance against Muniru. They therefore made sure that he abdicated in order that Ahmadu might head this last section of the Tukulor empire,[2] arguing that it was proper that the eldest son of 'Umar should be allowed to occupy the supreme position in the empire.

But to the men who brought down Muniru in favour of Ahmadu the attraction in the new situation was the opportunity they would

1 ASAOF, in 1D119/1, Le Commandant Supérieur du Soudan français à M. le Gouverneur du Sénégal, Nioro, 28 Jan. 1891; Archinard, *Rapport sur la campagne 1890–1891*, pp. 75–6

2 ASAOF, 1G158/1, Notice ethnographique et géographique sur le Macina, Bardot, Segou, Mar. 1892

have to strengthen their own positions. The new ruler was their own creation and since he was aware that other powerful interests led by Muniru were against him, he would, to preserve his position, always act in a way agreeable to them. To ensure this Ahmadu was not allowed to strengthen his own position by executing Muniru, as he wanted, for his role in the 1884–85 Muntaga rebellion.[1]

It was from this fettered position that Ahmadu was to continue the struggle against the French.

BAMBARA-TUKULOR COLLABORATION AND THE
REALIGNMENT OF FORCES, 1891–92

While Ahmadu was busy building up new forces with which to defend the empire against the French, Archinard was taking positive steps to put the conquered territories of Segu and Ka'arta under effective occupation. Direct French occupation was out of the question since Archinard did not possess the men and materials that would be involved. He therefore decided to continue to use the Bambara as instruments for attaining the desired goal. In contracting alliances with the various anti-Tukulor forces, he had assured them that the French had no territorial ambitions and had promised them, particularly the Segu Bambara, that he would restore them to their pre-Tukulor positions of authority and power as soon as the Tukulor regime was overthrown. His next strategy was to give the impression that this promise was being fulfilled at the same time as he kept for the French the fruits of the conquest. In doing this, he was eager that the administration evolved should be such as to make it easy for the French in the future to assume full control. This meant that the personnel of such an administration should not be in a position that would make it too strong to be effectively controlled. He said that he did not want to constitute 'de royaumes ou de puissances trop étendus ou trop considérables, de façon a éviter des difficultés pour l'avenir. . . .'[2]

A policy which aimed at creating a system that would guarantee

1 *Ibid.*, p. 406; 1G301/1, 'Sénégambie – Niger – Cercle de Bandiagara', Bandiagara, 15 Oct. 1903, p. 9
2 Jacques Meniaud, *Les Pionniers du Soudan* (1931), ii, p. 56

to the French authority and power over the newly conquered territories would certainly not meet the expectations of the Bambara, who had fought so long for their independence and who had been assured that alliance with the French would bring this to them. But Archinard went ahead to put his plan into effect. In Ka'arta he did not restore the Massassi Bambara to power in place of the Tukulor, on the ground that they too had been conquerors in the area, but neither did he give power to the Diawaras, in spite of the fact that they were the people who had been conquered by the Massassi Bambara. Archinard argued that both the Massassi and the Diawara had dispersed as a result of the Tukulor conquest and that those of them left in Ka'arta were not representative enough to justify a restoration of power to them. To restore them to power, he maintained, would be to encourage revolts among other ethnic groups. He then proposed to let each group return to its original home area and choose its own rulers there. For this purpose he reorganised Ka'arta, grouping it into three large administrative units based at Nioro, Bafoulabe and Kayes respectively. Each of these units comprised several districts – *cercles*.[1] Within each *cercle* each ethnic group was to have its own chief who would be responsible only to the French officer. Thus the administration of Ka'arta was based on the autonomy of the constituent ethnic groups.[2]

In Segu also, Archinard refused to give power to the Diara dynasty, generally accepted by the Bambara. He expressed the fear that if he gave them complete authority over Segu, they would use their position to victimise and penalise those of the Bambara, who for fear of being destroyed, had supported the Tukulor regime. He maintained that, having promised safety for all if they surrendered, it was his duty to protect them against would-be oppressors. Another reason why he would not give the Diara family power over the whole of Segu was that many Massassi Bambara had come to Segu during the jihād of 'Umar. The number of such Massassi Bambara, Archinard claimed, had increased through further immigration during the Tukulor regime. They now had Bodian as their chief and were certainly unwilling to be ruled by the Diara family, who had never governed them before. It was therefore only fair, he argued, to

1 *Ibid.*, pp. 58–60
2 *Ibid.*, pp. 61–7 for the structure of the administration which Archinard set up in Ka'arta.

allow them their freedom at Nango and the neighbouring villages which they occupied.[1]

Using this ingenious argument Archinard also organised Segu into three administrative units. He then appointed Mari Diara, head of the Diara family, in charge of the section with headquarters at Segu, gave Bodian control of the section controlled from Nango, and installed Mademba as *fama* of Sansanding. To supervise and control the activities of these men, he appointed a French resident to Segu.

In making this administrative arrangement, Archinard had been guided by a desire to create a situation in which the French would be masters even when campaigning against Masina to the east. In trying to achieve this he offended and disappointed the Segu Bambara, led by the Diara family. Ingenious as his argument for carving up Segu had been the Bambara found it dishonest. Worse still, the Segu Bambara did not feel safe in the little territory he had given them to govern because Archinard gave the impression that he had brought Bodian from Ka'arta to be used as a French agent to liquidate them. Bodian had not only been given a territory; he had been encouraged to group together all Segu Bambara who might prefer to be under him rather than Diara, and had been given a large quantity of arms and ammunition as well as horses captured from Segu.[2] In other words, Archinard not only encouraged subversion against the Diara, he also made sure that Bodian had the military means of carrying it out.

Archinard's cleverness notwithstanding, the Diara family were conscious of their right and were prepared to defend it. In fighting with the French against the Tukulor, they had made it clear that their aim was to recover the kingdom they had lost to the Tukulor. Archinard himself fully realised this, but he could not have helped the Bambara to realise their ambition because it was incompatible with his own, which was to conquer the Tukulor empire for the French.

The Segu Bambara showed their displeasure with what had been done, and were later accused of plotting to kill both Bodian and the French resident, Underberg, so that they could gain full control of Segu. Captain Underberg and Lieutenant Spitzer then

1 Archinard, *Rapport sur la campagne 1890–1891*, p. 77
2 *Ibid.*, pp. 77, 81

arrested Mari Diara and his councillors, under the pretext that they were foiling the alleged assassination plot. Mari Diara was subsequently removed from office and his territory given to Bodian to administer.[1]

Archinard probably had reasons to believe that Mari Diara and his advisers actually plotted to kill Bodian and the French resident. But it is equally probable that Mari Diara and his aides were accused of plotting mainly to find a pretext for removing them, since they were certainly not going to be willing tools of the French any longer. Whatever the case, the removal of Mari Diara provoked strong reactions from various parts of Segu and led to violent revolts aimed at dislodging the French and their instruments – Bodian and Mademba. The first of these revolts took place at Baninko in the eastern area of Segu, and it was organised by the Diara family and other Bambara leaders.[2] The uprisings later spread to several other parts of Segu and continued till 1892, before the French and their allies were able to bring the situation under control.

In the meantime the Tukulor continued their effort to oust the French from Segu and Ka'arta. For them the clash between the Bambara and the French created a new and favourable situation which should be exploited to make things impossible for the French. They, therefore, joined forces with the Bambara against the French.[3] More forcefully than ever before, the Bambara recognised that the French were as much enemies to the Tukulor as to themselves. They were therefore ready to collaborate with the Tukulor against the invaders.

At the same time Samori sent forces against Tiéba, chief of Kenedugu. As an ally or protégé of the French, Tiéba had been aided to carry on the war against Samori so that the latter had hitherto found it difficult to collaborate fully with Ahmadu. Samori's latest action, however, obliged the French to send forces to Kenedugu to fight in support of Tiéba. This was because if Samori defeated Tiéba the French in Segu would be open to direct attack from Samori and at the same time would have to confront the Bambara–Tukulor combine. Thus the uprising which started at Baninko as a Bambara affair now spread to various parts of Segu and Ka'arta, where the Tukulor and the

1 *Ibid.*, p. 78
2 *Ibid.*, pp. 78–92
3 *Ibid.*, pp. 92–3

Bambara were operating against the French and Kenedugu.[1] Consequently Ahmadu found himself in a stronger situation to fight for the survival of the Tukulor empire.

In spite of his improved position Ahmadu lost control of the situation in Segu mainly because the French had several other armies fighting on their side. These were the armies of people who saw their own interests closely tied to the preservation of the French presence in Segu. Among these were persons who had just been raised to new positions of power in Ka'arta and Segu, particularly men like Bodian and Mademba. There was also Tiéba who had been able to preserve his state against Samori so far mainly because of the military assistance which he had been receiving from the French.

Ahmadu, in spite of all odds, was relentless in his efforts to reconquer his empire. In this bid he employed both military and diplomatic means. As has been pointed out, he had succeeded in reconciling with the Bambara, if only temporarily, and in fighting a common war with them against the French. His alliance with the Bambara and Samori was not, however, as effective as it might have been because of the alliance of Tiéba with the French. Tiéba's state, Kenedugu, formed a barrier between Samori's Wasulu and Segu, and as long as the state of war between Samori and Tiéba lasted, the latter's alliance with the French would weaken the Tukulor position. Ahmadu therefore made moves to detach Tiéba from his French connection, with a view to making him at least neutral even if he would not join hands with the Tukulor.

In an attempt to settle the rift between Samori and Tiéba he sent envoys from Bandiagara to negotiate with both sides. In November 1891, for example, he sent al-ḥājj Ansoumoura Kouribari to negotiate with Tiéba in Sikasso, his headquarters. Ahmadu succeeded in reconciling Samori and Tiéba and in preventing the latter from further collaboration with the French. By the end of 1891, Tiéba had stopped fighting Samori. He refused, for example, to fight with the French against Samori in the campaigns of Nafana and Gankouna which took place on 20 November 1891,[2] and his son, N'Tou, did not join the French, as earlier agreed upon, in the expedition commanded by Lt

1 *Ibid.*, pp. 93–5
2 ASAOF, 1D120/3, 'Le Lieutenant résident du Kénédougou à M. le Colonel Commandant Supérieur – en Colonne, Koutiéni, 28 Feb. 1892

Marchand against Samori.[1] In 1892 Samori and Tiéba were reported to have exchanged gifts to mark the existence of friendly relations between them.[2]

Tiéba left the French alliance partly because the necessity for it had ceased to exist. He had joined forces with the French in order to protect his own state against Samori, who had attacked him in a bid to expand his Wasulu empire. With the settlement arranged by Ahmadu, Tiéba no longer had to fear Samori. Also, from the way that Archinard treated his Segu Bambara allies, Tiéba must have realised that the French only wanted to use him, like others, as instruments for fulfilling their colonising mission. He must have realised that in the existing situation, if he was not to be colonised, the wise policy to adopt was to ally with anti-French forces headed by the Tukulor.

The addition of Tiéba to the Tukulor coalition had several advantages. For once, Samori and Tiéba stopped dissipating their energy in fighting each other and henceforth, in alliance with the Tukulor, pursued the more noble role of fighting to preserve their independence against the French. In the fight against the French, Ahmadu had opened to him a new source of arms supply. Since he took refuge at Bandiagara (Masina), he had been finding it difficult to get arms and ammunition, since he could no longer get them from the French or the British agents. For some time, he had to content himself with getting his arms and ammunition through the Moors and the Arab traders of Timbuktu.[3] With the alliance, the barrier which Kenedugu had constituted was removed, and Samori's friendly relations with Futa Jallon and the British in Sierra Leone could be exploited to ensure constant supplies of arms to Ahmadu and his allies. The only hitch was that the French henceforth ceased their supplies of arms to Tiéba, for fear that he would use any weapons supplied to him against them.[4]

The Tukulor alliance pooled their resources to fight against

1 ASAOF, 1D128/10, Instructions pour le Résident de Ségou par le Commandant Supérieur, G. Humbert, Bissandougou, 27 Mar. 1892, pp. 55–6

2 ASAOF, 15G86/1, Remise de Service au Commandant Bourgey par le Lt-Col., Commandant Supérieur, G. Humbert, Kayes, 11 July 1892

3 ASAOF, 1D137, 2e Partie/I, Situation Politique et Militaire du Soudan français, 1893, p. 213

4 ASAOF, 1D128/10, Instructions pour le Résident de Ségou . . . G. Humbert, Bissandougou, 27 Mar. 1892

the French in Segu, Ka'arta, Kenedugu and Wasulu during most of 1892. Nevertheless they lost the battle for Segu, partly because the French intensified their campaigns against Samori so as to render him useless in the Tukulor war against them.[1] With their success in Segu, the French carried their campaigns against the Tukulor into Masina in 1893.

THE WAR IN MASINA AND THE END OF THE TUKULOR EMPIRE, 1893

In the war against Masina the French started from an advantageous position, encouraged as they were by their recent successes in Segu. The Tukulor, on the other hand, had invested most of their resources in the campaigns in Segu and Ka'arta, and their defeat in these places disorganised them and weakened their morale. An even worse affliction than the effect of defeat in Segu was the effect of the fact that they were, as before, still divided and their leaders at one another's throats in the competition for power. The French conquered Masina, not so much with military campaigns, but by carefully exploiting the unceasing rivalry among the Tukulor leaders. Some of the Tukulor readily allied with the French to ensure the defeat of Ahmadu in the hope that they would gain thereby.

The most glaring and perhaps the most devastating example of Tukulor cooperation with the French against the rest of the empire came from Aguibu, erstwhile emir of Dinguiray.[2] It may be recalled that Aguibu had capitulated to the French in 1890, when he was assured by Archinard that the French were not against the Tukulor in general, but against Ahmadu in particular. With the conquest of Ka'arta and the flight of Ahmadu to Masina, Aguibu came to put great hopes on his friendly relations with the French. On 20 May 1891 he went to Kita and made his submission to Archinard. He had come with all his sons, except the eldest who remained behind at Dinguiray to continue the administration of the emirate, accompanied by about three

1 ASAOF, 15G86/1, Remise de Service au Commandant Bourgey . . ., G. Humbert, Kayes, 11 July 1892; 1D122/244 (3e Partie), Rapport sur la mission à Ségou, mai–juillet 1892, G. Bonnier, A bord du Vaubau, 11 Sept. 1892
2 Saint-Martin, 'Un fils d'El Hadj Omar: Aguibou . . .'

hundred armed men.[1] In making his submission, Aguibu had
hoped that he would be allowed to replace Ahmadu at Nioro as
ruler of Ka'arta. In order to keep him loyal to the French,
Archinard assured him that this should be possible, but that
there was no need for hurry in sending him to Nioro. In the
meantime, Aguibu should prove his loyalty by policing the
activities of Samori, ally of Ahmadu. To make him useful in this
direction, Archinard sent Aguibu back to Dinguiray as chief.[2]

Seeing his position guaranteed in spite of the wars against the
Tukulor empire, Aguibu remained loyal to the French, in the
hope that after Ahmadu's defeat, he would succeed as the head of
the Tukulor empire: Ahmadu's fall would be his opportunity to
rise to power. The French recognised this ambition[3] and
continued to exploit it. Moreover there were also a number of
talibés who were either directly for Aguibu or had their own
reasons to want Ahmadu to fall. Through Aguibu, therefore, the
French could exploit a section of the Tukulor aristocracy. Given
this development Ahmadu was again on the defensive.

In the plan of war against Masina, the French tried to neutralise Samori and to use Aguibu to weaken the Tukulor forces.
Archinard sent Lt-Col. Combes against Samori, so that the latter
might be kept busy defending himself rather than come to the aid
of Ahmadu. This move was ruinous to Ahmadu's war plans. This
done, Archinard and his army, accompanied by Aguibu, left Segu
on 22 March 1893 for Masina, arriving at San on 7 April.[4]

From San he sent his secret agents to various parts of Masina to
report on the political situation. From their reports he knew that
the Tukulor ruling group at Bandiagara were divided on whether,
and how, to continue the war. Archinard therefore sent to various
parts of Masina messages designed to make the waverers among
the Tukulor refuse to fight. To all he gave the assurance that the
French wanted only commerce, and not Tukulor territory; it was
because Ahmadu had fought wars that made commerce impossible that the French had decided to fight against him. To Jenne,
a commercial centre, Archinard gave assurances that his desire

1 Archinard, *Rapport sur la Campagne: 1890–1891*, p. 172
2 *Ibid.*, pp. 174–5
3 ASAOF, 1G168/3, 'Rapport sur le Dinguiray – Notes sur Abuigou',
  Maritz, août, 1891
4 ASAOF, 1D137, 2e Partie/III(5) 'En route de Ségou à San, 1893, pp.
  319–52

was only to stop the raids going on, open up routes and make the Niger free and safe for commerce and navigation. When this had been done, he assured them, the French would withdraw and leave Aguibu, another of 'Umar's sons, in place of Ahmadu in Bandiagara.[1]

Although he still had to fight Ahmadu's forces at Jenne, Archinard's propaganda yielded dividends. Between San and Jenne several villages made their submission. For example, most villages in Pondori district, south of Jenne, and the villages of Koro, Dolola and Mantoura submitted to Archinard on 9 April 1893, deserting the army of Ahmadu, camped at Jenne. With so many desertions, it was not difficult for Archinard to defeat the rest of Ahmadu's forces at Jenne between 11 and 13 April.[2]

Jenne occupied a strategic position in the defences of Masina, and its conquest had always been crucial in any of the battles fought there since 1818.[3] Its fall to the French now virtually meant Ahmadu's fall. Its capture had a demoralising effect on many inhabitants of Masina, as could be seen in the way several villages submitted to Archinard as soon as he left Jenne, heading towards Mopti. For example, on 16 April Fulani chiefs from Gombo district came offering their submission to Aguibu as the new head of the empire. The head chief was given money and gold, and told to use it for winning over more people from the Tukulor side.[4] Archinard and Aguibu reached Mopti on 17 April to find that Ahmadu's garrison in the town had deserted. Aguibu was presented as the new head of the empire and the people submitted to him.[5] The story was the same for many of the places which Archinard and Aguibu reached before their arrival at Bandiagara.[6]

While Archinard and Aguibu were still heading for Bandiagara, the worst started happening to Ahmadu. His army was disintegrating with many of the *sofa* leaders deserting. Notable among the important deserters were Mahmoud, Bafi, Siba, Dondi, Niogomera, Moussa and Makoni, all described as 'chefs sofas déjà

1 *Ibid.*, pp. 352–4
2 ASAOF, 1D137, 2e Partie/III(6), Prise de Djenné, pp. 356–92
3 A. Hampate Ba, 'Archives Africaines: le dernier carré Toucouleur – récit historique', *Afrique en Marche*, no. 3, Dakar, avril–mai, 1957, p. 13
4 ASAOF, 1D137, 2e Partie/III(6), Prise de Djenné, p. 392
5 ASAOF, 1D137, 2e Partie/III(7), Séjour à Mopti, pp. 395–6
6 *Ibid.*, pp. 406–12

313

connus de nous pour leur importance et leur rôle dans le Ségou ou le Kaarta'. Several Tukulor *talibés* at Bandiagara had also sent messages welcoming Aguibu as their new ruler.[1]

It was in this situation that Archinard and Aguibu arrived at Bandiagara on 29 April 1893. The forces that confronted them – about 1,500 in all – were easily routed because most of them fought only half-heartedly.[2] Ahmadu fled and thereafter the people made their submission. On 3 May 1893 Archinard, with Aguibu, held a formal meeting with Tukulor, Habe, and Fulani chiefs. These pledged their loyalty and submission to the French and Aguibu. On 4 May 1893 Archinard installed Aguibu as the new ruler of Masina. He left Bandiagara on 5 May, with the people convinced that the only change had been the installation of one son of 'Umar in place of another.[3] But as they were to realise later, the Tukulor empire had in fact fallen. Aguibu was not as they thought, a Tukulor ruler, but a French agent.

It is evident that Archinard conquered more by diplomacy than by force of arms. In the varied manoeuvres, Aguibu had been a useful instrument. Having suffered from defeat and many desertions, Tukulor forces were already weak before Archinard and Aguibu arrived at Bandiagara. Politically, Bandiagara was already split into three groups. There was the faction headed by Muniru who remained unreconciled to Ahmadu, there were Ahmadu's own supporters, and there were the people who could be described as opportunists who would at any moment embrace the stronger party.[4] Already divided as they were, Aguibu's presence on the French side greatly weakened the resistance forces. The presence of a son of 'Umar with the French had a demoralising effect upon the Tukulor who were with Ahmadu. On those who were already tired of war, it had a reassuring and consoling effect. For them it was a question of another son of 'Umar, and therefore they saw nothing wrong in abandoning Ahmadu and rallying round Aguibu, thus unknowingly supporting the French cause which he represented. Thus Archinard, with great diplomatic skill, brought about the fall of the Tukulor empire by exploiting the unrecon-

1 *Ibid.*, pp. 411–16
2 ASAOF, 1D137, 2e Partie/III(9) Séjour à Bandiagara, p. 438
3 *Ibid.*, pp. 443–85
4 A Hampate Ba, 'Archives Africaines: le dernier carré Toucouleur ...', p. 13

ciled forces in its political system. He had started by using the resistance groups as instruments to conquer the Tukulor in Segu and Ka'arta and had completed the conquest through a careful exploitation of the internal Tukulor struggle for power.

But when so much has been said for Archinard's diplomacy, it is important to acknowledge the superior power of his army. This rested mainly on the possession and use of superior weapons. The French had all along controlled the arms trade to suit their purpose of equipping the Tukulor rulers for their internal wars and keeping the empire divided and consequently impotent against external aggression. When it came to a final confrontation the French harnessed all the anti-Tukulor forces in a massive operation. Too late, the anti-Tukulor groups, especially the Bambara, realised that the struggle against the Tukulor was as destructive to themselves as it was to their opponents and could only lead to their common subjugation to the French. They subsequently joined forces to repulse the French. In the battles that followed, the advantages which the French had as the controllers of the arms trade came into play. The Tukulor–Bambara coalition lost to the French because their long struggle against each other had proved mutually disastrous and because the French and their allies used superior weapons to advantage. Thus its ruinous internal conflicts and the superior weapons of its enemies brought about the fall of the Tukulor empire.

10 The Tukulor Experiment

The occupation of Bandiagara in 1893 marked the final collapse of the Tukulor empire. Timbuktu, particularly its Kounta Arab and Tuareg population, gallantly continued resistance to the French until January 1894. But from the point of view of the Tukulor this was no more than an action on the outskirts of their empire. Timbuktu was never totally integrated into the Tukulor system; the Kounta Arabs and Tuaregs enjoyed a great deal of autonomy and freedom and their main interests had always been to guarantee the independence of the city – other areas were significant only from the point of view of their relevance to trade for which the city was a major entrepôt. They had neither the interest nor the means to embark on a recapture and reconstitution of the Tukulor empire. Indeed, their heroic defence of Timbuktu ended in January 1894 when, in spite of the fact that in one of the encounters they killed Lt-Col. Bonnier, Commander of the French operations, ten of his officers, one native interpreter, two French N.C.O.s and sixty-eight troops,[1] they still lost the city to invading French forces.

At this stage it is legitimate to attempt an assessment of the meaning of all these events in terms of the Tukulor experiment. The Tukulor revolution which al-hajj 'Umar led had the purpose of spreading Islam of the Tijaniyya *tariqa*. It sought to institutionalise the ideals of revolution by creating a state based on the archetype of Islamic society and government. It would be utopian to imagine that this purpose could have been achieved within a decade or indeed within a generation. Turning people into good Muslims from their various primordial religions and cultures has never been achieved by the sword: it requires a long period of

1 Kanya-Forstner, *The Conquest of the Western Sudan* (1969), p. 221; an account of the invasion of Timbuktu and the reaction of the French public is given on pp. 217–23

proselytising and educating in order to tune the minds of those concerned in the right direction. For all this, the sword could create the opportunity by giving the revolutionaries power to control and direct society.

The earlier Tukulor experiment in spreading religion as an instrument for changing society and government in Futa Toro is a good illustration of this point. From the time of the overthrow of the non-Muslim Denyanke rule in the second half of the eighteenth century they acquired the power to control and direct society, and from then on the task of making good Muslims out of the population proved difficult and protracted. Even then, about a century later the result was still not satisfactory. This point is reflected in the attitude of a purist and scholar like 'Umar, who judged both the ruling elite and the population at large as falling short of the ideals of Islam. It was to raise the practice of Islam to the level of the ideal according to the tenets of the Tijāniyya, and to Islamise the non-Muslim areas of the Western Sudan, that 'Umar launched his revolution. In a sense he was carrying further the tradition of the Tukulor, especially the *toroBé* elements, in serving as the agent of the spread of the religion following in the footsteps of earlier jihādists in Futa Toro, Sokoto[1] and Masina. Between 1852 and 1864 he conquered the mid-nineteenth-century Western Sudanic states, creating a large empire that stretched over an enormous territory incorporating many political systems and groups. By 1864 he had succeeded in setting the framework of the institution within which the programme of Islamisation could be launched. He needed time to build and consolidate the emergent state and organise his men in pursuit of the ultimate goal. But he was not to have the time as he died in 1864, a victim of the violence which his revolution had engendered.

By the time 'Umar died he had only created a framework within which the objective of his revolution – which still remained a set of aspirations – could be realised. The task of doing this fell on his eldest son, Ahmadu, who had to build a nation-state, within an Islamic setting, out of the recently conquered and incoherently organised empire. Born around 1833, Ahmadu was only about thirty-one when he assumed leadership of the Tukulor empire in

---

1 The leaders of the Sokoto jihād, 'Uthman b. Fodiye and his men were mainly *Toronkawa* (people from Futa Toro), see Last, *The Sokoto Caliphate* (1967), p. lxxii fn

1864. As leader he consistently displayed considerable courage, energy and military as well as diplomatic resourcefulness in tackling what eventually proved intractable internal social and political problems which were complicated by the ever-threatening presence of French imperialism.

The revolution which gave birth to the Tukulor empire had a divisive impact on the Muslim community in general and, in particular, the Tukulor community which in consequence was split into warring Tijānīyya–Qadīriyya ideological camps. The first violent manifestation of the split within the Tukulor religious leadership took place between 1854 and 1860 when the defensive Qadīri ruling elites desperately went into alliance with the French against 'Umar's Tijāni revolution in the Senegambia. The split in the broader Western Sudan Islamic community was evident in the confrontation with Qadīri Moors, Masina and the Bakkā'iya group in Timbuktu. On a wider level, 'Umar's revolution rent the various Sudanic societies into discordant groups. Part of the explanation for 'Umar's success in conquering such a large area and so many states was that his revolution assumed different complexions and dimensions in the different areas. By being grafted to several primordial conflicts and schisms in the societies concerned, the revolution not only gained supporters who aided its spread, but also acquired enemies who proved irreconcilable and were to plague the empire with resistance wars that provided a crippling problem which contributed to the eventual collapse of the empire. On top of all, 'Umar's death deprived the ruling elites in the emergent empire of his charismatic leadership which was widely respected and alone had prevented the explosion of the ideological conflicts incorporated in the revolution. The latent conflicts of ideology, coupled with a struggle for power and position, came into the open in the succession problem which, in spite of the internal wars that it brought about, proved insoluble.

The convergence of the debilitating centrifugal forces within the empire and the expanding French imperialism finally overwhelmed Ahmadu and consequently he lost the state which his father had founded and which he had spent his own manhood defending.

The physical collapse of the state meant the frustration of the Tukulor experiment in empire-building. The unity of the *jamā'a* and coherence of organisation which, among other things, contributed to the success of the Toronkawa elements in controlling

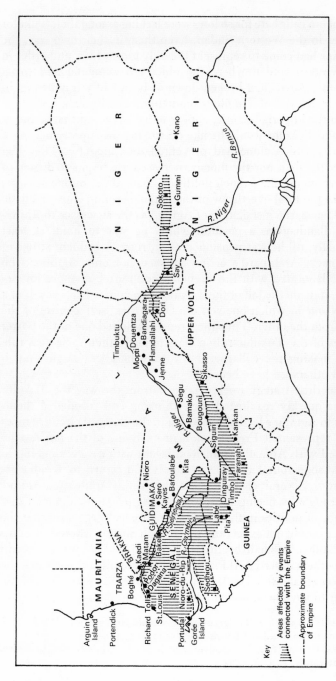

Contemporary states in the area of the former Tukulor Empire

the Sokoto caliphate for so long were lacking among their Tukulor
cousins in the Western Sudan. Even then, in their own way, the
Tukulor had come to represent the only force of law and order in
the Western Sudan where the older governmental and social
regulatory forces had broken down or been badly fragmented in
the four decades of Tukulor domination. The French, as successors to the imperial mantle, appear to have realised that to throw
away the Tukulor would be like destroying the superstructure of
authority which alone had prevented total anarchy. They had
neither the men nor the money, nor even the requisite degree of
support among the French political class and the public at large,
to make the total overthrow of the Tukulor ruling elite a realistic
idea. Hence, the installation of Aguibu as the successor to Ahmadu at Bandiagara, a position which he was to hold, at least
nominally, till he was pensioned off in 1907. A brilliant stroke of
diplomacy, Archinard's action satisfied not only Aguibu, who
had collaborated with the French since 1891 but, more impor-
tantly, it made the fall of the Tukulor rule appear like a result of a
coup d'état in which one son of 'Umar took over control of the
state from the other. Thus the French exploited one of the power
cliques of the Tukulor ruling class to strengthen their own rule
while making the collapse of the state look less tragic than it
would otherwise have been.

That this strategy worked is clear from the way the Tukulor
leaders quickly readjusted their thinking and reconciled themselves to Aguibu's leadership which in the changed circumstances
really represented French colonialism. Some of the *talibés* who
had fled with Ahmadu from Bandiagara with a view to going to
Sokoto soon found reasons to desert and return to Bandiagara
to settle. Several of them thought it was futile to continue
the struggle by fleeing to Sokoto. These people maintained that
the tone of politics in the Tukulor empire had been such that the
refugees could not expect any welcome in Sokoto, where Ahmadu's
liquidation of his half-brothers Abibu and Moktar, was resented.[1]
Some others deserted Ahmadu in the face of difficulties which the
refugees encountered on the way, particularly at Say.[2] Others still
appear to have been forced back by French diplomatic offensive.

1 ASAOF, 15G76/3 Télégramme: Commandant Région Nord-Est à
Gouverneur Soudan français, Kayes, 30 Aug. 1894
2 ASAOF, 15G76/3, Le Gouverneur à M. le Ministre des Colonies,
Saint-Louis, 10 Oct. 1894

For example one of Ahmadu's sons, Ahmadu Maki, who with fifteen *talibés* had been charged with protecting the route against any French offensive as the fleeing party continued its journey, found that they could not go on performing their functions and consequently they returned to Bandiagara to make their submission. The reason adduced was that the chiefs and traders in the area from Dori to Say were hostile to the Tukulor refugees and would not cooperate with them, claiming that they had concluded a treaty of friendship with the French[1] and could therefore not deal with Tukulor emissaries.[2] The most striking of those who abandoned Ahmadu was Ifra Almamy who had been a prominent figure in Tukulor politics for thirty-two years, during which period he was said to have been 'l'ami et le principal auxiliaire de l'Hadj Omar [et] de Tidiani'. There could be no doubt that Ifra Almamy was an important person in Tukulor politics; when he disagreed with Ahmadu and was returning to Bandiagara he was accompanied by twelve former chiefs and sixty *talibés*, all of whom asked to be allowed to settle with their families at Bandiagara and other parts of the state.[3] All these developments were stimulated by the feeling on the part of those involved that there was nothing terrible in Aguibu, who was as good a son of 'Umar as any other, taking over the leadership of the Tukulor. It was true he owed his position to the French, but for people who knew that the French had been part of the Senegambian society and had been involved in Tukulor politics right from the beginnings of the empire, Aguibu's association with them was not as reprehensible as it would have been in other circumstances.

However, to Ahmadu and the hard core of men who remained with him the collapse of the Tukulor empire was seen mainly as a temporary victory for the unbelievers and enemies of the faith. The flight from Bandiagara to Sokoto was therefore interpreted as a *hijra* which, following the example of the Prophet, they had to perform as a duty to protect the religion against the threat by infidels.

After experiencing some vicissitudes of fortune on their

---

1 Probably with the mission of Monteil, 1891
2 ASAOF, 15G76/3, Télégramme: Commandant Région Nord-Est à Gouverneur, Kayes, 4 Sept. 1894
3 ASAOF, 15G76/3, Télégramme: Ct. Région Nord-Est à Gouverneur Soudan français, Kayes – Urgent, 19 Nov. 1894

journey, Ahmadu and his *jamā'a* arrived in the Sokoto caliphate after about three years and were settled at Maykouki around 1896. Here efforts were made to continue to uphold and propagate the ideals of the Tijāniyya. The memories of the Tukulor empire normally lingered on. Ahmadu continued as the *amīr al-mūminīn* of his Tijānī Tukulor community until he died in 1898. In spite of his death, however, his followers were not despondent. There was the hope that all the crises that struck the Muslim peoples, and themselves in particular, were only a prelude to the arrival of the expected Mahdi who would set things right in the Western Sudan.[1]

Ahmadu's brother and former emir of Diomboko in the Ka'arta section of the Tukulor empire, Bassiru, was elected *amīr al-mūminīn* in succession to Ahmadu by the community. The Sokoto caliph was duly informed of the event and he offered the Tukulor Tijānī refugees another village to settle in. The community named the new place symbolically *Dār al-Islam*. While moving to the new settlement the remains of Ahmadu were exhumed and taken along for reburial. The Tukulor refugees shared the optimism of their hosts, believing in the imminent emergence of the Mahdi who would lead the forces of the faith to triumph over the unbelief institutionalised in the general European, especially French, conquest of the Western Sudan. Indeed, Bassiru and his *jamā'a* were so eagerly attached to the idea of the millennium that would come with Madhism that they apparently wanted to hasten the process by emigrating from the Sokoto caliphate and heading for the Sudan and eventually Mecca where they could meet the Mahdi.

It was in the course of their emigration that they arrived at the emirate of Missau and there the emir, Ahmadu, persuaded them to stay, offering them another town to settle in. It was to this emirate, especially the Mahdist town of Burmi, that the Sokoto caliph, Attahiru, fled. He was later joined there by a section of the Tukulor Tijānī under Bassiru. The Tukulor joined their besieged Sokoto hosts in fighting the invading British forces

---

1 For a discussion of the relevance of the theme of Mahdism in contemporary Sokoto, see Last, *The Sokoto Caliphate*, p. 10; R. A. Adeleye, 'The Dilemma of the Wazir: The Place of the *Risalat al-Wazir 'ila ahl al-'ilm wa'l – tadabbur* in the history of the Sokoto Caliphate', *JHSN*, iv, 2, 1968, pp. 285–311

under Sword in 1903.[1] In the encounter, Bassiru and some of his men were captured. The British conquest led to the dispersal of the surviving Tukulor refugees into various parts of the overrun Sokoto caliphate. The British Resident of Bauchi, C. L. Temple, compensated the section of the Tukulor who had not taken part in the war against the British by appointing their leader, Ahmadu Madani b. Ahmadu as the new *amir al-mūminīn* of the Tukulor Tijānī. Madani and some three hundred families were settled in Hadejia emirate at Yan Leman.[2]

With the conquest of Sokoto a fatal blow was dealt to the Tukulor expectation that they might still recover their lost empire. Some of them reconciled themselves to the new British rule, as indeed some of their hosts did;[3] but a fanatical core among those who survived the trauma that accompanied the British conquest escaped, and by 1906 were known to be fleeing to Arabia across Bornu, Wadai and Darfur. Traditions claim that this group finally settled in the Hidjaz under their leader Alfa Hashim, a nephew of the founder of the Tukulor empire. Like 'Umar, Hashim was said to have established his claim as the Khālifa of the Tijāniyya in West Africa,[4] thereby carrying on the traditions of the former.

The acceptance of the British rule by some of the group that had performed the *hijra* to Sokoto and the emigration to the Middle East by a few others, coincided with the removal of the last vestige of Tukulor prestige in what was their former empire. Hashim led his men out of Sokoto in 1906 and in 1907 Aguibu was removed and pensioned off from his position by the French who had installed him in 1893. Between the latter date and 1907 the French had had time to reorganise the empire they conquered from the Tukulor, and having created their own superstructure of control, the retention of Aguibu as a symbol of order became an unnecessary anachronism. His pension was obviously seen as a reward for services rendered towards spreading French imperialism.

All considered, it is clear that the events of the period 1893 to

1 Paden, 'The Influence of Religious Elites' (unpublished 1968), p. 190; Last, *The Sokoto Caliphate*, pp. 176–7n
2 Paden, 'The Influence of Religious Elites', pp. 236–8. Paden has earlier referred to the settlement as Dakkayawa.
3 Adeḷẹyẹ, 'The dilemma of the Wazir . . .'.
4 Paden, 'The Influence of Religious Elites', pp. 244–5.

1907 confirmed the destruction of the Tukulor experiment at empire-building as an inseparable part of the struggle to spread the Tijānī ideology of Islam. It also ended the dream of a possible recovery of the state from the French conquerors. The Tukulor case appears to demonstrate the falsity of the assumed oneness of religion and state in Islam. It is clear from the futility of the tortured effort of the Tukulor to transpose this idea into reality that in the Western Sudan, though the various societies might not resent proselytisation, especially through peaceful evangelisation, the attempt to merge the idea of religion with the state automatically represented a violent confrontation with the primordial cultures, as well as the political and social systems of the defending peoples; thus, in the circumstance, conflict was a necessity. In the Western Sudan the Tukulor experiment added another stage to the tradition of resolving such conflict by military violence. But when confronted with determined peoples, such as those the Tukulor encountered, violence could be protracted and crippling and did lead to the negation of the objectives of the movements. This can be illustrated by the damage inflicted by resistance movements.

The politicisation of the movement, which the idea of creating a state as a framework for the spread of Islam involved, not only engendered violence in non-Muslim areas, but also had the effect of fracturing the Muslim community itself and undermined the idea of the *'Umma* which emphasised the essential oneness of Islam. In the Tukulor venture the latter situation is illustrated by the antagonisms and wars between Muslims of different brotherhoods in the Western Sudan. Even internally within the Tijāniyya, 'Umar's total programme created rifts among adherents, as Tijānī men who were incumbent rulers rejected his leadership partly as a means of keeping their positions as political and social leaders of their states. For such groups the removal of the threat of political domination tended to make collaboration with 'Umar's successors possible.[1] The feeling of fellowship which later found expression in the collaboration of independent Tijānī rulers like Ali Bouri of Jolof, Abdul Bubakar of Futa Toro and Bubakar Sa'ada of Bondu on the one hand, with Ahmadu and his Tukulor rulers on the other, was made possible by the removal

---

1 I have discussed this idea in the introduction to a paper, see Qlqruntimęhin, 'Anti-French Coalition of States and Groups...'

of the threat to the independent, sovereign status of those concerned. In other words, cooperation was possible when relations of these leaders with the Tukulor no longer imposed a dependent, or subordinate status on the former.

For the non-Muslim a deterrent to conversion to Tijāniyya was that the Tukulor programme involved an overthrow of the existing political and social systems, a change that was bound to reduce the status of the elite groups in the prevailing systems. In such circumstances, it is understandable that the political aspect of the programme was an obstacle to conversion. The situation could be illustrated by the irony that it was mainly after the Tukulor had been divested of their political power that they achieved remarkable success in their other role of spreading Islam, and the Tijāniyya in particular. Under the French colonial rule, the Tukulor, especially *toroBé* elements, carried on their traditional function of spreading Islam by peaceful, personal contact with the would-be converts. They also built schools for the education and initiation of the youth and for the improvement of the practice of Islam among the adults who also increased their knowledge of the religion through instruction from, and the example of, their Shaikhs.

But even in the realm of missionary enterprise the story of Tukulor success has its limitations. The schism within the Tijāniyya which the 'Umarian Tukulor revolution had stimulated, and that between the Tijāniyya and the other brotherhoods which was an aspect of the revolution, have survived into the present time. Thus although 'Umar's successors have acquired a new significance as leaders of the Tijāniyya, they have done so in the face of stiff, though peaceful, competition with branches of the brotherhood led by others of Tukulor or Wolof origins. In the face of such competition 'Umar's successors have, on occasions, been able to keep their eminent position only because of the patronage and protection of the French colonial administration. This was the case for example in the rivalry between them and the more militant Hamallist branch under Shaikh Hamallah. Shaikh Hamallah and his men preached a more austere, radical adherence to Tijānī ideas and denounced the laxity of the 'Umarian and other branches of the Tijāniyya. To defeat his movement, Hamallah's rivals had to persuade the French authorities that he was anti-French and, consequently, the colonial authorities exiled him thrice between 1925 and 1942 when he died a prisoner in

France.[1] It is an irony that demonstrates the adaptation of the movement to changing circumstances when one realises that the movement which invoked French colonial power against its rivals in order to survive was the main obstacle to French imperialism in the nineteenth century. The changing role of the movement will not be too surprising, however, if one bears in mind that Islamic laws on the relations between Muslims and other elements in society are sensible rules of survival. Actions are legitimate once they can be explained as necessitated by a desire to protect Islam and the Muslims.

But whereas the Hamalliyya as a radical movement could be identified with subversion and its leaders persecuted, it was not so easy to deal with rivals who were subtle in their tactics. Such rivals of the 'Umarian Tijānīs demonstrated their acceptance of French rule and therefore enjoyed the protection and patronage of the French rulers. For all loyal Muslim groups, the French established *medresas* or Franco-Muslim schools, built mosques, sent their leaders on pilgrimage and decorated them with French honours.[2] In essence, French policy was to encourage the competition within the Islamic community and to regard the division and rivalry between Muslim groups as healthy in so far as they were a guarantee against concerted action which could undermine French rule.[3]

In the circumstances competing Tijānī groups spread, and so also the Qadīriyya, especially the Mouridiyya which is influential among the Wolof of Senegal.[4] In the latter country, the Tijāniyya is easily the most important brotherhood with over a million adherents, followed by the Mouridiyya branch of Qadīriyya with about half a million. Internally, the nineteenth-century division between the followers of 'Umar and others has persisted among the Tijānī. The brotherhood is divided into 'Umarians under 'Umar's grandson Sayyid Nuru Tall at Dakar, followers of Malik Sy based at Tivauane and the branch led by Ibrahim Niass whose headquarters are at Kaolack.[5] In terms of the

1 Gouilly, *L'Islam*, pp. 134ff
2 Crowder, *West Africa Under Colonial Rule* (1968), p. 361
3 In contrast to this attitude that treats Islam as a stabilising factor, there was an earlier one that regarded Islam as an obstacle to be broken. See Donald Cruise O'Brien, 'Towards an Islamic Policy in French West Africa, 1854–1914', *JAH*, vii, 2, 1967
4 See Monteil, *L'Islam noir* (1964), for a discussion of the Mouridiyya.
5 Paden, 'The Influence of Religious Elites', p. 223

nineteenth-century antecedents, Sayyid Nuru Tall is obviously
a successor to his grandfather's mission, while Malik Sy, a
Tukulor, could be seen as representing the tradition of the
Tijānī elements in Futa Toro and Bondu who did not accept
'Umar's leadership in spite of their ethnic affinity. In the
nineteenth century these Tukulor Tijānī were led by Abdul
Bubakar and Bubakar Sa'ada, and although they joined 'Umar's
son and successor in a coalition to fight French imperialism, their
example of not accepting 'Umar's religious leadership seems to
have been transmitted as a tradition to their successors. The
Wolof, Ibrahim Niass, could be compared to the *Buurba Jolof*,
Ali Bouri, who though he was a Tijānī and later joined forces with
others in resisting French imperialism, maintained the separate
identity and integrity of the Wolof against 'Umar's more per-
vasive, stronger movement.

Elsewhere in the Western Sudan, Tijāniyya has spread and has
been organised in competing groups as in Senegal. In Northern
Nigeria for example, the 'Umarian branch – started since
'Umar's visit and sojourn in Sokoto in the nineteenth century and
reinforced later by the Tukulor refugees under his son, Ahmadu –
has competitors in other Tijānī groups led by Shaikh Ibrahim
Niass and others who claim Maghribian connections. At the head
of the Reformed Tijāniyya, Ibrahim Niass leads the strongest
Tijānī group, accounting for about sixty per cent of the Tijānī
elements in Nigeria, a large proportion of those in Senegal and
Gambia and in other parts of West Africa like Chad, Ghana and
equatorial Africa.[1] The 'Umarian branch of the Tijāniyya and
others exist also in all these places. But Ibrahim Niass appears to
tower above all other Tijānī leaders and he enjoys an international
prestige and status derived from his leadership of an influential
modern movement.

Since Tijāniyya spread against the opposition of the older
Qadīriyya, it has largely been an opposition movement. This
strategy dates back to the time of 'Umar when the movement
started in Masina and the Senegambian states partly as a forum
for those who had grievances against the Qadīrī ruling elite. In
this century, it has spread to Nigeria and other parts of West
Africa by the strategy of 'oppositional politics'.[2] Since this is the

1 *Ibid.*, pp. 219–23
2 Brown, 'Towards a chronology for the Caliphate of Hamdullahi
  (Masina)', pp. 430–1; Paden, 'The Influence of Religious Elites', p. 219

case, as in the Tukulor empire, the spread of Tijāniyya tends to generate conflict and violence. This tendency can be illustrated with the northern Nigerian example, where conflict between the Sokoto ruling Qadīri, represented since the 1950s by the power of the northern Nigerian government under the Sardauna of Sokoto, a descendant of 'Uthmān b. Fodiye, and the ruling elite in Kano and leaders of Tijāniyya in Nigeria, has resulted in political violence. According to Paden, the deposition and banishment of the Emir of Kano, Muhammad Sanusi, the spiritual leader of the Reformed Tijāniyya in Nigeria, in 1963 resulted from Tijāniyya confrontation with Sokoto Qadīri religious authority, championed and protected by the premier of the region, the late Sardauna of Sokoto, Ahmadu Bello. The evangelical activities of the latter thereafter, coupled with the application of political pressure on some areas of the region, is also explained as an attempt to reunify northern Nigerian Islam in the name of Shaikh 'Uthmān b. Fodiye.[1]

It is obvious from this study of the Tukulor empire and its aftermath that religion, like any other ideology, if backed by sufficient force could be, and has been, a valuable instrument for bringing about large-scale political unification. When so used in such political, religious and social situations as those of nineteenth century Western Sudan it tends to generate conflict and violence which in turn lead to instability of regimes. This explains the endemic nature of wars in the Tukulor empire whose rulers, unlike their luckier Sokoto predecessors, were not sheltered from other problems like European imperialism and succession difficulties at the early stages of the processes of state formation. Given their own circumstances it is not surprising that unlike the Sokoto group, who also fought a series of wars, the Tukulor achievement did not last long. The Tukulor experiment demonstrates that the idea of the oneness of state and religion in Islam is largely an illusion. Whenever an attempt has been made to translate it into concrete social and political reality frustration has come either through opposition from competing Islamic ideologies or from non-Islamic resistance movements. Although Islam can be a uniting force like any of the other religions and high cultures, it also has potentialities which can be tapped to bring about disintegration. Perhaps Islam can spread best if it does not also mean a political programme. The spread of Tijāniyya and

1 Paden, pp. 219–20

328

other brotherhoods under French rule illustrates this point. During that period the conflict that plagued the Muslim groups in the nineteenth century was removed. The tension and political violence which resulted from the recent attempt to merge religion and state in northern Nigeria also confirms the point.

Although the fall of the Tukulor empire meant loss of power to the Tukulor, they have since gained in status and their reputation as leaders of Islam in the Western Sudan has been rehabilitated. Tijāniyya of the 'Umarian branch has spread even among Bambara elements, and Segu, capital of old Bambara and Tukulor empires, is still the base in the Western Sudan of 'Umar's successors. Moreover 'Umar's achievement in the missionary field is preserved and his memory is venerated, as is evident in the pilgrimages which Tijānī devotees still pay to Degembere at Bandiagara in Masina where he was known to have died fighting against resistance movements opposing the revolution through which the Tukulor empire was created.

Appendix

	Sons		*Daughters*
1	Ahmadu	1	Madina
2	Maki	2	Mariama
3	Habidou	3	Fadima
4	Hadi	4	Kadidiatou
5	Saydou	5	Djéinaba
6	Aguibu	6	Oumou
7	Moktar	7	Roukiatou
8	Bassiru	8	Hafsatou
9	Muntaga	9	Dioda
10	Hamidou	10	Saoudatou
11	Hassirou	11	Diouvéiratou
12	Sahidou	12	Aminata
13	Ahidou	13	Hindou
14	Lamine	14	Sana
15	Muniru	15	Lamiratou Yébé (Baba)
16	Daha	16	Safiatou-Bâ
17	Daye	17	Safiatou N'Din
18	Ouahidou	18	Assiatou
19	Siradiou	19	Sanou
20	Mamoudou	20	Oumakala
21	Ahidou	21	Diamilatou
22	Hassimi	22	Reihanatou
23	Nourou (father of Saydou Nourou of Dakar)	23	Bobo
		24	Safoura
24	Moubassirou	25	Bassekou
25	Nazirou		

Source: Ibrahima-Mamadou Ouane, *Pérégrinations Soudanaises*, Lyon, n.d., p. 180.

Bibliography

A. CONTEMPORARY SOURCES

1. Archives

The documentary material for this study was collected mainly from archives in Senegal and France. In Dakar, Senegal, I used the ASAOF, especially the papers in the following series: B: Correspondence Générale 1779–1895; D: Affaires Militaires 1763–1920; F: Affaires Etrangères 1809–1921; G: Politique et Administration Générale. The following sub-sections are the most relevant in the G series: 1G: Etudes Générales: Missions, Notices et Monographies 1818–1921; 13G: Affaires Politiques, Administratives et Musulmanes, Sénégal 1782–1919 and 15G: Affaires Politiques, Administratives et Musulmanes: Soudan 1821–1920.

In Paris, at the ANSOM, I used principally the Series Sénégal I–IV. Sénégal I: Sénégal et Dépendances, containing material on various subjects from 1850 to 1895 and classified in files labelled Sénégal I/1–95; Sénégal II: comprises, in bulk, memoires; Sénégal III: Missions et Explorations, AOF, subdivided in files dealing with various topics and numbered Sénégal III/1–11 *bis* dating up to 1884; Senegal IV: Expansion territoriale et Politique Indigène, with subdivisions in files Sénégal IV/1–133 dealing with various topics. At the MAE, the most useful materials were those in the bound volumes titled: *Mémoires et Documents: Afrique*. In particular, I used Afrique 46–50: Sénégal et Dépendances, 10–14, for the period 1852–1882; Afrique 74: Renseignements sur les possessions . . . 1843–1885; Afrique 85: Sénégal et Dépendances 16, for the period 1885–1887; Afrique 86: Possessions Anglaises de la Côte Occidentale, no. 4, for the period 1883–1888; Afrique 122–124 Sénégal et Dépendances nos 17–19, for the period 1886–1894; Afrique 128–31, Possessions Anglaises de la Côte Occidentale nos 5–8, for the period 1888–1894. The Series: *Angleterre*, 107–9, on Sierra Leone 1890–1895, also contains some useful information.

The following materials in the Bibliothèque Nationale are useful on Senegal: Nouvelles Acquisitions Françaises: 12079, 13528, 24260, 24525, 3634, 7485, 9339–9341.

The collection at the Institut des Sciences Humaines, Bamako was largely uncatalogued when I was there in 1965. Nevertheless, some information was collected from the Series IE, nos 3, 6 and 9.

The archival materials listed above embody: (*a*) reports of various missions, governmental and non-governmental; (*b*) correspondence between the French colonial administration and Tukulor rulers, in particular Ahmadu and his emirs; (*c*) correspondence between French officers in the field and the administration at St Louis, and vice versa; (*d*) documents collected from Ahmadu's palaces at Nioro and Segu; and (*e*) reports by serving military personnel from 1880 to 1893.

2. Monographs

These are in files of the Dakar archives. They contain collections of oral evidence on the ethnography and history of various areas as compiled by investigators who included some 'commandants des cercles'. These investigations were carried out mainly during and immediately after the conquest of the territories. Their object was to provide information which could assist the French government in formulating its policy towards the different societies. The list below comprises the monographs (all in manuscripts) that I came across and have consulted in the course of my research.

1G122/1   Notes sur l'histoire du Macina, Underberg (Ségou-Sikoro), 10 Oct. 1890

1G124   Pays du Ka'arta: Historique (n.d.), Anonymous

1G125/1   Notice géographique sur le cercle de Ségou, Le Capitaine, commandant du cercle, Ségou, 29 Nov. 1895

1G156/2   Notice historique sur la région du Sahel, de Lartique, 1897

1G158/1   Notice ethnographique et géographique sur le Macina, E. Bardot, 1892

1G158/2   Notes sur l'histoire et la situation actuelle du Macina, Ch. de la Bretesche, 1 Mar. 1892
1G184   Renseignements historiques sur le Sansanding et le Macina, capitaine Bellat, Sansanding, mars-avril, 1893
1G195/9   Notice générale sur le Soudan, Lt Sagols, 1897
1G209/1   Notice historique du royaume et du cercle de Ségou (n.d.)
1G301/1   Sénégambie-Niger – Cercle du Bandiagara, Ch. de la Bretesche, Bandiagara, 15 Oct. 1903
1G301/3   Organisation politique, administrative et judiciaire indigène (n.d.)
1G305/2   (2e Section), Sénégambie-Niger – Cercle du Djenné 1903–1904
1G320/1 & 2 Notice sur le cercle du Ségou, Le Commandant du cercle, Ségou, 1 Mar. 1904
1G351/5   Monographie du cercle de Ségou, L'Administrateur, Ségou, 8 Feb. 1921

3. Printed Books

Archinard, Louis. *Le Soudan Français en 1888–1889: rapport militaire*, Paris Librairie Militaire Berger Levrault & Cie. Nancy, 1890
— *Soudan Français: campagne de 1890–1891: rapport*, St Louis, Imprimerie du Gouvernment, n.d.
Bechet, Eugene. *Cinq ans de séjour au Soudan Français*, Paris, Librairie Plon, 1889
Binger, Gustave. *Du Niger au Golfe de Guinée*, vol. i, Paris, 1892
Burdo, A. M. *Niger et Benué*, Paris, 1880
Caillie, René. *Travels through Central Africa to Timbouctou and the Great Desert, to Morocco performed in the Years 1824–1828*, London, 1830, 2 vols
Carrère, Frédéric et Holle, Paul. *De la Sénégambie française*, Paris, 1855
Compte Rendu des Séances de la Société de Geographie et de la Commission Centrale, Paris, 1885
De Card, Rouard E. *Les Traités de Protectorat conclus par la France en 1870–1895*, Paris, A. Durand et Pedone-Lauriel, 1897
D'Ormoy, F. *Un Mot Sur le Soudan*, aôut 1858, in BN Paris

Clapperton, Hugh. *Journal of a Second Expedition to the Interior of Africa*, London, John Murray, 1829

Exposition Coloniale de 1889: les colonies françaises: colonies d'Afrique, Publiées par ordre du sous Secrétaire d'Etat des Colonies, Paris, Maison-Quintin, 1890

D'Eichthal, G. *Histoire et origine des Foulahs ou Fellans*, Paris, 1841

Durand, J. L. P. *A Voyage to Senegal*, English tr., London, 1806 (Fr. orig. 1802)

Faidherbe, L. *Le Sénégal, la France dans l'Afrique Occidentale*, Paris, Librairie Hachête, 1889

Frey, Col. Henri. *Campagne dans le Haut Sénégal et dans le Haut Niger 1885–1886*, Paris, Librairie Plon, 1888

Gallieni, Lt-Col. *Voyage au Soudan Français (Haut-Niger et Pays de Ségou 1879–1881)* Paris, Librairie Hachête, 1885

— *Deux campagnes au Soudan français, 1886–1888 par Lieutenant-Colonel Gallieni*, Paris, Librairie Hachête, 1891

Le Chatelier, A. *L'Islam dans l'Afrique Occidentale*, Paris, G. Steinheil, Editeur, 1899

Legendre, P. *La Conquête de la France Africaine*, Paris, Paclot, n.d.

Mage, E. *Voyage dans le Soudan Occidentale 1863–1866*, Paris, 1868

Mage, E. *Voyage dans le Soudan Occidentale*, abrégé par J. Berlin-De Lanncy, Paris, Librairie Hachête, 1877

Manuel, John. *Le Soudan, ses rapports avec le commerce Européen*, Paris, 1871

Mitchinson, A. W. *The Expiring Continent*, London, 1881

Mollien, G. *Voyage dans l'intérieur de l'Afrique aux sources du Sénégal et de la Gambie fait en 1818*, Paris, 1822, 2 vols

Monteil, P. L. *De Saint-Louis à Tripoli par le lac Tchad*, Paris, 1894

Pietri, Le Capitaine. *Les Français au Niger*, Paris, 1885

Raffenel, Anne. *Nouveau voyage dans le pays des Nègres, suivi d'études sur la colonie du Sénégal et des documents historiques, géographiques et scientifiques*, Paris, 1856, 2 vols

Ricard, F. *Le Sénégal: étude intime*, Paris, 1865

Sanderson Edgar. *Africa in the Nineteenth Century*, London, Seeley, 1898

Soleillet, Paul. *Voyage d'Alger à St Louis du Sénégal par Tombouctou Conférence de M. Paul Soleillet*, Avignon, Typographie François Séguin Aîné, 1875

— *Voyage à Ségou 1878–1879*, rédige par Gabriel Gravier, Paris, Challamel ainé, Librairie-Editeur, 1897
Wilson, J. L. *West Africa*, London, 1856

4. Articles

Anon. 'Notes sur le Sénégal par un Sociétaire', *Bulletin de la Société des études Coloniales et Maritimes*, mai 1879
Braouezec, J. E. 'L'Hydrographie du Sénégal et nos relations avec les populations riveraines', *Revue Maritime et Coloniale*, janvier et fevrier 1861
Collomb, Dr. 'Les populations du Haut Niger, leurs moeurs et leur histoire', *Bulletin de la Société d'Anthropologie de Lyon*, 1885
De Crozals, J. 'Trois états foulbés de Soudan Occidentale et Central : le Fouta, le Macina, l'Adamaoua', *Annales de l'Université de Grenoble*, Paris, Gantheinvillars, 1896, t. iii, no. 1
Monteil, Commandant. 'De Saint-Louis à Ségou', *Revue de Paris*, 15 mai 1894
Quintin, Dr. 'Etude ethnologique sur les pays entre le Sénégal et le Niger', *Bulletin de la Société de Géographie*, 1881, 2e semestre
Soleillet, P. 'Explorations dans le royaume de Ségou, conférence faite par M. Soleillet le 26 mai 1879', *Bulletin de la Société des Etudes Coloniales et Maritimes*, 1879
Tautin, Dr. 'Tombouctou', *Nouvelle Revue*, 1 fevrier 1885

B. LATER WORKS

1. Books

Abun-Nasr, Jamil. *The Tijāniyya: a Sufi order in the modern world*, London, 1965
Arcin, André. *Histoire de la Guinée français*, Paris, Augustin Challanel, 1911
Blake, John William. *Europeans in West Africa, 1450–1560*, Hakluyt Society, ser. 2, no. 86, 1942
Boahen, Adu. *Britain, the Sahara and the Western Sudan 1788–1861*, Oxford, Clarendon Press, 1964
Bodelsen, C. A. *Studies in Mid-Victorian Imperialism*, London, Heinemann, 1960

Boutillier, J. L., Cantrelle, P. *et al.* *La Moyenne vallée du Sénégal*, Paris, Presses Universitaires de France, 1962

Brigaud, F. *Histoire traditionelle du Sénégal*, Etudes Sénégalaises, no. 9, St Louis du Sénégal, 1962

Chailley, Ct. *Les grandes missions françaises en Afrique Occidentale*, Dakar, IFAN, 1953

Chailley, M., Bourbon, A. *et al.* *Notes et études sur l'Islam en Afrique noire*, Paris, 1962

Cooksey, J. J. and McLeish, A. *Religion and Civilisation in West Africa*, London, World Dominion Press, 1931

Cornevin, R. et Cornevin, M. *Histoire de l'Afrique des origines à nos jours*, Paris, Payot, 1964

Crowder, Michael. *West Africa under Colonial rule.* London, Hutchinson, 1968.

Cultru, P. *Histoire du Sénégal du XVe Siècle à 1870*, Paris, Emile Larose, 1910

de Clercq, A. J. H. *Receuil des Traités de France 1861–1919*

Darcy, J. *France et Angleterre: cent années de rivalité coloniale: l'Afrique*, Paris, 1904

Delafosse, Maurice. *Traditions historiques et légendaires du Soudan Occidentale*, traduit d'un manuscrit arabe inédit, Paris, 1913

— *Les Noirs d'Afrique*, Paris, Payot, 1922

— *Haut-Sénégal–Niger*, Paris, 1922, 3 vols

— *Les Noirs de l'Afrique*, Paris, Edition Definitive, Payot, 1941

Delavignette, P. et Julien, Ch. André. *Les Constructeurs de la France D'Outre-Mer*, Paris, Editions Corrêa, 1946

Deschamps, Hubert. *Le Sénégal et la Gambie*, Paris, Presses Universitaires de France, 1964

Dieterlen, G. in Fortes, M. and Dieterlen, G., eds., *African System of Thought*, Oxford University Press, 1965

Diop, Abdoulaye Bara. *Société Toucouleure et Migration*, Dakar, IFAN, 1965

Diop, Cheik Anta. *L'Afrique Noire pré-coloniale*, Paris, Présence Africaine, 1960

Dupire, M. *Peuls Nomades*, Paris, 1962

Faidherbe, L. *L'Avenir du Sahara et du Soudan*, annoté par L. Faidherbe, tome i, Paris, Larose & Forcel, 1907

Fyfe, C. *A History of Sierra Leone*, Oxford University Press, 1962

Gaden, H. *Proverbes et Maximes Peuls et Toucouleur*, Paris, 1931

Gatelet, Lt August L. C. *Histoire de la Conquête du Soudan* *français 1878–1879*, Paris et Nancy, Berger-Levrault et cie, 1901

Gerteiny, A. G. *Mauritania*, London, Pall Mall Press, 1967

Gibb, Sir Hamilton A. R., Shaw, J. and Polk, William R. *Studies on the Civilization of Islam*, ed. Stanford, London, Routledge & Kegan Paul, 1962

Gouilly, Alphonse. *L'Islam dans l'Afrique Occidentale*, Paris, 1952

Gray, John M. *The Gambia*, Cambridge University Press, 1940

Guebhard, Paul. *L'Histoire du Fouta Djallon et des Almamys*, Paris, 1909

Guenin, G. *L'Apogée coloniaux de la France Racontées par les contemporains*, Paris, Librairie Larose, 1932

Gwynn, Stephen. *Mungo Park and the Quest of the Niger*, London, John Lane, The Bodley Head, 1934

Hampate-Ba, A. et Cardaire, M. *Tierno Bokar le Sage de Bandiagara*, Paris, 1957

Hampate-Ba, A. and Daget, J. I. *L'Empire Peul de Macina 1813–1853*, Centre du Soudan, IFAN, 1955

Hardy, Georges. *La Mise en valeur du Sénégal de 1817 à 1854*, Paris, Emile Larose, 1921

— *Histoire de la colonisation française*, Paris, Librarie Larose, 1928

Hargreaves, John D. *Prelude to the Partition of West Africa*, London, Macmillan (1966 edition)

Holt, P. M. *Egypt and the Fertile Crescent 1516–1922*, London, Longman, 1966

Houdas, O., trans. *Tedzkirect En-Nisian fi Akhbar Molouck Es-Soudan*, Paris, Ernest Laroux, 1901

July, Robert W. *The Origins of Modern African Thought*, London, Faber, 1968

Kanya-Forstner, A. S. *The Conquest of the Western Sudan: a study in military imperialism*, Cambridge University Press, 1969

Khadduri, Majid. *War and Peace in the Law of Islam*, Baltimore, Johns Hopkins Press, 1955

Klein, Martin. *Islam and Imperialisn in Senegal: Sine Saloum 1847–1914*, Edinburgh University Press, 1968

Last, Murray. *The Sokoto Caliphate*, London, Longman, 1968

Levy, Reuben. *The Social Structure of Islam*, Cambridge University Press, 1957

Ly, Abdoulaye. *Compagnie du Sénégal*, Paris, 1958

Marty, P. *Etudes sur l'Islam et les tribus du Soudan*, tome iv, Paris, Editions Ernest Laroux, 1920

Méniaud, Jacques. *Les Pionniers du Soudan*, Paris, Société des Publications Modernes, 1931, 2 vols

Mill, Lady Dorothy. *The Road to Timbuktoo*, London, 1924

Monteil, C. *Les Bambara du Ségou et du Ka'arta*, Paris, Emile Larose, 1924

— *Les Khassonké*, Paris, Ernest Laroux, 1915

Monteil, Vincent. *L'Islam Noir*, Paris, 1964

Murdock, G. P. *Africa: its peoples and their culture history*, New York, McGraw-Hill, 1959

Niane, D. T. et Suret-Canale, J. *Histoire de l'Afrique Occidentale*, Paris, 1961

Ouane, Ibrahima-Mamadou. *Pérégrinations Soudanaises*, Lyon, n.d.

— *L'Islam et la civilisation française*, Avignon, 1957

Quellien, Nain. *La Politique Musulmane dans l'Afrique Occidentale*, Paris, Emile Larose, 1910

Réquin, Général E. *Archinard et le Soudan*, Paris, Editions, Berger-Levrault, 1946

Roberts, S. H. *The History of French Colonial Policy 1870–1925*, London, P. S. King, 1929; reprinted Cass, 1963

Robinson, R. *et al. Africa and the Victorians: The Official Mind of Imperialism*, London, Macmillan, 1961

Rodney, Walter. *A History of the Upper Guinea Coast 1545 to 1800*, Oxford, Clarendon Press, 1970

Rouche, J. *Contribution à l'histoire des Songhay*, Dakar, Mémoires de l'IFAN, no. 29, 1953

Ruxton, F. H. *Maliki Law*, London, Luzac, 1916

Shaw, S. J. and Polk, W. R., eds. *Studies on the Civilization of Islam*, London, Routledge & Kegan Paul, 1962

Stenning, D. J. *Savannah Nomads*, Oxford University Press, 1959

Suret-Canale, J. *L'Afrique Noire: occidentale et centrale*, Paris, Editions Sociales, 1961.

Tauxier, Louis. *Moeurs et Histoire des Peul*, Paris, 1937

— *Histoire des Bambara*, Paris, 1942

Terrier, A. et Mourey, C. *L'Oeuvre de la troisième République en Afrique Occidentale*, Paris, 1910

Trammond, J. et Reussner, A. *Eléments d'Histoire Maritime et coloniale contemporaine 1815–1914*, Paris, Société d'Editions Géographiques, Maritime et Coloniale, 1947

Tressanne, Lt de la Vergo. *La Pénétration française en Afrique*, Paris, Librairie Maritime et Coloniale, 1906
Trimingham, J. S. *Islam in West Africa*, Oxford, Clarendon Press, 1959
— *A History of Islam in West Africa*, Oxford University Press, 1962
Tyam, M. A. *La Vie d'El-Hadj Omar, Qacidar en Poular transcription, traduction, notes, et glossaire par Henri Gaden*, Paris, Institut d'Ethnologie, 1935
Vansina, J., Mauny, R. et al., eds. *The Historian in Tropical Africa*, Oxford University Press, 1964
Wane, Yaya. *Les Toucouleurs du Fouta Tooro (Sénégal)*, Dakar, IFAN, 1969
Welsh, G. *The Unveiling of Timbuctoo*, London, Gollancz, 1938

2. Articles

Abun-Nasr, Jamil M. 'Some aspects of the Umari Branch of the Tijaniyya', *JAH*, iii.2, 1962
Adelẹyẹ, R. A. The Dilemma of the Wrazī: The Place of the *Risālat Al-Wazīr 'ila Ahl Al-'ilm wa'l-tadabbur* in the history of the conquest of the Sokoto caliphate' *JHSN*, iv.2 1968
Adelẹyẹ, R. A. et al. 'Sifofin Shehu: an autobiography and character study of 'Uthman b. Fudi in verse', *Bull. CAD*, ii.1, 1966
Al-Hajj, Muhammad. 'The Fulani Concept of Jihād-Shehu Uthman dan Fodio', *Odu*, i.1, 1964
Al-Naqar, Umar. 'Takrur the history of a name', *JAH*, x,3, 1969
Anon. 'L'Empire Toucouleur d'El-Hadj Omar', *Bingo*, no. 64, Dakar, 1958
Bathily, Abdoulaye. 'Notices socio-historiques sur l'ancien royaume Soninké du Gadiaga', *Bull. IFAN*, B, xxxi.1, 1969
Bivar, A. D. H. 'The Wathiquat ahl al-Sudan', *JAH*, ii.2, 1961
Brown, William A. 'Towards a chronology for the Caliphate of Hamdullahi (Masina), *CEA*, viii.3, 1968
Cazemajou, M.-C. 'Journal de route', *BCAF*, 1900
Cissoko, Sékéné-Mody. 'Traits fondamentaux des sociétés du Soudan Occidental du xviie au début du xixe Siècle,' *Bull. IFAN*, B. xxxi.1, 1969
Coindard, M. A. 'Notes sur les indigènes du Tamgué dans le

Fouta Jallon (Guinée Française)', *Ann. et Mém. CEHSAOF*, 1917
Davidson, Basil. 'Guinea: past and present', *History Today*, ix.6, June 1959
Delafosse, M. 'Traditions Musulmanes relatives à l'origine des Peuls', *Revue du Monde Musulman*, xx, 1912
Delcourt, André. 'La France et les établissements français au Sénégal entre 1713 et 1763', *Mémoires de l'IFAN*, xvii, 1952
Dupuch, C. 'Essai sur l'emprise religieuse chez les Peulh du Fouta Djallon', *Ann. et Mem. CEHSAOF*, 1917
Eckstein, Harry. 'On the etiology of internal wars', *History and Theory*, iv.2, 1965
El-Masri, F. H. 'The life of Shehu Usuman dan Fodio before the jihād', *JHSN*, ii.4, Dec. 1963
Faure, Claude. 'La garnison européenne du Sénégal et le recrutement des premières troupes noires (1779–1858)', *Revue d'Histoire des Colonies françaises*, 2e semestre, 1920
Fisher, Humphrey J. Review of J. M. Abun-Nasr, *The Tijāniyya . . .*, *Bull. SOAS*, xxx.1, 1967
— 'The early life and pilgrimage of al-Hajj al-Amīn the Soninke (d. 1887)', *JAH*, xi.1, 1970
Ganier, C. 'Lat Dyor et le Chemin de fer de l'arachide 1876–1886', *Bull. IFAN*, B, xxvii.1-2, 1965
— 'Maures et Toucouleurs sur les deux rives du Sénégal: La Maison de Victor Ballot auprès de Sidi Ely roi des Maures Braknas, fév–juin 1884', *Bull. IFAN*, B, xxx.1, 1968
Goudiam, Ousman. 'San (Soudan Français)', *Annales Africaines*, Paris, 1958
Griaule, M. 'Philosophie et religion des Noirs', *Présence Africaine*, 1950
Hampate-Ba, A. 'Le dernier Carré Toucouleur: Récit historique', *Afrique en Marche*, no. 3, Dakar, avril–mai, 1957; no. 4, mai–juin, 1957
— 'Le Sultan de Ségou était-il Orgueilleux? Une anecdote qui illustre l'égalité des hommes devant la justice', *Afrique en Marche*, no. 9, Dakar, oct.–nov. 1957
Hardy, Georges. 'Un episode de l'exploration du Soudan – l'affaire Duranton 1828–1838, *Ann. et Mém. CEHSAOF*, 1917
Hargreaves, John D. 'The Tokolor empire of Ségou and its relations with the French', *Boston University Papers on Africa*, ii, ed. J. Butler, Boston, 1966

— 'The French Occupation of the Mellacourie 1865–67', *Sierra Leone Studies*, new series v, Freetown, 1955

Hecquard, M. 'Coup d'oeil sur l'organisation politique, l'-histoire et les moeurs des Peulhs du Fouta Djallon', *Revue Coloniale*, Nov. 1952

Hiskett, M. 'Material relating to the State of learning among the Fulani before the jihād', *Bull. SOAS*, xix, 1957

— 'An Islamic tradition of reform in the Western Sudan from the Sixteenth to the Eighteenth Century', *Bull. SOAS*, xxv.3, 1962

Johnson, James and Robinson, David. 'Deux fonds d'-histoire Orale sur le Fouta Toro', *Bull. IFAN*, B, xxxi.1, 1969

Kane, Abdoulaye. 'Histoire et origine des familles du Fouta Toro', *Ann. et Mém. CEHSAOF*, 1916

Kanya-Forstner, A. S. and Newbury, C. W. 'French policy and the origins of the scramble for West Africa', *JAH*, 1969

Labouret, H. 'Les Manding et leur langue' in *Bull. CEHSAOF*, 1934

Last, M. and Al-Hajj, M. A. 'Attempts at defining a Muslim in the 19th century Hausaland and Bornu', *JHSN*, iii.2, 1965

Loppinot, A. de. 'Souvenirs d'Aguibou', *Bull. CEHSAOF*, 1919

Mademba, B. 'La dernière étape d'un conquérant, *Bull. CEHSAOF*, 1921

Martin, B. G. 'A Mahdist document from Fouta Jallon', *Bull. IFAN*, B, xxv.1–2, 1963

Monteil, V., ed. 'Chronique du Walo Sénégalais (1186–1855) par Amadou Wade (1886–1961)', *Bull. IFAN*, B, xxvi.2, 3–4, 1964

Monteil, V. 'Le Dyolof et Al Bouri Ndiaye', *Bull. IFAN*, B, xxviii.3–4, 1966

N'Diaye, Francine. 'La colonie du Sénégal au temps de Brière de l'Isle 1876–1881', *Bull. IFAN*, B, xxx.2, 1968

Newbury, C. W. 'The development of French policy on the Lower and Upper Niger 1880–1898', *Journal of Modern History*, xxxi.1, 1957

— 'Victorians, republicans and the partition of West Africa', *JAH*, iii.3, 1962

Niane, D. T. 'A propos de Koli Tenguella', *Recherches Africaines*, 4, Oct.–Dec. 1960

Nyambarza, D. 'Le Marabout al Hadj Lamine d'après les archives françaises', *CEA*, 33, ix.1, 1969

O'Brien, D. C. 'Towards an Islamic Policy in French West Africa', *JAH*, viii.2, 1967

Ọlọruntimẹhin, B. Ọ. 'Resistance movements in the Tukulor empire', *CEA*, 29, viii.1, 1968

— 'Abd al-Qadir's Mission as a Factor in Franco-Tukulor Relations, 1885–1887', *Genève-Afrique, Acta Africana*, vii.2, 1968

— 'Muhammad Lamine in Franco-Tukulor Relations 1885–1887', *JHSN*, iv.3, 1968

— 'The treaty of Niagassola, An Episode in Franco-Samori Relations in the era of the Scramble', *JHSN*, iv.4, 1969

— 'Anti-French Coalition of African States and Groups in the Western Sudan 1889–1893', *Odu*, new ser., no. 3, Apr. 1970

— 'Senegambia – Mahmahdou Lamine', in Michael Crowder, ed., *West African Resistance. The Military Response to Colonial Occupation*, London, Hutchinson, 1971

— 'The Western Sudan and the coming of the French 1800–1893', in J. F. A. Ajayi and M. Crowder, eds., *A History of West Africa*, vol. ii, London, Longman, forthcoming

Pageard, Robert. 'Ségou (Soudan Français)', *Annales Africaines*, Paris, 1958

— 'Un mystérieux voyage au pays de Bambouc, 1789', *Notes Africaines*, 89, 1961

Petot, F. 'Sikasso (Soudan Français)', *Annales Africaines*, Paris, 1958

Ritchie, Carson, I. A. 'Deux textes sur le Sénégal (1673–1677)', *Bull. IFAN*, B, xxx.1, 1968

Rodney, W. 'Jihād and social revolution in Futa Jallon in the eighteenth century', *JHSN*, iv.2, 1968

Rouche, J. 'Contribution à l'histoire de Songhay', *Mém. IFAN*, no. 29, 1953

Rousseau, R. 'Le Sénégal d'autre fois, cahier de Toro Dyao', *Bull. CEHSAOF*, 1929

— 'Le Sénégal d'autre fois; Etudes sur le Cayor, *Bulletin du CEHSAOF*, 16, 1933

Saint-Martin, Yves. 'Les relations diplomatiques entre la France et l'empire Toucouleur de 1860 à 1887', *Bull. IFAN*, B, xxvii.1–2, 1965

— 'L'Artillerie d'El Hadj Omar et d'Ahmadou', *Bull. IFAN*, B, xxvii, 1965

— 'Une source de l'histoire coloniale du Sénégal: Les Rapports de Situation Politique (1874–1891)' *Revue française d'Histoire d'Outre-Mer*, lii.187, 1965

— 'La volonté de paix d'El Hadj Omar et d'Ahmadou dans leurs relations avec la France', *Bull. IFAN*, B, xxx.3, 1968

— 'Un fils d'El Hadj Omar: Aguibou roi du Dinguiray et du Macina (1843–1907)', *CEA*, 29, viii.1, 1968

Salenc, Jules. 'La vie d'Al-Hadj Omar, traduction d'un manuscrit arabe de la Zaouia tidjania de Fez', *Bull. CEHSAOF*, 1918

Samb, Amar. 'Sur al Hadj Omar à Propos d'un article d'Yves Saint-Martin)' *Bull. IFAN*, B, xxx.3, 1968.

Siddle, D. J. 'War-towns in Sierra Leone: a study in social change', *Africa*, xxxviii.1, 1968

Silla, Ousmane. 'Quelques particularités de la société Sénégalaise', *Notes Africaines*, no. 122, avril 1969

Sissoko, M. 'Chroniques d'El Hadj Oumar (1er et 2e Cahiers)', in *L'Education Africaine (Bulletin de L'Enseignement de l'AOF)*, janvier–juin, 1937

— 'Chroniques d'El Hadj Oumar (3e Cahier)', *L'Education Africaine (Bulletin de l'Enseignement de l'AOF)*, juillet-sept. 1937

Smith, H. F. C. 'Source material for the history of the Western Sudan', *JHSN*, i, 1958

— 'The archives of Segu', *Bulletin of News, Historical Society of Nigeria*, Supplement iv.2 1959

— 'The Islamic revolutions of the 19th century: a neglected theme of West African history' *JHSN*, ii.2, 1961

— 'Nineteenth-century Arabic archives of West Africa', *JAH*, iii.2, 1962

Suret-Canale, J. 'El-Hadj Omar', *Présence Africaine*, nouvelle serie, no. 20, juin–juillet, 1958

Villard, André. 'Peuls, Foulahs, Toucouleurs et autres', *Dakar-Jeune*, 30 avril 1942

Waldman, M. R. 'The Fulani jihād: a reassessment', *JAH*, vi.3, 1965

Wane, Yaya. 'Etat actuel de la documentation au sujet des Toucouleurs', *Bull. IFAN*, B, xxv.3–4, 1963

— 'De Halwaar à Degembere, ou l'itinéraire islamique de Shaykh Umar Taal', *Bull. IFAN*, B, xxxi.2, 1969

Willis, Ralph. Review article of Abun-Nasr, *The Tijāniyya* in *Research Bulletin* of the Centre of Arabic Documentation, University of Ibadan, ii.1, 1966
— 'Jihād fī sabīl Allāh – its doctrinal basis in Islam and some Aspects of its Evolution in 19th century West Africa', *JAH*, viii, 1967
Wolf, Eric R. 'On peasant rebellions', *International Social Science Journal*, xxi.2, 1969
Wood, W. Raymond. 'An archaeological appraisal of early European settlements in the Senegambia', *JAH*, viii.1, 1967
Zuccarelli, François. 'Le régime des engagés à temps au Sénégal', *CEA*, 7, ii.3, 1962

3. Unpublished Theses/Papers

Brenner, Louis. 'The Shehus of Kukawa: a history of the al-Kanemi dynasty of Bornu', Ph.D., Columbia University, 1968
Harris, J. E. 'The Kingdom of Fouta Diallon' Ph.D., Northwestern University, 1965
Hopewell, James F. 'Muslim Penetration into French Guinea, Sierra Leone and Liberia before 1850', Ph.D., Columbia University, 1958
Oloruntimẹhin, B. Ọ. 'The Interactions of Islamic and Pre-Islamic Concepts in Tukulor Constitutional Evolution', seminar paper, History Department, University of Ibadan, 1969
Paden, J. N. 'The influence of Religious Elites on Political Culture and Community Integration in Kano, Nigeria', Ph.D., Harvard University, 1968

C. ORAL SOURCES

During my stay at Dakar and Segu, I made efforts to collect oral information, especially from known descendants of al-hajj 'Umar. In the interviews that I had with these people I asked questions with a view to seeking information on specific issues. On some occasions, I experienced difficulties in obtaining information because people were uncommunicative either because of the existing political situation, especially in Mali, under which the various ethnic groups were suspicious of one another and therefore remained reticent, or because of language difficulties.

In Dakar, Bamako and Segu, some of the people concerned spoke either Wolof or Bambara only, and I had to use the services of interpreters. Whenever I succeeded in obtaining information, except in a few cases, the evidence obtained largely corroborated the documentary sources. The most rewarding of my interviews were those with the descendants of al-ḥājj ʿUmar at Segu, especially the patriarch of the family, Shaikh Madani Muntaga Tall, and his aide, Ahmadu Sanmori who was aged about ninety-five in 1965 and who claimed to have accompanied Ahmadu on the flight to Sokoto in 1893.

Index

Index

Index

Guimba, ruler of Tamla, 63–4, 69
gum trade, 29, 189

Habe people, 164–6, 172–3, 175–6
Hadi, son of 'Umar, 152
Hamadou Cheikou, 293
Hamalliyya brotherhood, 325–6
Hamdallahi (in Masina), 23, 139–40
Haoussidji, Abdullahi, *talibé* of Diagounte, 92
harvest tax (*Diaka*), 176
Hashim, Alfa, 323
Hausa people, 137
Hecquart, French commandant at Bakel, 47
hijra, 49, 53–4, 59, 321
Holland, trade interests of, 28
Holle, Paul, French commandant at Médine, 97, 98

Ibrahim b. Hamma Malik, Masina military leader, 138
Ibrahim Niass, Tijāniyya leader, 326
Ibrāhīm b. Nuhu (Alfa Ibrāhīm b. Nuhu), Futa Toro chief, 15–16, 34
imamate system, 8–9, 11–14, 15–16, 36; in Futa Toro, 154–5
Irlabé, 16
Irlabé-Ebiabé, 7
Islam, 22, 34; conversion to, 59–60; 'ideal', 54–5; political aspects of, 324; purification of, 45–6, 81, 147, 317; schisms in, 324–5; as state religion, 44–5; 'Umar's attitudes toward, 44–60
Islamic community, 'ideal', 54n, 147, 316
Islamic judiciary procedures, 173–5
Islamisation, 316–17; of Segu, 128–129, 131, 135–8
istikhāra (defined), 39n

Jauréguiberry, Admiral, 234
Jenne (in Masina), 312–13
jihād(s), 15, 22–3, 47, 53–4n (defined), 148; of Cissé dynasty, 22, 140; military organisation of, 55–

59; of 'Uthman b. Fodiye, 22; of 'Umar, 316–17; *see also* Tukulor revolution
Jolof, 293; and the French, 108; and Tukulor conflict, 110–11
judiciary, Tukulor, 173–6; Habe, 175–6

Ka'arta, 18–21, 90–1, 120–2, 129, 259–65; civil war in, 165–7, 179–185, 192–4; French administration of, 306; French conquest of, 298–304; and Segu, 259–65; Tukulor revolution in, 61–91; 'Umar's return to (1859), 112–15
Ka'arta Bine (in Ka'arta), 92
Ka'arta Bine Bambara, *see* Bambara, Ka'arta Bine
Ka'arta Massassi kingdom, 2
kafos (administrative units), 161–2
Kagoro people, 21
Kandia, Mamadi, *fama* of Ka'arta, 20, 80
Kaniareme (in Ka'arta), 92
Karabarou (Karakoro), 80
Karamoko (Ali Alfa Karamoko b. Ibrahim), Futa Toro ruler, 16
Karamoko Diara, Bambara leader, 278–9
Kartoum Sambala, 73–4, 79, 93–101
Karunka, Diawara chief, 122, 124
Katili, Merkoye chief, 122
Kayes-Bamako railway, 268
Kayor, *lamaan* of, 6–7
Keita, Siramakha, Soninke king of Segu, 19
Kenedugu, 300; and the French, 309; -Wasulu-Tukulor alliance, 309–11
Khaladian Koulibali, Bambara ruler, 19
Khalidou, Tierno, *talibé* of Ka'arta Bine, 92
Kharāj (land tax), 176
Khasso, 14 (map), 276; civil wars in, 18–19, 73–4, 93–4; and the French, 87–9; internal conflict in, 88, 205–23; Tukulor campaigns against, 73–9

Index

Moktar, emir of Diomboko, 157, 166, 169, 179–85, 186, 189–94, 229, 320
Moors, 6, 7, 26, 70–1, 91; Bamaku, 256–7; civil war of, 83; Dowich, 86; and the French, 30–2, 82–4, 86; Ludamar, 20; of Ludamek, 79, 81; and Tukulor, 82–5
Moriba Safere, rebel leader, 197–8, 204–5, 210
Mossi people, 23–4
Moudou (religious tax), 176
Mourgoula, 57, 255–6, 261
Mourtada, chief of Koulou, 281
Muhammad Aguibu, *see* Aguibu, Muhammad
Muḥammād al-Ghāli Abu Talīb, 38
Muḥammad Atiq (Atiku), *khālifa* of Sokoto, 41, 50
Muhammad Bello, *khālifa* of Sokoto, 40, 41, 50, 137
Muhammad b. Mustafa b. Ahmad b. Usman, 152
Muhammad Djelia, 159
Muhammad ibn 'Abd al-Wahhābi, founder of Wahhabiyya, 46
Muhammad Mahim, 'Umar's son, 152
Muhammad Sanusi, emir of Kano, 328
Muniru, 172–3, 263, 281, 304–5, 314
Muntaga, Muhammad, *wazir* of Ka'arta, 175n, 191, 195, 198–200, 304–5; and Aḥmadu, 193; -Abibu Moktar alliance, 192–3, revolt of (1884–5), 295–65; and Tijani, 261
Muslim-French relations, 325–6
Muslim–non-Muslim conflict, 8
Mustafa, emir of Nioro, 41, 150, 166, 178, 191, 228

Namouda, Tamla commander, 64
Nango, 239, 240; treaty of, 241–4, 255n
Natiaga (in Khasso), 79, 98
nationalism, African, 77n

nazr al-mazālim system of justice, 175
N'Diaye, Ali Bouri, *see* Ali Bouri N'Diaye
N'diaye, Samba, 145, 159, 193
N'Guénar, 7, 57
Niamodi (Niamody), ruler of Logo, 19; and Sambala, 205–7, 209–23
Niass, Ibrahim, Tijāniyya leader, 326
Nigeria, Tijāniyya in, 327–8
Niger mission, 235–45, 266–9
Niger river, 160, 243
Nioro, capital of Ka'arta, 80–1, 82 178, 180–2, 190–1, 259–65
non-Muslim peoples and Tukulor revolution, 59–60
Nuhu, Ibrāhīm b. (Alfa Ibrāhīm b. Nuhu), 15–16, 34
Nuru, emir of Diafounou, 196–7
Nyamina: Aḥmadu at, 261; French post at, 287–91; as a Tukulor base, 124–5

Ouitala (in Segu), 125–6
Ouled Embark, Moorish leader, 79, 81
Oumarou ('Umar), almamy of Futa Jallon, 70
Ouossébougou, French attack on, 297
Oussourou (caravan tax), 176

Paris, 218–20, 244–5, 246, 274–5, 279–80; -Senegal conflict, 247–51, 253–4
pilgrimage, 'Umar's, 37–40
political organisation: of Futa toro, 8–14; of Senegambia, 143–4; of Tukulor empire, 148–77; of 'Umar's revolution, 50
Portuguese trade interests, 26–7
pre-Islamic concepts of government, 62
Protet, governor of Senegal, 30, 31, 76, 85

Qacida, 67, 132n, 156–7

354

Index

DATE DUE			